A TREASURY OF NEEDLEWORK PROJECTS

FROM

GODEY'S LADY'S BOOK

Edited and Compiled by

ARLENE ZEGER WICZYK

New York

For my darling Hillah
When she grows up

Published by Arco Publishing Company, Inc.
219 Park Avenue South, New York, N.Y. 10003

Copyright © 1972 by Arlene Zeger Wiczyk

Library of Congress Catalog Card Number 72-3698

Library Edition: ISBN 0-668-02702-9

Paper Edition: ISBN 0-668-02692-8

Printed in the United States of America

INTRODUCTION

Godey's Lady's Book, founded in Philadelphia in 1838 and the first women's magazine to be published in America, is remembered primarily for its extraordinarily beautiful hand-colored fashion plates. Yet each issue of the magazine included a fancy work department which encouraged women to try their hand at home crafting of all kinds. Under the influence of Mrs. Sarah Hale, the editor of *Godey's,* women everywhere began to take up their needles and stitch delicate accessories, crochet lacy fichus, even create superbly decorated articles for their home: lampshades, picture frames, wastebaskets, linen bands, cigar cases, quilts and pillows. Berlin wools (today's brightly colored knitting worsteds) were used to decorate many things from samplers to baskets for bathing dresses, but nothing is more typical of the period than the antimacassar, designed, like the glass cases over clocks, to preserve the furnishings of the middle-class home.

Life is more hectic today but needlework remains a most enjoyable leisure-time activity. Today's woman is rediscovering this ageless craft and enhancing her modern home with the fruits of her labors. Here then are the best of the needlework and crafts projects worked by nineteenth-century women as they appeared within the pages of *Godey's Lady's Book.* Who could resist the charm of a feather flower, embroidered footstool or Turkish lounging cap, knitted chest preserver, Berlin wool work slipper, girl's gaiters, a latch-key pocket, gypsy jewel basket or netted sponge bag? You'll find strikingly different designs and patterns for these and hundreds of other knitting, crochet, embroidery, needlepoint, applique, quilting, crewel, bead, shell and leather work projects. All are designs you can copy as they are or adapt to scores of other uses. And all are so simply explained and illustrated that even the most difficult techniques can be mastered.

Beautiful handcrafted items reflect your own interests and taste and are personal treasures you'll cherish and enjoy for years to come. Whether you are an experienced needleworker or a beginner who has not mastered all the aspects of this age-old craft, you can, with just a little work and ingenuity, become an artist with your needle.

ARLENE ZEGER WICZYK

CLOUD AND SHAWL (KNITTING).

THE cloud, seen on the left-hand figure in the engraving, for which white, pink, blue, or scarlet Shetland wool may be used, and three long wooden needles, No. 10, without knobs, is an easy piece of work for those who are not experienced knitters, as it is merely a long straight scarf knitted plain. It has the advantage of being able to be drawn over the head, folded about the neck, and even tied around the waist, so as to be a protection to the whole upper part of the body. If wished still warmer, it may also be knitted in eider yarn, with needles No. 7 or 8. For the length of the cloud, cast on 424 stitches equally on the two needles, and knit 200 rows plain for the width, at the conclusion of which cast off very loosely. The ends of the scarf are finished with fringe, for which first work a row of double crochet on the ends of the rows of knitting, and then, for the heading, 3 rows of open crochet or trebles with 1 ch. between each, missing 1 of the previous row, and keeping the trebles one over the other. After the 3d row, 4 strands of the wool 8 inches long are to be tied into each space between the trebles.

THE SHAWL.—The shawl worn by the right-hand figure is a square of fully a yard and a half, which can, at pleasure, be either folded cornerwise, or as a scarf, or draped over the head like a hood. It consists of a centre, the pattern of which is shown in detail at Fig. 2, and a deep border, of which latter the four sides are separately knitted to the centre. Shetland wool, white or of any color preferred, and 3 or 4 long wooden needles, No. 10, without knobs, will be required. Neither the centre nor the border must be knitted too loosely,

Fig. 2.

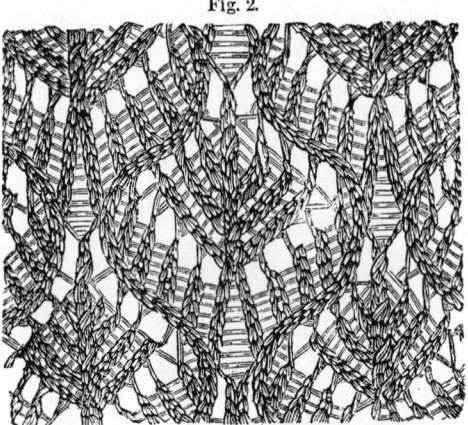

and for the former 318 stitches are to be cast on, and the rows knitted backwards and forwards, the uneven numbered rows being on the right side of the work. Knit a purl, a plain, and a purl row; then begin. 1*st pattern row.* 3 plain, * over, knit 2 together from the back of the stitches, 2 plain, over, slip 1, knit 2 together, pass slipped stitch over, over, 2 plain, knit 2 together as usual, over, 1 plain; repeat from *; the 3 last stitches of all the uneven numbered rows are to be knitted plain. 2*d* and all alternate rows are purled throughout. 3*d.* 4 plain, * over, knit 2 together from the back, 5 plain, knit 2 together as usual, over, 3 plain; repeat from *; at the end 5 plain instead of 3 plain. 5*th.* * 5 plain, over, knit 2 together from the back, 3 plain, knit 2 together, over, repeat from *, end with 6 plain. 7*th.* 6 plain, * over, knit 2 together from the back, 1 plain, knit 2 together, over, 7 plain; repeat from *. 9*th.* 2 plain, knit 2 together from the back, * 3 plain, over, 3 plain, over, 3 plain, knit 3 together; repeat from *; last time knit 2 together as at the beginning, instead of 3. 11*th.* 2 plain, knit 2 together from the back, * 2 plain, over, 5 plain, over, 2 plain, knit 3 together; repeat from *; end as in the 9th row. 13*th.* 2 plain, knit 2 together from the back, * 1 plain, over, 7 plain, over, 1 plain, knit 3 together; repeat from *; end as in last row. 15*th.* 2 plain, knit 2 together from the back, * over, 2 plain, knit 2 together, over, 1 plain, over, knit 2 together from the back, 2 plain, over, slip 1, knit 2 together, pass slipped stitch over, repeat from *; last time, knit 2 together from the back instead of slip 1, etc., and the rest plain. 17*th.* * 5 plain, knit 2 together, over, 3 plain, over, knit 2 together from the back, repeat from *; end with 6 plain. 19*th.* 4 plain, * knit 2 together, over, 5 plain, over, knit 2 together from the back, 3 plain, repeat from *. 21*st.* 3 plain * knit 2 together, over, 7 plain, over, knit 2 together from the back, 1

plain, repeat from *. 23*d.* 5 plain, * over, 2 plain, knit 3 together, 2 plain, over, 5 plain, repeat from *; at the end 6 plain. 25*th.* 6 plain, * over, 1 plain, knit 3 together, 1 plain, over, 7 plain, repeat from *. 27*th.* Commence again at the 1st row. For the whole size of the centre, these 25 rows have to be repeated 25 times, which will form a perfect square, after the completion of which the stitches are not to be cast off, but a purl, a plain, and a purl row, to be knitted so as to appear all three plain on the right side of the work, and then the border is to be begun, in which in all the uneven numbered rows, viz., the 1st, 3d, 5th, etc., a stitch is to be increased at the beginning and end, to make the slope at the corners. 1*st row.* 1 plain, * over, knit 2 together, repeat from * throughout the row. 2*d.* Purl. 3*d.* Plain. 4*th* and 5*th.* Like 2d and 3d. 6*th.* * over, 1 plain, repeat from * 3 times more, then † knit 2 together, and repeat from † 7 times more, ‡ over, 1 plain, repeat from ‡ 7 times more, then repeat from † again. At the end of the row, as at the beginning, there will be only 4 times "over, 1 plain." For the depth of the border, the 2d to the 6th row must be repeated 9 times, taking care as the number of stitches at the corner increase to add gradually to the number of "over, 1 plain" at the beginning and end of the pattern rows, till there are the full complement of 8 repetitions (as in the rest of the pattern). When that is attained, then as many of the diminutions (knit 2 together) before them as the number of stitches will admit, reversing these directions at the other end. For the borders on the other three sides, pick up and work as you take them up, the same number of stitches as on the first side, and knit them according to the directions given for it; then sew the corners together on the wrong side. When completed, the entire shawl should be dressed in the manner so often before described, by pinning it out with a clean sheet or tablecloth under it, laying a muslin wrung out of water over it, and letting both remain till perfectly dry.

WORK-BASKET OF NETTING AND BEADS.

This elegant little basket consists of a wire frame covered with crystal beads, to which is attached a piece of silk netting embroidered with chenille. It is ornamented with a bead fringe, a ruche of green silk, and green silk tassels. First prepare the frame by hemming a wire into both sides of a strip of double glazed linen, thirty-two inches long and one inch broad, and joining it to a circle. Bend the circle to an oblong with rounded corners, eight and a half inches long and seven and a half inches broad, and cover it with linen, over which is wound a string of small crystal beads. Then work a piece of netting with green filerelle on a mesh half an inch in diameter, beginning at one corner, and making the work forty stitches long and thirty-five stitches wide. Darn it with green chenille, and then join it to the wire frame by passing green chenille through the holes at the edge of the netting and around the frame, the corners of the netting fitting into the corners of the frame. Next prepare the feet and the scrolls by doubling a long wire, pushing a large bead to the point where the wire is bent, winding the doubled

handle, and ornament the sides with bows of chenille. If desirable, fasten a wire covered with beads underneath the network, passing from one foot to the other.

PENWIPER.

THIS is another design for a penwiper, and forms a pretty little addition to a writing-table, and will be found useful as a small thing for a fancy fair. You require a circular piece of

wire over first with cotton, and afterwards bending it to the required form with a string of crystal beads. The feet are attached to the square frame, according to illustration, and a chenille bow conceals the join. In order to make the fringe, first set a row of bead scallops, each containing twenty-six small beads, along the frame, and to these scallops work as follows : fasten the thread to the third bead of the scallop, thread four small beads, one cut bead, two small beads, and one long bead ; pass the needle through the following bead of the scallop, and back through the long bead * ; thread two small beads, one cut bead, two small beads, and one long bead ; pass the needle through the fourth following bead of the scallop, and through the long bead ; repeat three times from * ; thread two small beads, one cut bead, four small beads, and fasten the thread to the fifth following bead of the scallop. The handle, which is nineteen inches long and half an inch wide, is prepared precisely in the same way as the frames, covered with linen, and wound over with beads, and the ends are looped into the feet, according to illustration. Ornament the edge of the basket and the handle with a double ruche of pinked green silk ; sew a row of beads wound over a wire inside the

millboard for the bottom, about an inch and a half in diameter ; on this you glue your bristles, which are encased in card-board. This

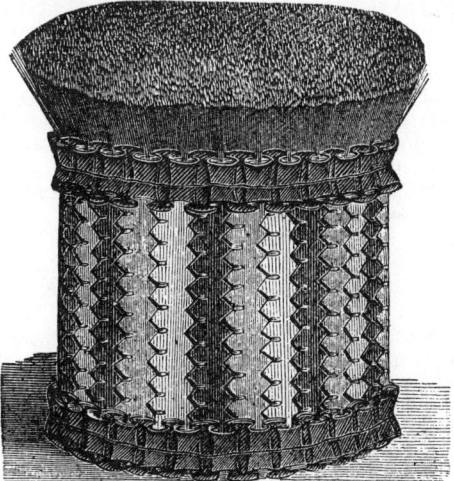

card-board is sewn or glued to the millboard around the bottom, and is about two and three-quarters inches high. The bristles project over this about half an inch. Horsehair cut in lengths, and firmly tied together, will answer the purpose of the bristles, if there should be any difficulty in procuring the latter. The card-board is ornamented with rows of different colored silks, or velvet pinked and over-cast with silks forming a good contrast. These are gummed on to the card-board. A ruche of ribbon around the top and bottom of the same completes the whole.

REEL STAND.

CUT out two circular pieces of card-board, divided into six scallops at the edge. Cover them on both sides with perforated card-board, and bind the edges with blue silk. To the upper piece sew a blue silk bag just inside the scallops, and then arrange six reels between

the two card-board plates, passing a double thread of strong silk through the lower plate, leaving a bead underneath to form the feet of the stand, then carrying the silk through the hole of the reel, and through the upper plate, and tying it firmly together with a knot. Conceal the knots at the top by small squares of perforated card-board, trimmed around with lace, and ornamented with bows of blue ribbon. Trim around the top of the bag also with lace, according to illustration.

SATCHEL, WITH COLORED SILK EMBROIDERY.

THE materials are Penelope canvas, eleven and three-quarters inches long and eight inches wide; a small bunch of Tuscan straw, the straws of which must be thick enough to cover every two canvas-threads; brown cloth in two strongly contrasting shades; woollen or silk stuff, with sarcenet ribbon of the darkest shade, three-quarters of an inch wide; shaded purse silk in brown, etc. The straws laid across, being three-quarters of an inch shorter than the canvas, are fastened down along the middle

with white silk; then the ends are completely secured by putting over and sewing down the edges of the canvas. The whole surface is afterwards lined with good calico. The strap trimming, one and a half inch wide, lying over loosely, is of a stripe of dark brown cloth, with a small scallop edge of the light shade standing over, and embroidered in flat and herring-bone stitch of brown-shaded purse silk; the straps

are fastened at the upper edge of the satchel. The double scallop stripe, with herring-bone stitch for the handle-strap, is one inch wide. Brown stuff stripes, three inches wide, give the folding sides set in plain at the sides in length. At the top these meet together plain, one and a half inch long, the rest of the stuff being drawn together in close folds. A ribbon quilling trims the satchel; to close it, an elastic loop, with tassel, and a black button, are needed.

POSTAGE CARD CASE.

THIS case serves to contain postage-cards, when it is desired to carry them with one, and consists of a bag cut out of fine gray linen, of

the shape and size shown in the illustration. It has a flap about three inches and one-fifth long, and one inch and one-fifth wide, which is scalloped. The trimming of the case is formed by a strap of Russia leather, cut out in squares through the middle, and worked with dark and light red silk in *point russe.* The strap as well as the case is scalloped and worked with dark red silk. The case is secured by a loop of Russia leather, attached to the case with *point russe* stitch, through which the strap is passed, and by a button and buttonhole.

BASKET FOR SWEETS.

THIS little basket is made of paper and thin card-board. For the bottom take a circle of card-board, two and a half inches in diameter; and for the side, a strip seven inches long, and one and a half inch wide. Join the strip around,

CROCHET BORDER FOR QUILTS, ETC.

THE materials are cotton, No. 8; medium-sized hook. Make a chain of twenty-two stitches. Work seven rows of double backwards and forwards, always taking up the back stitch. Increase one stitch at the end of the first, third, and fifth rows, so that when the seven rows are worked you have twenty-five stitches.

8th row. Four chain, one double-treble into third stitch of preceding row; one chain, one cross double-treble back into the first stitch of preceding row. (The cross double-treble is

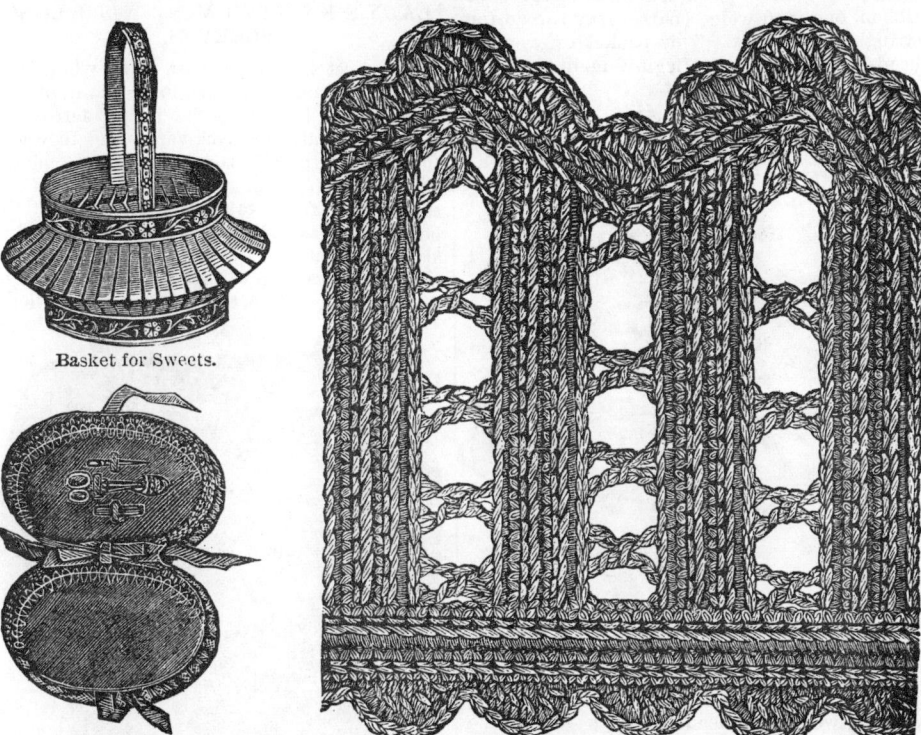

Basket for Sweets.

Lady's Companion.

Crochet Border.

and gum it to the bottom. Next take a strip of tinted note-paper, seven inches long, and two wide; fold it in half, lengthwise, and cut it in strips to within the eighth of an inch at the edge. Open it, and gum it at the two edges to the foundation, letting the cut part stand out, as seen in engraving. The edges are bordered with gilt, or other ornamental paper; the handle is of a narrow strip of card-board, also covered with ornamental paper.

LADY'S COMPANION.

THE foundation is of card-board, covered with silk or velvet, and ornamented with lace. Small straps of silk are sewn on for holding the thimble and scissors, etc.

worked thus: Put the cotton once around the hook, insert the hook through the middle of previously-worked treble; put the cotton once more around the hook, insert the hook into the specified stitch, and work back in the ordinary way.) * Two chain, pass over five, one double-treble into the next, one chain, one cross double-treble back into the third of the five just passed over. Repeat three times more from * [one chain, pass over one treble into the next]. The next seven rows are worked in the same manner as the first seven, decreasing one at the beginning of the second and sixth, so as to leave on twenty-three stitches the same as at the beginning.

16th. Same as the eighth, omitting that inclosed in brackets.

For the heading, work four rows of double to correspond with the stripes; then, lastly, a row as follows: Six graduated treble in successive stitches—viz., * two treble, two double-treble, two treble, one double. Repeat from * to the end. The edge is worked in the same manner as the heading; but only two rows of double are worked instead of four.

BASKET FOR KNITTING MOSAIC PATTERN OF WOODEN BEADS.

THE materials are ninety-six dozen common wooden beads; blue sarcenet; blue sarcenet ribbon, one inch wide; coarse gray thread for stringing the beads. This basket of wooden beads is of two parts. Beginning in the mid-

Fig. 1.

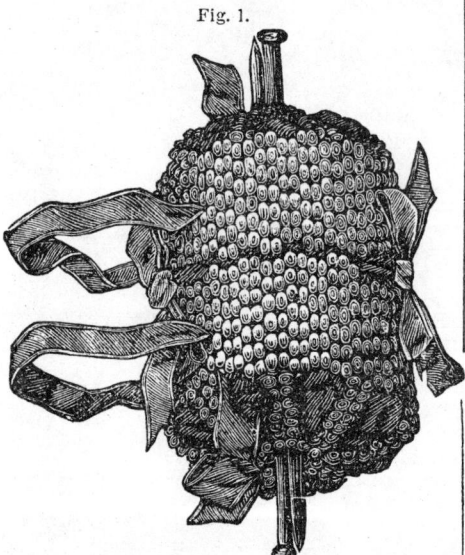

dle of the bottom, sixteen beads strung on a piece of coarse gray thread are to be knotted to a round, to which are added eight slings, each of twenty-two beads (always drawing the needle through two beads of the round). The firm edge of each half of basket worked in the round, the first bead row of which joined to the six middle beads of each sling, is made by alternately threading two beads, and drawing the thread through two beads of the foregoing row, as seen in the full size in Fig. 2. Six such

Fig. 2.

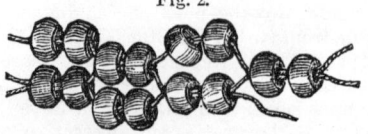

reversed rows of beads form the edge, which is two and a half inches deep. The open-work bottom is lined with sarcenet, put in full, which comes out in a puffed way through the bead slings. To fasten on the blue ribbon straps,

each eleven and a quarter inches long, as also the two strings, each ten and a half inches long, which, tied in bows, close the basket, the required end of ribbon is put through between the beads at the back, a wooden bead strung on, and close behind this a knot slung in the ribbon. Around the place where the two basket halves are joined together is a piece of ribbon, which is tied in a bow above. At each opening of the bottom a blue ribbon bow is also added.

LADY'S KNITTED VEST WITH LONG SLEEVES.

THIS vest is knitted with 3-ply white wool on wooden needles. Begin a chain of 370 stitches, the length of the jacket across the shoulders, and knit backwards and forwards 10 rows. In the 11th row cast off the 28 middle stitches for the slope of the neck, and work 70 rows for the front, taking off 4 stitches at the beginning of the 2d and 4th rows, and 2 stitches at the beginning of the 6th, 8th, and 10th rows, increasing again on the same side at the end of the 61st, 63d, 65th, 67th, and 69th rows. Knit

70 rows with the same alterations for the back, and then 11 rows along the whole length, adding 28 stitches in the first of the 11 for the shoulder. Cast off the first and last 123 stitches, and knit 130 rows with the middle 124 stitches for the sleeve, knitting 2 together at the end of every alternate row, up to the 49th row, and then at the end of every 3d row to the end. Cast off, and knit the 2d sleeve on the middle 124 stitches. Sew up the sleeves and the jacket at the sides, and work along the top of the jacket and the wrists a row of crochet points with 3-ply white wool as follows: * 1 double, 4 chain, 1 double into the 1st of the 4, missing a space underneath; repeat from *. Run a ribbon through the crochet.

LAMP MAT.

Materials.—Round cord, wool in three shades of green, rose-color, and white; black spangled wool; wire.

THE centre of this mat is worked in double crochet over cord with three shades of green, commencing with the darkest shade. The mat is then ornamented with sprays of sweet peas both are arranged on wire. The flowers, when completed, are disposed in groups of six or eight.

For the crochet leaves make a foundation chain of 11 st; go back over it, working 1 treble first on one side and then on the other of the foundation chain. This forms the middle part of the leaf. Edge these stitches with one round

with crochet leaves between; the sweet peas are worked with white and pink wool.

Fasten four threads crosswise on a card-board mesh, then pass the wool over these threads so as to form a circle of six rounds; now take a piece of similar wool divided in two, and pass it slanting across the six wool circles which are held down by the above-mentioned stitches; the latter are then cut away and the petals taken off the mesh. Two petals are required for each flower, one quite flat, slightly turned back towards the bottom, the other folded heart-shaped; the latter is placed in front and of double with spangled wool; a piece of wire is placed down the veining of the leaf to make it firmer.

KNITTED FRINGE.

CAST on 9 stitches. *1st. row.* Slip 1, 2 plain, over, knit 2 together, 1 plain, knit 2 together, 1 plain. Every row the same. When the length is completed cast off five stitches and unravel the rest.

These directions are for fringe in which the loops are formed by unravelling.

PAPER ROSE.

Materials.—Pale yellow, white, or red, and light green tissue-paper; thick gum, fine wire, paint-brush, pincers, hyacinth hook, the thickest wooden rounding pin, green leaves, and green wax calix; light green wool.

double, and then cut. The stamen calix, represented in Fig. 2, consists of a few light green loops of wool fastened to a wire. These are carefully combed out and surrounded with stamens of gold thread, touched at the points

Fig. 1.

Fig. 2.

Fig. 3.

Fig. 4.

OUR model is a light yellow rose, with a reddish pencilling; any pink will do as well.

The coloring is painted with carmine. The several leaf parts are folded four or eight times with fine white sand. Six double leaves, curled with what is called a hyacinth hook, are then pressed together at the under end, as shown in Fig. 3, and bound round the calix. They are one inch and a quarter long and half an inch wide, with a little piece cut out of the middle in a tapering form to within a quarter of an inch of the bottom of the paper. Then make three hollow pads, each formed from one inch and a half square by inclosing and pressing the corners together carefully (see Fig. 4). The again laid in the palm of the hand, and pressed up with the hook several times, so as to form the shapes represented in Figs. 7 and 8. First the four smaller, then the four larger petal parts; the latter, reversed, are bound round the hollow pad; then follow three circles of the petals cut four in one piece, with a little open-

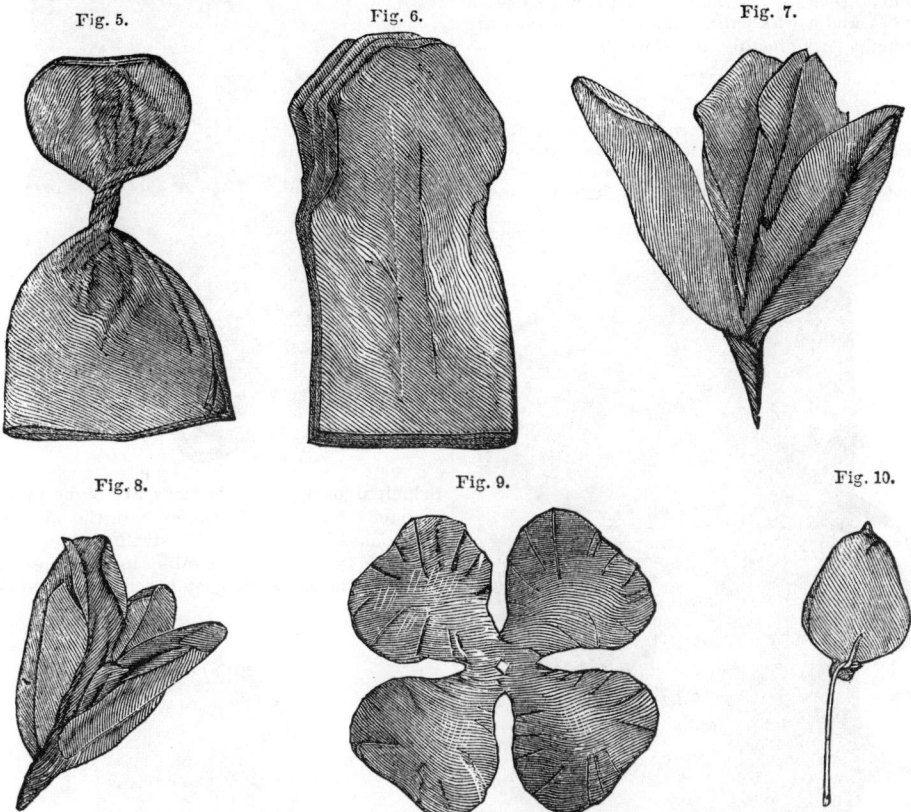

Fig. 5. Fig. 6. Fig. 7.

Fig. 8. Fig. 9. Fig. 10.

our leaves, which are all cut in one piece, are for the smaller size, two inches long and one inch broad, quite straight at the bottom, folded together at the top, and slightly rounded, so as to give a little curve exactly in the middle. The larger ones are one inch and a quarter broad, two inches and a half long, shaped at the top as described for the smaller one. Four of both sides (see Fig. 5) are pressed between the thumb and fore-finger of both hands, then opened out again, and, lying fourfold upon each other upon the palm of the hand, are crimped with the hyacinth hook, according to Fig. 6. The scalloped edges are then drawn lightly over the scissors in order to give the part that turns over the delicate form natural to the rose-leaf. Then the separate parts of the petal must be quite unfolded and separated from each other, and the four petals in one piece must be pressed together at the under end; then the so-far prepared petal part is

ing in the middle for pushing on. These are cut in the exact form shown in Fig. 9.

Each leaf is two inches and a quarter at the widest part, and is the same length from the highest point to the hole shown in the middle to draw the wire of the stamen calix shown in Fig. 2. The largest round of the wooden pin will be needed for rounding the large petals. As soon as a separate circle of the so-far finished rose is closely pushed on, the edges of the petals are very carefully gummed over each other at the side edges. Twelve leaves taken from this pattern are placed in reversed lines, and again carefully gummed over each other at the under points and side edges.

Suitable branches of moss are firmly gummed at regular distances under the roses. The stalks are covered with light green tissue paper, and a calix of green wax completes the rose. The mode of placing on the wadding and yellow tissue paper bud is shown in Fig. 10.

The large buds are easily made, and require a long or short strip of paper, according to their size, about one inch and a quarter or one inch and a half broad. Every leaf must be scalloped, and rounded, and turned back, according to Fig. 6, and squeezed together from the inside outwardly in the usual manner. The buds are also ornamented with branches of moss and a wax calix. The green leaves are bought very cheaply at a florist's.

PORTABLE BOX.

Materials.—American cloth, light brown cloth, embroidery silk, black, two shades brown and white, gold beads, little gilt ornaments, two buckles, striped ticking, pasteboard, leather for border, wooden frame.

Fig. 1.

THIS box opens in the middle, forming two equal halves, and measures fourteen and a half inches in length, and ten inches in breadth, and is eight and a quarter inches high at the sides. It is made of pasteboard covered with American cloth, and ornamented with leather scallops round the outer edges, borders covering the straps, and large palm-leaves in *appliqué* of light brown cloth, worked with a little black, and two shades of brown silk, with a few gold beads, and pretty little gilt ornaments. The arrangement of the tray, which is covered with ticking, is clearly shown in Figs. 2 and 3. The parts must be very firmly joined together with paste and glue; holes must be bored with a thick needle, and strong waxed thread used.

For the outer box, cut a piece of thick pasteboard, fifteen and a quarter inches long, and fourteen and a quarter inches broad for the

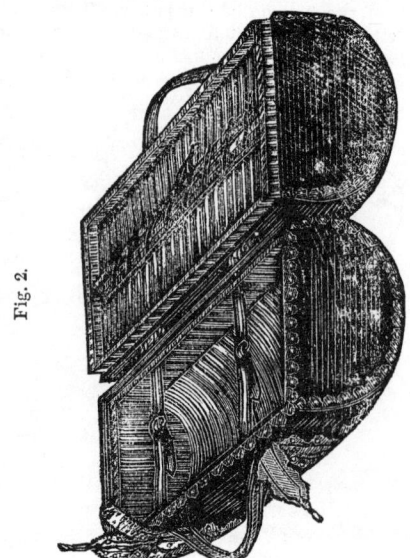

Fig. 2.

principal part; the side parts are eight and a quarter inches broad; the ends in the middle, five inches high, and at the straight sides, two inches. In order to be able to arrange the under rounding, each pasteboard part must be

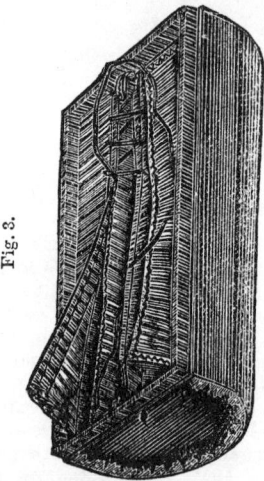

Fig. 3.

covered with American cloth, and a piece left to turn over at the outer edges only. The other sides must afterwards have holes bored in them, and be firmly sewn together. The pieces of pasteboard for the inner box must be cut with great accuracy, and arranged according to the outer box, so that one-half of the inner box advances three-quarters of an inch above the outer, and the other half is as much below the outer box. The ticking must be glued on, and one and a half inch must be left to turn over everywhere. The parts must be afterwards sewn together at the edges. The four large pasteboard parts are cut through with a sharp knife exactly at the places where the sharp bend comes (for the outer box two inches from the edge; for the inner box, at a corresponding distance) upon the side that is not gummed for the requisite bend at the corners. Above this bend, a thin wooden edge, one inch broad, must be glued on to the outer box, and an edge of corresponding height must be also placed on the outer side parts. For the leather scallop on the seams and outer edge, a strip of leather one and a quarter inch broad, is cut out in scallops. For covering the joining seams, the strips of scallops must be sewn on underneath. Previously to fastening the scallops at the edge of the cover a strong cord must be placed in to make a firm finish. After fastening on the palm-leaves, and the little border in brown chain stitch, with a brown edge and slanting white stitches, the inner box with cord and straps (see Figs. 2 and 3) must be fastened to the box with almost invisible stitches. The handles are stitched over a cord, and the straps are lined with tick, and embroidered, and holes are bored for fastening them and the handles in the places where the wooden ledge renders it most secure. The buckles must be made secure with silk braid.

INFANT'S FLANNEL SHOE, WITH KNITTED SOCK.

THIS pretty little shoe is made of white flannel, worked round with button-hole stitch of red wool; the sock is knitted with colored

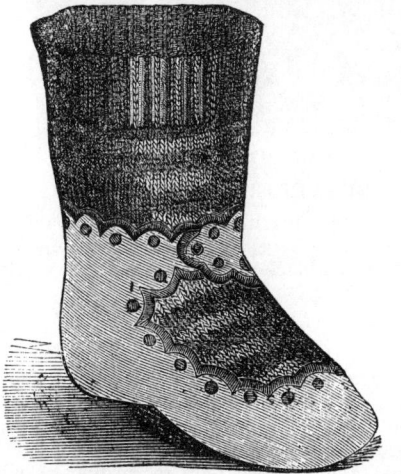

wool. Cast on for the sock a sufficient number of stitches with red wool; begin at the upper edge, and work 16 rounds alternately 2 stitches knitted, 2 purled; then begin the striped pattern, which is worked in plain knitting, 2 rounds with red wool, 3 rounds with white

wool, 2 rounds red, and 1 round black. The sock is worked like a stocking, only shorter and looser. The shoe is made of flannel taken double; it is embroidered with red wool, from illustration. The lappets of the shoe are fastened with a button and button-hole.

SPECTACLE CLEANER.

NOTHING damages an eyeglass or spectacles more rapidly than wiping them with any harsh, rough fabric. This small contrivance will be found very useful for the purpose. The shape is cut in paper, and the back is covered with

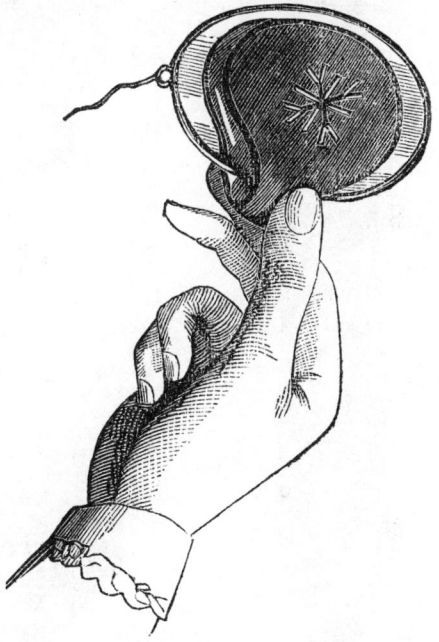

green silk, ornamented in the centre with a few fancy stitches; a little wadding is added, and the lining consists of either soft wash leather or a piece of white kid glove, the inside being turned outwards. The edge is finished off with a piece of cord. Both sides are alike.

SCISSOR-SHEATH AND STRING.

Materials.—Drab crochet cotton, blue filoselle, blue purse-silk, steel beads, blue satin ribbon three-fifths of an inch wide.

THIS scissor-sheath consists of a strip eighteen inches long, three-fifths of an inch wide, worked in crochet with drab cotton, and darned with blue filoselle in a damask pattern. At the lower end of the string there is a small pocket finished off into a point; it is worked with blue purse-silk. At the upper end fasten a hook, by means of which the strip is fastened on to the waistband. At the same place a rosette of blue satin ribbon is sewn on. For working the crochet strip, wind some gray crochet cotton closely over a mesh three-fifths of an inch wide, work along one side of the mesh one slip stitch round each piece of cotton. Draw the thus covered cotton off the mesh, leaving only the last three or four, cover the mesh again, and continue to work on in this manner till the strip is nineteen inches long. Work slip stitches in the same manner along the other side of the

into a point. Then sew the lower end of the crochet strip on to half the upper edge of the pocket, after passing the handle of the scissors through, in the manner seen on illustration. Lastly, ornament the pocket round the edge with steel beads, from illustration, fasten a large hook at the upper end of the holder on the wrong side, and a rosette of blue satin ribbon on the right side.

SCISSOR-SHEATH AND STRING.

BUTTERFLY WORKED ON NET.

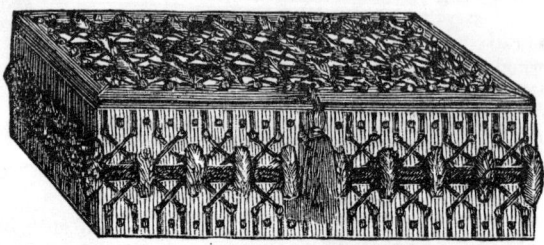

ORNAMENTAL BOX.

strip; at both ends work the slip stitches round the last piece of cotton. Then darn the loose cotton between the two rows of slip stitches with blue filoselle in the damask pattern, fold the strip in two, so as to form a point in the centre, and so that the selvedge stitches of one side meet together. These selvedge stitches are sewn together five inches from the point with buttonhole stitch of blue purse-silk, taking up two corresponding stitches with one buttonhole stitch; a steel bead must be threaded with each stitch. When the strip has been thus far joined together, work on the free side one buttonhole stitch in every selvedge stitch, likewise threading on one steel bead for every stitch. For the pocket, make a foundation chain of twenty-eight stitches, join them into a circle, and work eighteen rounds in double crochet, decreasing in such a manner that the pocket is finished off

BUTTERFLY WOKED ON NET.

THESE butterflies are used for ornamenting evening dresses; our model is composed of white and black net worked with pink silk.

ORNAMENTAL BOX.

THIS small box, intended for holding the knick-knacks on a dressing-table, is made of the new gold canvas, and can be of any size, according to requirement. The foundation, sides, and lid are all cut in card-board, which is covered with pink satin at both sides. The gold canvas is then cut the size of the card-board, and worked with black chenille, according to the illustration. The small round dots are gold beads. A gold cord is sewn at the edges to conceal the joinings.

BIB IN CROCHET TRICOTEE.

Materials.—This bib is crocheted with knitting cotton, No. 16, and a long coarse steel crochet hook; a finer cotton and hook are required for the edging. If worked in wool it would make a capital chest preserver for children in cold weather.

COMMENCE at the bottom of the point in front with 3 ch, take up the 2 chain, and work back as usual.

2d row. Make a stitch by taking up the horizontal stitch running between the 1st and 2d loops, take up the 2d long loop, make another stitch as the first between the 2d and 3d long loops; work back.

3d. Make a stitch as in last row on each side the centre long loop in the row. Work back; repeat this row until you have 59 long loops; this should bring you to the 28th row.

29th. Take up 29 loops only with the one on

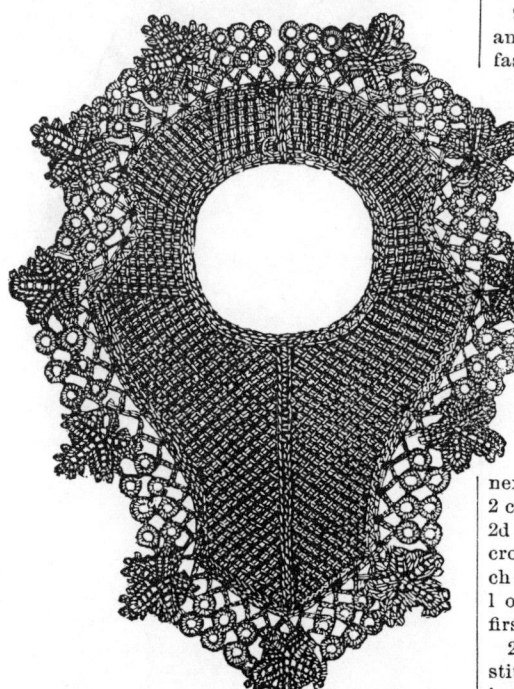

the needle. Work back. This is the first row of the right shoulder.

30th. Take up 28 loops. Work back. 31st row to 37th row. Take up one stitch less each row.

38th. Leave 3 loops unraised at the end of this little row; repeat this row 5 times.

44th. Take up each 3 stitches left in each of the last 6 rows. Work back. Work the 2 last on the needle off together, so decreasing 1 stitch.

45th. Take up all the loops of last row, work back the 2 first together, decreasing one, and the two last on the needle also.

Then work 6 rows, decreasing one each row at the end of each row in working back.

52d. Take up all but the last loop, work back plain.

53d. Make a loop between the loop on the needle and the 2d long loop, as in the first rows; leave 1 loop unraised at the end of the row, work back. Work 7 more rows like this.

61st. Leave 1 loop unraised at the end, and make no increase in commencing; work back. Work 4 more rows like this.

66th. Raise 2 loops besides the one on needle; work back.

67th. Raise the loops of 66th row and all the stitches left at the end of the rows to the 46th row.

9 rows plain.

77th. Leave 1 loop unraised at the end; work back; work the next 16 rows as the 77th.

94th. Raise all the loops left between this and the 77th row; work back; 8 plain rows, fasten off.

Join to the 3d stitch from the centre of the work in the 29th row, and repeat from that row for the left shoulder, with this difference, that all the stitches are left in working back at the end of the needle instead of in raising the loops, and where you decreased in commencing the row, decrease in ending it—the same with the increasings—when this left shoulder is worked, work a row of double crochet all round and in the neck.

The border consists of 11 ivy leaves worked in the finer cotton; these ivy leaves are joined by 12 sets of 6 rings.

1st ivy leaf. 11 ch for 1st vein, 1 l on the 7th ch, * 2 ch, miss 2, 1 l on the next * twice. 2d vein, 14 ch, 1 l on the 10th * 2 ch, miss 2, 1 l on next * 3 times; repeat the 2d vein twice more; after the 4th vein is worked crochet 1 l on the 1st l of the 1st vein, then 11 ch for the 5th vein, 1 l on 7th, * 2 ch, miss 2, 1 l on the next twice, 1 dc on the 1st ch in the first vein.

2d round. Double crochet, work 1 dc in each stitch, excepting in the top stitch of every vein, in it work 3 dc, and at the bottom of each vein miss 3 stitches; at the end of the 5th vein leave 1 stitch, and commence the 3d round in the 2d dc of last round.

3d round. Dc in each of the 2d and 3d stitches, * 3 ch, 1 dc in each of 2 next stitches; repeat. At the top of each vein only leave 1 dc between the little loops of 3 ch; at the bottom of each vein leave 2 stitches unworked, besides the centre stitch, and 2 on the other side the centre stitch, making 5 stitches altogether. Always begin the next vein with 2 dc. At the end of the round leave 2 stitches unworked, and join with 1 s in the 1st dc of the round; fasten off. Work 11 of these leaves; when 2 are worked, join them with the rings.

1st ring. 13 ch, unite, work inside half only of this ring with dc, then 16 ch, join into a ring, 1 s on the last dc in last ring, fill half this ring with dc. 16 ch, join as the last, fill half of it with dc, and draw through the picot at the top of the first vein in a leaf; work back in each half of the 3 rings with dc, and join with 1 s to the 1st dc in 1st ring, and at the same time to the top of 1st vein in another leaf; fasten off. Work the next row of 3 rings in the same manner, joining to the picot at the top of the side in the 2d vein, and drawing the centre dc in each half of the ring through the middle dc of each ring below. You will observe that two leaves are joined on both sides the bib with 4 rings in the 1st row. At the back end the border with a set of rings on each side.

You join the border to the bib in the following manner: Commence on the point of the bib in front with 1 dc, 6 ch, join with 1 dc on the dc of leaf between the top of first vein, to which the ring is joined, and the one to the outside of it; 6 ch, * 1 dc on bib, 6 ch, 1 dc on ring; repeat, taking up each ring and first and last veins of the leaves, making the border fit nicely; fasten off. Add 2 little buttons and loops at the back.

KNITTED DUSTER.

SHOWS part of a duster, full size; it is knitted with narrow tape, in rows backwards and for-

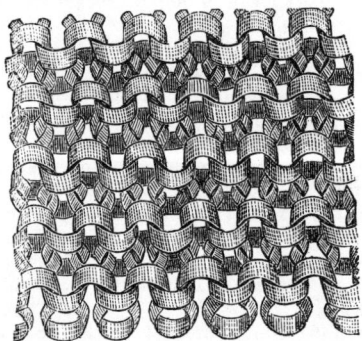

wards, with thick wooden knitting-needles. At both ends the duster is finished off with a fringe of the tape. The duster can be made of worsted braid or wool, if preferred.

CROCHET SCARF.

Materials. — White wool, mauve-colored wool, a bone crochet needle to correspond.

MAKE a foundation chain of 22 stitches with white wool; join the stitches into a circle. *1st round.* Insert the needle into the 1st stitch, work 1 stitch, draw out a loop three-fifths of an inch long, keep the loop on the needle, work 1 stitch more, and draw out another loop of the

same size. *2d.* Take the needle out of all the long loops, and take them up separately one by one by slip stitches of mauve-colored wool.

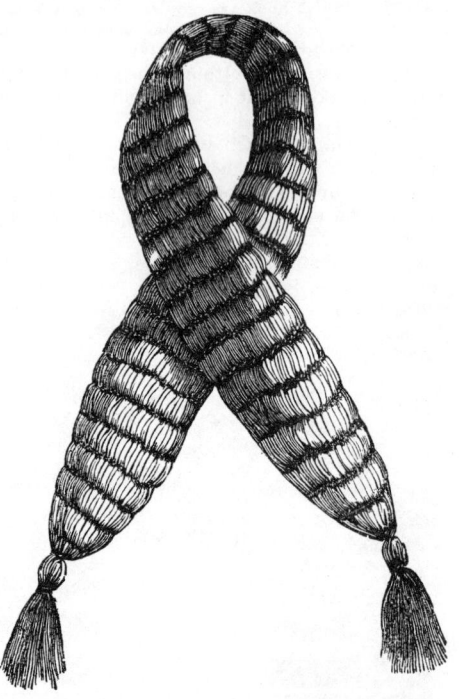

Work thus 34 rounds. Gather up the ends, and fasten a small tassel of white and mauve wool.

LETTER FOR MARKING.

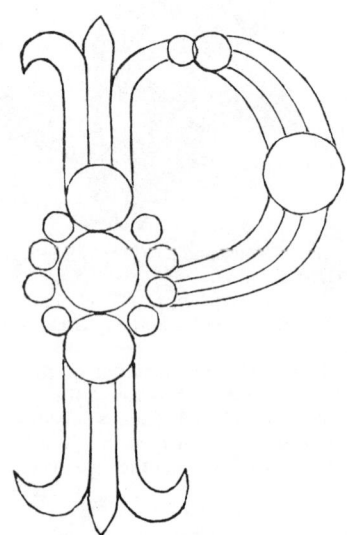

PATTERN FOR A LADY'S WRAPPER.

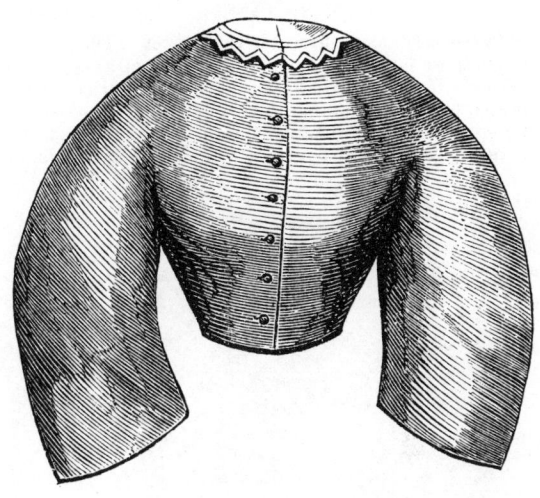

THIS wrapper pattern possesses peculiar advantages in its simplicity and adaptation to any figure—the back and front being exactly alike, and the only alteration necessary being in the size of the neck. It can be made of any material, perfectly plain, or very richly trimmed. It does not require the aid of the dressmaker, as any lady can make and trim a dress for herself. Cashmere trimmed with velvet, lawn with ruffles, or white material with flouncing, look equally well. Plain chintz, with puffs of the same. The connecting seam is on the shoulder. The waist should have a string run in the hem to make it fit smoothly.

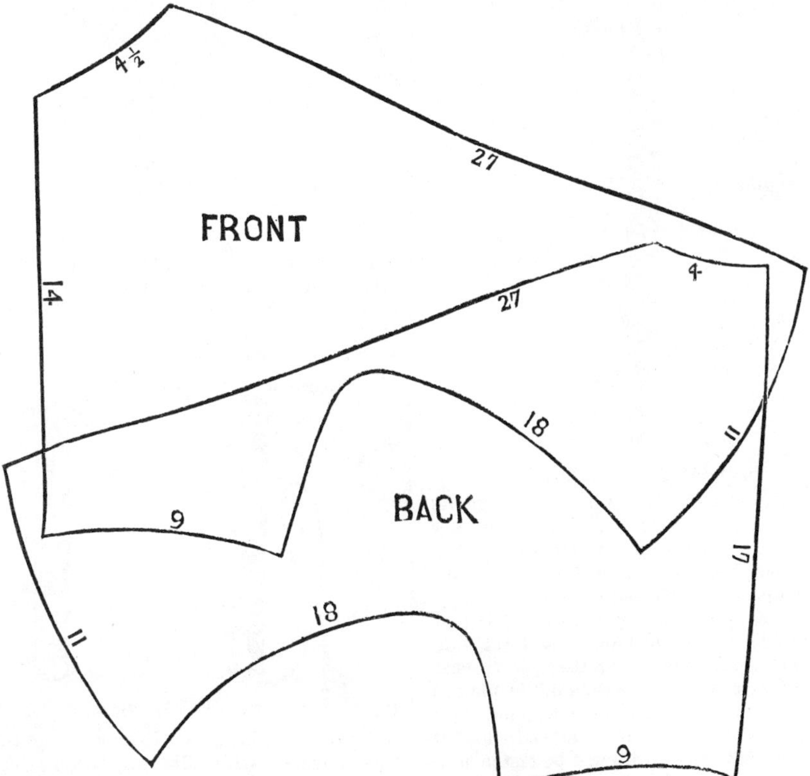

POCKET FAN.

THIS fan is easily carried in the pocket. The upper part is made of white silk, plaited and ornamented with *point russe* embroidery. It is drawn into the handle by means of a cord; the handle consists of a tube of card-board seven inches long, measuring four-fifths of an inch

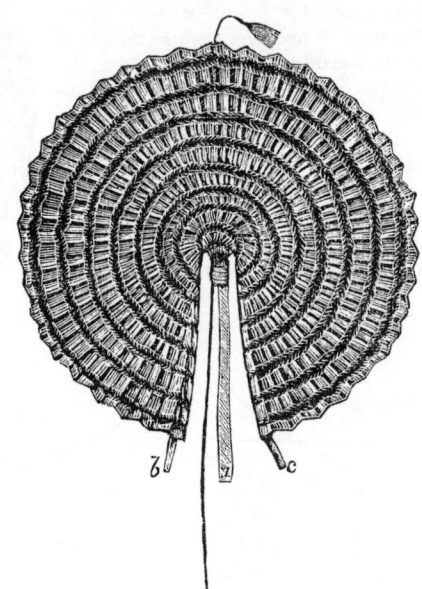

Fig. 2.—Detail of Fan.

out. The plaits are sewn together on one side, and wound round with a thread, as can be seen on Fig. 2. Fasten on at the same time a piece of ribbon two-fifths of an inch wide, four and four-fifths inches long. The ribbon, as well as

and twelve inches at the bottom. Then fasten the folds of the middle plait over one another, covering the strip of card-board in this manner. Then plait the fan, fasten the plaits with a few stitches, and press them slightly with a hot iron, so that the plaits are marked and remain in the silk when the fan is drawn in and

Fig. 1.—Pocket Fan (Open).

across, covered with silk. Fig. 1 shows the fan open; Fig. 3 as it is drawn through the tube. The piece of silk for the fan must be twenty-eight inches long and four and three-fifths inches wide. It is then embroidered from illustration, and plaited all round; the plaits must be two-fifths of an inch deep, and the folds must come exactly one over the other. Paste a strip of card-board into the middle plait; it must be four and two-fifths inches long, three-fifths of an inch wide, and folded in half its width. A white silk cord must be fastened beforehand into the strip of card-board, hanging one and one-fifth inches beyond it at the top,

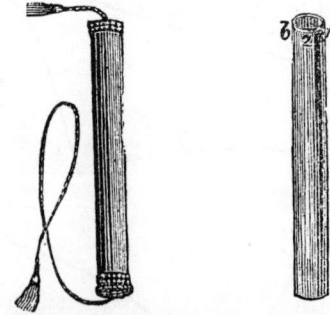

Fig. 3.—Pocket Fan (Closed).   Fig. 4.—Tube for Fan.

the silk cord, is drawn through a card-board tube covered with silk, which must be two-fifths of an inch shorter than that which forms the handle, and thin enough to be pushed into it. Fasten the ribbon at the bottom, at the place marked *a* on the tube 1. Then open the fan, from Fig. 2, and fasten the ribbons *b* and *c*, each being four-fifths of an inch long, at the top of the tube 2 at the corresponding letters, drawing in the fan and the tube 1 into the

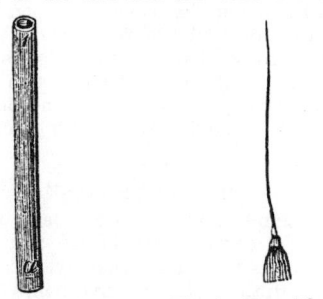

Fig. 5.—Tube for Fan.   Fig. 6.—Tassel for Fan.

handle. These stitches are covered with a circle of beads. At the bottom the cord is drawn through a case made of beads. These beads are threaded on wire; form with them a flat circle, corresponding in size to the width of the handle, join on to it a border two-fifths of an inch high. Then wind the wire in coils, and fasten the separate coils to one another by means of finer wire. This case is fastened on the handle by a few stitches. The cord is finished off with small silk tassels.

CROCHET CIGAR-CASE.

THIS cigar-case is made of two pieces of card-board, made to slide into each other in the manner seen in illustration, the inner piece being rather smaller than the outer, so that it may slide in and out with ease. The inner part is covered on both sides with brown silk, only the round end having a covering of crochet. The outer part is lined with brown silk, and covered outside with crochet. Commence by cutting out the card-board, and when you have laid on the silk for the lining, gum the sides together, and cover the outside of the inner piece also with silk. Then work the crochet covering for the end of the inner piece as follows: Make with brown netting silk a chain of six stitches, join it into a circle with a slip stitch, and work on this 13 rows of double, increasing gradually at the opposite ends of the work, so as to form a flat oval three inches long and two inches and a quarter wide. Round this work 6 rows of double without increase, and then fold the piece lengthwise; press the rounded edge of the card-board into the crochet, to form a crease, and work on the wrong side a row of double stitches on the stitches marked by this crease. In the middle of this crease sew outside a small ribbon loop, and draw the crochet over the end of the card-board. Now begin the crochet cover for the larger piece in the same way, allowing for the

larger dimensions, and working 15 instead of 13 rows for the oval. When the covering for the end is finished, proceed to work in connection with it as follows: 2 rows of double with light brown silk, 1 row with middle brown, 1 row with dark brown, then 10 rows with middle brown, putting in the 4th, 6th, and 8th rows spots in treble stitch, according to the illustration. Each spot consists of three treble stitches worked over the front thread of the double stitch in the last row but one, the double in the last row being missed. In the 4th row these spots occur at intervals of 7 double, in the 6th row at intervals of 3 double, in the 8th row at

intervals of 7 double. In the 5th, 7th, and 9th rows these spots are passed over, and 1 chain-stitch worked. After these 10 rows work 1 row of double with dark brown silk, 1 row with middle shade, two rows with light brown. The last row must be divisable by 8, and if necessary a few stitches added. Work 41 rows of double as follows: Without cutting off the light brown silk, take up the dark brown, and draw the dark silk through the loop with the light silk in the last light stitch. (Throughout the work the different shades are taken up and laid aside without cutting off the silk, which is slipped at the back of the work.) *1st row.* * 1 dark brown, 2 light brown, 3 middle brown, 2 light brown, repeat from * to the end of the row. *2d.* * 1 middle brown, 1 dark brown, 2 light brown, 1 middle brown, 2 light brown, 1 dark brown, repeat from *. *3d.* * 2 middle brown, 1 dark brown, 3 light brown, 1 dark brown, 1 middle brown, repeat from *. *4th.* * 3 middle brown, 1 dark brown, 1 light brown, 1 dark brown, 2 middle brown, repeat from *. *5th.* * 2 middle brown, 2 light brown, 1 dark brown, 2 light brown, 1 middle brown, repeat from *. *6th.* * 1 middle brown, 2 light brown, 1 dark brown, 1 middle brown, 1 dark brown, 2 light brown, repeat from *. *7th.* * 2 light brown, 1 dark brown, 3 middle brown, 1 dark brown, 1 light brown, repeat from *. *8th.* * 1 light brown, 1 dark brown, 5 middle brown, 1 dark brown, repeat from *. Repeat these 8 rows 4 times, and then work 1 row like the 1st row. Now work 2 rows in light brown, 1 row in middle brown, 1 row in dark brown silk, then 10 rows in middle brown, in spots, 1 row in dark brown, 1 row in middle brown, 2 rows in light brown. Draw this cover over the card-board, and fasten it down. Slip the inner piece inside the outer piece, and the case is complete.

CROCHET POPPY.

Materials.—Purse silk, wire, and zephyr.

TAKE some fine wire and work over it 1 treble, 1 plain, and 2 treble in succeeding stitch, 3 treble in the next, and 3 treble again in the next. On the other side of the flower you

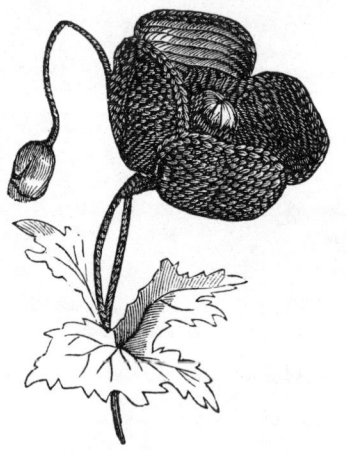

work all over the wirework, 4 treble in one stitch (the same in which you worked 3 before), then 3 treble in next stitch and 2 treble in each of the 3 following, 1 double in the next, 3 single. Then work as follows all round the petal : 1 double and 1 treble in 1st double, 1 treble in each of the next 7 stitches, 2 treble in each of the next 11 stitches, 1 treble in each of the next 7 stitches, 1 treble, and 1 double in the next, 1 single ; fasten off. Four such petals are required for each

flower. For the stamens, take the black silk and make a chain about three-fifths of an inch long, leave a long end of silk hanging from the chain, thread a needle with this silk and work a bit of fringe upon the mesh with it, inserting the needle into the chain after forming each loop. Draw out the mesh, cut open the silk loops, roll up the bit of fringe very tight, and fasten it up so that the chain forms a little round ball. Add a small wire stem covered with silk. Dispose the petals round this centre upon a thicker stem covered with green wool.

SPECTACLE CASE.

THIS simple and useful article is made of card-board, covered with brown silk on both sides, the inside having a thin layer of wadding underneath the silk. It is five inches long and one inch and three-quarters wide, and is composed of 5 pieces—the bottom, the rim, the top,

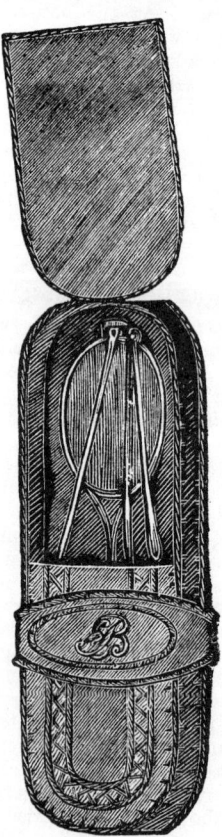

half of which is cut off to form the lid and the slide. The top is neatly embroidered with braid and herring-bone stitch, and the pieces are joined together with overcast stitch. The slide is made of 1 piece, the ends of which are stitched together at the back, and a piece of elastic fastens it to the bottom of the case.

SOFA TIDY OF TATTING.

IN tatting it is far more puzzling to work from written instructions than from an engraving, which, in this design, is a fac-simile of the work itself. It is commenced in the centre with 1 tat, having 8 loops, 2 stitches between each loop. Into each of these loops 3 plain stitches are made, then a loop, then 3 more stitches, a loop, then the two tats are worked

Fig. 1. Begin with the cup of the upper blossom of the spray, the 1st 3 rounds of which are like the 1st 3 rounds of the spray Fig. 2. 4th and 5th rounds. 15 double stitch in each, then turn and work the 6th round; 10 long double divided by 1 chain stitch in the 10 following stitches of the preceding round (the 1st long double is formed by 2 chain), in the following 5 stitches, 7 double. Fasten the last stitch of

and joined as in engraving, and the tat first commenced is finished. When these two circles of tats are finished, the outside row, consisting of 2 rows of tats, is worked, consisting of a centre tat having 4 loops, round which 5 tats are worked, then the 2 tats, which are joined in their places to the centre piece of tatting which was first worked. The tidy, when finished, is lined with the llama, which is first fringed out three nails in depth.

CROCHET SPRAYS OF FLOWERS.

Materials.—Twilled crochet cotton of two different sizes.

THESE sprays of flowers are suitable for trimming collars and cuffs, cravat ends, children's frocks, etc.

every round to the first with 1 slip stitch. 7th round. On every long double of the preceding round 1 treble, 1 chain stitch between, now and then work 2 treble, divided by 1 chain on 1 long double; on the following, 7 double, 12 double. 8th round like the 7th. Leave 1 purl after every treble, as has been explained already; and after the 6 double stitches worked on the 1st 6 double of the preceding round, work the three following loops; 5 chain, 1 slip stitch in the last worked double stitch, 7 chain, 1 slip stitch in the same double stitch, 5 chain, 1 more slip stitch in the same double. The 3 other larger leaves are worked in the same way, but in larger dimensions, by making 20 stitches in the cup, and by working the 7th round twice, fasten the blossoms together at the places marked on illustration. Work the stem last; make a foundation chain of 10 stitches; and after the last stitch, work the small leaf. 1st round. 12 chain, miss the last 3, turn and work alternately 1 long double, 1 chain, missing 1 chain stitch under the latter. Work the 2d round over the 1st in the same manner; after every trefoil leaf make 1 purl, and do not miss any stitch 4 times following in the upper part of the middle of the leaf. After having fastened the last stitch of this round with 1 slip stitch, work 22 stitches for the stem, fasten this with 1 slip stitch on the lower blos-

Fig. 1.

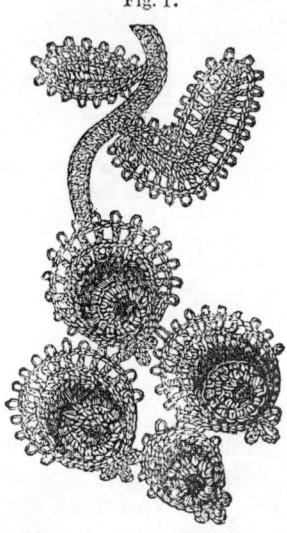

som, turn and work 1 treble in each chain stitch of the stem. After 16 treble, work the large leaf as follows: 1st row of the large leaf, 81 chain stitch, miss the 2 last, turn and work the 2d row; 3 double, 15 treble, miss the 2 next chain stitch under them, 9 treble, 2 double. The 3d row is worked round the leaf thus: Alternately 1 treble, 1 purl, 1 chain, missing 1 stitch under the latter; in the 2d stitch missed in the preceding row, work 2 treble, divided by 1 chain stitch; on the opposite side miss 3 stitches, but do not divide the 2 treble stitches by 1 chain. This gives a curved shape to the leaf.

Fig. 2. Begin with the cup of the flower; take the coarsest cotton and make a foundation chain of 5 stitches; join them into a circle, and work 5 rounds in the following manner: 1st round. 2 double in every stitch of the foundation chain. 2d. On the 10 double stitch of the preceding round, 15 double. 3d. 15 double. 4th. 20 double. 5th. 20 double. Then turn the work. Fasten the finer cotton on the last stitch of the cup, and begin the first flower leaf; * 11 chain, miss the last turn, and work 2 double, 2 treble; to join the different leaves together, work 1 purl after the 2 treble; make the purl by drawing out the loop on the needle a little longer, take the needle out carefully, insert it in the upper part

of the last stitch, and then work 5 treble, 1 slip stitch in the 6 following stitches of the foundation chain. When you work the stitch after the purl, take care not to draw the latter too tight. Work 1 slip stitch on the cup, and repeat 15 times more from *. As the outer edge of the cup has 20 stitches, miss 1 stitch now and then. When you make the foundation chain of the following leaves, work, instead of the 7th chain, 1 slip stitch, inserting the needle in the purl of the preceding leaf. After the last flower leaf, work the stem of the spray with its leaves; but before doing this, the middle veinings must be worked. For each veining of the two small upper leaves make a foundation chain of 9 stitches, miss the last, turn and work as follows: 1 slip stitch, 5 treble, 1 slip stitch, 1 chain, fasten the cotton carefully at the beginning and end. The veinings of the larger leaves are worked in the same manner, only begin with a chain of 11 stitches. Then, for the stem, make a foundation chain of 14 stitches; then a smaller leaf on the left side of the stem; this leaf is worked in rounds as follows: 1st round of the leaf. 7

Fig. 2.

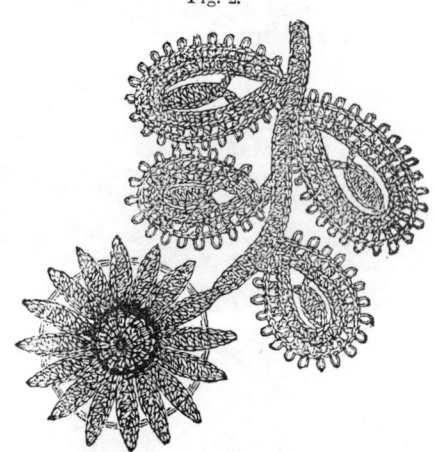

chain, 1 slip stitch in the 1st chain stitch left free in one of the small veinings, 12 chain stitch, 1 slip stitch in the upper part of the middle of the veining, 12 chain, 1 slip stitch in the last chain left free in the veining, 4 chain, 1 slip stitch in the 5th of the 1st 7 chain of this round, so that the 1st 4 chain stitches of the same remain free for the stem of the leaf. 2d round. Alternately 1 long double, 1 chain, miss 1 stitch of the preceding round under it (the 1st long double is formed of 2 chain stitch); only in the upper part of the middle of the leaf do not miss any stitch three times following; at the end of the round work 1 slip stitch in the 1st slip stitch of the preceding round. 3d round like the 2d round. After every long double, make 1 purl in the way above described; at the end of the round, crochet 4 long double in the 4 chain stitches left for the stem of the leaf. Then work 14 chain stitches for the large stem of the next large leaf, which is worked like the one just described, only in larger proportions, by working in the 1st round a greater number of chain stitches round the larger veining. After you have completed this leaf, work 6 chain stitches for the large stem, turn and work 1 treble in each chain stitch, working the 2 leaves on the right side of the stem when you come to their respective places.

STAR IN BEADS OR BERLIN WOOL.

PATENT EAR-RING HOOK.

FIG. 1 shows it applied to the ear-ring. This is a new invention to prevent ear-rings from being lost. We fear the sensation of the rough

Fig. 1.

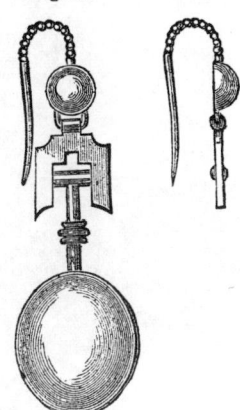

part entering the ear would not be pleasant but we like to give our readers all that is new

ANTIMACASSAR MADE OF BRAID.

THIS is quite a new kind of antimacassar and very pretty when executed with neatness and accuracy. It consists of seven separate

Fig. 1.

Fig. 2.

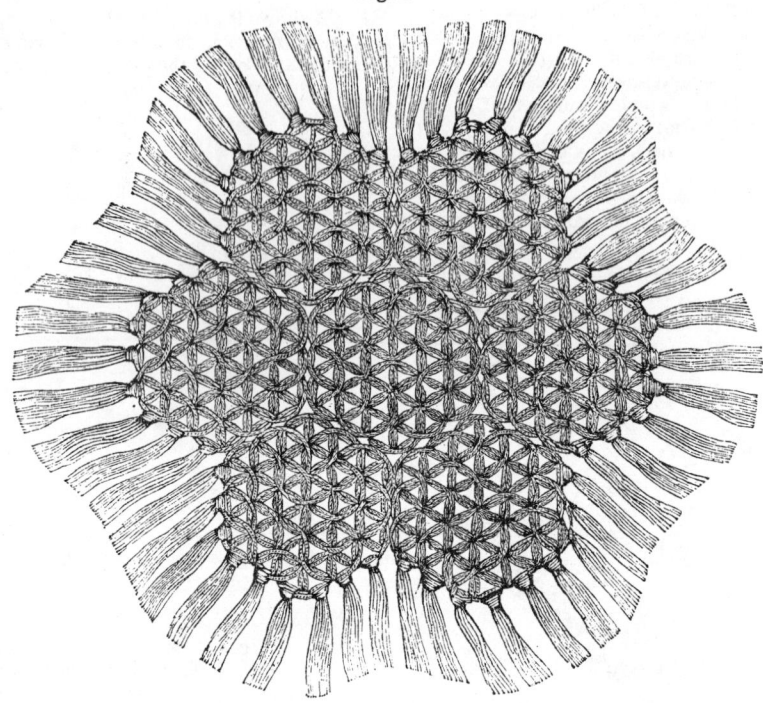

rosettes (like that shown in Fig. 1) sewn together with fine thread, and surrounded by cotton fringe, as seen in Fig. 2. In order to make the rosettes, draw the pattern first on paper, and then run the braid along the lines, observing to avoid cutting the braid, and stitching the points where the braids cross each other firmly together. When the rosette is finished, tear away the paper at the back without breaking the threads.

PURSE.

KNIT in blue worsted and gold thread, with small gold tassels to finish it at the edge. A very pretty purse.

HANGING TOWEL RACK.

MADE of oiled walnut, with looking-glass in centre, and embroidered pieces at each side.

SAMPLER PATTERN FOR OUR YOUNG READERS.

FEATHER TRIMMINGS FOR BALL DRESSES, ETC.

Some of the newest and most uncommon trimmings of the present season are composed of feathers arranged in a variety of ways, either as ornaments for the hair, in separate shapes, or in continuous rows forming a border of any desired width, very suitable for trimming ball dresses—ostrich, pheasant, and even partridge feathers being called into requisition. Ladies residing in the country, and keeping fancy and other poultry, may easily make a collection of useful and effective feathers for the purpose, while those living in towns may obtain them from their poulterers. The white poultry feathers are particularly useful, as, by the aid of dyes, they may be made to assume any tint required to match or contrast with any ball dress. From the Magenta dye a beautiful rose pink may be obtained by putting in a small quantity of it. Scarlet, cerise, mauve, violet, yellow, blue, orange, gray, and many other colors may be had. For dyeing the small feathers, pour into an earthen basin two quarts of boiling water, and let the feathers soak in it for a minute or two, then lift them out with a perfectly clean quill pen or piece of stick, and pour in a little of the dye. The quantity must depend on the shade required ; but it is better to put in too little than too much, as it is easy to add more if requisite. The feathers must never be allowed to remain in the basin while the dye is poured in. When the dye is thoroughly mixed with the water, put the feathers

Fig. 1.

in, and stir them about well with a pen or stick in each hand, that the color may take effect equally. When the feathers are of the shade you wish, take them out of the water with your little implement, and hang them to dry. We will now proceed to describe the various trimmings, illustrations of which are given in

Figs. 1 to 7. Fig. 1 is a pretty ornament for the hair, and looks extremely well with lace, ribbon bows, or flowers. It admits of great variety in the combination and arrangement of the colors ; and, after describing the manner in which it is made, we must leave each lady to exercise her taste and ingenuity in the matter, merely remarking that the feathers of all kinds of foreign birds are very available for this purpose, as they need only match each other in pairs. For the foundation take a piece of rather thin Bristol board, three-quarters of an inch in depth and one inch and one-eighth in width ; slope the outer corners towards the centre, leaving one-quarter of an inch in the middle for the body, which must be sloped and rounded at the extremities, and slightly fold the card-board straight across, depth ways, on each side of this. This piece is for the support of the wings (it is better to be colored black on the under side), and to it the feathers composing them must be fixed with strong gum-Arabic. For these, feathers having a larger and stronger shaft than those forming the trimmings hereafter described must be selected ; those for the two upper wings cut to about an inch and three-quarters in length, and for the lower ones an inch and a quarter ; these last must overlap the former, part of one side of the feather being cut away that they may not do so too much. The feathers for the upper wings must also be shaped with the scissors, and sloped to meet the under ones, and both sets notched at the edge. Scarlet looks well for the upper wings, and buff or sulphur color for the lower ones (but these can be varied in any way) ; white spots may be painted on the scarlet with body or oil color, and black on the buff with lampblack, with which also the notches may be edged. The breast feathers of pheasants are very pretty for the centre, arranged something in the manner shown in Fig. 1, their natural markings coming in to great advantage. The very small neck feathers of the peacock, too, may be advantageously used for the same purpose. Having arranged the wings to your satisfaction, proceed to cut the shape of the butterfly's body in the Bristol board, about an inch and three-quarters in length, rather pointed at one extremity, and rounded at the other for the head ; paint the under side black, and cover the upper with black velvet gummed on ; but, before doing so, put between it and the former piece of card-board two of the thinnest filaments of a peacock's feather (or, if not thin enough, cut them narrower), about one inch and three-quarters in length, for the antennæ; these, being so very light, are the best things for the purpose, as they

Fig. 2.

put through the loop in the wire fastens it to the hair in any required position. Figs. 2 and 3 are well adapted for bands to loop up the tunic of a white tarlatane or crape ball dress.

Fig. 3.

move with the air, and give a more natural appearance. Now insert into the centre of the under piece of card-board a short length of fine wire (such as is used for artificial flowers)

A foundation must be made by folding a double piece of the same material as the dress, rather narrower than the feathers will cover, and on it, for Fig. 2, are to be fixed a row of five

Fig. 4.

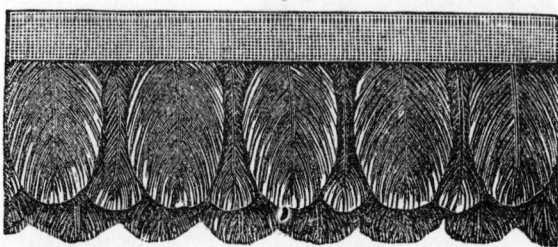

twisted round a knitting needle, and make a small loop at the disengaged end; it only remains now to gum on the body in its proper place, and the butterfly is complete. A hairpin

feathers in breadth, of any light or bright color preferred, placed not quite straight across, but in the manner shown in the illustration. There are to be five rows of the same feathers also in height, as distinctly seen in the illustration, and then by way of contrast the tip of a large dark green and black cock's feather, or a peacock's eye, which would have the best effect at the same purpose, for a mourning dress, is composed entirely of black feathers, arranged in the form there shown, and edged with very light narrow ones. Some gray feathers might

Fig. 5.

night, with a very small feather of the same color as the rest on each side of it to make up the width. There are two ways of fastening on the feathers. Some people fix them with very strong gum-Arabic at the quill end of be intermixed in any way preferred to lighten this trimming; and, in order to adapt them to any desired shape, all and any of the feathers may be cut with sharp scissors to give them the proper form and make them fit in where re-

Fig. 6.

each, but the most secure way is sewing over every feather twice on each side the top of the quill. The peacock's feather and the smaller colored ones are to be repeated in the manner shown in the illustration till you have the required length. Fig. 3, which is intended for quired. Fig. 4 is a narrow trimming for the edge of the tunic, to correspond with the looping up, and, in the choice and arrangement of the colors, must be made to match the others. Fig. 5 is a rosette, which may be used for many purposes, composed of single white or colored

Fig. 7.

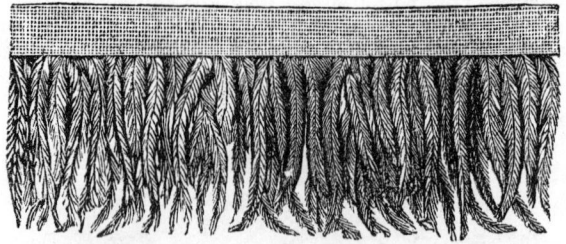

feathers, which, being rounded at the tip with scissors, are arranged in circles on a foundation of stiff tulle; the centre is filled up with a few longer, slightly curled feathers, prepared before fixing with the back of a heated knife. Fig. 6 is peculiarly adapted for trimming the low bodice of a ball dress, like a bertha. It is composed entirely of the single barbs of white ostrich feathers, curled as before directed, arranged in the manner shown in the illustration in a kind of continuous row of rosettes, which appear as if tied together by loops of white floss silk placed in the centre of each. Ostrich feathers, which have become worn at the tips, or otherwise damaged, may be made available for this trimming, which is to be repeated in a narrower width round the short sleeves; and Fig. 7 is a fringe for the edge of the tunic to correspond. Strong gum-Arabic will be the most expeditious way of fastening these barbs to the foundation either of stiff tulle or tarlatane. The same trimming looks still lighter and more delicate if made with marabout instead of ostrich feathers.

CROCHET BANDS FOR LINEN.

THE bands for tying the linen together, of which Figs. 1 and 2 show a part about the real size, may be knitted, crocheted, or made of soft cotton tape, with a simple pattern in *point Russe* worked on it with Turkey red cotton. Those of which illustrations are given, are crocheted with white and red cotton, about one yard and five-eighths in length, and form a loop at one end. For Fig. 1, make a chain of the required length, and join to the 40th stitch to make the loop. Work on each side of the foundation chain (but only on the outer side of the loop part) a row of dc, taking up every chain, and in the round part at the end of the loop putting two stitches in one, so as to keep it flat. Then, still going round, a chain of trebles (thread once over the needle), with 1 ch. between, and missing 1 of the last row; when the round end of the loop is reached, 2 ch. or 3 ch. between (still only missing the 1 stitch) as may be found necessary to keep the outer row flat; and, having completed the row by joining to the commencement by a single stitch, fasten off. With the red cotton, work a row of close scallops all round the edge, thus

(taking up every stitch of last row): * 1 dc., 1 treble, 2 long (twice round), 1 treble, 1 dc., and repeat from *. The other band, Fig. 2, is commenced with the red cotton, making a chain of the required length; join in a loop as before and work on both sides, except at the loop, 1 dc., 1 ch. alternately, missing a stitch. On

Fig. 1.   Fig. 2.

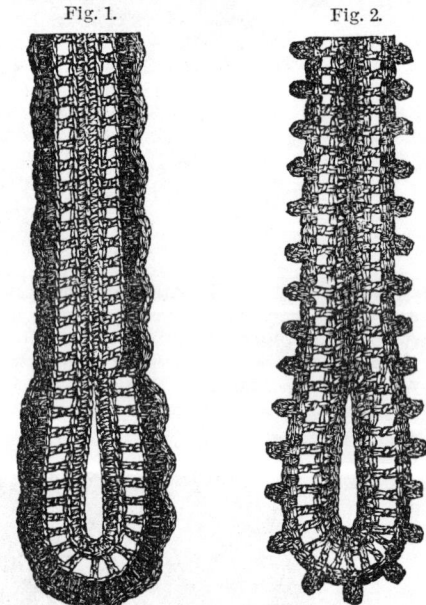

both sides of this centre strip, dc. round each ch. is to be worked, in white cotton, and 1 ch. after it; repeat. Then follows a row all round of trebles, with 1 ch. between, missing 1 of the last row, keeping the end of the loop as before; and, lastly, a row of picots, with 2 dc. between, with the red cotton, each picot consisting of 4 ch., and dc. into the first of them.

TRAVELLING-BAG.

THE pretty bag made with a strap to hang over the shoulder—the practical arrangement of the inside being shown in Fig. 2—is, in our model of glazed holland, made up with a somewhat darker embroidery of silk braid stitched on, and silk stitches, a cord of the same color going all round, and tassels. A skilful hand will find no difficulty in the making up of such a bag; we shall, therefore, confine ourselves to the most needful directions. The front, hind parts, and flap of this satchel, eight and a half inches high, ten and three-quarters inches wide below, and seven and a quarter inches above, are of one piece of the stuff taken double.

On the front, plain half of the bag, three-quarters of an inch from the upper edge on the upper layer of the stuff, must be put a pocket, which, as seen, stitched with brown and made in single stuff, being four and a half inches long, five and a half inches wide at the top, and four and a half inches below, is stitched on in two rows. A similar pocket, yet somewhat larger, is to be sewn for the inside space to the inner stuff layer of the hind wall. After the two stuff parts have been finished so far, they are then joined to the flap by a run and fell, and for the bottom part are stitched six divisions, each half an inch from the outer edge for the putting in of whalebone.

Fig. 1.

The upper edge is to be turned over as a hem and arranged by the stitched-on lining to put in two pieces of whalebone; three lines of stitching for two smaller pieces of whalebone mark the upper edge of the hind wall. The rounded folding sides, each at the top with a piece of whalebone cracked in the middle, of double stuff, and two and three-quarter inches wide, are next to be joined to the lined part by a run and fell and to the largest part by the side stitches. Brown silk cord edges round the folding sides and the bag flap.

The two *straps* for bearing the bag, with each a button-hole at end—the pointed ends of which lead through each of the button-holes of the flap—make at the same time the end straps two and a half inches long of the inner bag; and of double stuff are each twenty-eight and a half

Fig. 2.

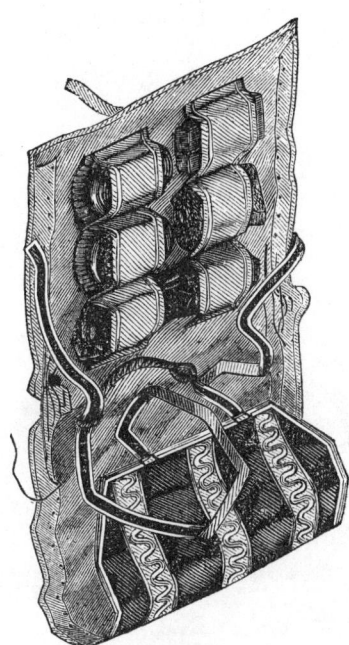

inches long and three-quarters of an inch wide, decorated with two rows of braid stitched on, and to be button-holed with brown silk at the lower pointed ends. The place where each strap is securely fastened in the button-hole of the flap is hidden on the outside by a gimp-button.

A small steel buckle lock, of two parts, joins in the manner usual for leather-bags; the two straps may be made longer or shorter, the part going under having a cord strap to slip through the other strap, with a silk tassel attached. Two tassels put on the flap finish the decoration of our model.

TENT PENWIPER.

Materials.—Red and black leather, and some black, stiff muslin.

THE outer covering of the little tent consists of two equal parts of different colored leather, plaited into each other, as represented in the design. Fold a red and a black strip of leather, each measuring one inch and five-eighths broad, in the middle, to three inches in length. From the folded size make five straight cuts, one inch and five-eighths, so that there are six equal narrow strips. These somewhat rounded ends may be cut in corners, in round or pointed scallops. Then plait the prepared leather parts into each other, so that the closed side of one strip incloses the open side of the other (see Fig. 2), beginning from the under

Fig. 1.

plain ends. When the plaiting is finished, cut the inner double muslin leaves (a little smaller than the outer part). In order to support the leather walls, a kind of stick of rolled pasteboard, gummed together, two and three-eighths

Fig. 2.

inches long, and nearly half an inch in diameter at the bottom, and tapering at the top, is pushed in at the point of the tent, and fastened there, together with the points of the muslin leaves. A stick, two inches long, the under end of which is hidden in the pasteboard-stick, is cut out of wood, around which red silk is

twisted, and upon it is placed a black, red, and white silk braid flag.

GOLD POCKET WITH BELT.

THIS pocket is intended to hold gold, jewelry, and similar articles, and will be found very useful in travelling. The original is made of a double piece of linen sixteen inches long and eight inches wide; the top is cut slightly convex, while the bottom is rounded. In the middle of the upper piece, cut a slit five inches and a half long, beginning about three inches from the top. Work the edges of the slit in buttonhole stitch with red cotton. Work the edges of the pocket in the same manner, putting the

needle through the double material of the pocket. Bind the top of the pocket between the linen band, in doing which, catch the end of a red cord ten inches long, the other end of which is attached to an oval ring drawn over the pocket. For this ring, take three pieces of bonnet wire, and over them work button-hole stitches with red cotton. A brass ring worked in single crochet may be used instead. Sew hooks and eyes to the belt for fastening.

COVER TO BE PLACED OVER DISHES,

FOR KEEPING EGGS WARM ON THE BREAKFAST TABLE.

THIS cover is made of white linen lined with red flannel, which has previously been slightly quilted. A square of guipure d'art is sewn into the linen on the upper part of the cover; a lace border to correspond, one inch and one-fifth wide, is sewn on all round. Cut two pieces of linen, or stiff gauze, and of flannel, each ten inches square; quilt each flannel part, stitch it through in diamonds, and line the cover with them. The upper part of the cover is ornamented from illustration with a square of guipure d'art; the latter consists of a centre of plain netting, five and three-fifths inches square, darned in *point d'esprit* and darning stitch. The upper half of the cover is then ornamented with lace; work a row of herring-bone stitch with thread along the outer edge of the cover, and a similar row with red wool along the inner edge. The netted square is likewise shown, and labels on each, the sheets, table-cloths, or whatever it may be, fastened together by the bands, of which we give an illustration. The labels for the packets of linen are cut out in card-board in the form shown in illustration, and covered with shirting—calico or linen—previously ornamented in front in point russe with ingrain red cotton; the initials worked in

Fig. 1.

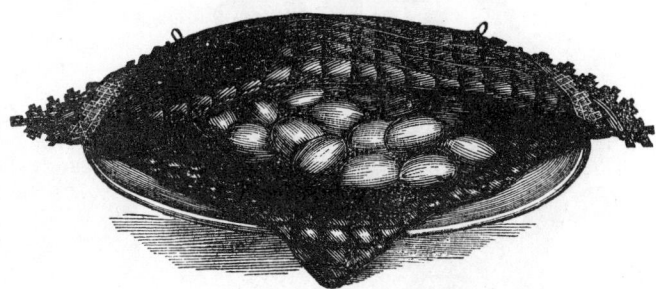

Fig. 2.

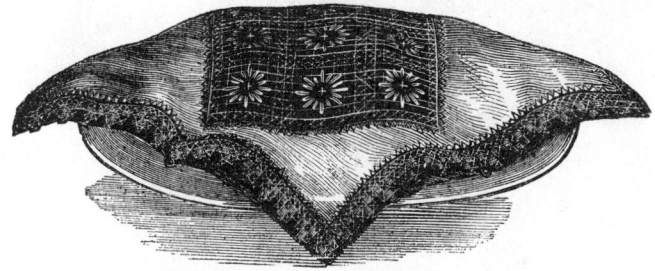

edged with a herring-bone stitch row, worked with thread. Sew both parts of the cover together along two sides; sew on loops and buttons round the two other sides, as can be seen on illustration.

------◆◆------

LABEL FOR PACKETS OF LINEN.

KEEPING a linen closet in order is such an

satin stitch, adding the name of the article contained in the packet, either in single point russe or in marking ink. For the table linen it is well to give a more particular description, such as "Tablecloths for twelve," "for eighteen," etc. Two slits are cut horizontally in front of the label, of the length requisite to allow the crochet band to pass through, and these slits are worked over with long overcast stitches

important branch of housekeeping that we give our readers this month a plan, which, if followed, will save much trouble. Have a shelf devoted to each suit of articles, with covers, as (not close together) with the red cotton, and the outer edge of the label is ornamented round in the same manner.

PAPER FLOWERS.

ALPINE RHODODENDRON.

WHITE, mauve, red, or yellow flowers can be

with gold and red silk, and a little spray of flowers worked; the rounds of cloth are put between, and the edge is composed of ribbon plaited and sewn on.

Fig. 1.

Fig. 2.    Fig. 3.

Fig. 4.

Fig. 5.    Fig. 6.

made. The centre is of six stamens of cotton tied together, dipped in gum. The gummed ends are next dipped in fine sand, and, while still wet, in yellow ochre. The stamen is fixed to the wire stalk, Fig. 2. The flowers are cut and bent like Fig. 4. To make the raised parts, a small screw is taken; the flower is held in the palm of the left hand, the screw pressed lightly from the tip of each point over the flower part towards the bottom. The ends of each flower are pasted neatly over a lead pencil.

Fig. 3 shows how the flower is pressed together at the lower edge. The stalk, with stamens attached, is now passed through, and the stalks are wound over with green silk, Fig. 5. The leaves are cut like Fig. 6. These may be of green paper or cloth.

DESIGN FOR PENWIPER.

IT is made with rounds of cloth. The stand is wood or bronze; the front (represented) and the back are alike, and are made of rich blue satin, stretched over card-board; on this satin seven circles of white velvet are *appliquéd*

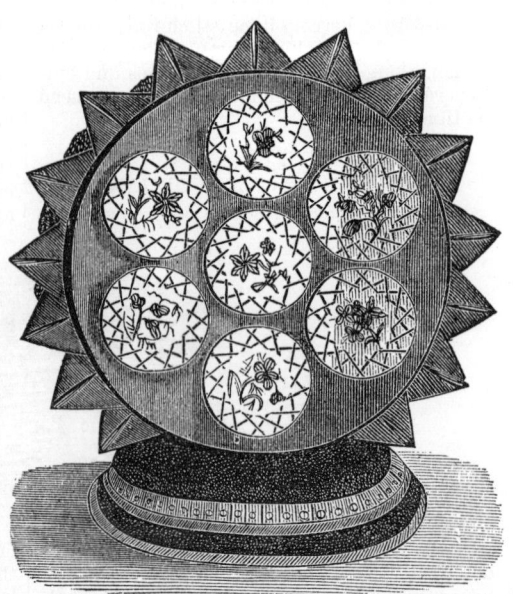

Design for Penwiper.

Materials.—White French merino or cashmere; and either white silk, or purple, green, and brown silk.

WE give the two parts of which the entire shoe is composed, and the design may be either worked entirely in white silk or in the appropriate colors. If the latter, the veinings of the leaves must be in a darker shade of green than the leaf itself. The upper petals of the flowers are worked in French knots; the scrolls in *point de chainette;* the calyx of the buds in pale green; the buds in purple silk.

To make-up these shoes, quilt some finest of twill-muslin, with flannels for the lining; binding this lining and the outer part together with a piping-cord, covered with white silk. The soles of these very small shoes are usually also made of merino, quilted; but they may, if preferred, be cork-soles, bound with white ribbon.

EMBROIDERY PATTERNS.

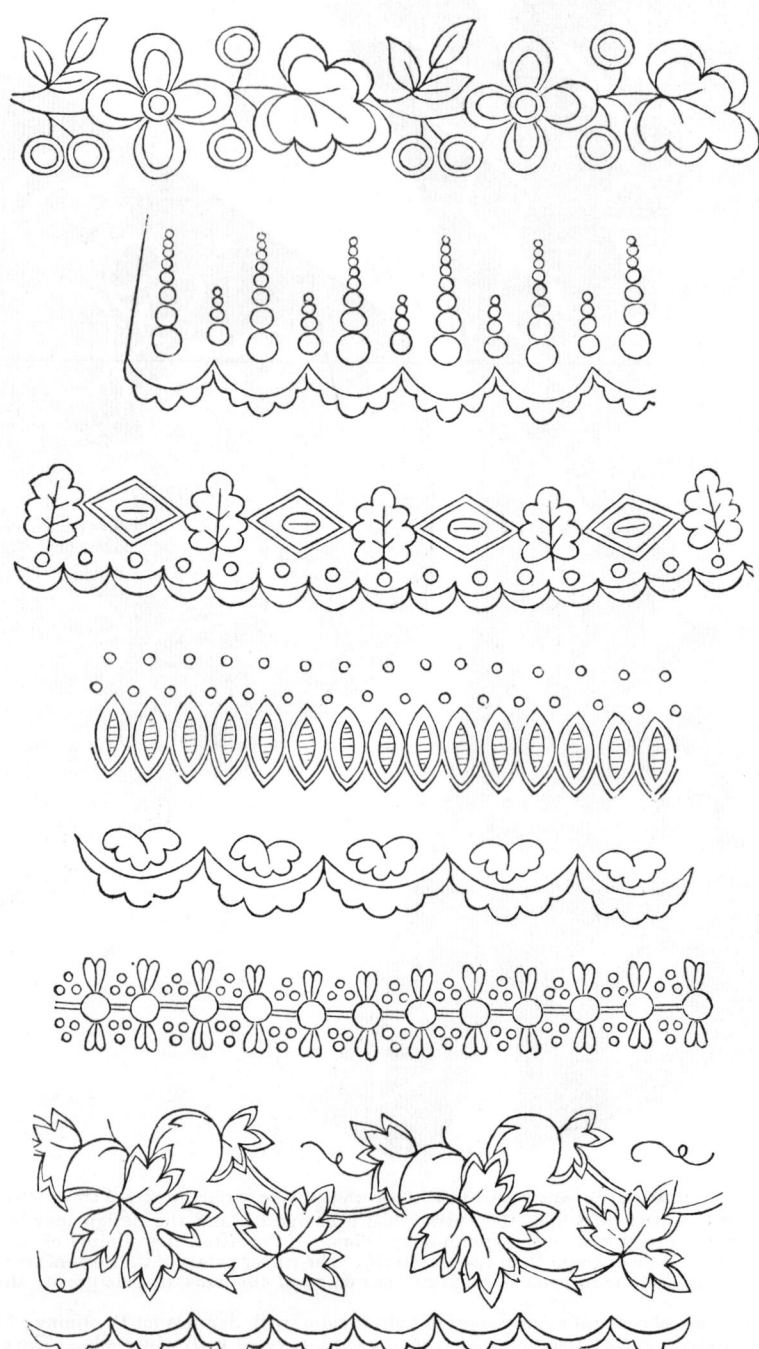

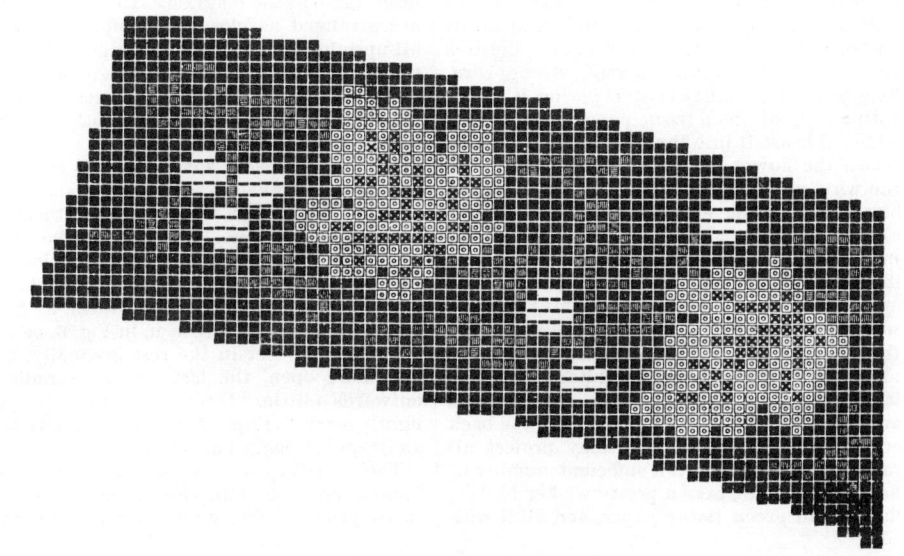

The Vine-Leaf Slipper.

EXPLANATION OF THE COLORS.—■ Fawn brown.   ▦ First (darkest); ▣ Second; ▨ Third (lighest) Green.   ▮ Red.

SHELL FLOWERS.

BEAUTIFUL groups of artificial flowers may be made very simply with shells of a common kind. Some are made simply of white shells, buff, or pink-tinted shells, of the common kind, so abundant on many of our coasts, and which resemble somewhat the nails of the fingers. These shells can also be purchased in any quantity at the stores where articles for fancy work are sold. Other shells are painted entirely, or in stripes.

BASKET OF SHELL FLOWERS.

Most of the shell flowers are made by means of a cement in the first place. Melt to a moderate consistency a quantity of gum-tragacanth and a little alum; mix this into a thick paste with plaster of Paris and a small piece of sugar of lead. Make a ball of this, the shape of an orange—that is, a flattened round—and about half or a third the size of an orange. Let this nearly dry. Then take a stiff, strong wire, long enough for a flower-stem; wind it round with a strip of green tissue paper, half an inch wide. Thrust it into the ball of cement, upon which the flower is to be constructed. Place the wire, with the cement at the top, in a tumbler or vase, long enough to hold it comfortably; first taking a stout card, larger than the mouth of the bottle or vase, with a hole cut in it, just of a size to admit the wire stem easily, and placing it over the tumbler; this keeps the work steady. Set in the shells according to the flower to be represented, and let it remain untouched till the flower is quite dry. Then take a few short leaves, with the stalks cut off and wires removed, and gum them to the back of the flower, so that they may project all round partially. When a sufficient number of flowers are made, take a pretty wicker basket, line it with green tissue paper, and fill it with

the cement. When this is nearly dry, stick the flowers in, and place sufficient leaves about them. The basket should be so well filled as entirely to conceal the cement. Do not move it until the cement is quite dry. The leaves used are the ordinary muslin ones, such as are employed for bonnets. Fig. 1 shows the lump of cement attached to wire ready for the shell-work.

To Make a Rose.—Dip the shells (Fig. 2) into a strong mixture of powdered carmine and liquid gum. Let them dry. They ought to be of one uniform deep crimson. Put three together in the centre of the cement, folded one over another as closely as possible, to form the heart. Place a row round these, also closely, and so on, row after row, each shell slightly overlapping the other, till the cement is completely filled, and the flower finished. The shells are placed lengthwise, on end, as shown in Fig. 3. Add some leaves all round the flower, which are to be fixed on at the under part of the cement, covering it at the bottom completely. Fig. 4 is a small representation of the rose. The shells that form the rose are about half an inch long. To make a rosebud, choose shells at least half as large again; fold them over the same way in the centre, and close the succeeding shells closely round them; also, instead of placing the shells in the cement upright, as shown in Fig. 3, arrange them lengthwise, as shown in Fig. 2, and put a large rosebud calyx on the stalk after the cement is quite dry. The centre of cement for a rosebud is very much smaller than for a rose, not being quite a quarter of the size.

For a *China Aster* the white transparent shells are cut in pieces, like Fig. 5, the centre being as small as possible, the largest half as large again as the diagram. In the centre they are arranged as close as possible. They are all upright, and towards the edge inclining to radiate outwards slightly. When the cement is quite dry, charge a small camel-hair brush with carmine and gum, and lightly variegate the flower here and there.

For a *Ranunculus*, shape the ball of cement like Fig. 6. Take the same kind of shell as for the rose, but rather smaller. Paint them well with a bright yellow. Set them into the cement as the rose was set, only very much closer together, each one wrapping over the other, as close as it is possible to make them, as far as the dotted line from A to B, in Fig. 6, or even lower down. Set in the rest gradually, more and more open, the last two rows radiating outwards a little. Dip a brush in carmine, and lightly mark the tips of the shells, to give them an irregular, jagged appearance.

The *Passion-flower* is set upon a cement foundation, resembling Fig. 7, only larger. A small piece of fine wire covered with green silk, such as is used for the making of paper and wax flowers, is placed in the centre, twisted. The stamens are made of the fine ends of porcupine quills dyed blue, and set in two rows, thirty-six in the outer row and twenty-four in the inner one. The shells (Fig. 8) of transparent white form the flower. They are laid on in two rows of seven each, placed these fixed to a larger wire, and cover that with paper. Add lily of the valley leaves; nine make a spray. There is a small shell of the same kind, lined with a deep pink, which makes well into flowers. For the construction of these, make a perfectly flat piece of cement, the size of a two-cent piece; attach the shells in flat-looking rows, like pink May, after fixing in

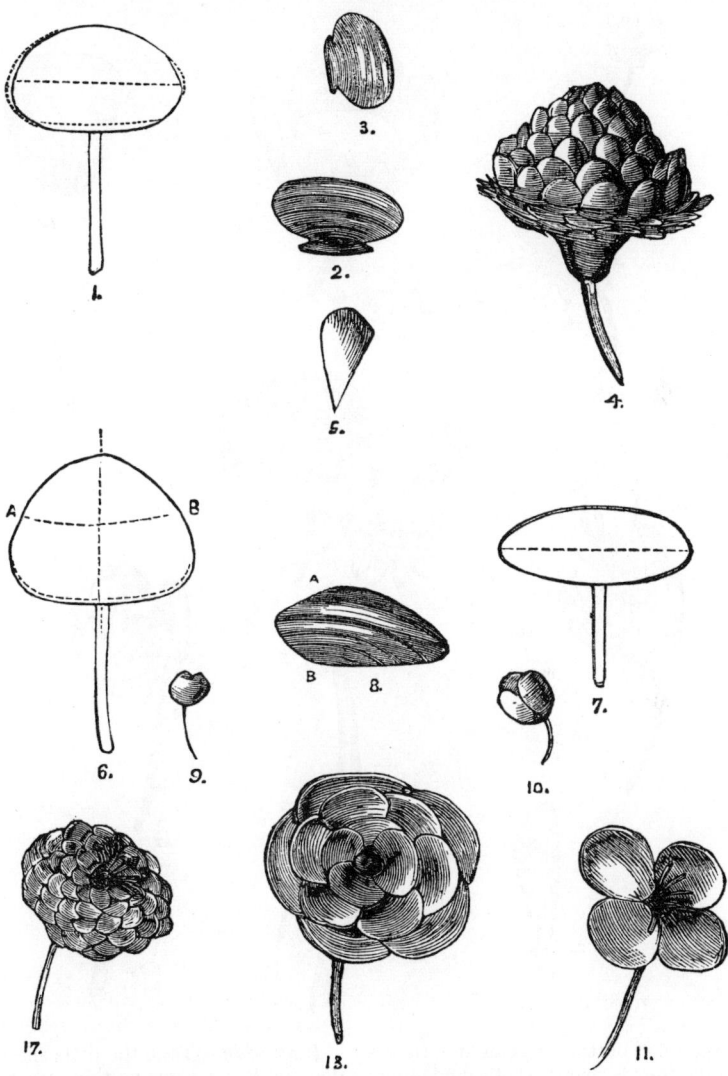

alternately. The passion-flower looks pretty laid over some large camelia leaves, which may be cemented underneath it, in the manner already described.

Lilies of the Valley are made with very small, white, finger-nail shaped shells. Make a little ball of cement, the size of a small pea (see Fig. 9), and attach it to fine wire. Place round it three small shells (see Fig. 10); make a row of the centre a green heart, such as is sold for paper or wax flower making.

White May Blossoms (Fig. 12).—Make a flat piece of cement like a button, and attach it to a wire. In the centre place a May-heart, such as is sold for paper or wax flowers. Place round it four white and transparent shells. Make four or five of these, and mount again on a larger stem. Make another group of the

same kind. Mix some powder-blue, cobalt, or
French ultramarine with gum-water, and mark
the edges with it, streaking the inside a little.
Vary the marking as much as possible. Tip
two shells out of the four, and leave the others;
or tip three, and leave one. Let the coloring,
in this case, be careless.

Fig. 13 represents another kind of flower.

Laburnum.—Take a pair of small shells,
smaller than those used for the passion-flower,
like Fig. 8, white. Paint them bright yellow.
Insert a little piece of the cement between the
pair of shells. Close them over it. Attach a
wire. Make about eight of them, and then
form them into a spray with leaves upon a
stronger wire.

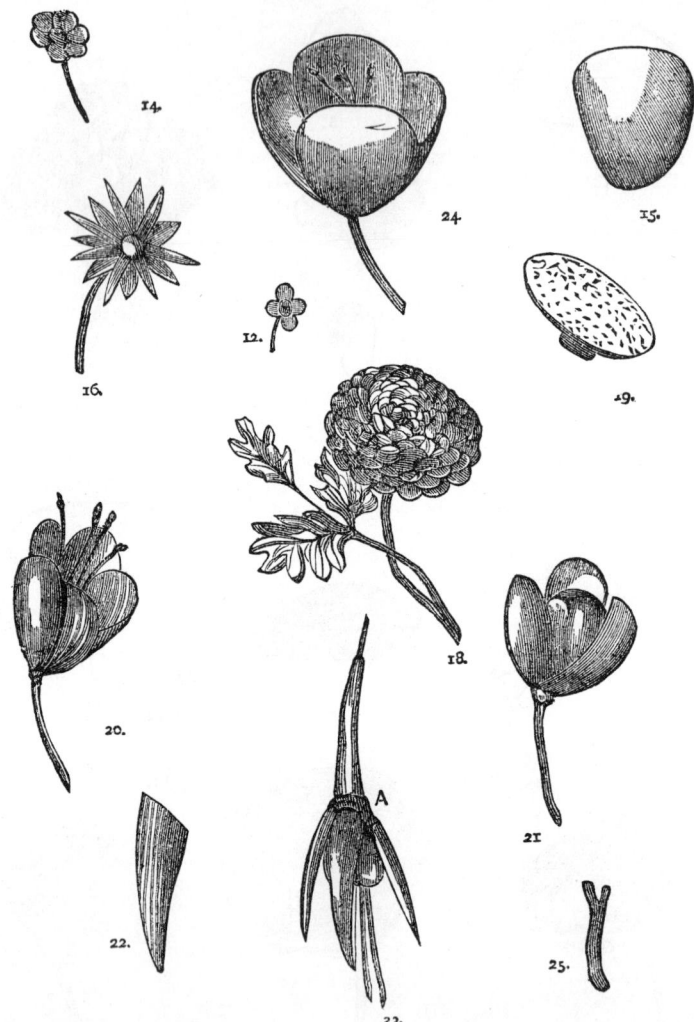

Make a larger flat button of cement. In the
centre arrange four flat white shells, and others
round them. Make a round ball of cement,
like a bead, and place it in the centre. Tip
and streak the shells with blue.

Pink Rosebuds.—Beautiful imitations of flowers may be made with the pink nail-like shells.
Place them endwise, in the manner shown by
Fig. 3, and arrange them to resemble a rose as
closely as possible. No artificial coloring is
needed. Roses may also be made this way,
with a very charming effect.

Pink May.—Take the little shells lined with
deep pink, the same as those used for Fig. 13.
Make a small flat button of cement. Place a
May-heart in the centre (a "heart," as it is
technically termed, means stamen and pistils).
Set round it six of the small shells (see Fig.
14). Make a group of four or six.

Geranium.—Make a cement foundation the
size of a large pea. Put in it a large green
heart, as before described. Round this are
four shells, arranged like Fig. 11, either shells
the shape of Fig. 8. filed flat across the top, or

shells so formed. Paint the upper half of each deeply and abruptly with carmine ; or two may be painted thus, and two streaked—some have all four only streaked (see Fig. 15).

Forget-me-nots.—A small pea should be made of cement. Attach it to wire. Paint some of the small shells, such as were used for pink May, a deep blue. Put four on the pea. In the centre, put a little ball of cement and color it yellow. Make a round group of about six (see Fig. 12).

Make a large pea of cement and place it on wire. Cut white shell into two sets of spikes, place six small ones round the pea, and nine larger under these. Color the centre of the cement pale yellow (see Fig. 16).

A Camellia.—Take shells like Fig. 8, and other shells of the same kind, one or two sizes larger. File them all off from A to B. Make a cement foundation in shape between Fig. 1 and Fig. 7, and of a large size. Take a few much smaller shells, stick them in the centre close together, points upward and upright, to make a centre. Round these arrange the filed shells in rows, the smallest first, and curled backwards like a camellia petal. The shells used for this should be thick, white, and not too transparent. Some of the camellias can be streaked with carmine ; irregular shell flowers may also be made, like Fig. 11, without a heart in the centre, but with another shell of the same kind fixed on the top of the centre to the cement, or with a little bit more cement (see Fig. 17).

A Dahlia.—Make a cement foundation, in shape between Fig. 6 and Fig. 1. Put a green heart of four little pieces, like Fig. 25, in the centre. Arrange in rows, row and row, shells the way up of Fig. 3. They may be gradually larger towards the edge. When finished, mix vermilion and gum and a little carmine mixed to a deep color, inclining most to vermilion. Speckle every shell well, to variegate it completely, and most so at the edges.

Snowdrops.—Take a few thick white shells, with raised dotted backs, like Fig. 19. Make a large pea of cement on wire. Fix in the centre an azalea head. Round this place five of the shells, overlying one another a little, and half open, like a snowdrop. The part of the shell where the shells meet when in pairs is towards the edge. Fig. 20 shows the flower.

Crocuses.—Take the same kind of shells as those used for the snowdrops (Fig. 19), and paint them bright yellow, and make them up in the same way. Or make a large pea cement ; use no heart. Close three shells together first in the centre, and place three half-open shells round them, in the way shown in Fig. 21.

In making the snowdrop, crocus, and geranium, it is the best plan to procure some very large rose calyxes. Cut off the projecting leaves. Fix each calyx to a stem, and then fill the calyx with the cement. Proceed afterwards with the flower as directed already. Flowers

that show the join between the cement and stem white, when quite dry may be painted with powder-color, mixed with thick gum, at that part.

Fuchsia.—To make a fuchsia, put a pea of cement on a stem, place in the centre a fuchsia heart. Round this close four small white shells, like Fig. 10, the heart hanging down in the centre. Then make the slender part of the fuchsia, marked A in Fig. 23, of the cement. Cut four pieces of shell the shape of Fig. 22. Color them deep carmine. Fix them round in the way shown in Fig. 22, and then color A in Fig. 23 also red.

China Aster.—There is a very pretty looking transparent white shell, rather oval. Make a cement foundation like Fig. 1, only larger. Set it with this shell, extremely close in the centre, and gradually more open.

Periwinkle.—Take some of the shells like Fig. 3, of a good size. Stain them a deep blue inside with powder-blue and carmine. Fix six of them on a pea of cement. Make a little pea of cement, place it in the centre, and paint it white. The shells to form this flower are fixed by the edges, like Fig. 3 (see Fig. 24).

A Yellow Rose is made like a pink one, of the pale yellow shells of the kind shown in Fig. 2, not colored, but naturally tinted.

A pretty flower, much like the periwinkle, may be made of nine shells placed on in the same way as the periwinkle, white, and tipped with blue at the edges ; the ball in the centre one tipped with white, tinged with green.

The object in filling the basket with cement is to have a material to hold the flowers, strong enough to keep them in place—for they are rather heavy—and also to prevent the basket from easily tipping over. The shells are very brittle, and great care is needed not to damage them when made ; but, with proper security from injury, they will last more than one generation. Place the basket on a crimson, velvet-covered stand.

The closer the shells are set together, and the more shells are used to compose such flowers as the dahlia, rose, and anemone, the better the flower looks. If any of the color is removed from the painted shells in making them up, when the cement has become quite dry and hard, take a brush charged with the right color, and touch up all the damaged places. In the basket (see page 244) will be observed on the left a passion-flower, lilies of the valley, May, and some other flowers ; on the right, a dahlia, a small ranunculus, and part of a rose. In the centre of this basket, which is engraved from a photograph taken from shell flowers, is a damask rose ; on the reverse side are a yellow rose, a large ranunculus, and China aster, crocuses, and snowdrops, and the basket is complete with rosebuds, cineraria, geranium, a camellia, fuchsias—in short, all the flowers here described with buds and leaves.

DESIGN FOR PATCHWORK.

Our page compels us to reduce the size of the pattern ; but, by a little attention, sections may easily be cut of any dimensions desired. Take a piece of clean stout white paper, and fold it in all the parallel sloping lines seen in our engraving. These may be at any distance from each other ; only regular and equal. It will be seen that a line drawn exactly between every pair of parallels will take in the points. Draw these lines with a pencil, to distinguish them from those caused by the folding, and the proper forms can be readily obtained. Cut them out, and from them others in card-board, if for a large piece of work, and you have all your sections ready, without the possibility of a misfit. The two eight-pointed figures are differently arranged. A may be filled up in eight pieces, while B should be composed of nine—a star of eight points to the centre, and

eight diamonds round it. Or, if on a sufficiently large scale, the inner star may be of eight pieces. Two very distinct shades of the same color will look better for A than many different tints. B may have a dark centre and bright points, or *vice versa*. The intermediate figure, C, should be of such neutral tints or dark shades as may throw up the brilliant hues of which the star should be composed.

We have said that this design may be applied to another purpose. Worked on canvas, in wools, the outlines done in black, it would be both rich looking and easily worked. Elderly people and children can often do a piece where they can count threads, where a painted pattern would puzzle them. No. 14 or 16 canvas, and eight-thread wool should be used. Orange, claret, blue (if good), and brilliant greens look well in such a pattern.

BED-QUILT OF JAVA CANVAS, WITH CROCHET BORDER.

THE materials required for this bed-quilt are a piece of Java canvas the size of the bed, and

Fig. 1.

thick white knitting cotton. Begin with the squares in the middle, leaving a sufficient space at the sides for the border. First work the

Fig. 2.

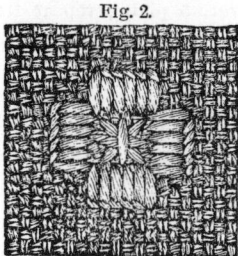

Fig. 3.

squares in overcast and Smyrna stitch according to Fig. 1, which represents a quarter of the square in full size. Then work in the small crosses according to Fig. 2, to fill up the spaces between the squares. Now begin the border by working the rows of herring-bone stitch according to Fig. 3, so as to leave open spaces for the medallions, as seen in Fig. 4. Work the

medallions in *point russe* and Smyrna stitch according to Fig. 5, and then overcast the cover all round, working over 4 threads of the canvas, and cut away the edges beyond. The crochet edging is worked as follows : *1st row.* Alternately 1 long treble, 1 chain, the treble caught into a loop of the overcast edging, and stitches added at the corners to make the work lie flat. At the end of the 1st row loop into the 1st treble stitch with a loop stitch, work a slip stitch on the chain stitch, and commence the *2d.* * 3 double, 11 chain, missing 5 underneath ; repeat from * ; at the end of the row loop into the first double with a slip stitch. *3d.* 3 chain to form a long treble, 2 long treble, 13 chain, * 3 long treble on the next 3 double of the previous row, 13 chain, repeat from *. *4th, 5th,* and *6th* like the 3d row, observing to work the treble stitches on the treble of the previous row. *7th.* 1 double on the middle stitch of the 3 treble of the previous row, * loop the chain scallops through each other as seen in Fig. 6, drawing the scallop of the 3d row through that of the 2d row, and the scallop of the 4th row through that of the 3d row, and over the last scallop drawn through in the 6th row work 13 treble ; then 1 double on the middle stitch of the 3 treble, and repeat from * to the end of

Fig. 6.

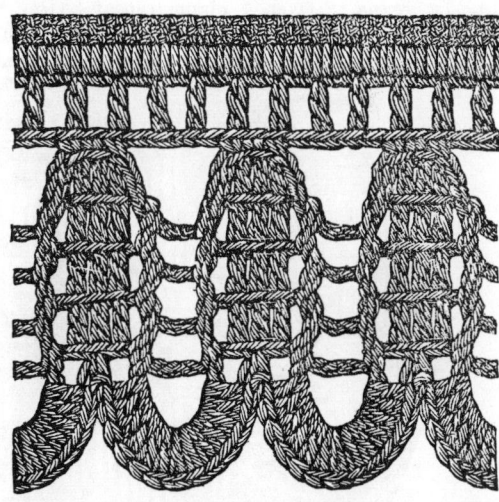

the row, where the thread is looped into the 1st double and fastened off.

KNITTED CHEESE CLOTH.

COTTON No. 16, and four needles No. 12. Cast on 8 stitches, and knit them off, 3 on each of two needles and 2 on the third ; this is easier

Fig. 4.—Bed-Quilt.

than to cast on 2 stitches only on each of four needles. *1st round.* * Over, 1 plain; repeat from * 7 times more. *2d* and every alternate from *. 9th. Over, 5 plain; repeat from *. *11th.* * Over, 6 plain; repeat from * *13th.* * Over, 2 plain, over, knit 2 together, over,

Fig. 5.—Bed-Quilt.

round plain. *3d.* * Over, 2 plain; repeat from * *5th.* * Over, 1 plain, over, knit 2 together; repeat from *. *7th.* * Over, 4 plain; repeat knit 2 together, 1 plain; repeat from *. *15th.* * Over, 2 plain (over, knit 2 together, 3 times); repeat from *. *17th.* * Over, 4 plain, over, knit 2 together, over, knit 2 together, 1 plain; repeat from *. 19th. * Over, 10 plain; repeat from * 7 times more. 21st. * Over, 11 plain; repeat from *. 23d. * Over, 12 plain; repeat from *. 25th. * Over, 1 plain, over, slip 1, knit 1, pass slipped stitch over, 10 plain; repeat from *. 27th. * Over, 3 plain, over, 2 plain, over, knit 2 together, over, knit 2 together, knit 2 together, 3 plain; repeat from *. 29th.

card-board, allowing for turnings, and also a double piece for the souffle at one end. Embroider the design, seen in the illustration, on the silk in *appliqué* of velvet, with gold twist sewn around the edges of the design, and figures in *point russe*, and satin-stitch with brown silk. Gum the silk to the card-board, putting in the soufflet, and sew a fine cord around the edge. Make the inner case precisely in the

Over, 5 plain, over, 1 plain (over, knit 2 together 3 times), knit 2 together, 1 plain; repeat from *. 31st. * Over, 7 plain, over, knit 2 together, over, knit 2 together, over, knit 2 together, 3 plain; repeat from *. 33d. * Over, 3 plain, over, knit 2 together, over, knit 2 together, 2 plain, over, knit 2 together, 6 plain; repeat from *. 35th. * Over, 3 plain (over, knit 2 together 3 times) 2 plain, over, knit 2 together, 5 plain; repeat from *. 37th. * Over, 1 plain, over, knit 2 together, 2 plain, over, knit 2 together, over, knit 2 together, 1 plain, knit 2 together, over, 1 plain, over, knit 2 together, 4 plain. 39th. * Over, 3 plain, over, knit 2 together, 5 plain, knit 2 together, over, 3 plain, over, knit 2 together, 3 plain; repeat from *. 41st. * Over, 1 plain, over, knit 3 together, over, 1 plain, over, knit 2 together, 3 plain, knit 2 together, over, 1 plain, over, knit 3 together, over, 1 plain, over, knit 2 together, 2 plain; repeat from *. 43d. Over, 3 plain, over, 1 plain, over, 3 plain, over, knit 2 together, 1 plain, knit 2 together, over, 3 plain, over, 1 plain, over, 3 plain, over, knit 2 together, 1 plain. 45th. * 1 plain, over, knit 3 together, over, 3 plain, over, knit 3 together, over, 1 plain, knit 3 together, 1 plain, over, knit 3 together, over, 3 plain, over, knit 3 together, over, 1 plain, knit 2 together; repeat from *. 47th. Pass the first stitch to the last needle, then on the first needle, * over, 3 plain, over, knit 3 together; repeat from *. 49th. Plain. 50th and 51st. Purled; then cast off loosely. Knit a narrow edging, and sew around it.

SPECTACLE CASE.

THIS spectacle case consists of two parts, the one sliding into the other. Begin with the outer case, and cut a piece of card-board the length of the spectacles and double the width, with rounded ends. Join this down one side after lining the inside with glazed paper; then cut out a piece of brown silk the size of the

same way, only a trifle smaller, omitting the embroidery, and put in a loop with the soufflet, with which to draw out the inner case.

CANDLESTICK ORNAMENT.

THE ornament consists of a piece of flat glass three inches square, with a circular hole an inch in diameter cut out of the middle. Around the edge of the glass plate, as well as around the edge of the hole, is a row of cut glass beads strung in wire. These are fastened in their place by means of strings of small glass beads, passing from the outer to the inner edge, and fastened to the wire on which the cut beads

are strung according to illustration. There are five of these strings at each corner, meeting at a point between two beads of the middle ring. The tassels are arranged in the same way, nine strings of beads, fastened to the wire at the edge, meeting below, and passing through a large cut bead, and then forming loops of beads, with a large cut bead at the bottom of each loop. The smaller tassels at the corners are composed of three graduated cut glass beads, small round beads and long cut beads, and are arranged according to illustration. The larger tassels are made with one thread passed up and down, so that there are ten threads within the large cut bead in the centre.

CURTAIN-HOLDER.

THIS curtain-holder is made of white blind cord, according to Fig. 2, by first twisting the cords into an open plait, and then scalloping loosely around the edges. It consists of a band, to which are attached tabs of different lengths, the middle one being seven inches long. Work the band first, then the tabs separately, taking care to fasten off the cords well. Then line the band and tabs with colored

double row of steel beads across the tubes, according to illustration. Finish the edges of

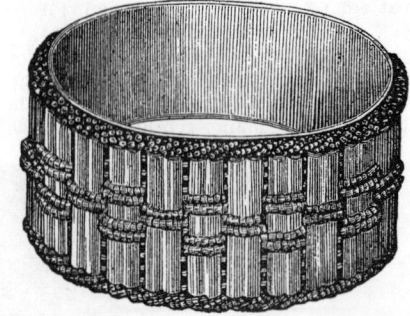

the ring with steel beads sewn on in slanting lines to imitate a cord.

Fig. 1.

Fig. 2.

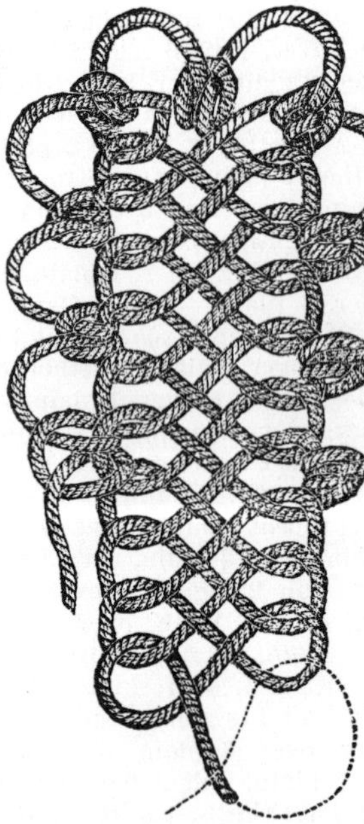

worsted binding, letting the scallops protrude beyond the lining, and stitch the tabs to the band as seen in Fig. 1, and add a tassel of thick crochet cotton at the end of each tab.

BEAD TABLE-NAPKIN RINGS.

COVER the card-board ring with long silver bugles, by threading them singly on double thread, and passing the needle inside between the card-board and the lining. Leave a small space between every two bugles, and fasten a

CHILDREN'S GAITERS.

No. 11 needles. Cast on 22 stitches, and knit 18 plain rows, increasing a stitch at the toe end in every alternate row (when within 2 stitches of the end, lift up the thread between 2 stitches of the former row, put it on the left hand pin and knit it as a stitch; this increases without making a hole in the work). There will then be 30 stitches on the needle, 14 of which must be taken off at the heel end on a third needle, then knit 24 plain rows without increasing. Now cast on 14 stitches to correspond with the 14 taken off, and knit 18 rows, decreasing one stitch every alternate row at the toe end until 22 stitches are left. This completes the foot. For the leg, take up the 14 stitches on each side and pick up 12 in the centre, knit 20 plain rows without increasing, and afterwards increase one at each end every 3d row until 54 rows are done. Knit 20 plain rows, decreasing one every other row, then knit 10 or 12 rows in ribs, 2 plain, 2 purl, and 6 plain rows, and cast off. The ribbing may be continued to the end, and makes the gaiter keep up better. A strip of patent leather of proper length is to be sewn across the foot, to go under the sole of the boot. If not large enough, knit a few more rows on the leg.

GENTLEMAN'S MORNING BOOT.

This warm boot is of gray cloth, embroidered in chain stitch with black silk, lined with flannel and furnished with a thick felt sole. At

Fig. 2.

■ Black. ✕ Green. ▨ 2d shade. ▢ 3d shade.

a design suitable for this purpose, and may be worked in black and three shades of green.

Fig. 1.

the top it has a trimming of black 8-ply fleecy, knitted in loop-stitch. Instead of this, fur may be used, and the boot may be worked in cross-stitch on canvas like a slipper. Fig. 2 is

BABY'S BOOT.—KNITTING.

This little boot, in imitation of a shoe and stocking, the model of which came from Germany, is, perhaps, rather longer in the stocking part than we generally see them; but this is no disadvantage, as it makes it keep on better. It is knitted with blue and white (or any color preferred) single Berlin wool and two needles No. 12, and is a very easy pattern, as it is commenced in the middle of the sole and entirely worked in rows backwards and forwards, the edges being sewn together on the wrong side when the boot is completed. Cast on 62 stitches, and knit 10 rows plain with the blue wool; the next two rows are knitted so as to appear both

2d. The stitches that appear plain must be purled, and the purl stitches knitted plain throughout the row, in order that the pattern may alternate, and of course the 2 centre stitches must be purled. In this 2d row, to begin forming the instep, a stitch must be taken-in by knitting 2 together on each side of the 2 centre purled stitches. *3d.* Like 1st, but taking-in on each side of the 2 plain centre stitches by purling 2 together; continue in this way, decreasing on each side of the centre

Baby's Boot.—Knitting.

Brooch; Painting on Satin.

Flower-pot Cover.

purled on the right side. The blue wool is now to be exchanged for the white, and the rest knitted in moss stitch in the following manner: *1st row.* On the right side, * 1 plain, 1 purl, repeat from * till 30 stitches are knitted; the 31st and 32d, which are the 2 centre stitches, must be plain, and these 2 centre stitches are kept plain on the right side, all the way up the boot; continue * 1 purl, 1 plain, and repeat to end of row.

stitches till the 16th row is completed, when the stitches will be reduced to 32; then follow 12 rows of the moss stitch without any decreasing, still keeping the 2 plain stitches in the centre, which bring it to the 29th row, in which a stitch must be increased immediately after the 1st stitch, also on each side of the 2 centre stitches, and before the last stitch of the row by knitting twice (once from the back) in the same stitch before taking it off the needle, and the same increase is also to be made in the 36th row, so that there will then be 40 stitches, with which the moss stitch must be continued for 6 rows more till the 42d row is completed. The 5 next rows, from the 43d (which will be on the right side of the work) to the end of the 47th, are to be knitted all plain, so that two of them will look purled on the right side. Through all these the two plain stitches in the centre must be kept up. 48*th*. 1 plain, * over, knit 2 together, repeat from *. This will make a row of holes, through which to draw, when the boot is finished and joined, a narrow plait of blue and white wool, about half a yard in length, finished at the ends with small tassels. 49*th to 52d*. Knitted so as to appear all plain on the right side; and to finish the top of the boot, take the blue wool again, and crochet 2 rows as follows: 1*st row*. Take up the first 2 stitches together from the needle with a dc, * 4 ch, take up the two next in the same way, and repeat from * to end of needle. 2*d*. * dc in the centre of space of 4 ch, make 4 ch, and repeat from *. Turn the boot on the wrong side, and sew the edges carefully together, the blue part with blue wool, and the white with white. Work a length of chain stitches with blue wool, and make them up into a small double rosette with needle and thread, to be placed on the front of the shoe.

BROOCH; PAINTING ON SATIN
(*See Engraving, Page* 48.)

THIS pretty brooch, which may be considered among the fashionable novelties of the day, has a rose bouquet in the centre, on a white satin ground, which has an extremely nice effect, increased by the black edge, of copal varnish, intended to imitate enamel. It is advisable to mix a little sugar with the colors. A wooden button carved out half an inch in the middle, is to be taken for the shape, and this covered on the outside with a round of satin half an inch larger than the button, gathered at the edge, put over so as to lie smooth, and drawn tightly at the back; a second round of satin, only a little larger than the back of the brooch, is turned over, and sewn against the first round, so that the gathered part of this is hidden. After the outside has been painted, a brooch, or safety pin, is fastened at the back.

FLOWER-POT COVER.
(*See Engraving, Page* 48.)

THIS cover consists of canes united by enamel and glass beads. Take eighteen pieces of cane, five inches long, and pierce a hole in the centre of the canes at each end, to the depth of half an inch; also pierce each cane transversely in the middle, and at three-quarters of an inch

from each end. A small gimlet will answer the purpose best. Then fix with gum into the holes at each end of the sticks, small pins with glass beads, and an enamel bead threaded on them. Unite the canes by passing a fine wire, threaded with enamel and bronze-colored glass beads, through the transverse holes, according to illustration; and then add the bead fringe, which is made as follows: Thread on a strong gray thread, 6 times alternately, 1 bronze bead, 5 enamel beads, then 1 bronze bead, for each of the scallops at the head of the fringe; then tie the thread to the 1st bronze bead of the scallop*, thread 13 enamel beads, 1 bronze bead, 1 large enamel bead, 1 bronze bead, 13 enamel beads, and pass the thread through the next bronze bead of the heading; repeat from * and loop the scallops into each other, according to illustration.

EMBROIDERED FOOTSTOOL.

THE frame of this footstool is of carved oak or walnut, and is sixteen inches long, eleven inches wide, and three inches high at one end,

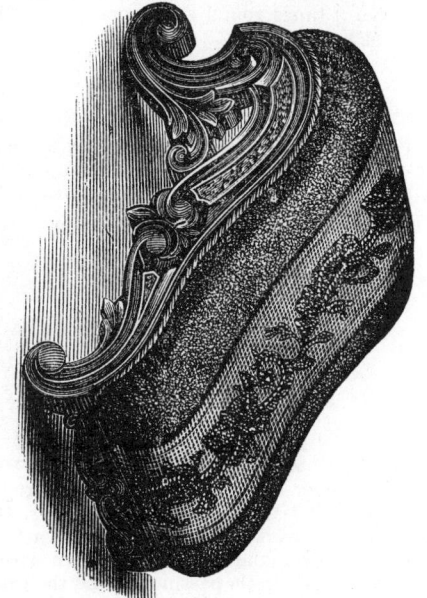

six and a half inches high at the other, exclusive of the cushion. The cushion is covered with two stripes of dark brown velvet and one stripe of Berlin wool work, according to illustration.

ROUND MATS.—KNITTING.

THE round mats in two colors in brioche stitch, with looped fringe around them, are done in the following way: Cast on 16 stitches on bone needles No. 10, say with scarlet. 1*st row*.

Insert the needle in the first stitch, pass the wool between the two needles, and twice round the first and second fingers of the left hand, bringing it between the needles each time, and then knit the stitch; repeat and knit the 3 next stitches in the same way (this is for the fringe); then * wool forward, slip 1, knit 2 together; repeat from * to end of row. 2d. * wool forward, slip 1, knit 2 together; repeat from * until you come to the 4 stitches at the end that form the loops, which must be knitted plain, taking up the 2 loops and the stitch together, in each case, as one stitch. 3d. Same as 1st, but leave 3 stitches unknitted at the end, and turn back. 4th. Same as 2d. 5th. Like 1st, but leaving 6 stitches at the end; turn back. 6th. Same as 2d. 7th. Like 1st, but leaving 9 stitches at the end; turn back. 8th. Same as 2d. 9th. Only knit the 4 stitches with the loops plain; knit them back. Then taking the other color, say white, commence again at the 1st row, and continue these divisions with the two colors alternately, till the mat is finished; join the first and last rows, and draw it together in the centre. The loops of the fringe are not to be cut. If the fringe be wished thicker, bring the wool 3 times round the fingers in each of the first 4 stitches.

KEY CASE.

THIS neat little case for a latch key is made of brown silk, embroidered in chain-stitch, with two shades of brown silk, lined with

quilted brown silk, and edged with a brown silk cord. It is composed of two pieces, the front and the back, which extends into a flap, that turns over and is fastened down with a button and an elastic passing around the case.

OPEN TRICOT.

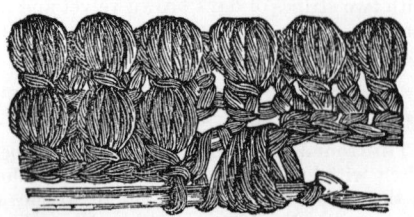

For this work, commence with a chain the required length, and work the first row forwards and backwards as in ordinary tricot; but in the following forward rows the hook must be inserted under the chain formed by the preceding backward row, instead of into the perpendicular stitches. It is suitable for comforters, wraps, etc.

ROSETTE FOR SHOE.

THE rosette consists of five large and five small pieces cut into scallops, buttonholed

around the edge, and worked with holes inside the scallops. The ten pieces are arranged, according to illustration, on a stiff net foundation, and a button forms the centre.

TUFT-STITCH.

MAKE a chain the length required, two to turn. * Twist the cotton once around the hook, insert the hook into a stitch, draw up a

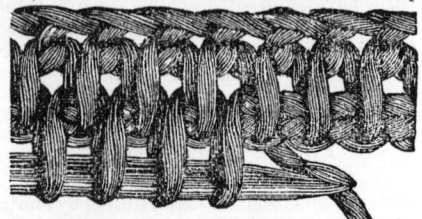

loop; repeat twice more from *; then work all the stitches that are upon the hook off together as one double, one double into the next stitch. Repeat from first *.

A NORWEGIAN MORNING OR BONNET CAP, IN SHETLAND WOOL.

Materials.—Half an ounce each of cerise and white Shetland wool ; two steel knitting pins, No. 12; crochet hook, No. 2.

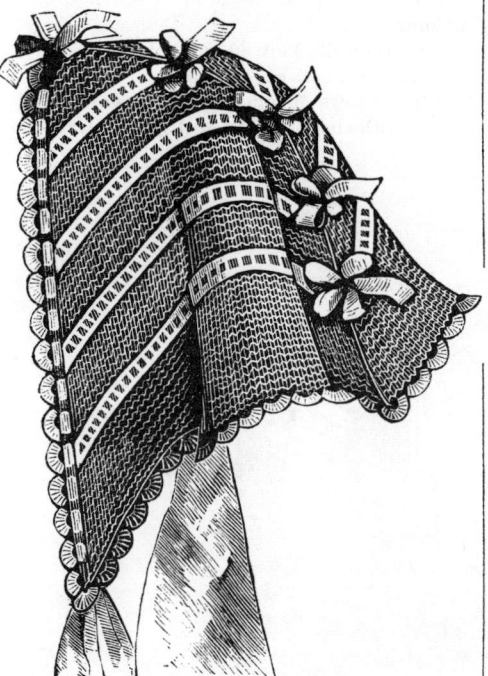

CAST on 240 stitches. K (or knit) two plain rows * ; now knit one stitch ; take two together ; knit 115 stitches ; take two together, and take two together again ; now K the remainder, taking two together before the last stitch. The next row back is plain ; now repeat from * till there are 18 ribs of knitting in which there are 36 rows alternately decreased and plain. Take the white wool—knit three rows in the same way, which is one rib and one row, decreasing as before : K one stitch ; take two together ; wind the wool twice over the pins ; take two together, wind twice over the pin again till there are 41 holes ; then take two together twice ; make 41 holes again ; take two together ; K 1 ; now knit three rows plain, again decreasing as before.

Now, with cerise wool, knit six ribs or twelve rows, decreasing as before. Then with white the same as the first white stripe. Then continue with white and cerise alternately till there are four white and four cerise stripes irrespective of the first deep border. Now, with cerise, knit 16 rows, decreasing as before. This finishes with one stitch. For the border along the

front, with cerise, make 2 L stitches, with 1 ch between each L ; in one loop of the knitting 3 ch ; 2 more L as before in *an equal space to the 3 ch : this is along the front only.* 2d row, 9 L with 1 ch between each *u* the 1 ch ; 1 ch dc between next 2 L ; 1 ch 9 L with 1 ch between each *u* next ; 1 ch repeat. This last row is worked with the knitting at the back within the row of L stitches. Run cerise ribbon in the alternate holes of the white rows, and the same in the alternate L stitches of the border.

THE KNITTED WINTER SPENSER.

Materials.—Seven skeins of dark fleecy four-thread ; one skein each of gray fleecy, four shades ; No. 8 pins ; No. 1 Penelope crochet hook.

Stitch Brioche, thread forward, slip 1, knit 2 together, the same backwards and forwards.

Cast on 141 stitches, knit 2 plain rows.

Knit 40 rows.

Knit 4 ribs besides the outside half rib. Increase, *do this by picking up two of the back stitches with the right hand needle, placing them on the left, wool forward, slip 1, knit 1,* knit 39 ribs, increase as before, knit 4 ribs.

Knit 10 rows.

Knit 5 ribs, increase, knit 39 ribs, increase, knit 5 ribs.

Knit 10 rows.

Knit 6 ribs, increase, knit 39 ribs, increase, knit 6 ribs.

Knit 10 rows.

Knit 7 ribs, increase, knit 7 ribs, cast off 2 ribs, knit 21 ribs, cast off 2 ribs, knit 7 ribs, increase, knit 7 ribs.

Pass off the *fronts* on to a thread, knit 44

rows for the back, increase a rib on each side nearest the shoulder.

Knit 10 rows.

Decrease by casting off 1 rib 8 times—that is, 1 rib at the beginning of each row; there will be 8 ribs, and 7 ribs on the top of the neck.

Knit a plain row, cast off.

Take up the front, knit 7 ribs, increase, knit 7 ribs.

Knit 10 rows.

Knit 8 ribs, increase, knit 7 ribs.

Knit 30 rows.

Increase a rib the side nearest the shoulder.

Knit 10 rows.

Cast off three ribs, then decrease every row equally till to a point.

FOR THE SLEEVES.—Cast on 81 stitches, knit 22 rows.

Increase a rib, knit 60 rows, decrease a rib, knit 22 rows, cast off.

Work 4 rows of long stitches in crochet all round with the four shades of gray fleecy.

KNITTING —GENTLEMAN'S TRAVELLING-CAP.

Materials.—Three ounces of double brown Berlin wool, three quarters of a yard of brown silk, one yard of brown ribbon, one quarter of an ounce of brown silk, and leather peak pins No. 14.

Cast on fifty loops, and knit two rows.

3d row.—Knit 3, *a*, thread forward, knit 2 together; repeat to 2 stitches of the end of row; leave these unknitted on the pin.

4th.—Thread forward, knit 2 together; repeat, finishing the row with knit 3; repeat these two rows five times more, increasing the number of stitches which are left unknitted in the alternate rows. Thus, in the 5th row leave 4; 7th row, 6; 9th row, 6; 11th row, 10 stitches, unknitted; 13th row, plain, knitting every stitch; 14th row, plain, every stitch.

One division of the cap is now worked. Commence again at 3d row, and repeat, till four divisions are completed; after which cast off twelve stitches at the bottom of the cap; knit four more divisions (in all eight) on the remaining stitches, and cast off. Join the two sides together, leaving twelve stitches to correspond with the twelve which were cast off. After the 4th division, this piece forms a cape. Line with silk; make a tassel with the sewing-silk, and attach to the centre of the crown; sew on the peak, and the strings at the corners of the cap.

INDIAN CANOE WORK-BASKET.

FOR CARRYING ON THE ARM, WITH A LITTLE PIECE OF WORK OR KNITTING.

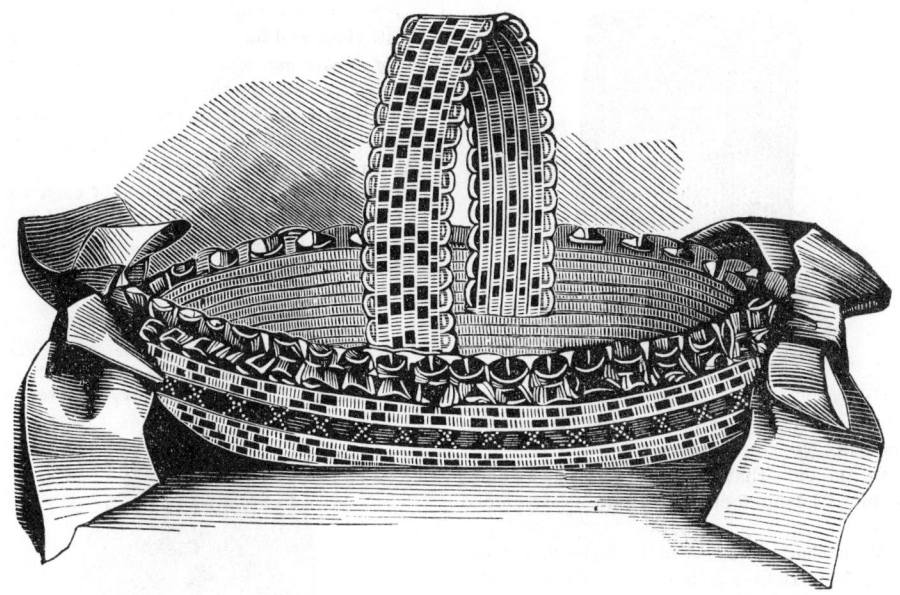

Materials.—One ball of crochet cord, gray or drab; one knot of colored satin cord; satin ribbon, and a coarse crochet hook.

MAKE a chain loosely, nine inches long, and work on it one row of sc. Then hold on the cord, and work over it, 4 stitches, 2 ch, miss 2, 1 stitch over cord ; 2 ch, miss 2, repeat to the end. At the finish of the row, cut off the crochet cord, but not the satin, which bend back along the next row, and work in the same way ; only the last of the four stitches must come on the second chain stitch after the four of the previous round. The third row the same. At the fourth you again bend back the satin cord, and do the same stitches, making the fourth crochet stitch come over the third of last row. In the fifth row, the satin cord is, as in the third, ready to work over ; do the same as the fourth. After these five, cut off the cord nearly close. Do one row of sc without the satin cord. Then the open row, thus: 1 long tc stitch, 1 diamond open hem; repeat to the end. Then a row of sc. Now resume the satin cord ; repeat the five rows with it, and the three without, until five cord stripes are done. Do one row of sc, and then a row *round;* that is, on the foundation chain as well, to close the two sides for the top of the basket.

With a needle and crochet cord join up and fasten the threads at the two ends.

Run a narrow ribbon through the open rows under the diamonds, and over the straight bars.

Make the handle exactly like one stripe, with the satin cord ; with a simple scallop edge on each side, thus : * 1 sc, 3 ch, miss 2. * repeat to the end.

2d row.—* 1 sc on each ch, 1 sc over sc, inserting the hook in the row beneath it. * repeat to the end.

The handle should be about eleven inches long, and sewed inside the basket, which may be lined with silk, or not, according to the taste of the worker. The ends of the basket are drawn, so as to be rounded. Quill some ribbon, and set it on round the top, with a bow of broader ribbon at each end.

The diamond open-hem is worked thus : begin with the thread three times round the work, as for long treble crochet : do half the stitch, having drawn it twice through. Pass the thread twice more round, miss two, and work an ordinary long tc stitch, only draw the hook through at the third movement ; 2 ch, put the thread once over the hook, and do a dc stitch where the two bars join. A perfect cross or X is thus made.

KNITTED CUFF IN BRIOCHE.

STITCH WITH CROCHET EDGE.

Materials.—Six skeins of colored four-thread Berlin wool; one skein of black Shetland wool; No. 15 pins; No. 2 Penelope crochet hook.

CAST on 57 stitches, knit two plain rows, knit 70 rows, knit two plain rows, cast off. Sew up the cuff.

On the side that was cast off make 5 chain, dc into 2d loop, 5 chain, dc into every second loop.

With Shetland dc *under* the 5 chain, 5 chain, dc *under* next five, 2 chain, *twist the wool twice over the hook*, 7 long *under* next 5, 2 chain, *repeat.*

Dc *under* the 2 chain, 5 chain, dc *under* the 2 chain, 5 chain, dc *under* the 5 chain, 5 chain, *repeat.*

Five chain, dc *under* the 5 chain, *repeat.*

WINTER CUFFS IN DOUBLE KNITTING.

Materials.—White four-thread Berlin wool, and four skeins of scarlet; two bone or wooden pins of such a size that a string put tightly round shall measure half an inch.

DOUBLE knitting is one of the best stitches

that can be used for comforters, cuffs, and chest-protectors, also for babies' cot-covers, being very light, soft, and elastic, and not liable to get hard in the washing, and, of course, being double, the warmth is very great.

For a Lady's Cuff.—Cast on in scarlet wool 56 stitches, and for a gentleman's 66 (*the number of stitches must always be even*). Knit 4 plain rows, then join on the white, and *; knit 1; bring the wool in front (*but not over the pin*). Slip 1, pass the wool back. Repeat from *. Each row is precisely the same.

Observe that the last stitch of each row is always slipped, and also that the *back* loop in each row is the one which is always slipped.

A CRAPED NECK-TIE.

Materials.—Cotton, No. 60; a pair of bone knitting pins, No. 12; two lumps of sugar dissolved in half a pint of hot water, and let remain till cold; two chenille tassels.

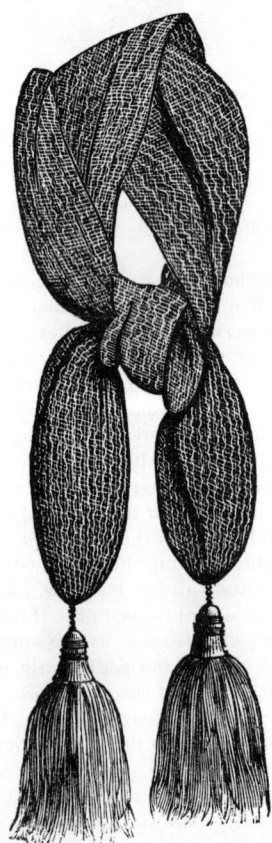

THIS is one of the prettiest articles for a neck-tie that can be made; having, when finished, all the appearance of soft white crape, and may be adopted either in mourning or out, by adding either black, colored, or white tassels.

Cast on the pin 460 stitches, and knit in plain garter-stitch till it is five nails wide; then cast off, but not too tight; then sew a strip of calico on to each side, but only so that it can be easily untacked. If the work is at all soiled, wash it with white curd soap and water; then rinse it perfectly, and squeeze it in a cloth very dry; after that dip it in the sugar and water, squeeze it slightly, and lay it out on a doubled sheet to dry; afterwards take off the calico, sew it up, and add the tassels. The washing and rinsing in sugar and water will always give it the appearance of being new.

KNITTING BASKET.

PERHAPS there are few kinds of work which require a basket expressly arranged for their own reception so much as knitting, on account of the almost fatal injury which it sustains when needles are drawn out and loops are dropped. The central opening is in bright blue Berlin wool, as well as the small part within the loop at each end. The ground within the diamonds is in maize-color. Both of these are much improved by being worked in floss silk. The ground on the exterior of the design is shaded crimsons, dark, medium, and light. It requires three pieces of this form to make the basket; the two sides must be worked alike, but the third, which is the bottom of the basket, only requires to be worked in the stripes of the shaded ground. All three must be stitched on card-board of the same shape and size, neatly lined with silk or German velvet, and sewn together on the outside, the stitches being concealed by a row of beads. After this the handle must be attached, which may be of double wire, twisted round with a little cotton-wool, and then with ribbon and beads. All this being done, a silk cord must be taken, the end fastened down close to the handle, and the cord wound round and round, each twist touching, but not over-wrapping the last, until about an inch and a half of the end of the basket is enclosed, this being an important point for the safety of the needles.

A NEW STYLE OF BIB.

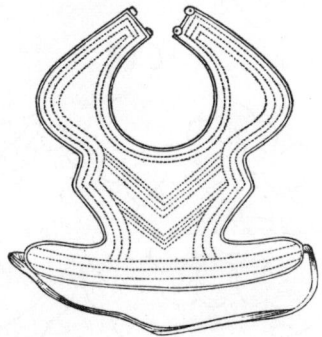

MADE of Marseilles, with rows of machine stitching on it. It buttons round the neck, and is fastened round the waist with a band.

NEW STYLE OF DRAWERS, VERY COMFORTABLE, AND EASILY MADE.

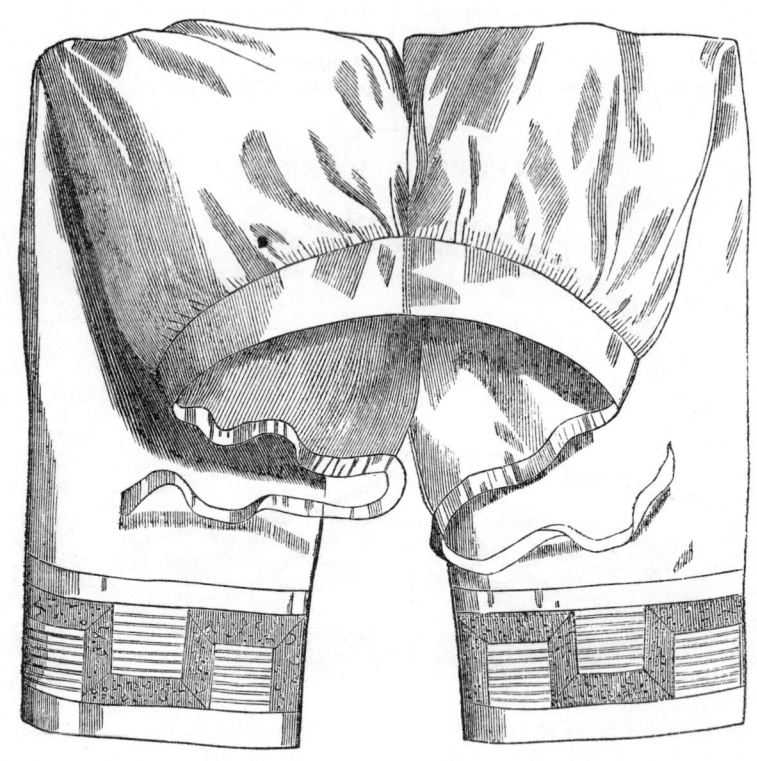

EMBROIDERY.

CROCHET TIDY.

TO BE WORKED IN SQUARE CROCHET.

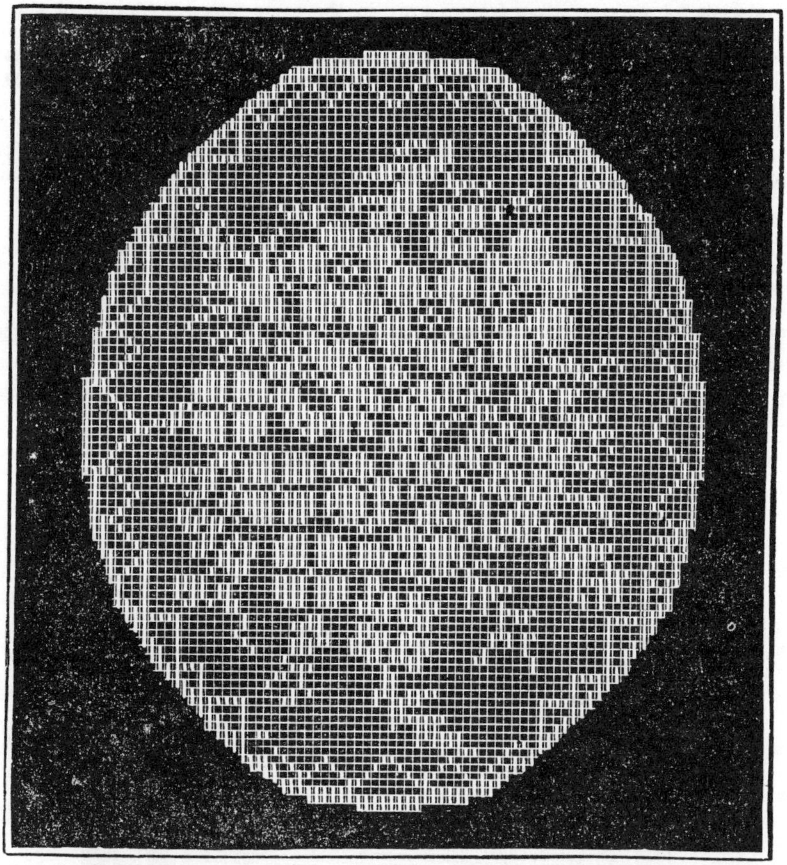

Count the number of squares in the extreme width and multiply by three, with the addition of one for the length of chain ; and then select a cotton which will bring the tidy to the size you require. In an oval tidy, you do not commence on a chain of the full length, but on one that will make the number of squares at the side. In this tidy, as there are twelve squares, thirty-seven chain must be made. Break off. In the next row, as there are six squares extra on each side, make a chain of eighteen, then work on the chain for the twelve close squares ; then finish with eighteen chain. Go on increasing in this way till the extreme width is obtained. To decrease, if by one square only, miss the first stitch of the last row, slip the next, single crochet the next, and double cro-

chet the third. Reverse this to decrease at the end of the row. If two or more squares are to be decreased at each end, begin with the slip stitch over the second, third, or any other. Always work in the ends if possible. This tidy will be greatly strengthened and improved by a line of double crochet being worked entirely round it. A fringe trimming is the prettiest for round or oval tidies.

EMBROIDERY.

STRAW FRAMES.

THE materials for making straw frames are card-board, colored paper, sewing silk, dark blue and straw-colored purse silks, and dark blue China ribbon, with wheaten straw, or reed as it is called in the country, both whole and split. From the sheaf select such reeds as are of good color and unbroken, and cut them into the required length. For the patterns in split

The foundations for the frames are all made in the same way. A frame of the required shape and size is cut out in card-board, and covered with colored paper, which must be wide enough to turn back over the edges. Gum tragacanth, made as thick as ordinary starch, is the best paste for the straw frame. The front is ornamented with the straw, strips of the same colored paper are gummed to the back to

Fig. 1.

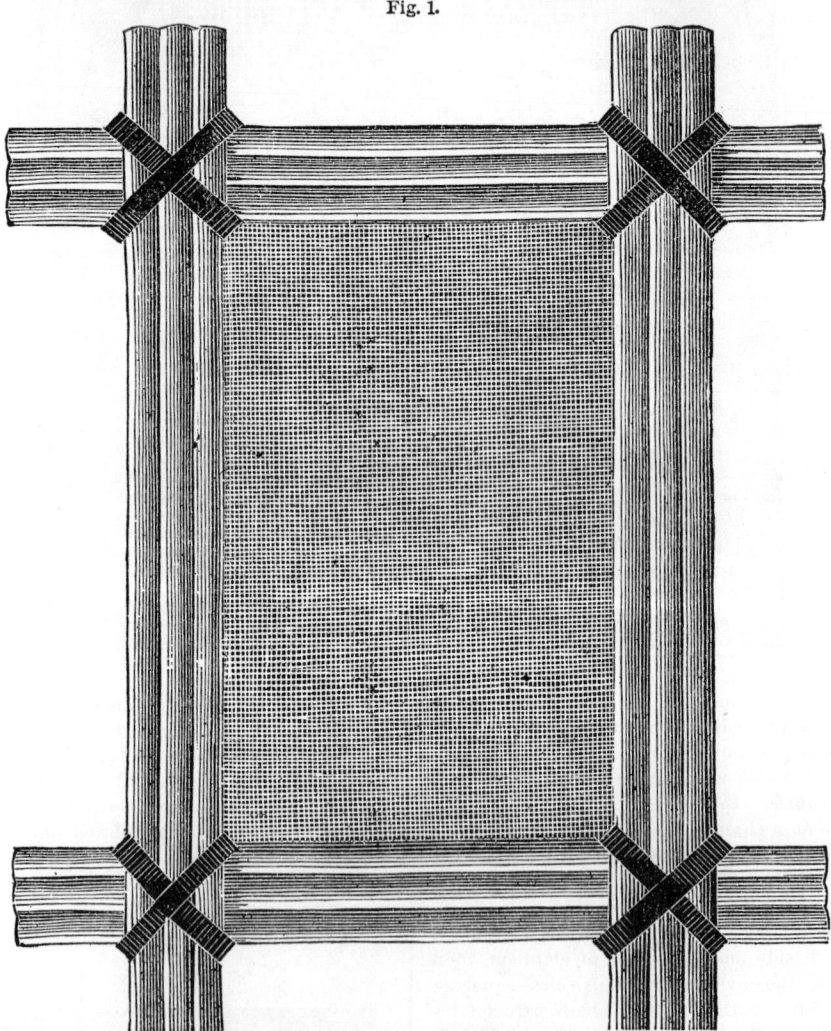

straw the reed may be slit with a knife, but the straw plait makers use a little bone instrument for the purpose. The special care requisite in handling the reed is not to bruise or crack it, as, though strong, it is brittle.

hide the stitches. The back for the photograph is next cut out, rather larger than the opening, and covered with colored paper. Either a support with a ribbon hinge may be added to it, or a ring sewn on to hang it up by; it is then laid

Fig. 2.

Fig. 3.

on the frame, colored side outwards, and secured to it by strips of colored paper pasted around three sides, the upper being left open to slip the photograph into. This may be covered with thin glass or talc.

Fig. 1. This frame is the easist to make. The foundation must be cut rather narrower than the three reeds. Take three reeds for the top of the frame and three for the bottom, of exactly equal length, and with sharp scissors cut away two-thirds of their circumference for the width of the crossing. With a needle and straw-colored silk secure them to the frame, notched side uppermost, taking the stitches through their lower side, and passing the silk at the back of the frame; turn it, and with the back uppermost make about four more stitches in the same way as the top, and proceed as before for the bottom. Now take the six reeds for the sides, notch them, and lay them on the frame notched side downwards, so that the ends and sides fit into each other exactly. Make a few diagonal stitches at the crossings, and when they are all secured add the crossing of blue

fasten them as before, and so on until the diamond is complete. Now form the inner square, and then the outer, and last of all add the single straws for the middle crossing. Cover the crossings with China ribbon to match ground, gild oval in centre with gold-leaf, adding the back and a ring, this frame being more suited for hanging up than for the table.

Fig. 3. Make the cabinet-sized frame as follows: Cover the frame with dark-green paper, split the reeds into the required width, and cut them to the length required for the stars. Make the diamond first, securing each end with straw-colored silk. Next fasten on the perpendicular straws, and lastly take a split one for the central line. Work the centre stars and divisions with scarlet purse silk, for the edges take small whole reeds, notching them at the crossing, and securing them as directed for Fig. 1, crossing each at the intersections with straw-colored silk, and covering this afterwards with the scarlet, the last thing to do being to work the corner stars with the purse silk. Great care is requisite in this frame to make the holes

Fig. 1.   Fig. 2.

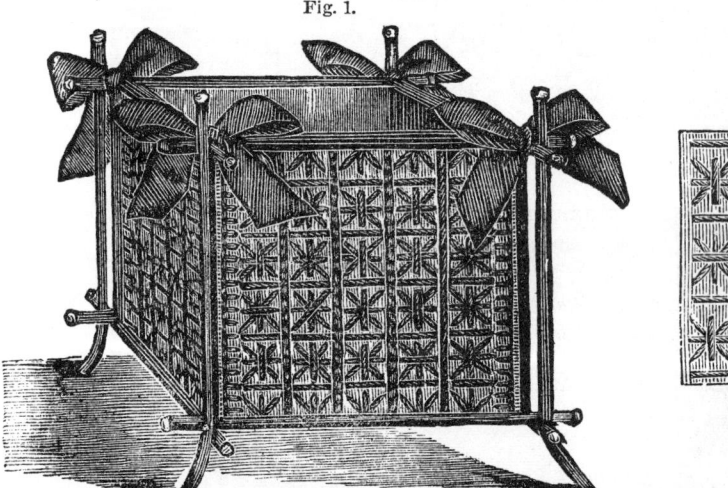

China ribbon, which must be double each way. Add the back and support as directed. If the ends become split they may be cut off at the crossing, and bits of reed the required length slipped in.

Fig. 2 is made of split reeds, which should be cut longer than required, and the ends afterwards clipped off. The place of each crossing should be measured with compasses, and marked with a pencil. Begin with the diamond; take three split straws, and fasten down each end with a needle and blue silk in this as in the next frame, making all the holes first from above, and taking the stitches so that they will be covered with the ribbon afterwards. Take the next three, and slip them under, or lay them over, as shown in the design, and

from the right side, and the strips of paper for the back must be laid on colored side downwards, or the white will show through the holes. Add a back and support to the frame.

WASTE PAPER BASKET.

This basket is intended for the drawing-room or boudoir, and forms a very useful and elegant addition to a room. The framework is of black cane highly polished, with gold tips to each part of the frame; this framework can be made any design. The sides are formed of gold or silver canvas; this canvas is very coarse perforated card-board; it is worked according to the detail Fig. 2 in rows of double cross-stitch, with a row of back-stitch or chain stitch between;

the stars are in alternate rows of red, green, and blue, with very dark chocolate or black between; the sides must be lined through with silk. The sides are then bound around with black velvet, which is sewn together at each corner, and a bow of colored silk fastens it to the framework. The bottom of the basket is plain card-board, covered with silk to match the other parts of the basket.

CIGAR BASKET.

THE materials are gray thread, split cane (the same that is used for seating chairs), six and a half dozen of wooden buttons, three dozen of beads, green wire, chenille, thick bonnet-wire, copal varnish, etc.

This basket, which is six and a half inches high, might be made of leather, or Java canvas, with a pattern worked with chenille or silk. Our model may be entirely made by a lady. The two feet, which are three inches high, are made of wire from six to seven inches long (with

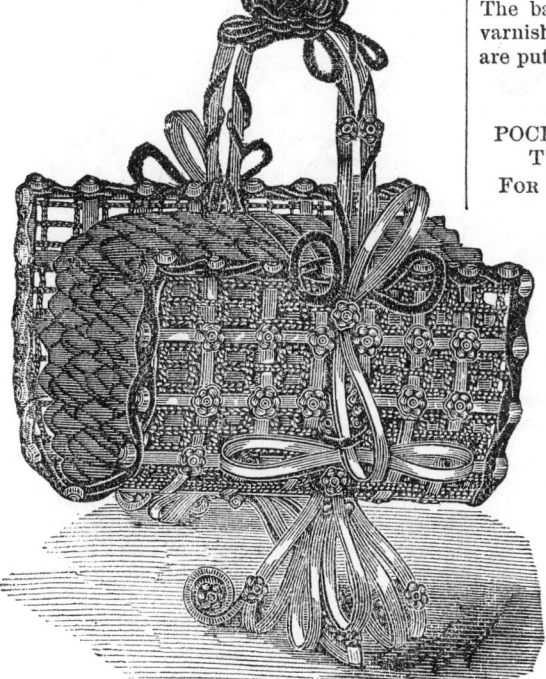

thus formed reaches to the top end of the basket, and to it are joined the six eyes falling over the foot, the two upper double bows, and the ends of the eight inches long cane handle. The cane bars for the handle must have holes bored in them, and fastened across. The frame and basket are sewn together with a needle and thread. A bow of cane four inches long, with covered wire placed over it, inclosed in the middle by a little loop ornamentation, and fastened with each of the loop eyes to the foot part standing sidewise. For the gray thread basket part, crochet perpendicularly upon fifty-two stitches, twenty-six rows of treble, separated by three chain, in which the trebles must meet trebles; then a wire is placed around the crochet, and fastened with a row of double, and so placed that the ends projecting a little are crossed at the corners. Cane bare are then drawn through the foundation in the form of squares, and holes are bored in the projecting ends, which are fastened with a few stitches. The ends are ornamented with wooden beads (see design). Our model is ornamented with wooden rosette buttons fastened on with glue. The basket is then painted over with copal varnish; the handle and place where the feet are put on are ornamented with green chenille.

POCKET-CASE FOR HOLDING COMB, TWEEZERS, AND TOOTHPICK.

FOR the outside case, cut two pieces of card-

cotton twisted around it) in three parts. The basket consists of a straight piece four and a half inches broad and eight inches long, bent half round; for this the middle wire is bent outwards to form an eye an inch and three-quarters in length, and the two others are bent at the ends in a serpentine form sidewise; commencing from the eyes, these three wire parts are united by twisting cotton around them. The bar

board, five inches long and three and a half inches broad; cover with ticking, embroidered with scarlet and green purse silk.

For the inside, the card-board must be cut four and a half inches long and three inches broad, covered with scarlet silk, with a ribbon strap across to hold the comb, tweezers, and toothpick. The inside and outside are bound with a silk braid.

BUTTON-CASE.

Fig. 1 represents the case closed; Fig. 2 represents it open.

Fig. 1.

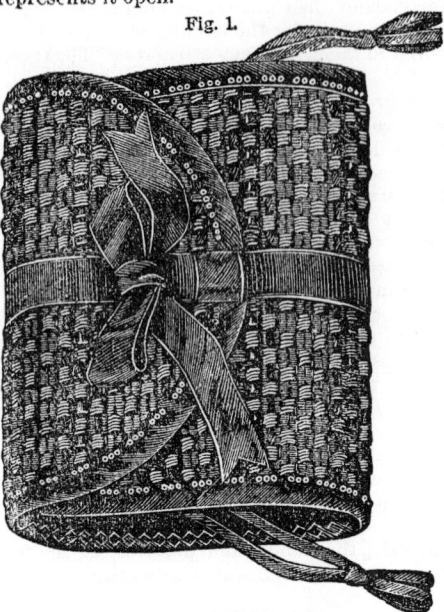

The materials are curled canvas, colored silk, narrow ribbon, and card-board.

Fig. 2.

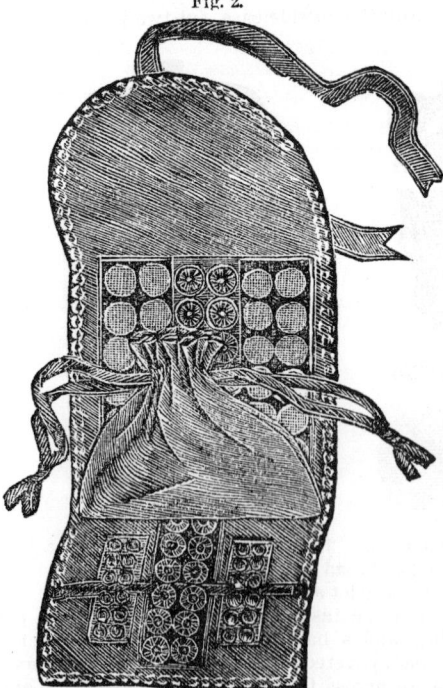

The canvas must measure four inches in breadth, and eight inches in length, and re-

quires to be a little rounded at the top (see Fig. 1). Our model has violet Berlin wool, and separate black beads drawn through. Card-board is placed beneath, and the case is lined with silk to match the ribbon; it is also turned over on the outside to appear like a narrow binding, and fastened down with three steel beads. The lining, according to Fig. 2, is ornamented all around with loose stitches of white silk and little black cross stitches. Two small ribbon straps are placed to fasten in the paper of buttons. A ribbon is required for closing the silk bag, which is two and a quarter inches high; this ribbon is two inches long and about a quarter of an inch broad, fastened by a ribbon strap on the rounded side. The bag is for loose buttons.

INSERTIONS OF TAPE WORK.

Our two designs are intended for insertions for children's linen, dresses, etc., and are excessively durable and strong for the purpose. You require tape the width of the figures in the engraving; cut each piece double the length of each figure in the design, fold them, and sew

Fig. 1.

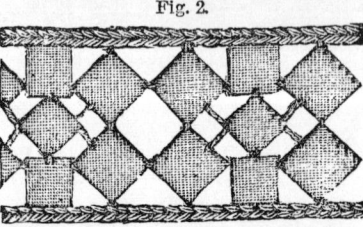

Fig. 2.

them together with a needle and thread, joining them to each other as you proceed. The edge is made of fine braid, to which the tape is sewn, or it may be crocheted in chain stitch. The bars are worked with a needle and strong cotton, in the same manner as the lace bars.

BONNET-BOX.

(*See Engravings, Page* 63, 64.)

A STRONG wood box, made in the circular form, is the foundation. The lower part is covered by a plaited valance, made of chintz or glazed calico of some bright color, covered with plaited muslin.

Fig. 2 shows a part of the border falling around the upper part. The top is ornamented with the same pattern. White or colored braid,

Fig. 1.—Bonnet-box.

Case for Tablets.

muslin and colored silk or cambric, may be used for the top. When the button-hole work is finished, the muslin is cut away according to design.

--- ◆ ---

CASE FOR TABLETS.

A CARD-BOARD foundation is required rather larger than the tablets. This is covered with velvet, ornamented with a small pattern in embroidery or braid, and bound around with braid. A small piece of velvet is separately stitched on one side to hold the pencil. An oval in the middle of one side is cut and button-holed around, and a photograph or embroidered medallion may be inserted.

Fig. 1.

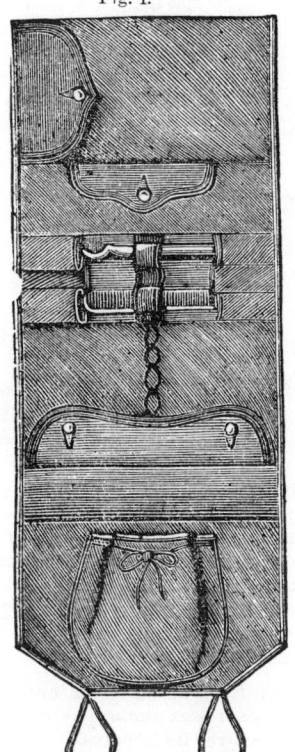

Fig. 3.

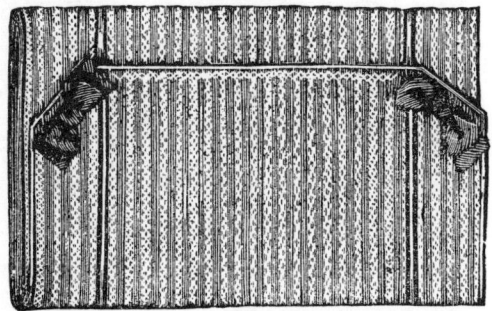

Fig. 2.

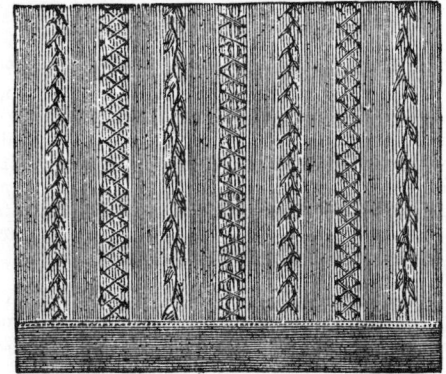

HOUSEWIFE.
(*See Engravings, Page* 63.)

The engraving illustrates a very useful and compact model of a housewife. The material used for the case is red and white striped ticking. The white stripes are worked with green

EMBROIDERED JEWEL CASE.

This case is lined with rich crimson corded silk. The feet and margin are covered with crimson Russian leather, and ornamented with bronze work. The foundation of the medal-

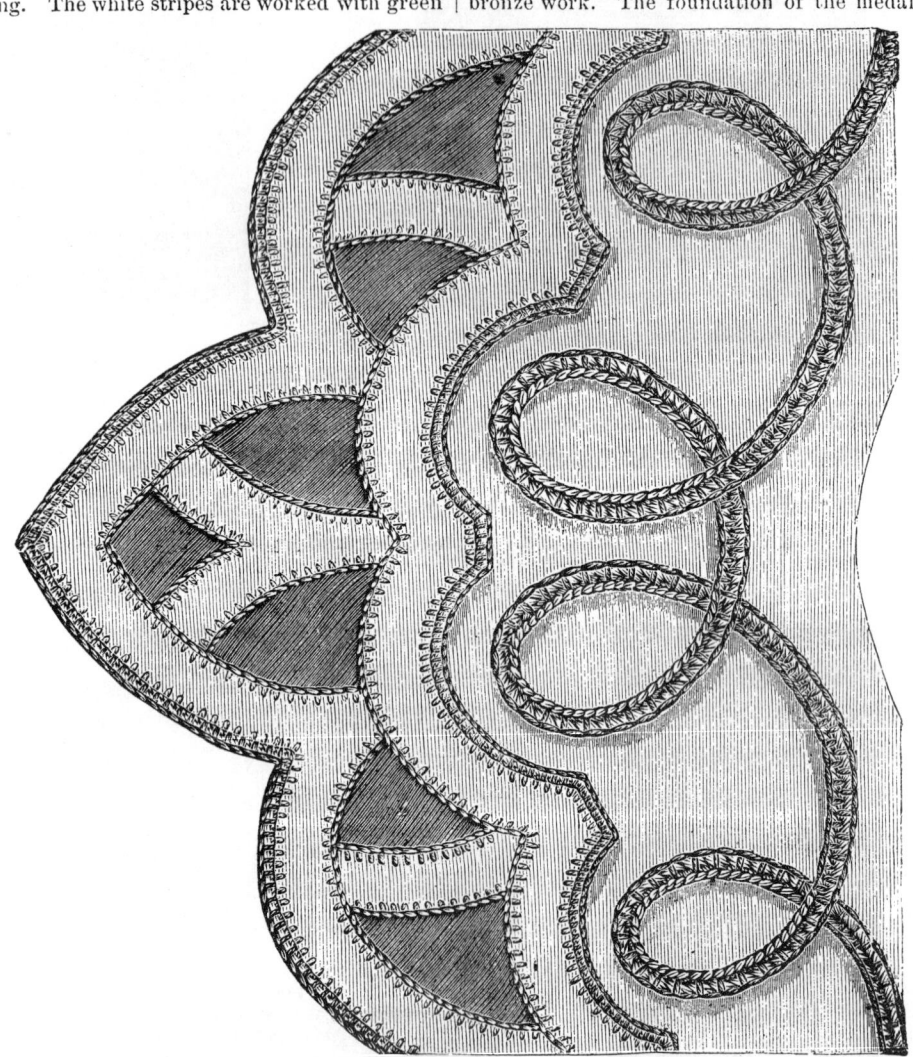

Fig. 2.—Bonnet-box.

feather stitch, black backstitching, and blue herringbone, as illustrated in the detail, the ticking is cut fourteen inches long and five and a quarter inches wide; it is lined with red silk; the sides are bound with ribbon or braid. The engravings represent the housewife open, showing the pockets, and Fig. 2 closed and finished, Fig. 3 the detail for the embroidery.

Pictures should be dusted lightly with cotton wool, or with a feather brush.

lion, which is framed in bronze, is of gray corded silk, embroidered with flowers of doubled crape, in the natural colors. These flowers are fastened down with the veins of chenille in *point russe*. The tendrils are also worked in *point russe*, and the case is lined with gray taffetas.

A neat, clean, fresh-aired, sweet, and well-arranged house, exercises a moral as well as a physical influence over its inmates.

WRITING CASE.

THIS writing case of cedar-wood consists of two equal halves, and opens like a backgammon board; one half has an inner cover, and holds the writing materials; the other half is

knit 2 together, over, knit 2 together, knit 2 together again, and pass the 1st over the 2d, over, knit 2 together, over, knit 2 together, over, 3 plain, over, knit 2 together; repeat from *. 2d and all alternate rows. Purl. 3d.

Fig. 1.

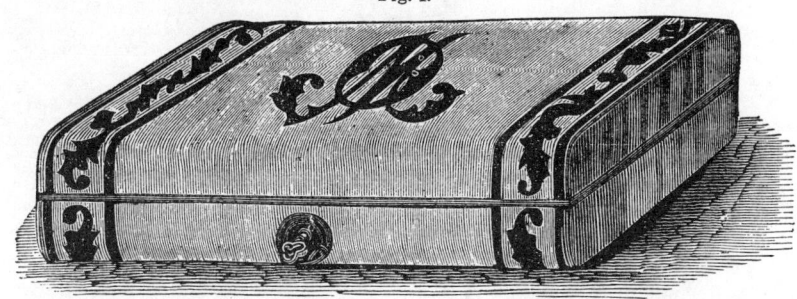

furnished with a number of pockets, as seen in Fig. 2, for holding letters and papers. The pockets and the covers are of pasteboard, covered with maroon-colored leather and white

* 1 plain, knit 2 together, over, 3 plain, knit 2 together, over, knit 2 together, over, knit 2 together, over, 1 plain, over, knit 2 together, over, knit 2 together, over, 3 plain, knit 2 to-

Fig. 2.

watered paper; and the soufflets are of linen, covered on the outside with leather, and inside with paper. The box is ornamented on the outside with a monogram in brown velvet, and with a border of brown silk and arabesques in velvet, according to illustration.

KNITTED ANTIMACASSARS.

CAST on 24 stitches for each pattern, and allow 2 or 3 stitches as preferred on each side for the edge; these are not included in the directions, but are always knitted plain, taking off the 1st stitch. 1st row. * 2 plain, over, knit 2 together, 3 plain, over, knit 2 together, over,

gether, over, 1 plain; repeat from *. 5th. * 2 plain, over, knit 2 together, 1 plain, knit 2 together, over, knit 2 together, over, knit 2 together, over, 3 plain, over, knit 2 together, over, knit 2 together, over, knit 2 together, 2 plain, over, knit 2 together; repeat from *. 7th. * 1 plain, knit 2 together, over, 1 plain, knit 2 together, over, knit 2 together, over, knit 2 together, over, 5 plain, over, knit 2 together, over, knit 2 together, over, knit 2 together twice, over, 1 plain; repeat from *. 9th. * 2 plain, over, knit 2 together, 1 plain, over, knit 2 together, over, knit 2 together, over, knit 2 together, 1 plain, over, knit 2 together, 2 plain, over, knit 2 together, over, knit 2 together, over, knit 2 together, over, knit 2 together; repeat from *. 11th. * 1 plain, knit 2 together, over, 3 plain, over, knit 2 together, over, knit 2 together, over, knit 2 together, 2 plain, knit 2 together, over, knit 2 together, over, knit 2 together, over, 1 plain, knit 2 together, over, 1 plain; repeat from *. 13th. Commence again at 1st row.

Easy Leaf Pattern.—Cast on any number that will divide by 11, adding 2 stitches on each side for the edge, which are to be knitted as in the preceding pattern. After a purl row, begin. 1st row. * Over, 3 plain, slip 1, knit 1, pass slipped stitch over, knit 2 together, 3 plain, over, 1 plain; repeat from *. 2d and all alternate rows. Purl. 3d and 5th. Same as 1st. 7th. 1 plain, * over, 2 plain, slip 1, knit 1, pass slipped stitch over, knit 2 together, 2 plain, over, 3 plain; repeat from *, and end with 2 plain instead of 3. 9th. 2 plain, * over, 1 plain, slip 1, knit 1, pass slipped stitch over, knit 2 together, 1 plain, over, 5 plain; repeat from *; at the end 3 plain instead of 5. 11th. 3 plain, * over, slip 1, knit 1, pass slipped stitch over, knit 2 together, over, 7 plain; repeat from *; at the end 4 plain instead of 7. 13th. * 4 plain, over, slip 1, knit 1, pass slipped stitch over, over, 3 plain, slip 1, knit 1, pass slipped stitch over; repeat from *. 15th. * Knit 2 together, 3 plain, over, 1 plain, over, 3 plain, slip 1, knit 1, pass slipped stitch over; repeat from *. 17th and 19th. Same as 15th. 21st. * Knit 2 together, 2 plain, over, 3 plain, over, 2 plain, slip 1, knit 1, pass slipped stitch over; repeat from *. 23d. * Knit 2 together, 1 plain, over, 5 plain, over, 1 plain, slip 1, knit 1, pass slipped stitch over; repeat from *. 25th. * Knit 2 together, over, 7 plain, over, slip 1, knit 1, pass slipped stitch over; repeat from *. 27th. 1 plain, * over, 3 plain, slip 1, knit 1, pass slipped stitch over, 4 plain, over, slip 1, knit 1, pass slipped stitch over; repeat from *; at the end 1 plain, instead of taking one stitch over the other. Commence again at 1st row, but knit 1 plain before the pattern.

EMBROIDERED CIGAR CASE.

THIS pretty cigar case is made of card-board covered with silk, and embroidered with brown silk in *point russe*. Take a piece of card-board ten inches long and five inches wide, cut one end into a curve, according to illustration, cover it on the inside with brown silk, and on the outside of the straight end with a strip of silk four inches wide. Then make the pockets of pieces of silk lined with calico, five inches long and three and a half inches wide, and sloped out at one end. Turn in the edges and stitch them together with brown silk, stitch on an embroidered medallion to one of the pockets, and then, making a plait down the sides, sew them to the case, according to illustration. Then make the flaps two inches long and three

inches wide, lined and stitched around the edge. For the outside of the case take a piece of silk and lining the required size, slope it at one end, and work on it the design, according

Fig. 1.

to illustration, with brown sewing silk. Line the sloped end three inches deep with silk, bind it with brown ribbon, and tack the outside to

Fig. 2.

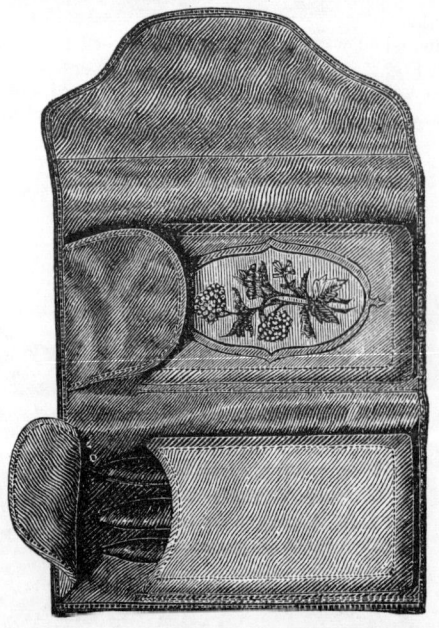

the inner part of the case. Bind the case all around with ribbon and furnish it with a loop. In closing the case the curved end is slipped between the outside and the inside of the sloped end.

GENTLEMAN'S SCARF PINS OF OXYDISED SILVER.

BOTTLE HOLDER.

THIS holder for a champagne bottle is made of four pieces of gray cloth cut according to illustration. The leaves and grapes are of brown cloth, gummed on to the foundation; then work

the veins and stalk in corded silk, line the gray cloth, and turn the edges of the lining over on the right side, and fasten them down with open overcast stitches and a row of single stitch. Sew the pieces together on the wrong side.

CROCHET SOAP-BAG.

MAKE a chain of thirty-eight stitches with thick white wool on a wooden or bone crochet needle, and work around this chain one row of double, increasing at the ends to make the work lie flat. Finish the row with a slip stitch into the first stitch of the row, one chain, and

Fig. 1.

turn the work. Work six rows of double on the back threads of the previous row, at the end of each row making a slip stitch as above, and one chain, before turning the work, and increasing at the round ends so as to keep the work flat. Between every two ribs of this piece work two rows of double, according to

Fig 1. Then work the front of the pocket as follows: Make a chain of twenty stitches, and work around it as in the first piece; but in order to make one end straight, omit the slip stitch and only work one chain before turning the work. Work rows of double stitches over this

Fig. 2.

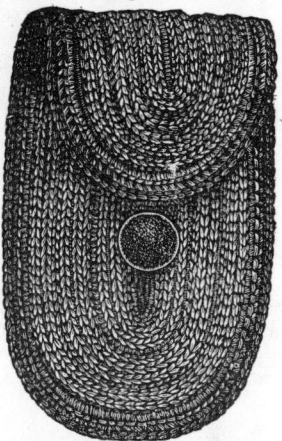

piece as before, and two rows of double across the straight end, finishing with a row of red wool. Join the two pieces together with a row of red wool, and work around the flap with the same, fasten a button on for the flap to fasten on, and a cord can be added to hang the bag up if desired.

GIMP ORNAMENT FOR POLONAISES, ETC.

DRESSING-SLIPPER.

THE cork sole may be bought of the required size. A piece of cloth should be placed over the upper side, and the edge bound with braid. The upper part of the slipper may be a piece

HANDKERCHIEF SACHET

(*See Illustration, Page* 69.)

THIS sachet measures twelve inches in width and twenty-four in length, which allows four and a half inches for the flap, cut to the shape

of the plush-like cloth of which jackets are made. A little revers is put on over the front. This and the edge of the slipper all around are bound with braid. The lower edge is sewn to the binding of the cork sole, and the upper edge is ornamented with scallops of crochet, made of three chain, one double, worked into the braid at regular distances.

shown in Fig. 1. It is of white honeycomb canvas, worked with red and black Berlin wool, the design for which is given in the full size in Fig. 2. The sachet is fastened at the edge with a narrow waved braid, and fastened with elastic loops and pearl buttons.

SQUARE FOR ANTIMACASSAR: TAPE AND CROCHET.

THE small squares in the centre are of fine tape, folded double, the edges sewn neatly to-

KNITTED BODICE IN SHETLAND WOOL

KNITTED with Shetland wool and two long bone needles, No. 10. Cast on 201 stitches. 1*st. row.* Plain. 2*d.* Knit 2 together, 3 plain, * over, 1 plain, over, 3 plain, knit 3 together, 3 plain ;

gether, and the squares joined at the corners. The double row of rings must next be worked. For each ring make a chain of twelve, close around, and work under the chain twenty-four double ; join the rings in working with four double. Sew them to the tape squares, and fill in the corners with twisted bars.

repeat from * 18 times ; over, 1 plain, over, 3 plain, knit 2 together. Repeat these 2 rows 9 times. 21*st.* Plain. 22*d.* Knit 2 together, 7 plain, * knit 3 together, 7 plain ; repeat from * 18 times ; knit 2 together. 23*d.* Plain. 24*th.* 2 plain, * over, knit 2 together, 4 plain ; repeat from * 25 times ; over, knit 2 together, 1 plain.

25th. Plain. There are now 161 stitches. Knit 16 rows plain. You now begin to increase in front and back. *1st row.* 22 plain, over, 33 plain, over, 51 plain, over, 33 plain, over, 22

9th or next increasing row there will be 24 plain, over, 33 plain, over, 55 plain, over, 33 plain, over, 24 plain. In the 13th row, 25 plain, and so on. When all the increasings are com-

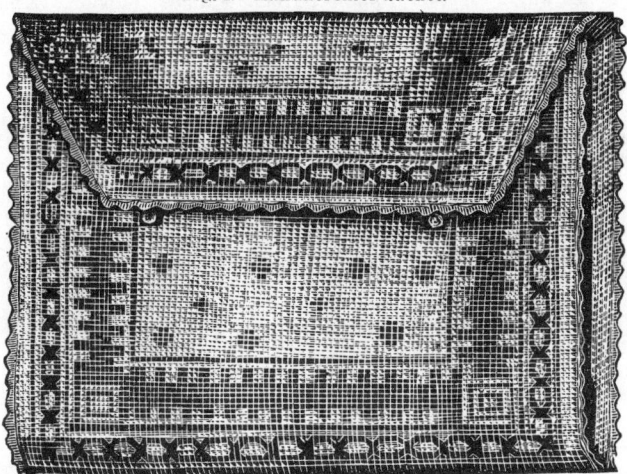

Fig. 1.—Handkerchief Sachet.

plain. Knit three plain rows. *5th.* 23 plain, over, 33 plain, over, 53 plain; over, 33 plain, over, 23 plain, then 3 plain rows. Increase in this man-

pleted, knit a plain row, then knit 56 stitches for one front, turn, 1 plain, knit 2 together, then plain to the end. Knit a plain row of 55

Fig. 2.

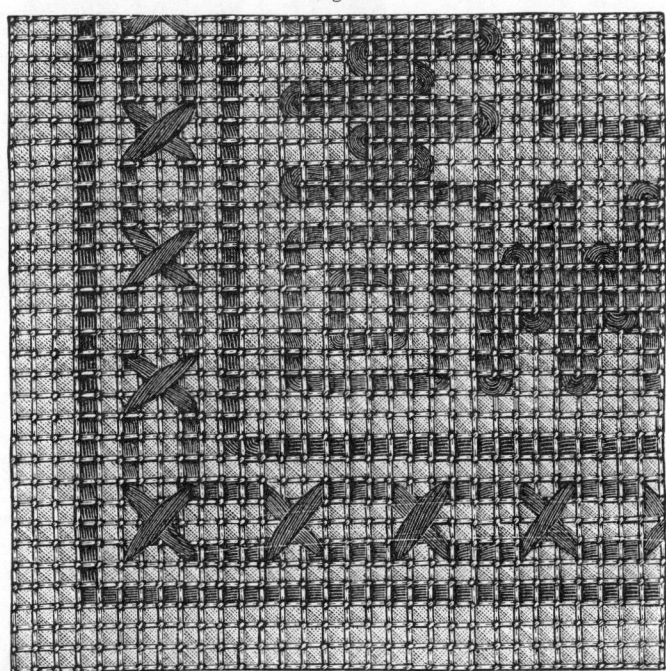

ner 16 times more, with 3 plain rows between the increasings. At the beginning and end of every increasing row, knit 1 stitch more, and at the middle knit 2 stitches more; thus, in the

stitches, and repeat from * 3 times. Knit 60 rows plain and break off the wool.

For the Back.—Cast off 8 stitches, knit 105 plain, turn, leaving 64 stitches, * 1 plain, knit

2 together, knit to end of row all but 3, knit these, 2 together, 1 plain. Knit a plain row. Repeat from * 3 times. Knit 70 rows, break off and begin the other side of front. Cast off 8 stitches, knit to the end. *Next row.* * knit plain all but 3 stitches, knit 2 together, 1 plain. Knit a plain row; repeat from * 3 times. Knit 60 rows, then knit all the stitches off the other needle. *1st row.* 50 plain, knit 2 together twice, 93 plain, knit 2 together twice, 50 plain. *2d.* Plain; repeat these 2 rows 23 times, knitting 1 stitch less at the beginning and end, and 2 less at the back every decreasing row, and at the end of the 14th time, leave 3 stitches unworked at the end of row, turn, and leave 3 stitches unworked at the end of next row, and continue to leave 3 more stitches at the end of every row till the last; then knit to the end of the needle, pick up the stitches down the front (one for every 2 rows), knit a row, decreasing at the shoulder the same as before, and pick up the stitches down the other side of front. Knit 1 row plain. *Next row.* 18 plain, over, knit 2 to-

1 plain, over, 3 plain, knit 3 together, 3 plain; repeat from * 4 times; then over, 1 plain, over, 3 plain, knit 2 together. *3d.* Plain. Repeat these 2 rows 9 times. *Next row.* 9 plain, knit 2 together, * 8 plain, knit 2 together; repeat from * 3 times; 10 plain. Knit 10 plain rows. *Next row.* 1 plain, increase 1 by knitting again in the same stitch from the back, knit to within 1 of the end, increase 1, 1 plain. * Knit 16 plain rows. Increase 1 at each end of the row; repeat from * 7 times. Knit 2 plain rows; then knit 2 together at each end of the needle, every alternate row, 7 times, and cast off. Sew up the sleeves, and put them into the armholes. Sew on 8 pearl buttons up the front, and run a ribbon in at the top of the border around the waist.

----◆◆----

FANCY MAT FOR SMELLING-BOTTLES, CANDLESTICKS, ETC.

This little mat is made of thin gray card-board, embroidered in *point russe* with red cot-

Fig. 1.

Fig. 2

gether, * 8 plain, over, knit 2 together; repeat from * 7 times. Increase 1 at each corner, and decrease at the shoulder same as before; knit 4 rows and cast off rather tightly.

For the Sleeves.—Cast on 61 stitches, knit a plain row. *2d.* Knit 2 together, 3 plain, * over,

ton, and finished around the edge with a plaited frill of colored paper. Each mat is seven inches square, and when the work is finished, it is lined with white paper. Fig. 2 represents the border in full size.

SOFA OR CARRIAGE PILLOW, IN CROCHET.

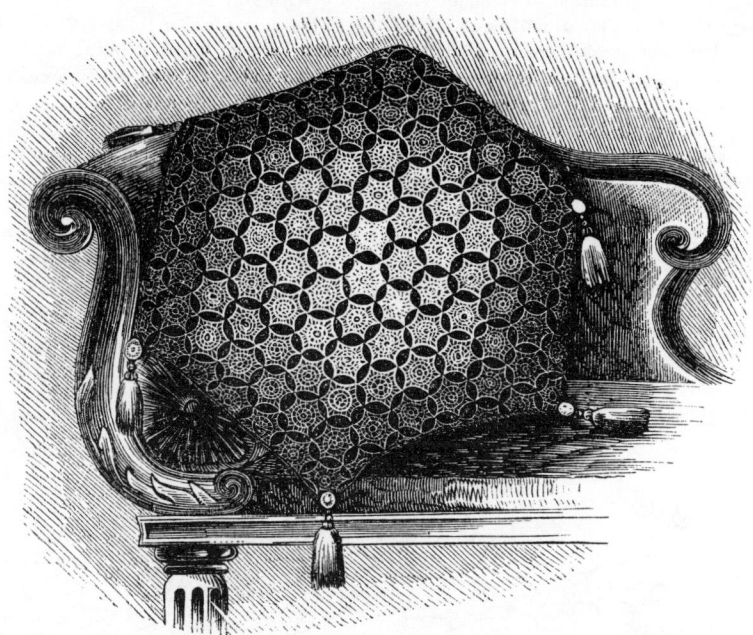

Materials.—Seven shades of scarlet, four thread Berlin wool; the third shade from the lightest to be a bright military scarlet, the darkest to be nearly black. Seven shades of bright emerald green (*grass green must never be used*), three-quarters of an ounce of each shade, except the lightest of both colors—six skeins of each of these. No. 2 Penelope crochet hooks.

1st row.—With lightest scarlet make a chain of 9 stitches, unite the ends; 5 chain, dc *under* the 9 chain; repeat this 5 times more (*in all*, 6 *chains of* 5). Cut off the wool, tie it securely at the back. (*This must be done at every row.*)

2d.—Same color. 2 long *under* the 5 chain; 3 chain; 2 more long *under* the same; 3 chain; repeat this 5 times more.

3d.—Next shaded scarlet. 2 long *under* the 3 chain, between the 4 long stitch; 3 chain; 2 more long *under* the same; 3 chain; dc *under* 3 chain; 3 chain; repeat this 5 times more.

4th.—Military scarlet. 2 long *under* the 3 chain, between the 4 long; 4 chain; 2 more long *under* the same; 4 chain; dc on dc; 4 chain; repeat this 5 times more.

5th.—Palest green. 3 long *under* the 4 chain, between the 4 long; 5 chain; 3 more long *under* the same; 3 chain; dc *under* 4 chain; 5 chain; dc *under* 4 chain; 3 chain, *repeat*.

This forms the centre star.

Now work 6 more stars in precisely the same manner, only varying the shades as follows: Commence with the lightest shade scarlet, and work the 2d row with next shade instead of the same; taking the next shade green for the outside row; sew with green wool these 6 stars to the points of the centre star, sewing them also at the side.

Now make 12 stars, beginning with the 2d shade scarlet, making the 1st and 2d rows of the same color.

3d row.—Military scarlet, same as 3d row of 1st star.

4th.—Next darker shade, same as 4th row.

5th.—Next darkest green.

Sew these 12 stars round the last six, attaching them as before.

Now make 18 stars, commencing with military scarlet, making the 2 first rows in the same shade.

3d row.—Next darker.

4th.—Next darker.

5th.—Next darker green.

Sew these round the other stars.

Make 24 stars, commencing with military scarlet, but making the 2d row of the next darker shade, instead of the same.

Use the next two darker shades in gradation, and the next darkest green.

Sew these stars round the others.

Make 30 circles, commencing with the next shade darker than the military scarlet ; use the 3 darker shades in gradation, and edge with the darkest green but one. It will be observed that seven shades of scarlet are used on this side, and 6 of green : for the reverse of the cushion, 6 of scarlet and 7 of green. Damp well, and press by placing it between folded linen, with a heavy weight upon it, till dry.

Line this side with white cotton velvet, white satin, or watered silk.

For the Reverse.

Make exactly the same number of stars, and worked precisely the same way with respect to the tints, but commencing with the palest green, instead of scarlet, and edging the outside row with scarlet.

This side may be lined either with white or green velvet ; make a lining of strong calico, the exact size, fill with four pounds of feathers.

Trim with green silk cushion cord, and 6 shaded bullion tassels.

Great care must be taken to arrange the colors precisely as the instructions given, as the effect will be to give a most intense and brilliant color, and in selecting the wools, they should be of the brightest tints.

EMBROIDERY.

PATCHWORK.

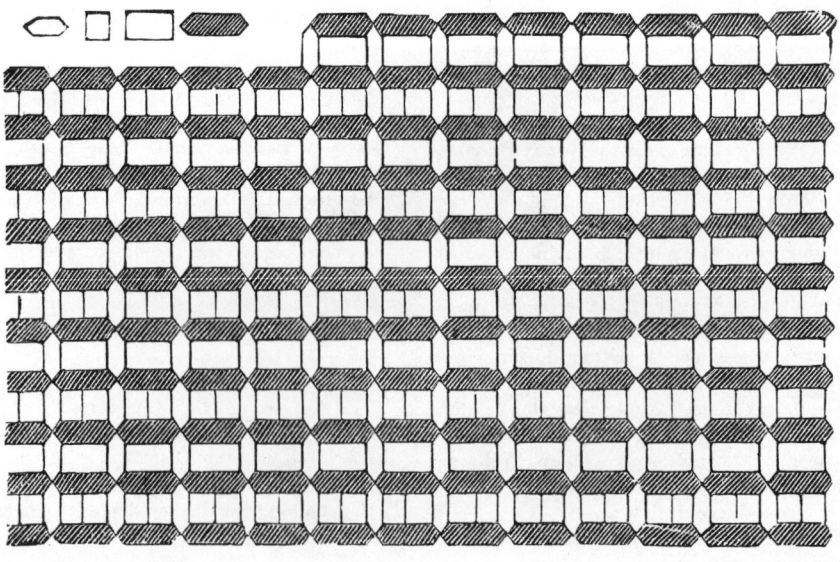

LAMP MAT IN CROCHET.

The centre is of white, the star in black; then alternate rows of deep crimson and orange. The border is formed by making balls of worsted of three shades of green, and sewing them on in regular order, the lightest being outside.

DESIGN IN BERLIN WOOL-WORK FOR MATS, SLIPPERS, ETC.

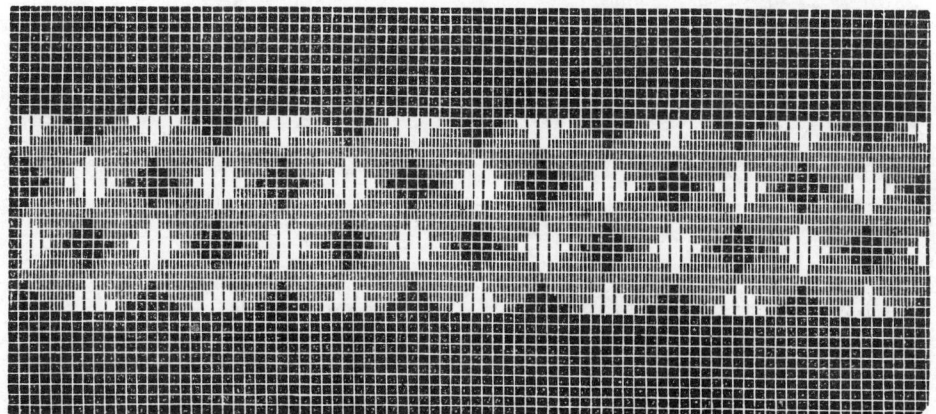

Simple patterns in Berlin wool-work, producing lively and pleasing effects, are amongst those supplies for the work-table which every lady finds most useful for various purposes, enabling her with perfect ease to make many pretty articles, which, if great arrangement were necessary, would never be undertaken. The little design which we have now given is one of these, being perfectly easy of execution, and especially pretty when completed. Wools of three different colors are all that are required, worked in the following manner: The lines which form the sides of the diamonds are in a brilliant green, inclining to a blue; when they appear to cross, the small square becomes a very dark green, approaching to a black, the ground or under diamonds being white. Another pretty arrangement of colors is to take a ruby for the sides of the diamonds, a black for the crossings, and a white for the ground; or a blue may be substituted for the ruby with equally good effect. This little design will be found well suited for cushions, mats, slippers, and many other articles, and it may be worked on either fine or coarse canvas, according to the article for which it may be required.

BORDER IN BRODERIE ANGLAISE AND BUTTON-HOLE STITCH.

FOR A LOUNGING CAP.

QUILTING DESIGN.

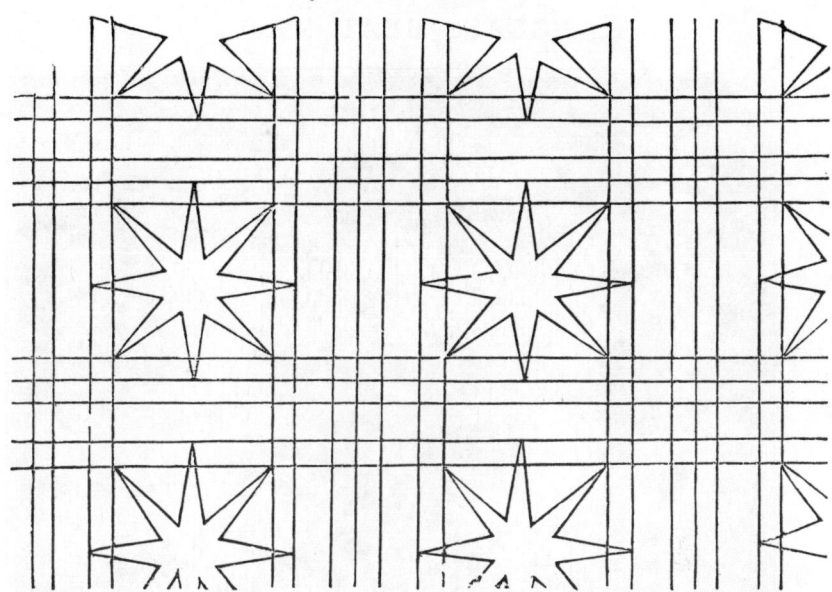

FANCY TIDY.

GLASS BEAD MAT.

Materials.—Three rows dark red beads, seven rows middle red, seven rows light red, seven rows dark blue, eight rows light blue, one row yellow, twenty-one rows white, one row black.

THIS mat must be commenced the same way as No. 1, October number, at A, beginning with but two beads and working alternately two and one to the opposite side, afterwards with only one needle at each side. The white beads on the outer border of this one should be dead white. These two mats will only require a very simple fringe.

OTTOMAN, IN BERLIN WORK.

Materials.—Penelope border canvas, about 50 stitches in width, and of a size which will allow the beads to cover a stitch completely; amber pound-beads of two shades, rich green, and claret wool; also the Mecklenburg thread No. 71.

THE beads are chosen of shades which contrast somewhat strongly, the darkest being of a decided orange, and the others straw-color. The borders and stars are done in the dark shade; the outlines of the medallions in the other.

Fill in the medallions in green, and also the inner part of the scroll; the rest in claret in cross-stitch.

The ottoman is to be made up in alternate stripes of work and velvet, and trimmed with rich cord and tassels.

Stripes of work and velvet being also much used for *Prie-dieu* chairs, this pattern would be very effective done in straw beading and wool. It will not do to use Penelope canvas for this, as the grounding is done in tapestry stitch, that is, taken over two threads in height and one in width. Select a canvas of which the straw will cover two threads, and run a line on, across the width of the canvas, in small neat stitches. Work with the wool all the parts which form the grounding, leaving the straw to represent the beads.

HANGING PINCUSHION AND NEEDLE-BOOK.

This little article is extremely ornamental when completed, and possesses the advantage of being also useful. A little case, like a book-cover, is cut out in card-board; a similar-shaped piece of velvet or silk, a little larger, is also required, on which is worked the sprig given in the illustration. This may be done in white beads, or embroidered in colored silks, or worked in gold thread. This is then stretched over the card-board, brought over the edge, and gummed down. A little square mattress cushion, covered in silk, is then gummed to one side of the cover; two or three cashmere leaves are stitched to it at the top edge, and the other half of the cover, which is loose, is lined and brought over them. It is now in the form of a book. A bow of ribbon is placed at the back, and it is suspended by a chain of either gold or white beads, to correspond with the sprig. A fringe of the same beads is attached to the two sides, and two tassels are added from where the chain proceeds. This forms a pretty little article for a fancy fair sale, as it may be made very showy; it is also very easy to execute.

Gentleman's Slipper,

IN

BERLIN WOOL WORK.

———◆———

If our young lady readers are not too much frightened by this race of monkeys upon velocipedes, they can, by copying it, make a very original pair of slippers. The design, *en silhouette*, is worked entirely in black, with outlines of yellow silk, upon a bright red ground.

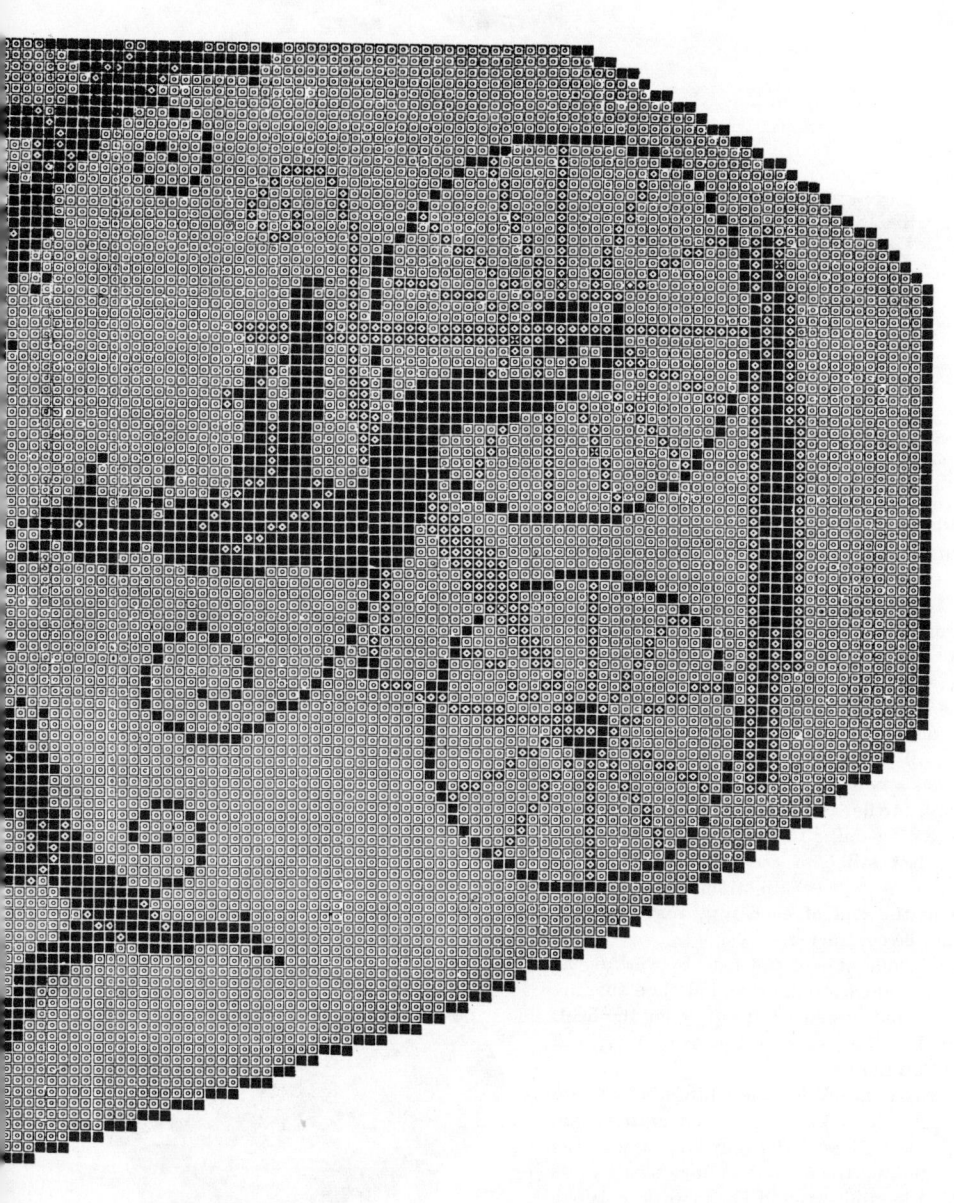

CHILD'S WARM SHOE, IN CROCHET,

TRIMMED WITH IMITATION ERMINE FUR.

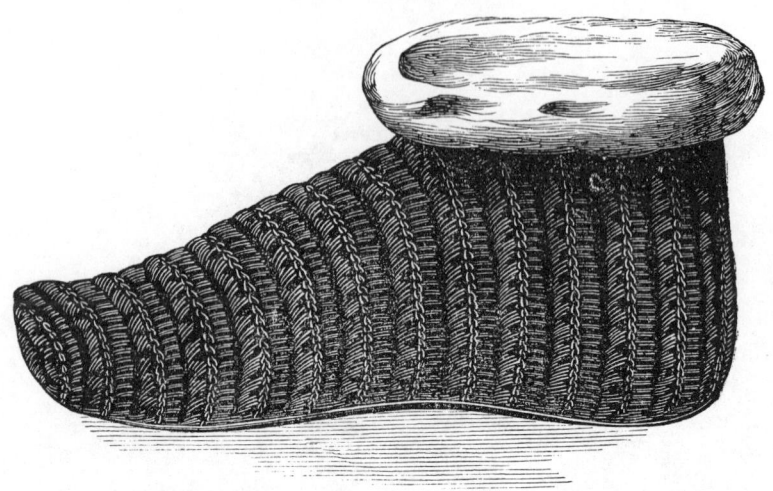

Materials.—One ounce scarlet or green shaded 4-thread wool; one ounce white ditto; a skein of black and pale straw-colored ditto; a pair of cork soles; crochet hook, No. 15; a pair of knitting needles, same size; and a mesh, half-inch wide.

BEGIN by working the shaded wool for the shoe. Nine ch, work in single crochet on it, with three stitches in the centre one. Turn, and work in single crochet, a stitch on every stitch; turn again and increase as before by doing three in the centre stitch. The next row is without increase. Continue to work thus, increasing two stitches in every alternate row, until you have done eight ribs. If the child has a very high instep, it will be necessary still further to increase the size in the last three ribs, by doing two stitches, in lieu of one, in the last stitch of *every* row. In working ribbed crochet, a chain-stitch must also be made at the end of each row, that the edge may not be contracted.

Now do one side of the foot, by working as far as the centre-stitch only, and then turning back. About six ribs will suffice for the heel. Work the other side in the same way, and crochet up the heel.

FOR THE FUR.—With the white wool cast on six stitches, and knit in common garter-stitch as much as will go *easily* round the top of the shoe. Making the fur is then done by a process exactly resembling raised Berlin work, only the ground is knitting instead of canvas. Thread a coarse rug-needle with a double strand of wool, so that you will work with *four* thick-nesses. Work on the rib of knitting in cross-stitch, taking the wool over the mesh. Cut each line before you withdraw the mesh. After three lines of white only, do in the centre two yellow stitches, and in the next row two black over them. When combed and cut, this makes a very pretty, washable fur.

Bind the cork soles with ribbon, or strips of thin leather, and sew on the shoe, also the fur round the top.

These directions, applied to 8-thread Berlin wool, with a coarser hook and a longer foundation-chain, will suffice for a lady's dressing-slipper or over-shoe.

The number of ribs may, of course, be increased, according to the size of the wearer's foot.

BUTTERFLY ROSETTE.

EMBROIDERED SCARF IN COLORS.

(*See Instructions, Page* 82.)

EMBROIDERED SCARF IN COLORS.

Materials.—A strip of black filet, No. 2, forty-eight inches by nine, cut on the square; a skein of ombre pink and violet silk, a skein of plain cherry, two of emerald green, and part of one vertislay.

THIS design is simply darned with the various silks on the filet, in the natural colors. The ombre pink answers admirably for the carnation, and the violet for the anemone: the vertislay for the leaves of the former, and the emerald green for those of the latter. To form the border, the filet is folded along the sides and ends, the depth of four squares, and the design is then darned on it, the stitches being taken, when necessary, through the double material. The Greek border is done in emerald green, and the stars in cherry. The fringe is knotted on the lowest row of holes, thus: Cut lengths of shaded violet and cherry, and of each green nearly half a yard long; take four strands of violet, pass them through the corner hole of the end, and tie in a knot; miss two holes, and tie in the third four strands of green, then cherry in the third from that, then the other green. Begin again with the violet: now knot four threads of violet with four green, the other four violet with four cherry; the rest of the cherry to the next violet, and green with green. Another row of knots will unite the same set of strands as at first—that is, the eight ends of violet together; then green, then cherry, then green again. This makes a very handsome fringe, and may be made richer by using six, or eight, instead of four threads.

No engraving can really give an idea of the beauty and novelty of this scarf, as the colors cannot be represented in it.

FANCY PURSE.

MADE of two round pieces, worked the long open stitch, and sewed together; trimmed at

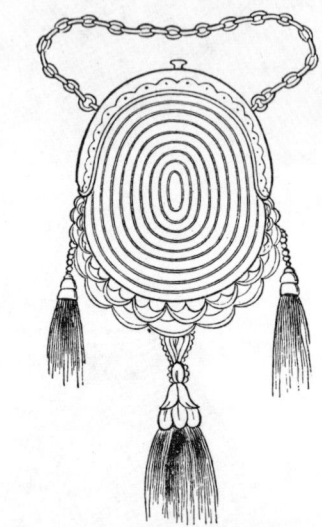

the bottom with a fringe of gold beads and three tassels. A gilt clasp fastens the purse.

SHOE ROSETTE.

PATTERNS IN CROCHET.

WE give this month two patterns for the centres of either antimacassars, berceaunette covers, or toilet mats. They are worked in solid and chain crochet, and are extremely durable, as well as pretty. The cotton used for working them should be about No. 10.

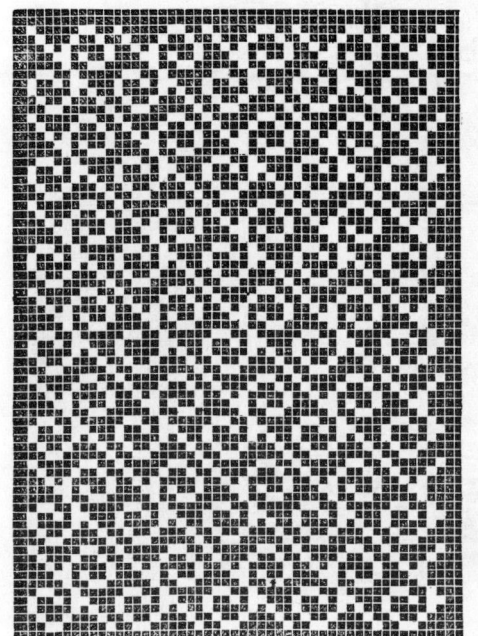

They may be finished with either a fringe or a lace. A border round them, of a light, open description can be added, if they are intended for drawing-room antimacassars; but they are more simple to execute if a square is worked of the pattern, and finished with a fringe tied in to every loop, a row of crochet being added all round for the purpose.

LITTLE GIRL'S SACK.

FOR CHEMISE YOKES.

TURKISH LOUNGING-CAP.

Materials.—Rich crimson cloth, black velvet, Albert braid of both colors, gold thread, gold braid, and a tassel made in passementerie to combine all these colors.

THE ground of the cap is in cloth, the lower part only (which is *appliqué*) being in black velvet. The centre of the crown is in the same material. In the engraving those parts that are in velvet are represented black.

The broad white lines indicate gold braid, which is used to cover the edge of the velvet where it joins the cloth, as well as to form certain scrolls. The double lines on the cloth are in black Albert and gold thread. On the velvet they are crimson Albert and gold thread, sewed down in the usual manner.

This sort of work especially commends itself from being so easily and rapidly executed; and in the opinion of many, it is far richer and more effective for this purpose than either crochet or anything else. It is extremely warm

TOP OF CAP.

and light, and, if small pieces are added for ears, it forms a delightful travelling-cap.

To make it up, procure some black silk and common bed-ticking, also a little black silk cord.

Cut out the silk lining the full size; but that of ticking about an inch narrower in the head-piece, so that it may not reach the edge where the velvet and cloth give already sufficient thickness. Gather the silk head-piece into the round for the crown, so as to make the lining *separately from the cap;* but work the ticking and cloth together. Tack the lining in round the crown, and down the joining at the side; turn in the edges round the head, and sew round the black silk cord, and the tassel in the centre of the crown.

CROCHET FLOWERS.

SPIDER WORT.

THIS flower is formed of three small petals, and requires two shades of violet Berlin wool; one rather deep, the other lighter, though it must not be too pale.

Take the lightest color, *not* split, and make a chain of three stitches ; fasten off. Take the second shade, and work in the first loop of the chain one plain stitch, in the second loop one stitch of double crochet, and one plain stitch ; then make a chain stitch, and begin the second round in double crochet, putting a wire in the edge. In this second round, you must increase one stitch in the first, third, and fifth long stitches of the preceding row. This round being completed, break off the wool, twist the ends of the wire together, and cut off one of them.

The stamens of this little flower are very beautiful—they are of violet color with a top of the richest golden hue—and spring from a little tuft of silky violet threads. It would be better to buy them ready made, if possible ; but, if preferred, they can be made thus : Take a bit of floss-silk, of a bright golden color, make a knot at the end of a piece of violet silk, or wool, insert the bit of gold-colored silk in the knot, and tie it as tightly as possible ; cut the end of the gold silk quite short. Make another knot about half an inch from the first, insert a bit of gold silk, tie it like the first. Cut short the violet and gold silk, and make another knot at the end of the latter ; tip it with gold in the same manner ; place your silk across the half-inch, tipped at both ends, and tie it in the middle, so as to make three stamens of equal length ; place them in the middle of a little tuft of violet silk, or wool, and fix the whole in the middle of the flower. Cover the stem with green wool, split.

The Spider Wort grows on a long stem, without leaves, and generally with two or three flowers on one stalk. The leaves are always close to the bottom of the stalk ; they have the appearance of a blade of grass, and are about a foot long, and an inch broad, and are of a very bright green color ; but the little bunch of flowers will form a pretty ornament for mats, &c., without leaves or buds.

FANCY FLOWERS FOR CAPS.

TAKE two shades of floss silk, of any color you please ; they must both be of the same size, neither too fine nor too coarse.

With the darkest shade make a chain of seven stitches ; cut off the silk, make a loop on your needle with the lighter shade, and work round the chain ; the first two stitches, and the last two, in double crochet—the remainder in long stitches (putting three stitches in the top loop)—some leto must be worked in the edge ; this completes one petal. Three similar ones must be made, and the four petals twisted, or

tied together securely, after having placed a little white stamen in the centre. Cut off all the wires but two, which forms the stem; cover this with a bit of green floss silk, split.

LEAVES.—Make a chain of nine stitches, with a pretty shade of green floss silk —it should be rather dark ; then, with a lighter shade, work a row of long stitches round it, the first and last two stitches being in double crochet ; a wire must be worked in the edge, leaving a little bit as a stem.

These little flowers have a pretty effect, and are very quickly done. They can be mounted according to taste—three or four flowers and three leaves will form a nice little spray.

BOURSE IMPERATRICE.

Materials.—Broad gold braid, gold thread No. 0, two dozen rings nearly three-quarters of an inch in diameter, a skein of purse silk of any color that may be desired, and passementerie tassels, bars, and cord, composed of the same color, with gold.

THE star in the centre of this purse is the part first done. Bend the end of the gold braid down an inch, draw an end of the silk through the doubled braid an eighth of an inch from the fold, and wind it round the braid for rather more than half an inch ; fasten off the silk. There will be an end of braid uncovered with silk. Leave it in both thicknesses of braid, and again fold down an inch. Treat this the same. Do this ten times, which will take up twenty inches of the braid. Arrange the piece in the form of a star, as seen in the engraving, and sew the centre firmly, to keep all the points in their true position.

Do another star, exactly like this, for the opposite side. Now cover all the rings with crochet, sew them together, as in the engraving, and work a gold rosette in the centre of each. Tack them down on a piece of *toile cirê*, with the star in the centre, and unite them by button-hole bars, carrying a line also round the star, just above where the silk is wound round, to form a wheel; all the points of the wheel must also be connected with the bars and rings.

Both sides, being done precisely alike, may be united at the sides. A flat ornament in passementerie (termed a Macaroon) is sewed in the centre of each star, and the trimmings, tassels, and bars are added.

THE CHINTZ WORK BASKET.

This basket is made of bright colored furniture chintz. As will be seen by the picture, its construction is very simple, being merely pieces of pasteboard, cut any size the maker may fancy, and the shape of those in the engraving. These are covered neatly with chintz, and sewed together. The little box to the left is for buttons; it is made of pasteboard, cut to fit accurately into the basket, with a cover of tin, covered with chintz. The advantage of tin is, that it will not curl as a pasteboard one would. There is a little stuffed cushion, fitted into the button box, for pins. The little bag is of chintz, and intended for a thimble. The two little bags to the right of the button box, are for spools of cotton; a needle-book comes next, having a cover of pasteboard sewed over the flannel. The bag to the right is made of chintz, very full, gathered in at the bottom, and confined at the top by a ribbon; this is for tape, and the many little trimmings to be found in a lady's work basket. At the side opposite the needle book, there is a bag of chintz for the scissors, and a strip sewed down tightly, and fastened at proper distances, for papers of needles, and bodkins. The handle is a strip of tin covered with chintz, fastened at the sides by bows of ribbon.

KNITTED BABY'S SHOE AND SOCK.

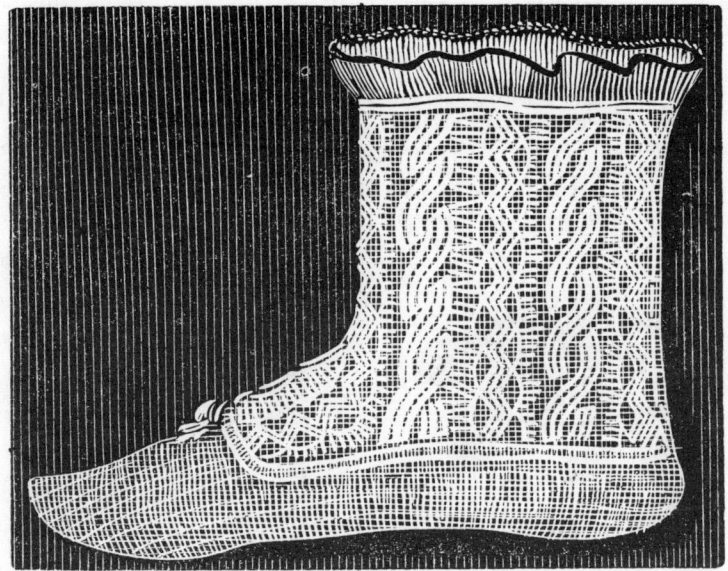

THESE are knitted on steel needles, in Berlin wool of two colors. The shoe in one color, and the sock in white, form the prettiest contrast; pink and white, maize and white, or blue and white, are all suitable. The shoe is in plain knitting, and ought to be worked tight and even; the sock is in the cable and hem-stitch pattern, the top being completed by two rows of netting, the first row being on a larger mesh than the second, one stitch of the netting in every stitch of the knitting. A narrow ribbon, the color of the shoe, is interlaced round the ankle, which ties in the front with a bow, and keeps it from slipping off the foot. The row of netting on the fine mesh ought to be in the colored wool.

EMBROIDERY.

CROCHET CAP FOR BOYS FROM TWO TO FOUR YEARS.

THIS cap is worked with dark blue Berlin wool in double crochet, and trimmed with a border of crochet loops in gray speckled wool to imitate Astrachan. The feather worked in the same stitch, and dark blue bows ornament the sides. Begin in the centre with a chain of 5 stitches joined to a circle, and work on it 25 rows of double, gradually increasing in each row so that the work may lie flat, and have 180 stitches in the 25th row. Then work 15 more rows, decreasing 4 or 5 stitches in each row by

LADIES' COMPANION.

THE materials are gray checked linen, white flannel, blue and brown sarcenet ribbon, each half an inch wide; brown silk braid, blue purse-silk, thin gold cord, etc.

The inner arrangement of this companion is quite novel, and will be found of great use to ladies afflicted with weak sight in keeping a supply of needles threaded ready for use.

The outside is a straight stripe of gray checked linen, eight inches long and three inches wide, decorated in the length, half an inch from the edge, with a border worked in

Fig. 1.—Ladies' Companion, Open.

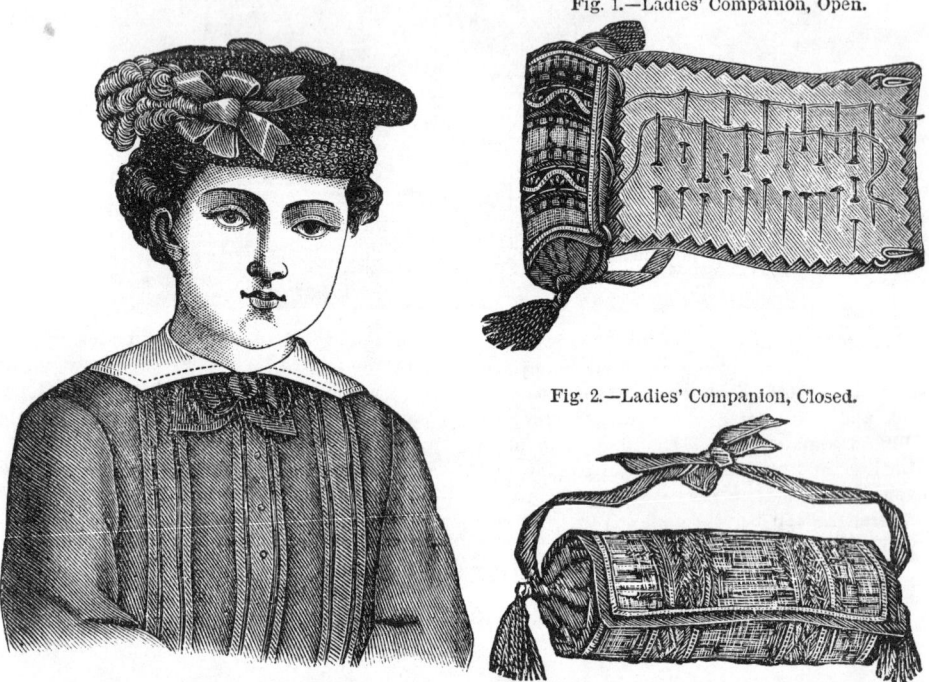

Fig. 2.—Ladies' Companion, Closed.

working 2 stitches together, so that the last row has 105 stitches. Now take the gray wool for the band, observing that the wrong side of the work should be the right side of the cap, and work 6 rows in loop stitch as follows: *1st row.* * 1 double on the 1st stitch, take up a loop from the following stitch, 4 chain, and draw the loop through the last chain and the stitch on the needle; repeat from *, observing to reverse the chain loops in the succeeding rows. Finish the band with a row of double. Knit the feather in loop stitch with speckled wool on a chain of 4 stitches in 40 rows, adding 1 stitch at the end of the first 6 rows knitted with the single thread, and taking off 1 stitch at the end of the last 6 rows knitted with the single thread. Put in the feather according to illustration with a bow, and add another bow in the centre of the crown.

coral stitch, with brown purse-silk and gold cord on blue sarcenet ribbon, edged with narrow brown silk braid, then lined with blue sarcenet ribbon, and bound with brown ribbon, which fastens at the same time a thin gold cord. A pocket is made at one end of the stripe to hold the two reels of cotton by sewing in with the binding on each long side of this a piece of blue sarcenet ribbon, three-quarters of an inch wide and three and a quarter inches long, which, drawn together a quarter of an inch from the edge on the second long side, gives the bottom at each end, with rosette in the middle, a tassel, an inch and a quarter long, of blue purse-silk, and a brown sarcenet ribbon or cord, five and a quarter inches long, tied in a bow above, being sewn into each of these. The flannel stripe, four inches long and two and a half inches wide, is pinked at the edge and fastened at each end to the case. The companion is closed with small buttons and loops of elastic.

EMBROIDERED TOILET PINCUSHION.

THIS ornamental pincushion is made on a circular cushion six inches in diameter, the bottom being of thick pasteboard, the sides of strong calico, and the stuffing of bran. Cover the bottom with calico, sew a strip of calico six inches wide around the edge, draw up the other side of the calico strip so as to hold the bran, and stitch a small round piece of calico over

slipped stitch over. Repeat this, decreasing in the 117th, 123d, 129th, 135th, 141st, 147th, 153d, 159th, 165th, 171st, 177th, and 183d row. Knit without decreasing from the 184th to the 243d row. Then divide the stitches into 2 halves, and work with the first 200 stitches, the front; knitting backwards and forwards alternately plain and purled, so that the work may appear plain on the right side. In the 244th row begin the front gore as follows: Knit 59, thread forward, knit 1, thread forward, knit 80, thread forward, knit 1, thread forward, knit 59th, 245th, 246th, and 247th row plain. Repeat the increasing in every fourth row up to the 324th

the gathers. Then take two strips of blue silk two inches wide, and pinked on one side; one strip must be fifty-two inches long, the other thirty-six inches; plait up the long strip into sixteen double plaits, the short strip into eight plaits, and sew them on the cushion according to illustration. Now cut out the star-shaped figure in white cloth, pinking out the edges, and embroider the design with colored braid and silk, and fasten it to the top of the cushion, so that the points of the star fit in between the plaits of the silk.

LADY'S KNITTED VEST WITH SHORT SLEEVES.

THIS vest is knitted on thick steel needles with pink fleecy. Make a chain of 450 stitches, join it to a circle, and knit 44 rows plain. Then take up the stitches of the chain on separate needles, and knit them with the stitches of the 45th row, to form a hem about an inch and a half wide. Knit up the 110th row without decreasing, then form a gore, by knitting in the 111th row, the 199th and 200th stitches together, and slipping the 224th stitch, knitting the 225th, and drawing the slipped stitch over. Make the gore on the other side, knitting the 423d and 424th stitches together, slipping the 448th stitch, knitting the 449th, and drawing the

row, always leaving 59 stitches at each end, and 80 stitches in the middle. Knit without increase up to the 339th row, and in the 340th row cast off the 152 middle stitches, and knit

on the 66 stitches at each side for the shoulder-straps, taking off 2 stitches on the side of the neck in the 342d and 344th rows; 3 stitches in the 346th and 348th rows, 4 stitches in the 350th, 352d, and 354th rows, 3 stitches in the 356th, 358th, and 360th rows, 2 stitches in 362d, 364th, and 366th rows. Knit without decreasing up to the 420th row, and then cast off. At the back work 96 rows without increase or decrease, cast off the 70 middle stitches, work the shoulders on the remaining stitches on each side as above, and sew the back and front shoulder-pieces together. For the sleeve make a chain of 225 stitches, and knit backwards and forwards alternately, 1 row plain, 1 row purled, 55 rows. In the 56th row cast off the first 55 stitches, work on the remaining 170 stitches up to the 83d row in ribs, alternately 2 plain, 2 purl, and then cast off. Sew the pieces together so as to form a three-cornered gusset, and sew the sleeve into the arm-hole. Bind the neck with ribbon, and run in a string to tie in front.

BOOK-WEIGHT.

The materials are sarcenet ribbon; middle size glass or steel beads; small shot. A piece of sarcenet ribbon ten inches long and three

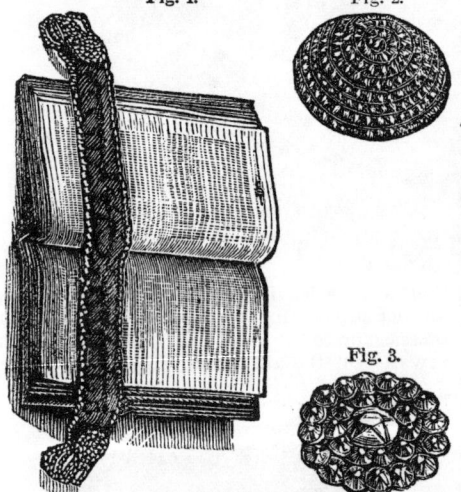

Fig. 1.   Fig. 2.

Fig. 3.

inches wide will be required. The edges must be folded exactly to the middle of the ribbon, and all seamed together so as to form two divisions. These are to be filled with shot, which must be kept in place by occasional stitches where required. The weight is edged with beads, and finished at the ends with bead-fringe and buttons, as shown in designs. Fig. 1 is covered with silk, and ornamented with steel beads. Fig. 2 is of cut steel.

DISH DOYLEYS.

For the foundation of these doyleys, a firm material, such as *piqué* or good Irish linen, is required. For the ornamental borders, we must refer our readers to back numbers, which contain several suitable designs. Fig. 1 is edged with a trimming of crochet and waved braid. Fig. 2 is bordered with rosettes in crochet or crochet and waved braid, according to fancy.

Fig. 1.

Fig. 2.

FRAME IN LEATHER WORK.
(*See Illustration, Page* 92, 93.)

This beautiful design is in leather, and for those who have not been accustomed to the work we will give full directions how to proceed. Procure at a saddler's one or two skins of leather, one very thin, for covering the woodwork of the frame, the other thicker, such as they ordinarily use for saddles (the skins should be of a light color), some glue, which should be kept warm during use by a little spirit lamp—a night lamp used for infant's food could not be better for the purpose —a small hammer, small brass tacks, plenty of small pins, a large flat board—any plank will answer the purpose—a basin of water, a fine-pointed bone knitting needle, a mould for indenting the round parts of the leather (these are made of boxwood), and some old rag—the rag is for the worker to dry her hands on, as it must be borne in mind that this leather when wet stains the handkerchief so that it is impossible to remove the marks—a rule, and pair of scissors. The oval frame should be made by a carver and gilder of wood. The first thing to be done is to cover this frame; lay it down on the thinnest leather, and mark the shape out, leaving at least an inch margin on each side. Cut it out, then soak for one or two minutes in the water, take it out and wring it, stretch it out immediately, and lay it on the frame; tack it at the top and bottom to hold it in its place, and then stretch it well over the rest of the frame, and nail it in its place on the wrong side, and place it in the air to dry. You next proceed to make the different flowers and ferns illustrated from Fig. 1 to Fig. 11 with thick leather. Those who have the natural flowers at hand cannot do better than draw them out on paper, laying the leaf of each flat upon some paper, from this cut it out in cardboard; with a pencil draw the different veinings and markings, pull a flower to pieces in the same manner petal by petal, and trace out, as you then have them for any occasion. Figs. 1 and 2 are fronds of ferns; trace these out on the leather with the bone pin, soak the pieces for one or two seconds, cut them out, mould each leaf with the head of your pin in your hand or on a cushion. After marking them,

and leave it to dry; afterwards the stalks, stamens, etc., must be glued to it. For the passion flower, Fig. 8, the petals must be cut separately, *moulded*, and glued together. The auricula, Fig. 10, is cut in one piece and moulded like a convolvulus. Some shreds of leather must be cut and rolled together while damp, and slightly glued, for the inside parts of the flower. The grapes require a mould of boxwood or sycamore for each one; any turner will supply them. The thin leather must be used for these, damp as before; put the mould into a piece of the leather, cut it out, and screw the leather up in the corner. When dry, cut the end off; these must all be glued together over each other for the proper shape. Make all the different parts before you attach them to the frame, pin them on the frame until you have got them all well arranged in their places, and then tack them on with nails wherever you can; hide the tacks, and glue them here and there in other parts, but use as little of the

pin them on to your board in the shape you wish them to lie on the frame, and let them dry; all the leaves must be made after the same manner.

The convolvulus, Fig. 3, should be made with a mould the size of the flower. You cut out a circle of leather to the shape of the flower, and when damp press it into the mould

glue as possible, for the more lightly they are arranged the better.

EMBROIDERY ON CHIP.

THIS is an entirely new style of work. It will answer for mats. The chip is plaited in and out, and then embroidered in colored silks.

Frame

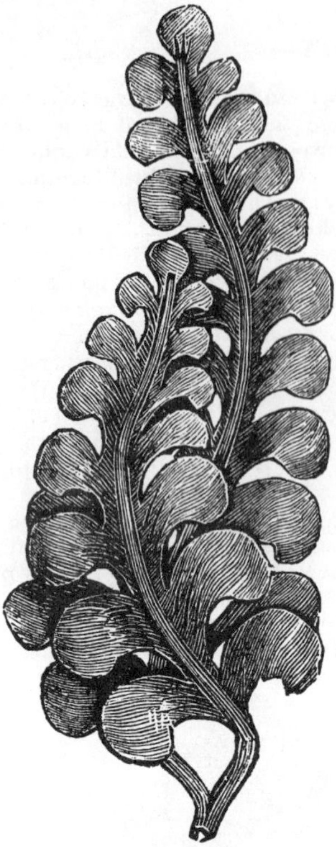

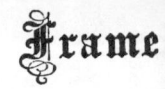

Fig. 1.

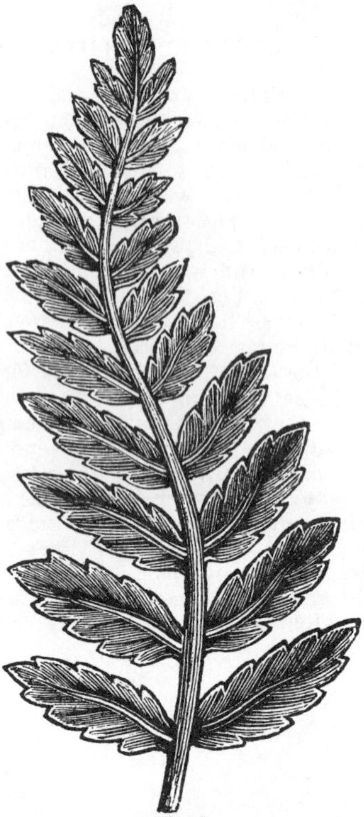

Fig. 2.

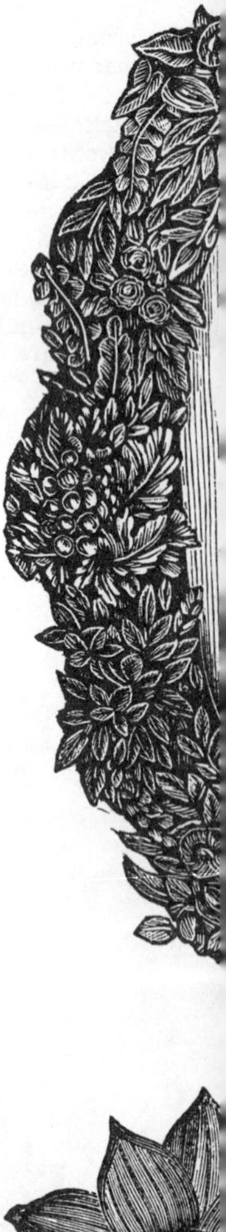

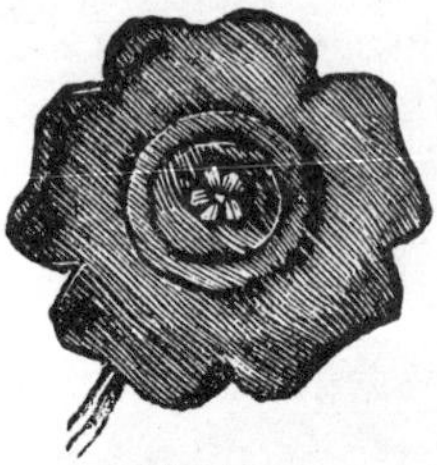

Fig. 10.

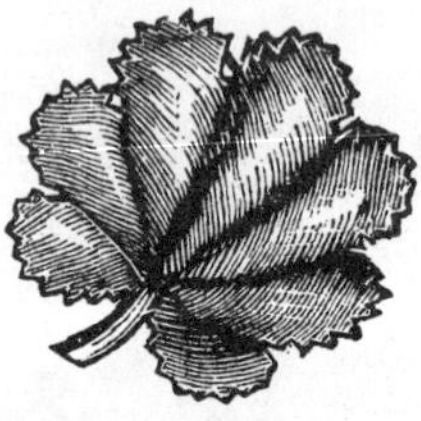

Fig. 11.

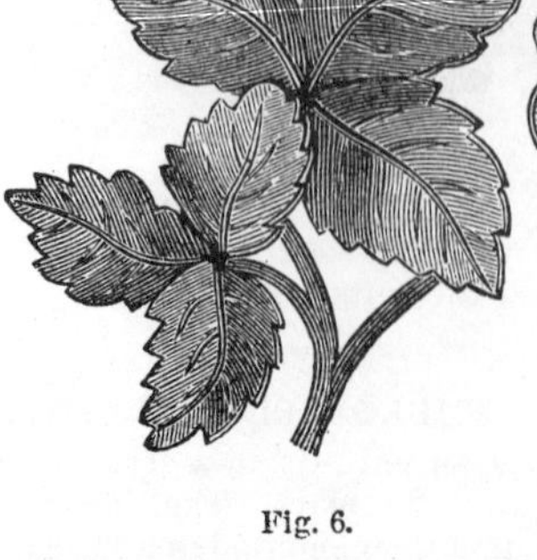

Fig. 6.

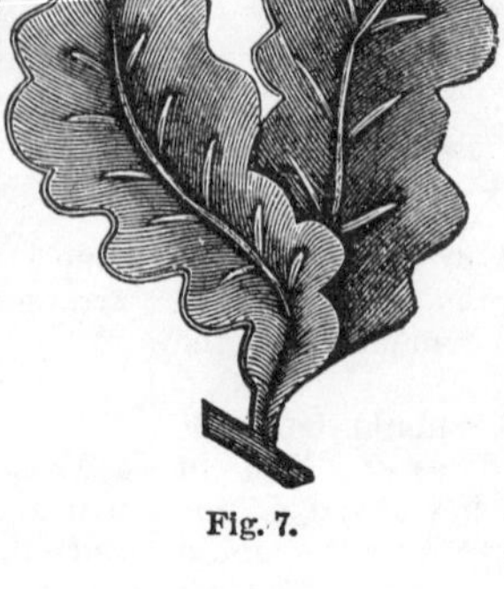

Fig. 7.

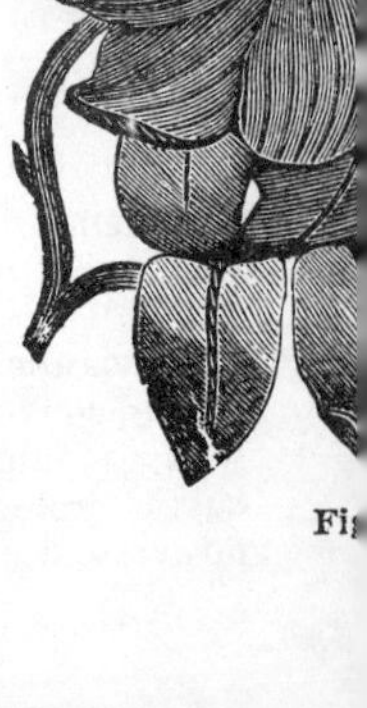

Fi

Fig. 4.

Fig. 5.

Fig. 3.

Fig. 9.

HANDKERCHIEF SATCHET.

THIS satchet consists of two squares, ten inches each way, one of canvas, the other of blue silk. The canvas is worked in small

INFANT'S CAP IN CROCHET.

THIS cap is intended for a child of twelve months to two years of age; it is crocheted in white and pink or blue eider wool, and a hook,

Fig. 1.

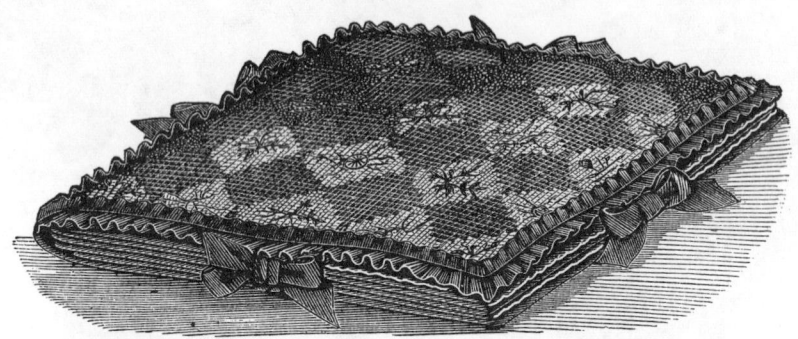

Fig. 2.—Detail of Handkerchief Satchet.

squares of white wool and blue silk. The white square is worked in tent stitch, over two threads each way, and on this ground flowers are embroidered in *point russe* with different colored silks. The blue squares are worked in Smyrna stitch, over four threads each way. Both canvas and silk are lined with scented wadding and white quilted silk. It is trimmed all round with a ruche of blue satin ribbon, and tied together with satin bows.

No. 8. The hat is round in shape, and is worked in a very simple pattern, which is given in a large size in Fig. 2. When the foundation is finished, it is ornamented with bands of color, which are laced through the holes as illustrated in the pattern. Cut a round in paper measuring nine and a half inches in diameter, and you crochet by this round a piece for the head. Commence with a chain of 12 stitches in white wool, turn, 3 long in the 9th ch, 3 ch, miss 3 ch,

Fig. 1.

Fig. 2.

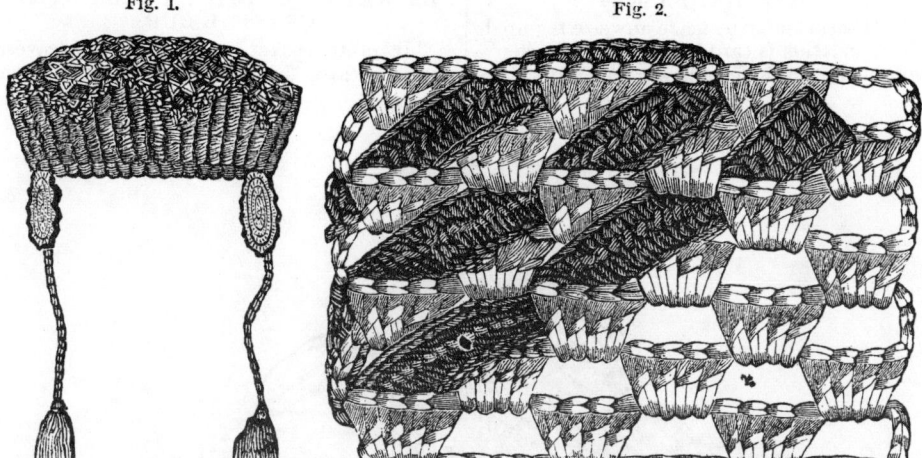

3 long in the next 3 ch, miss 3 ch, 3 long in the next, turn.

2d row. 1 single on the first long stitch, 6 ch, 1 long in the 3d, 2d, and 1st of the 6 ch; * 3 ch, 4 long in the next space of last row; repeat from * once more, then repeat again, working on the 6th of the 9th ch in commencing the last row; turn.

3d. 1 single on the first long, 6 ch, 1 long on the 2d and 1st of the 6 ch, * 3 ch, 4 long in the next space; repeat from * to the end of the row, where work 4 long on the last long stitch, then repeat this row until you have worked to the middle of your paper, which should make the work about 7 rows deep, then 3 more rows with no increasings, then decrease every row by turning after the long stitches in the last space on the next row, work 2 single on the first 2 long stitches, then in the next space 4 long, decrease until you have only 3 sets of long in the row. You next work a row of dc all round the edge of the piece worked, taking care to keep the shape well. When this round is finished work upon it a round of 1 dc on the first dc, * 1 ch, miss 1 dc, 1 dc on the next; repeat from *. The engraving Fig. 3 gives the

Fig. 3.

position of the stitches in this round. 1 dc just by the dc of last row and under the ch, * 1 ch, 1 dc just by the side of the next dc; repeat

from *, work 8 more rounds like the 2d, or a piece one and a half inches in depth, and you fasten off. You next work the bands of colored wool, and lace them through the work; make a ch sufficiently long to go through three or four rows of holes without a break, and on it work a row of long crochet, working it close and firm, then lace it through the holes in a slanting direction, and fasten it off neatly; work the rest in the same manner. When this is finished you work a Vandyked border in looped crochet with white wool, make a chain of 7 stitches, take up the 6th stitch, wind the wool three times round the tip of the first finger of the left hand, and over the hook, then finish the stitch as a double crochet; repeat this stitch to the end of the row, making 7 loops, turn, work 1 ch and 2 dc in the first stitch, so increasing a stitch, then 1 dc on each to the end of the row; repeat these two rows until you have 10 loops in the row, then decrease until you have 7 only; this forms one Vandyke. Work enough to go round the hat, then join neatly the first and last rows together with a row of dc. Work on the scalloped side of this border with blue wool the following edge: 1 dc in the first stitch, * 3 ch, miss 1 stitch, 1 dc in the next; repeat from * and fasten off. Sew this border to the hat, sewing the two plain edges together, and on this edge work a row of dc with blue wool. The rosettes may be worked in plain double crochet with white wool, or in looped crochet; in either case commence by a chain of 5, and unite, and increase gradually until the size required; edge them with a round of blue wool worked in the same manner as on the border When you work the last stitch in the round make a chain long enough for strings to tie the hat, and add a tassel of the two wools mixed; then line the hat with flannel and silk.

KNITTING BASKET.

This basket may be made any size required. The foundation is card-board, and it is covered with puffings of blue satin separated by stripes

BASKET OF CRYSTAL BEADS WITH CRYSTAL CUP.

This pretty basket consists of flowers, leaves, and grapes of fine crystal beads, strung on

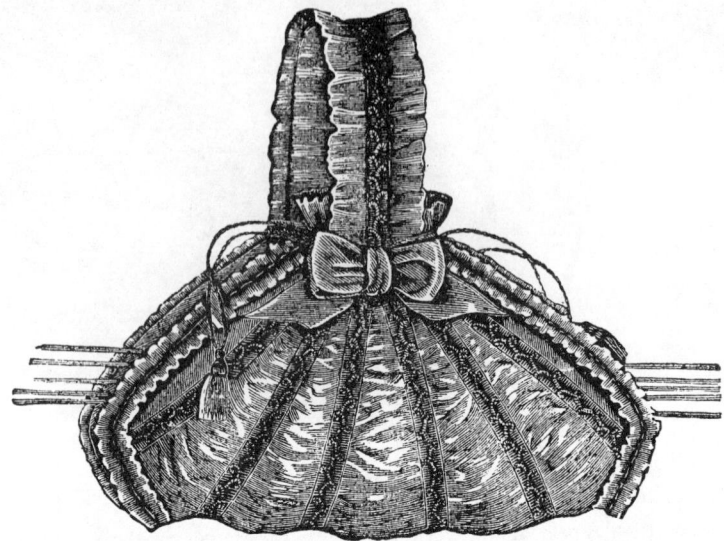

of black velvet; it is edged on both sides with a blue satin ruche. The handle is thin whalebone covered with a ruche, and terminating

silver wire; the glass cup inside is of blue crystal, and contrasts prettily with the white basket. The shape of the basket is made of

Fig. 1.

with a black velvet bow. The inside is cased so as to contain knitting-needles, and a bag of blue silk is added for the wools or cottons. The bag is drawn at the top with a silk cord.

thick wire from Fig. 2; this wire is covered first with soft white cotton, and then with crystal beads. Our pattern measures twenty inches round the top; the bottom measures

Fig. 3.

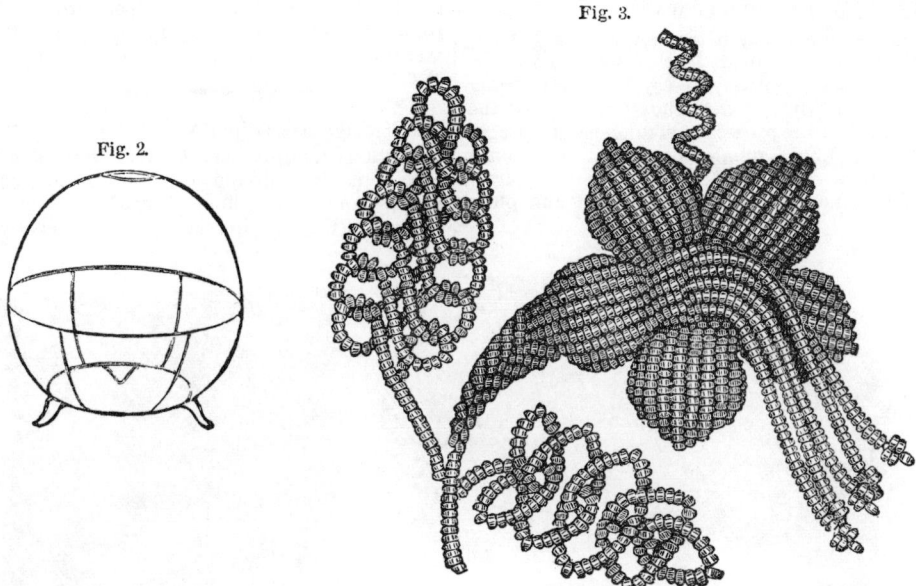

Fig. 2.

twelve inches round; the whole basket, including the handle, is nine and two-fifths inches high. On both sides of the basket the beginning of the handle is covered by a bunch of grapes and leaves, as seen in Fig. 4. The berries of the grapes are worked separately, and lying above each other, not quite as far as the edge; and then cover it in the same manner the long way. The cross rows must be somewhat raised in the middle of the leaf, so as to have a curved shape. The middle of the flower is covered also by two cross rows of beads, lying

Fig. 4.

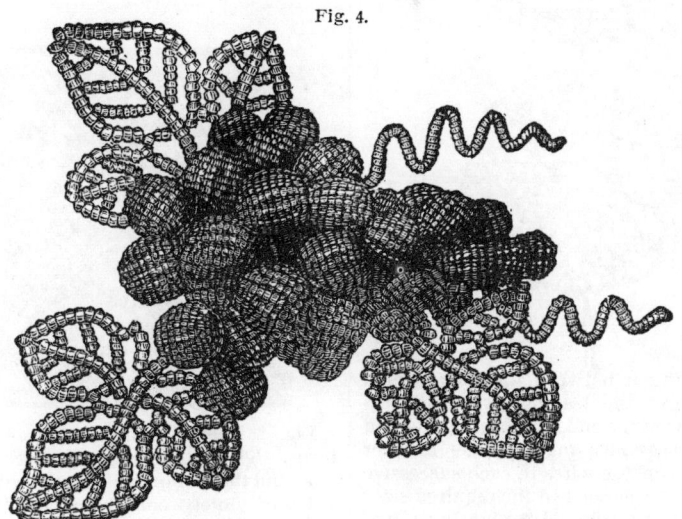

joined on to one another with cotton; the centre is formed of one alabaster bead, which is covered with crystal beads. The leaves and tendrils are to be worked from Fig. 3. Between the two bunches of grapes, the basket is ornamented with a large 5-petalled flower. Cut the foundation shape of this flower in strong gummed linen; cover each leaf on the top, the cross-way, with double rows of beads, one over the other. The stamens are made of five rows of beads from illustration. The other leaves are also worked from illustration. The tendrils, as well as the remaining small leaves, which occupy the free space between the grapes and flowers, are easily worked from Fig. 4. A blue crystal cup completes this very pretty model.

BEAD MAT.

THIS round mat or tray for glasses, bottles, or little ornaments, is four inches in diameter, and is made entirely of crystal beads strung on silver wire. Fig. 2 shows the size of the beads, and the process of arrangement. Begin by threading a number of crystal beads on a silver wire about three yards in length; draw up the first eight beads into a loop, and place

Fig. 1.

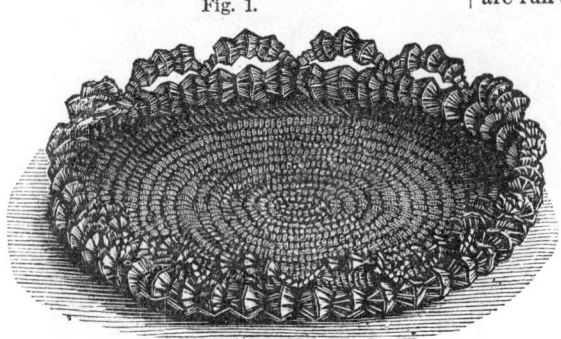

eight wires, five inches long, in between the beads, doubling them over the loop, and twisting the two ends together close to it. Then wind the long wire threaded with beads round

Fig. 2.

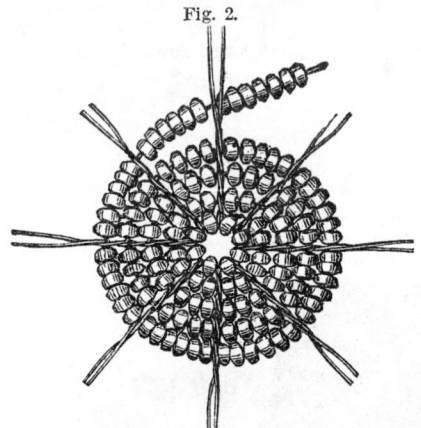

the loop, passing it between the open ends of the double wire, and leaving two beads between them, twist the ends together again, and repeat this process, leaving a greater number of beads between the wires in each successive row, till the mat has reached the required size; the ends of the wires should be tightly twisted together, and fastened down underneath the mat. Now proceed with the raised rim. Make a ring of large cut crystal beads round the mat, observing that the number of beads must be divisible by three. Take another wire and fasten it between two of these large beads, * thread three small crystal beads, three large cut beads, three small beads, pass the wire round the wire of the edge, missing three of the beads of the last row; repeat from * all round, cut off the wire and fasten in the end, and turn the scallops upwards to form a rim.

FANCY STITCHES (PANAMA CANVAS).

FIG. 1 is a stitch suitable for slippers, satchets, etc. The groundwork is brown Panama canvas, and on this lines of scarlet silk braid are run at regular intervals; one line is crossed

Fig. 1.

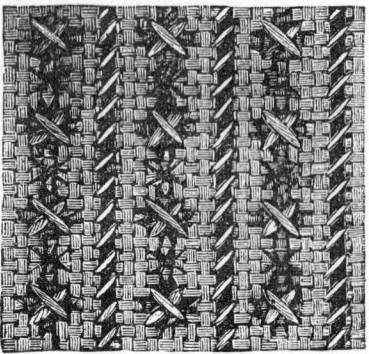

with yellow filoselle, and the alternate line with double cross-stitches of black and yellow filoselle. Any effective contrasts can be used for this simple design with advantage.

Fig. 2.

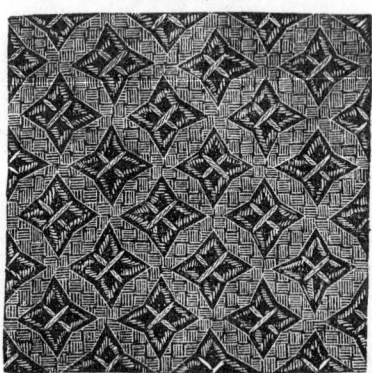

Fig. 2 is composed of lozenge-shaped patterns. The outline of each is traced with green silk, and the star in the centre is a double cross-stitch of violet wool and amber filoselle. The groundwork is Panama canvas.

DRAWIN-LNEN WORK, OR SPANISH STITCH.

Materials.—Cotton, No. 24, and a fine sewing needle.

THIS is admirable work to be used for insertions; for borders, for pillow-cases, and sheets;

and for the chemisette, piece of a chemise, or night-dress. It is economical, for old linen is better than new for the work. It is rapidly done, and requires no effort of the mind, no numbering of stitches, and is further valuable for its durability. The method of working will be better understood by reference to the engraving rather than description. The threads are drawn out from old linen, ten, eight, or twelve, according to the fineness of the material. A variety of patterns can be produced. Cut out the shape needed, and draw the threads only as required to finish a given space in a given time.

SAVING PURSE.

THIS purse is for money in reserve, to be kept in some safe place. Cut a strip of card-board as wide as the top of the purse, leave the lid to wrap over, and a diamond point at each end of the bottom. Lay a strip of silk over each end, simply giving them the required folds to form the shape. Then lay a piece of fancy ribbon over the central part, if possible, making the fastening fall in the middle of the pattern, and adding a pretty button with a loop. Place a small silk tassel on each side, at the ends of the silk and strings.

UNDER VEST AND DRAWERS FOR CHILD OF TWO YEARS.

DIRECTIONS for this description of under vest have often been asked for by our subscribers, and we now publish one, with directions for both knitting and crochet, that has been designed expressly for us. It is worked in white Saxony wool. The size for a child of three

years old will require from eight to nine ounces; for two years old, about six or seven ounces; and a smaller size may be still made if wished by casting on about twenty stitches less than the number given in the following directions: You require two pairs of No. 12 steel knitting needles. Though directions are given for the vest in crochet at the end of the pattern, it is not to be compared with a knitted one. Commence with the sleeve. Cast on one needle 56 stitches, knit a plain row, work 20 rows of knit 1, and purl 1; then cast 24 more stitches on to the needle at the end of the 20th row, and knit 36 plain rows; cast off loosely. The extra stitches cast on in the 20th row form the gusset to the sleeve, and the gusset must be so folded that the foundation row of the extra stitches can be sewn to the side of the plain rows on the back side of the sleeve. When the sleeves are finished commence a leg. Cast on 100 stitches, knit a plain row, then knit 20 rows of purl 1, knit 1; after that 4 rows plain knitting. In the next row knit 3 (the edge stitch should always be slipped if you wish for a good even edge); these 3 stitches include the edge stitch. Then increase a stitch; this increase is made by knitting a stitch in the front part of the stitch, and, before you lift the stitch from the

left-hand needle, knit 1 in the back part of the stitch also. Knit plain to the end of the row, leaving 4 stitches; in the first of these 4 stitches increase; then knit the 3 next. All the increasings in the pattern are worked in the same manner throughout. Knit 5 plain rows, and increase again in the following row, then * knit 3 plain rows, increase as before in the following row; repeat from * until you have 20 more rows. Then increase in every alternate row for the next 12 rows, and in every row for 8 more rows; this concludes the increasings for the leg. Then 20 plain rows. Now decrease for the front of the leg on one side only of the knitting; the other side is left plain for the back. * In the next row slip the edge stitch, knit 2 together, knit plain the rest of the row, then 3 rows plain; repeat from the last * until you have knitted 70 rows; leave the stitches on the needle, and commence the other leg. This is worked in exactly the same manner as the last, but, when finished, care must be taken to keep the two plain sides of the two legs together. You will now require the four needles. The knitting is left open in the front, where the front piece is in the engraving, but the number of stitches will make it necessary to use three needles. The knitting is still worked backwards and forwards. Begin the row that joins the two legs together from the side of one of the legs on which the decreasings are knit, and knit plain until you have about three-quarters of the stitches knit; then take another needle, continue the knitting until within 20 stitches from the end. Now take the other leg, see that the plain sides are together of the two pieces of knitting, and knit together each stitch from the two needles, knitting of course 20 plain stitches; by this means one side the work wraps over the other; knit plain to the third of the next leg, then take the third needle and knit to the end of the row; turn back, and knit plain about 44 more rows. Some very loose knitters may find these rows too many, and that they will make the vest too long under the sleeves; if so, reduce or increase the number as may be necessary. You next divide the number of stitches on the needle into four parts; the first quarter knit in plain rows backwards and forwards until you have a piece the necessary length for the armhole to the sleeve already knit. When you are about half an inch from the shoulder cast off five stitches in the neck, and decrease one stitch on the same side the work as these five stitches are cast off every alternate row, until you have knitted a piece that will reach about half an inch beyond the half of the sleeve, and cast off. Now knit the last quarter of the stitches left on the work in the same manner as this quarter, and cast off. You next knit the remainder of the stitches which form the back or middle half of the work in plain knitting, until you have worked to about half an inch from the top of the armhole; put the front and one side of this back part together, and see if you have sufficient for the sleeve, if so, continue knitting, and decrease one stitch on each side the work in every alternate row, until the side of the decreasings matches the shoulder of the front; then cast off, sew the shoulders together and the sleeves into the armholes; put a piece of fine calico down the front, as shown in the engraving. If the vest is to be crocheted, you must knit the ribbed part of the sleeve and leg as described for the knitting, but in brioche stitch begin with the sleeve. Use the same needles and number of stitches the first row, *bring the thread forward, slip 1, as if for purling, knit 1, repeat from *. The 2d and all following rows are knitted with bring the thread forward, slip 1, as if you were going to purl the stitch, knit 2 together, repeat this row until you count 30 stitches on one side the work. Now take a fine crochet tricotee needle, No. 12, and with the wool left on the work draw a chain stitch through the last needle, make a ch of 24, then raise 23 loops on this chain, and take off the knitting on the needle as crochet loops on to the crochet needle, taking off the double stitch as one loop, work them all back as usual in crochet tricotee, work enough rows to fit the gusset exactly when folded properly, and cast off. The remainder of the vest must be followed by the directions for knitting. All the increasings are made in the crochet by working a loop between the first two and the two last loops in a row, and the decreasings by crocheting the two loops together.

BOWL FOR SCRAPS OF WORK, ETC.

CUT six gored pieces of stiff linen and of brown silk, according to illustration, sew the

Fig. 1.

linen pieces together and tack in the silk for a lining, covering the point where the pieces meet

with a small round bit of silk buttonholed at the edge. Then sew a wire in at the top, and proceed to cover the outside in the following manner: Pass fine string across the bowl so as to form twelve ribs, crossing the ribs in the centre, twisting the string around the wire, and passing it on to the next section. Weave a gray thread several times through the ribs in the centre, and then wind around the ribs with gray cotton, working from right to left in the

Fig. 2.

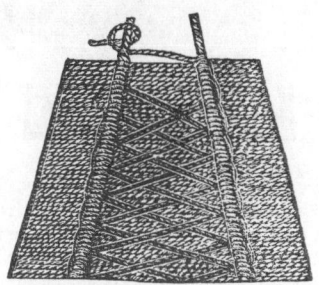

manner indicated in Fig. 2, till the bowl is entirely covered with a layer of cotton. On the threads work with brown netting silk the pattern in *point russe*, and then put on the silk-scalloped border around the top. For the plaited bag cut out a circular piece of brown silk and brown lining, overcast the edges with brown silk, arrange the plaits according to the illustration, pressing the edges firmly down, sew in the bag to the top of the bowl, and cover the stitches with a brown silk cord.

SILK-WINDERS,
CARVED AND PAINTED ON WOOD.

THE carving can be readily executed with a leaf-saw apparatus; but those of our readers who do not possess such can buy the winders ready carved at a trifling cost.

Fig. 1.

In Fig. 1 the black ground is edged with gold; the carved shapes are also edged with thin gold lines, and then filled in with lilac (of cobalt and carmine mixed together).

Fig. 2.

Fig. 2 shows black lines, each bordered with gold on the wood ground, these again bordering each triangle point. The dots filled in with blue (cobalt), and the interlaced bands around the red (carmine) middle rosette, are also edged with gold.

FEATHER FLOWERS.

THE feathers of which these pretty flowers are made are those of common poultry. White are preferable, as with water-colors and a

Fig. 1.

camel-hair pencil they may be painted to resemble natural flowers. Fine flower-wire, green tissue paper, water-colors, gum and cotton are the materials need. The feathers must be cut to the shape of the petals shown in the

design, gummed at the lower parts, and neatly fixed to the wire stalks with cotton; then the stalks are covered with paper. The stamens in Fig. 1 are of cut feathers, but the centre must be of cotton, first tied up into a little bunch, next gummed, then dipped into silver sand, and afterwards into yellow ochre. The leaves must be painted into two shades of green.

Fig. 2.

Fig. 2 is a bunch of lilac. This may either be white or mauve, according to taste. The buds are of feathers cut according to design.

CAP-BASKET.

THIS basket, similar in shape to a travelling hand-bag, is of plaited straw, worked with cross

stitch in colored wool. The monogram or initials are worked on cloth or silk, with embroidery silk.

DRESS TRIMMINGS IN ARMENIAN LACE.

THIS is an entirely new kind of work, and very simple, being worked with a needle and cotton. The material for working is white or *écru*-colored cotton, or, when intended for a gimp-like trimming, of tightly-twisted silk. The work is made in one single stitch, similar to a buttonhole one, which forms the pattern required, by the way of setting together in rows and joining on these stitches.

Fig. 1.   Fig. 2.

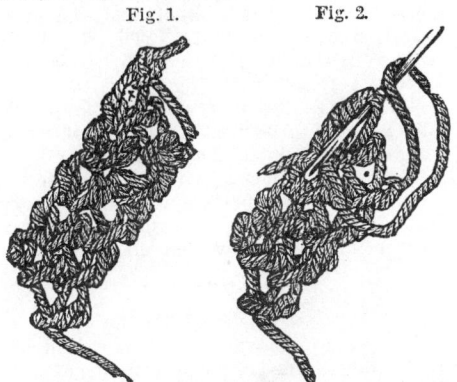

Fig. 3 shows the stitch in an increased size made on a foundation of braid. The letter *a* on the right side shows the manner of placing the needle; and, on the left, *b* shows the stitch

Fig. 3.

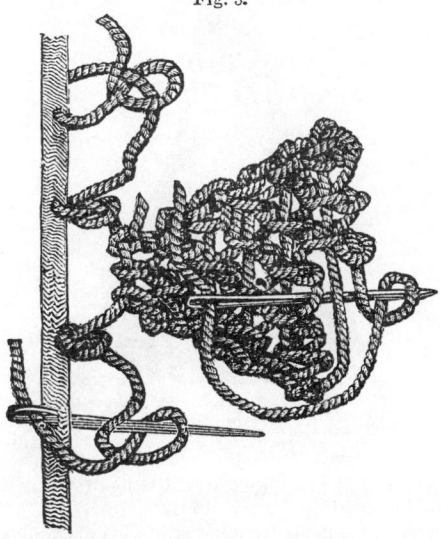

completed, but not yet knotted tightly. The braid, which is not used otherwise for this kind of work, serves here only to make the thread windings of the stitch easier to follow. To

begin with the stitch, a sling is made with the working thread from right to left (see Fig. 3) on the first finger of the left hand, and held firmly with the thumb. The needle is now put through the braid below, behind the thread across and through the sling (loop), as seen clearly. Always holding the sling firmly with the left hand, the thread is drawn tight. The stitch is worked throughout in the same way. The

Fig. 4.

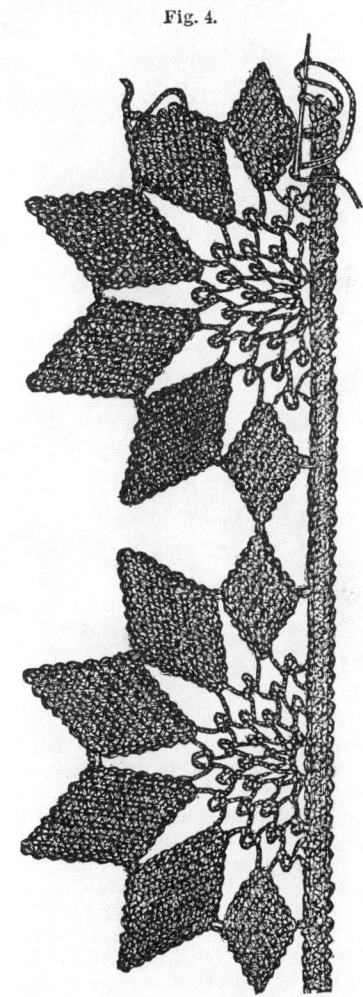

thread is to be put under, and joined to the foregoing row (see letter *c*). The needle is to be put under the three threads before putting through the sling. The way of placing the under-thread is shown in Fig. 2. After the row of stitches is finished, the needle is slipped in at the beginning, and the thread put around the point of the needle. Drawing the needle through the thread the knot is made, as seen in Fig. 1; and now the next row is to be worked as shown in Fig. 3, letter c.

Fig. 5.

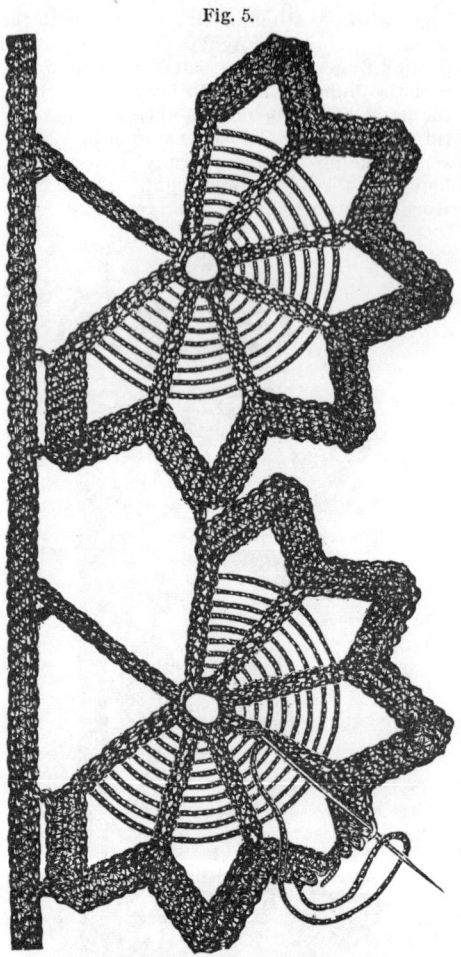

The work is never to be turned. The way of joining each row to the former one will be understood from the patterns, Figs. 4 and 5, without further explanations, showing clearly at what distance the new stitch is to be put in.

We shall now proceed to explain the separate parts of each pattern. These two show first a narrow edge, being a kind of foot to which the pattern shapes are joined. The way of making this edge two stitches wide is shown in Figs. 1 and 2. To begin, a knot is slung one and a quarter inch from the end, and two stitches joining this are made over the thread end. After the thread laid over has been slung tightly for the first stitch of this second, as for each of the next rows (as seen in Fig. 1), the needle is inserted in the whole with a cross, and for the second in that marked with a dot. The rows form themselves sloping, as in open

tunic crochet or tricot. The well-known stitch is also the best guide for the gore-like increase and decrease required for the pointed diamonds of the border. Figs. 4 and 5 show also very clearly the join on and commencement of the pattern, and the way the separate stitches are made at the outer edges can be followed out very well. The manner of pointing the pattern is shown plainly in Fig. 4. The designs being so well drawn, we shall only add that the small 'diamonds are seven stitches wide in the middle, the following ones increasing always in breadth two stitches, therefore to eleven stitches for the large diamonds.

For the trimming (Fig. 5), we would mention next the narrow stalk to each pattern, to be worked as the joining knot, and one stitch exactly like the small edge. The ring in the middle of the open part is made by crossing the thread over, as for a sling (loop), and then fastened with the first stitch. The pointed edge is again to be worked like the small flat one, and the pointed shapes form themselves in rows, already mentioned as peculiar to this stitch, which in the parts continued in an equal width go in a sloping direction. Every two diamonds are joined by their side stitches.

RING STAND.

THIS stand consists of two short and long supporters of fine yellow rushes, each of which has a ball of red wool at the top, and is wound around with fine red silk cord, by means of which they are joined together. The basket is made of spiral twists of yellow straw, with a

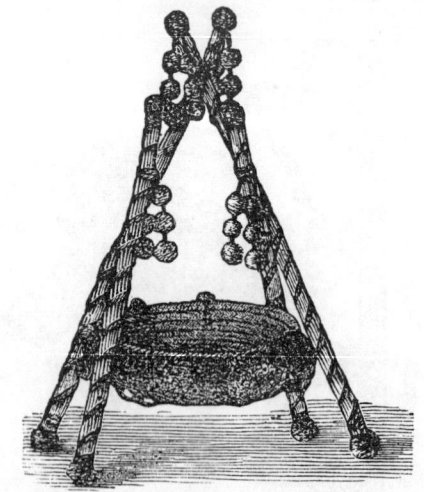

valance of red silk cord and balls of wool, and is fastened by the cord to the supporters. The valance is made by sewing for every scallop six short and long loops of cord on to the cord around the edge of the basket, and tying two knots opposite each other into each of these loops, and also between the scallops at the top; the joins of the loops of cord are held on by a ball of wool. Tassels of silk cord and balls of wool ornament the supporters.

POCKET FOR A LATCHKEY.

THIS neat little pocket is made of brown silk and cloth, ornamented with embroidery in *point russe* with two shades of brown netting silk. Begin by cutting out the back in silk and cloth, and the front only in silk. For the lining of the top cut out two pieces of cloth, with a point to turn back, according to illustration. Then work the border on the silk destined for the top,

and make a slit down the centre, put in the lining, and work around the flaps with overcast stitch in brown silk, fastening them down to the silk with a row of slanting stitch. Sew on silk buttons at the corners of the revers, and a button and loop of elastic in the middle of the slit to close the pocket. Work the silk for the bottom in the same style as the top, and then sew the two pieces together, finishing the edge with a silk cord. The pocket may also be made entirely of cloth or of leather.

PHOTOGRAPH CASE.

CUT out the back of brown cloth and brown silk. Then cut three pieces of card-board of equal size to fit into the back, and one piece for the flap that folds over. Cover the flap piece on one side with brown silk, the other pieces with white watered paper, and gum on to the latter the frames of brown silk with a stiff lining on which a pattern has been worked in *point russe* and knotted stitch with two shades of brown silk, leaving one side open for the reception of the photos. Now fasten

the pieces of card-board to the cloth, work an embroidered monogram or other device on the brown silk for the outside, and finish the other part and the flap with gold braid and silk

Fig. 1.

stitches according to Fig. 1. Make a round ornament of silk, worked with overcast stitches and gold cord, to cover the slit into which the

Fig. 2.

flap slides, and then fasten the inside to the silk with a row of herring-bone stitch, according to illustration.

DESIGNS IN BERLIN WOOL WORK, FOR SLIPPERS, CUSHIONS, COVERS, BAGS, SMALL CARPETS, ETC.

FIG. 1.—The ground is worked in ordinary cross-stitch, with two shades of one color, leaving spaces for the lighter pattern, which is worked afterwards, also in two shades; the centre stitch of the four leaves with the darker, then the two side stitches with the lighter shade. The illustration shows the place where,

Fig. 1.

after the needle is drawn out, it is to be inserted, by a cross.

Fig. 2.—This pattern is worked with three shades of one color. It consists of small checks, which cover four squares of canvas, and are worked as shown in the illustration,

Fig. 2.

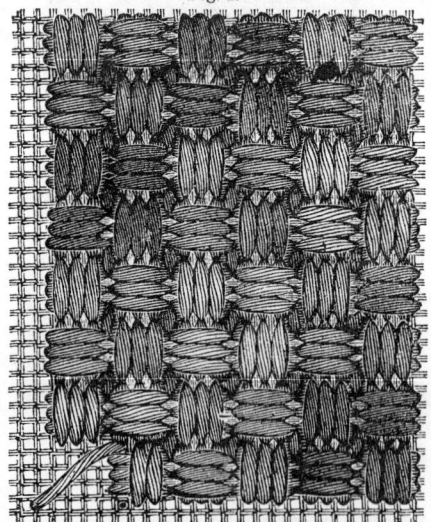

with three long stitches in one direction, then three long stitches across them in the opposite direction. Four of these squares are worked with one shade, and form a pattern. Between the squares little cross stitches are made.

Fig. 3 is also worked with one color, and

consists, like the former, of long cross-stitches, each of which has a stitch worked across the centre. The illustration shows one of these stitches loose, and by means of a cross and a

Fig. 3.

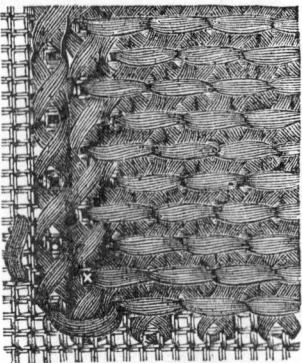

dot marks the place where the needle is to go in and come out for the next stitch.

Fig. 4 is worked with one color in long cross-stitches, each of which covers four rows of canvas in height and two in breadth. The

Fig. 4.

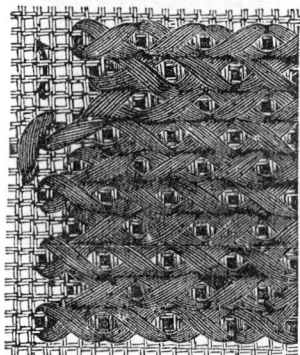

illustration shows by means of a cross and a dot where the needle is to go in and come out next time, and the canvas threads to be taken up for the next stitch are shown by an arrow passed through them.

TRIMMING FOR UNDER-LINEN.

THIS trimming is of tucks of the material alternated with insertion of point lace braid. For the crochet border, make a chain the required length.

1st row. Double.

2d. 2 chain, pass over 2, 1 treble into the next. Repeat.

On the other side of the chain work 3 chain, pass over 1 of foundation chain, 1 double into the next; repeat. This is then sewn to the material, and the edge is finished with a tape trimming.

EMBROIDERED JEWEL CASE.

THIS box is made of card-board, covered with blue velvet, embroidered in gold, with a framework of gilt wood, including which it is

about sixteen inches long, eight and two-fifths inches high, and six and two-fifths inches broad. The embroidery, which forms a mono-gram on the cover, and a narrow border on the front and sides, is worked in gold braid and gold thread. Inside the box is divided into two halves, each of which has a nest of three little card-board boxes, one above another, lined with white silk, to contain various ornaments.

DOG'S COLLAR.

THE collar consists of a strip of blue Cashmere sixteen inches long and about an inch wide, ornamented with *appliqué* figures of red cloth, as well as with a variety of stitches in red and blue silk. It is lined with red cloth, and trimmed with a fluting of red worsted braid. It is fastened around the dog's neck

by means of a button covered with blue Cashmere and two loops of red worsted cord, from one end of which hang cords with worsted balls and small bells according to illustration. On

Fig. 1.

one side of the collar is fixed a brass ring, to which is attached by a button and buttonhole a band of blue Cashmere an inch in width, embroidered in *point russe* with red silk and lined with red satin ribbon. Fig. 2 exhi-

Fig. 2.

bits the band with the holder attached. The latter consists of a steel hoop, covered to correspond with the band, which is fastened to it with a bow of red and blue ribbon. Other materials may be used instead of these above named—such as gray or brown leather, and silk to match.

HANDKERCHIEF-SACHET.

THE foundation is of five pieces of cardboard, two being nine inches square, and the other three, the same length, are to be cut two and a half inches wide; how the separate

Fig. 1.

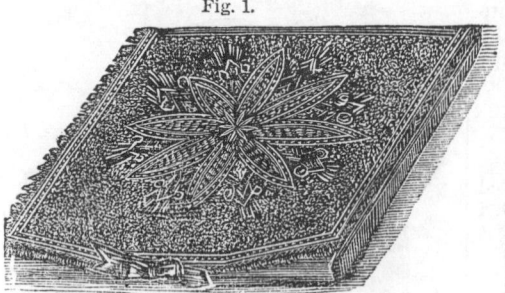

parts are to be shaped will appear from Fig. 1. These parts are covered with velvet, and lined with watered silk. The outside is embroidered in colored silks, and the edge is bound with

Fig. 2.

satin ribbon, with a narrow lace over it; strings fasten it in the front, as seen in Fig. 1, which shows it closed; Fig. 2 open.

HANDKERCHIEF BORDER (TATTING).

THE border to this handkerchief is worked in one length, and is about an inch and a half wide. You must work it in No. 90 thread, and when the insertion is ready, lay it over the

cambric; trace a line along the sides of the pattern with embroidery cotton, and work it over with button-hole stitch. The insertion consists of two rows of double ovals—that is, an oval to the right, then an oval to the left.

The thread between these ovals is so left that the work forms a small scallop. The second row is joined to the first, as shown in the engraving, and at the bottom of each scallop two more small ovals are worked, and joined to the edge by a twisted bar. It is best to lay the three parts over stiff paper, and join them on it. The outside ovals in the row are worked with 6 double, 1 purl, 6 double; the smaller ovals with 5 double, 1 purl, 5 double.

DESIGN FOR ANTIMACASSAR.

THE rosettes forming this design are of four loops of white tape, finished with a linen but-

ton, overcast with thread. The spaces may be left open, as shown in the design, or filled in with lace stitches.

FOOTSTOOL IN WOOL WORK.

THIS footstool is corner-shaped, and about four inches and four-fifths in height. The cover is of canvas, worked with Berlin wool of

through the loop so formed, and draw it together. Of course the rows of loops—since the loops of the last row fall over those of the former—must be worked upwards; also the first knot of each row of loops be fastened on to the

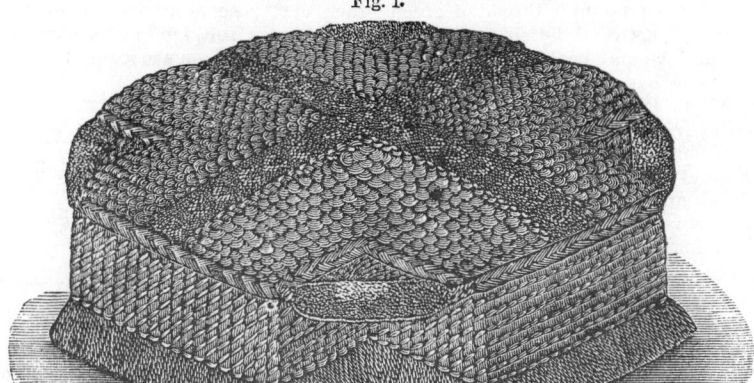

Fig. 1.

different shades of green in the ordinary cross stitch and raised (knotted) stitch. First draw the pattern of the cushion on moderately coarse canvas; then work the stripe which crosses the centre with black and green wool and silk in cross stitch, commencing in the centre. Now the remaining canvas is worked with light green fleecy wool in a kind of fancy loop stitch. This is worked, as shown in detail in Fig. 2, in knots, between which loops are formed by

last two stitches o. two rows of cross stitches in the stripe which crosses the cushion. Further, it must be noticed that a fresh thread is

Fig. 2.

Fig. 3.

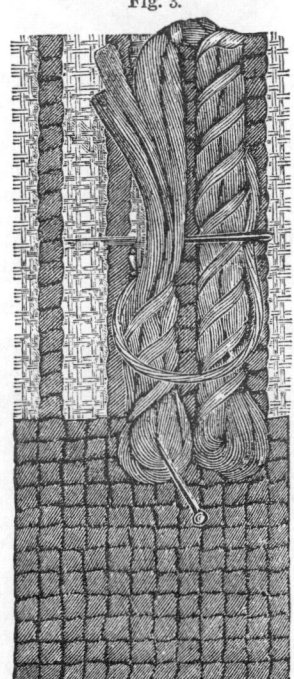

about three-quarters of an inch of wool. The knots cover four threads of canvas lengthwise, with a space between of eight threads, and worked in straight rows one over another; for each one first make a buttonhole stitch, then pass the needle close to this stitch upwards through the canvas, following the line of the illustration, ending in an arrow-head, back

to be taken for each row, commencing at the first knot of the former row, in order to cover the intermediate canvas threads. After this the border is to be made according to Fig. 3, which represents a portion of it on a smaller scale. First work single rows of half stitches with black wool, leaving a space of four threads, joined to which is a thick grounding of half stitches, which is afterwards covered by the fringe. Then a double thread of green fleecy wool is laid between the single rows of cross stitch, and wound backwards and forwards, then sewn over with light green filoselle, as shown in Fig. 1; to the loops formed by these skeins fringe of black and green wool is attached. When the cover is on the cushion the seam around the top edge is concealed by a plait of black and green wool, the bottom of the cushion is covered with black leather, and in each of the four incisions is placed a handle

Fig. 4.

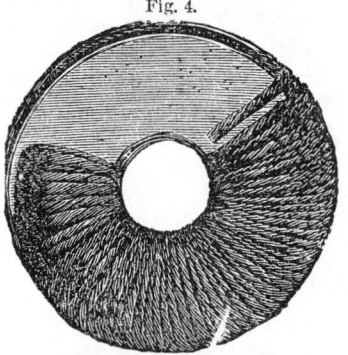

made of cord and balls of wool. These are formed by threading little balls of black and green wool, of different shades (the lightest in the centre) on a strong black worsted cord as follows: Take for each ball two round pieces of card-board of equal size, with a hole in the middle, thread them on the cord, wind them around thickly with several layers of wool, cut the threads around the outer edge of the card-board, as seen in Fig. 4 (which shows the pro-

cess by which the balls are made *without* the cord to which they are attached), and then tie the threads around several times in the middle between the pieces of card-board, which are then removed. Continue in this way until the requisite length of cord is covered with balls, then cut these around quite evenly, so that they form a roll, and fasten the ends of the cord to the cushion according to Fig. 1.

NEW STYLES OF BRAIDING.

QUITE a novel style of braiding has been introduced lately. Silk cord is used instead of flat braid, and the design arranged so that the

Fig. 1.

cord forms a compact mass, and thus the ornamentation when completed has all the effect of being in relief. The two accompanying designs illustrate the styles when complete, and the manner of working.

Fig. 2.—New Style of Braiding.

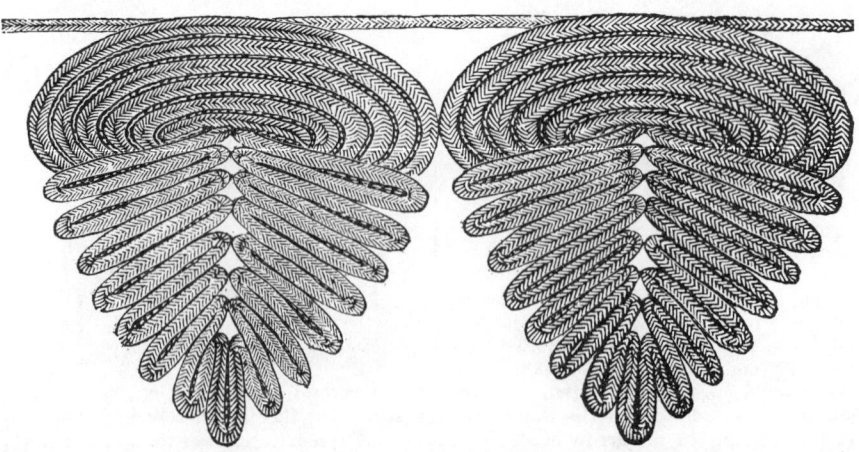

Sofa Tidy, or Top of Sofa Cushion

To be worked with black wool, on red Java canvass, or in any color to
suit the taste of the worker.

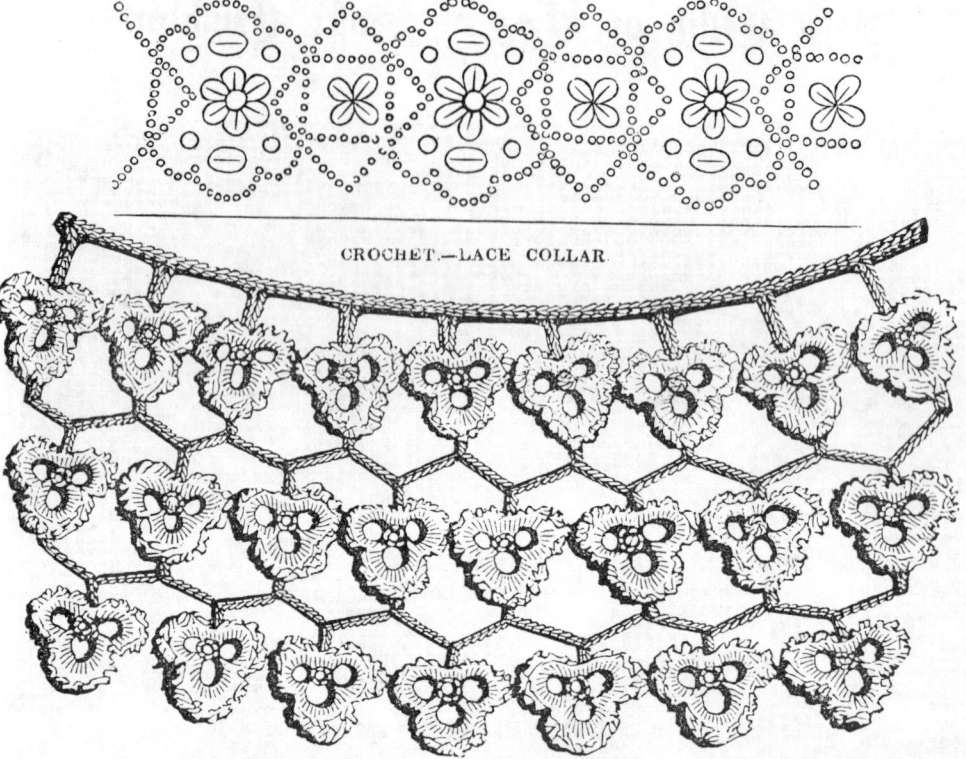

CROCHET.—LACE COLLAR.

Raworth's crochet thread, No. 70.

EXPLANATION.—c h, chain stitch; d c, double crochet; s c, single crochet; l, long stitch; d l, double long stitch; t l, treble long stitch; c s, common stitch.

THE OVALS, FORMING THE BORDER.—*1st round.* 10 c s, 1 l s into 8th stitch, *, 2 c s, miss 2, 1 l s into 3d; repeat from * twice more; then 5 c s, s c into last c s.

2d round.—5 c s, d c into 1st space; 5 c s, d c into next; repeat all round, and, at the end spaces, d c into them twice, after the 5 c s.

3d round.—S c up three of the 5 c s, *, 6 c s, s c round the 5 c s of last round; repeat from * all round and into the end spaces; 5 c s, d c again into same space.

4th round.—1 d c, 2 l s, 3 d l s, 2 l s, 1 d c round every chain of 6 in last round.

5th round.—6 c s, s c into centre d l s of scallop; 6 c s, s c into same stitch; 6 c s, s c into s c stitch between the 6 c s of 3d round; repeat all round.

Twenty-two ovals are required for the collar.

THE SMALL FLOWERS, WHICH FORM THE SPRIGS. —9 c s; unite; *, 6 c s, d c round the ring; repeat from * five more times.

In next round, 1 d c, 5 l s, 1 d c into every space formed by 6 c s.

Thirty of these flowers are necessary.

THE LEAVES.—30 c s, d c back fifteen of these; *, 5 c s, 1 d l s into last d c; 1 l s into next; 1 d c into next, repeat from * three times more; 3 c s, s c into top stitch; 3 c s, s c into 3d stitch down the other side; 1 d c into same stitch; *, 1 l s into next; 1 d l s into next; 5 c s, 1 d c into next; repeat from * three more times, finishing with 5 c s, 1 d c.

Pass the thread under the stalk; s c up three of the 1st, 5 c s, 7 c s, s c into the next point; 7 c s, s c into next; repeat all round. Fasten off.

Commence again on the same stitch as last round; 8 c s, s c into centre of 1st 7 c s of last round; 8 c s, s c into middle of next 7; repeat once more; 8 c s, s c into 3d of next 7; 7 c s, s c into 6th of the same 7; 8 c s, s c into 2d stitch beyond the point; 7 c s, s c into 3d stitch from last; 7 c s, s c into middle of next 7; *, 8 c s, s c into centre of next 7; repeat from * twice more. S c the remaining 15 for stalk.

Twelve of these leaves must be worked; four with fifteen stitches for the stalk, and eight with ten stitches.

Tack these flowers and leaves upon colored paper, wrong side up; fasten the ovals together by uniting the small loops. Arrange the sprigs as in the ILLUSTRATION, and unite them by bars of fine thread passed from the edges of the flowers to the ovals and each other, and working round the same thread a few times to form a twist.

Make a chain the length of the collar, and work 1 l s, 2 c s, miss 2 along this chain; then *, 4 l s into space; 3 c s, miss 1 space; repeat from *.

Tack this on the paper, and unite it to the flowers by the same twisted bars.

TOWEL HOLDER.

THIS is an article of German manipulation. We give the pattern, as it may possibly answer

some other purpose in a bedroom or nursery, and the stitch used for the crochet is so very novel and effective, that we strongly recommend our crochet workers to try it in wool or cotton for quilts, sofa covers, carriage rugs, etc. The directions are given for the towel holder as engraved; but, if wished for any of the things named instead, the crochet should be worked in stripes, making a chain of any number of stitches that will divide by three, adding one extra for the edge on the left side the stripe.

For the towel holder you require a quarter of a pound of coarse knitting cotton, a steel crochet hook No. 10 or 12, some red worsted braid. Make a chain 12 inches long, work two rows in double crochet, working throughout in ribbed or Russian crochet; this is worked from the back of the loop.

3d row, or the first pattern row. 1 dc on each of the first three stitches, * work 1 treble in the 5th dc of the first row of double crochet, working the stitch at the front of the other rows, and taking up the front half of the stitch

in that row, 1 treble in the 6th stitch of the first row, then 1 treble in the 4th stitch, so crossing over the other two stitches. Miss 3 dc stitches in the 3d row, work 1 dc in each of the next 3 dc; repeat from *, taking up the 5th stitch in the first row from the last used. At the end of the row make 1 ch, turn. *4th.* Work 1 dc on each stitch of last row, taking up the back of the loop at the end, 1 ch, turn. *5th.* * Work 1 treble in the 2d dc of the 3d row, 1 treble in the 3d dc, then 1 treble in the 1st dc, miss 3 dc of last row, 1 dc in each of the three next; repeat from *, taking care to work the treble stitches on the dc stitches in the 3d row, therefore between the treble stitches worked in that row. Repeat from the 4th row until you have worked 80 rows in all, and fasten off. You now bind the work round with worsted braid, and make a ruching of the same, which you put round the edge. The handles are crocheted, and sewn on firmly, and ornamented at the top with a bow of braid. For the handles make a chain of nine stitches, unite; on this work 9 dc, then work round and round in dc until you have made them 12 inches in length.

GIRL'S KNITTED COLLAR AND MUFF.

Materials.—Scarlet fleecy, white Shetland wool.

THIS collar and muff are knitted in a stitch which imitates fur. For the collar (Fig. 1), begin at the back edge; cast on 3 stitches with red fleecy, and knit plain in rows backwards and forwards, always increasing and decreas-

Fig. 1.—Girl's Knitted Collar.

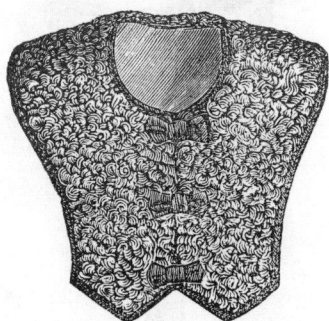

ing at the edges, according to a good-shaped paper pattern; work in also 3 rows of loops with white Shetland wool, which must have been wound 20 times double. Fasten this wool on the wrong side, * work 2 stitches, place the wool on the right side, knit 2 more, make a loop two-fifths of an inch long with the skein of wool, and draw it back to the wrong side of the work. The loops must be alternated in the following rows. When the knitting is finished, sew the loops down on the wrong side, so that they are not drawn out on the right side; then line the collar with scarlet silk, and bind it with red ribbon two-fifths of an inch wide. Sew on in front 3 lappets of red silk ribbon four-fifths of an inch wide, which are

Fig. 2.—Girl's Knitted Muff.

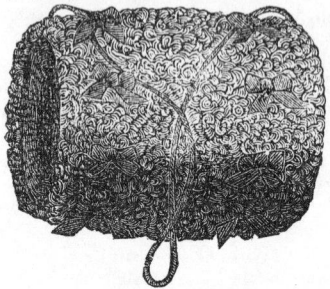

tied into bows. For the muff (Fig. 2), work in the same manner as for the cape a piece of knitting about twelve and four-fifths inches long, eight and four-fifths inches wide; sew the ends together on the wrong side; then quilt and line the muff, and ornament it with bows from illustration.

BLACK SILK WATCH-CHAIN.

Materials.—Black silk, lyre or lutal.

THIS mode of working watch-chains, and, indeed, of producing a thick braid, is an old style of work revived. It is exceedingly easy

Fig. 1.

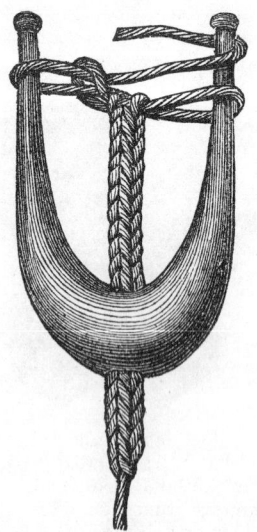

to do. The lyre or lutal, as it is called by some, is of wood or ivory. A slip-knot of silk is placed over one end of the lyre, as shown in Fig. 2; the end is wound round *a*; the loop

first formed is slipped over this thread of silk; the thread is passed over *b*, and the slipping re-

Fig. 2.—Detail of Watch-Chain.

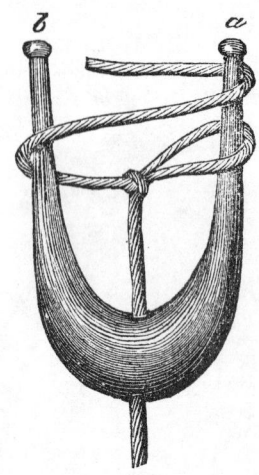

peated until a sufficient length of chain is completed, which is kept in place by being passed through a hole in the lyre.

BOY'S CROCHET CHEST PROTECTOR.

THIS chest protector is crocheted in Tunisian cross crochet stitch with violet and reddish-brown zephyr wool, in a square design imitating plaid. Join the back and fronts on the sides by means of a narrow belt, which is crocheted in connection with the backs, and is buckled over on the fronts. Cut a pattern of

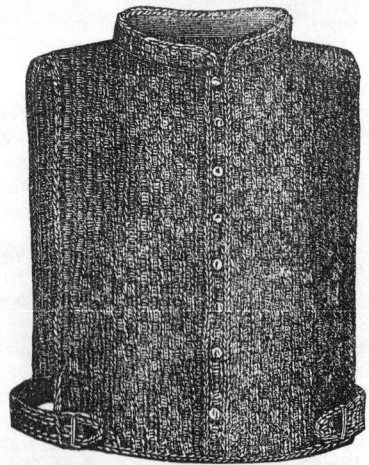

the requisite size of thin lining, then begin on the under edge of one of the fronts with the requisite number of stitches, with the darker wool, and crochet the first pattern row in Tunisian stitch, alternately four stitches with the darker and four with the lighter wool; the thread of each color is run along on the wrong side of the work; in the second round of the first pattern row these four stitches are worked off with the same colors. The second and all the remaining pattern rows are worked in Tunisian cross crochet stitch, but in the second pattern row the order of the wools must be changed. Continue in this manner so as to work alternating squares. Begin the back on

fine silk braid. This bow consists of 4 *gros grain* loops bound with satin one-tenth of an inch wide; the sewing-on of the loops is covered under an ornament of silk braid of different sizes, on to which 4 silk tassels are joined.

Fig. 2.—Bow with crochet ornament. The bow consists of 5 loops of *gros grain* one inch wide, bound with a strip of satin one-tenth of

Fig. 1.—Bow with Braid Ornament.

Fig. 2.—Bow with Crochet Ornament.

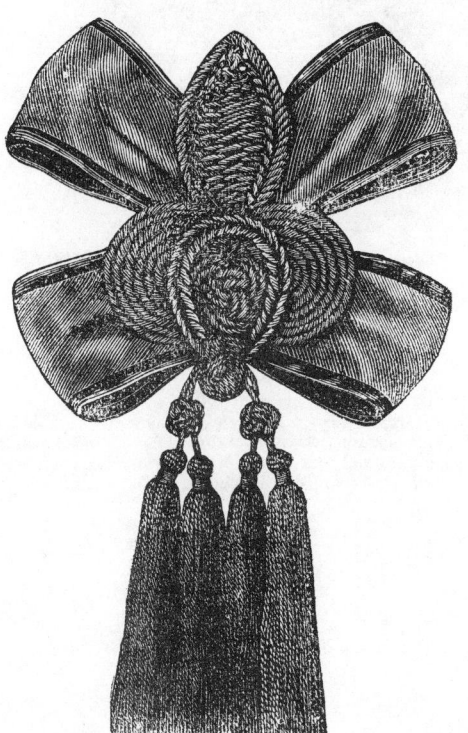

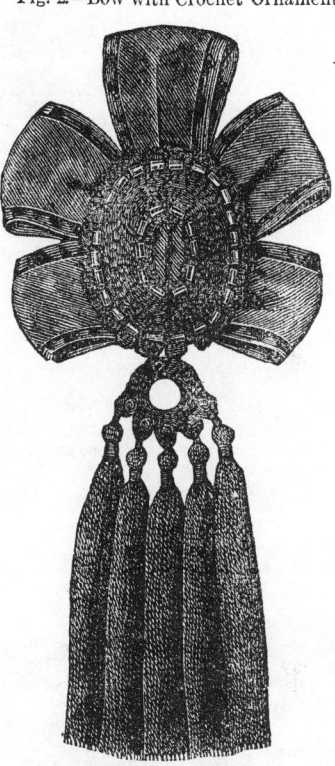

the under edge, and crochet it in the same manner, Join the shoulders on the wrong side with slip stitches, and crochet a neck binding an inch wide in the same manner. Edge the front of the left front, in the manner shown by the illustration, with two rounds of slip stitches of red wool, in working which the threads must lie under the work, as in tambour-work. This imitates a hem. Face the fronts with twilled muslin, set ornamental buttons on the left front, and sew button-hole loops on the under side. To correspond to these, sew little pearl buttons on the edge of the right front. Line the neck binding, and the upper edge of the back, and the belt parts, with drilling.

ORNAMENTS FOR MANTLES AND JACKETS.

Fig. 1.—Bow with ornament of thick and

an inch wide, sewn on a round piece of stiff net. The sewing-on of the loops is covered under the following ornament worked in crochet with black purse silk. Make a foundation chain of 40 stitches, join them into a circle, and work 4 rounds of slip stitches, increasing so as to keep the circle flat. Then work on the foundation chain stitches, as well as on the stitch of the last round, always alternately 1 slip stitch, 1 purl (3 chain stitch 1 double in the 1st), at the outer edge miss 1 stitch under every purl, at the inner edge miss 3 stitches. The small circle fastened below the larger one consists of 2 rounds of slip stitches worked round a circle of 12 chain stitches, working 5 purl in the 2d round, as can be seen in illustration. This small circle is sewn on to 2 purl of the larger one. Then ornament the purl of both circles with jet beads, and fasten 5 small silk tassels on the purl of the small circle.

BOX PINCUSHION.

EITHER a soap or a cigar box would be suitable for this cushion; the box is convenient for holding jewelry and pocket handkerchiefs. It is covered with blue satin, and the lid is edged

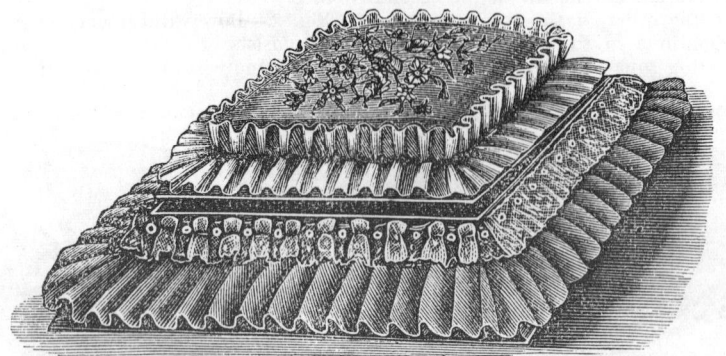

with a box-plaiting of blue satin ribbon; the sides are decorated with white lace and a ruching. The top may be either embroidered or decorated with guipure d'art.

PAPER FLOWERS.—DOUBLE VIOLET.

Materials.--Leaves from a florist's; two shades of violet-colored tissue paper; green paper; yellow floss silk; fine flower-wire.

THE circles for the flowers are cut to the dia-

makers. The petals are slipped over the wire and tied with a piece of green silk. The buds are formed of the small circles rolled tightly together, and finished with a strip of green tissue cut in four points at the top; this is continued over the stalks. Little knots of the yellow floss silks are fastened over the wire in the centre of the flower.

BAG FOR SKATES.
(See page 117.)

Materials.—*Toile cirée*, or American cloth, a piece measuring two yards and four inches in length, and a yard and nine inches in width; six yards of crimson worsted braid, one inch wide; narrow braid to match;

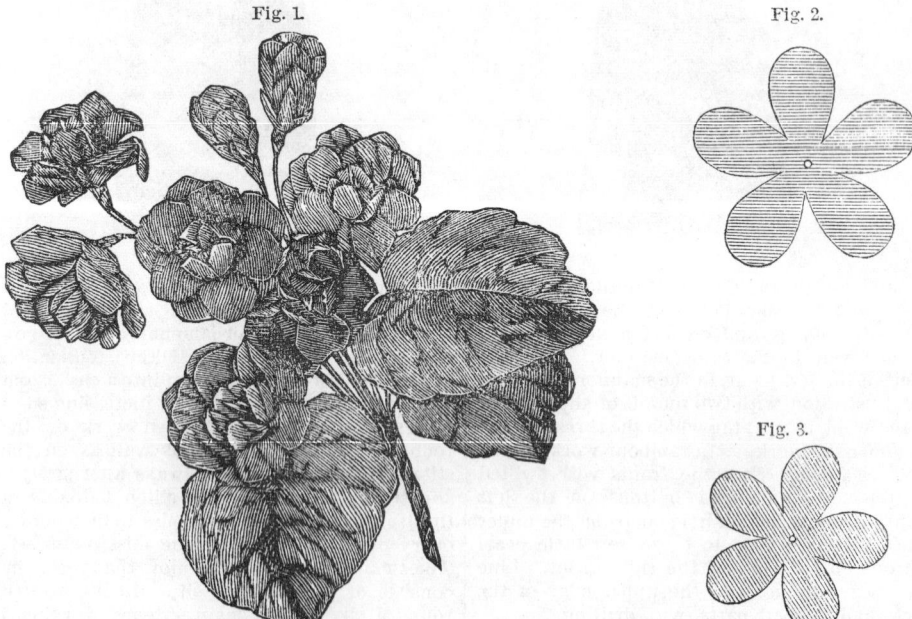

Fig. 1.

Fig. 2.

Fig. 3.

grams 2 and 3; the smaller are of the darker, the larger of the lighter shade of mauve paper. Each little scallop of the petals is rounded with a small wooden instrument used by flower-

chalk-white beads, crimson sewing silk; four brass rings, one inch and a half in diameter.

THIS bag, which is a German invention, is made of strong useful materials. As skating

Fig. 1.

Fig. 2.

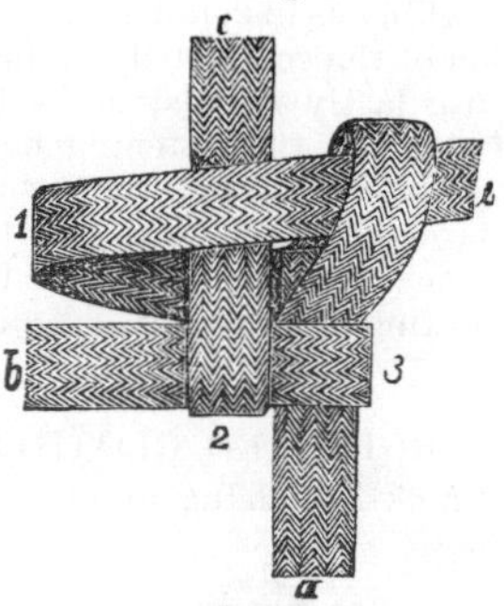

Fig. 3.

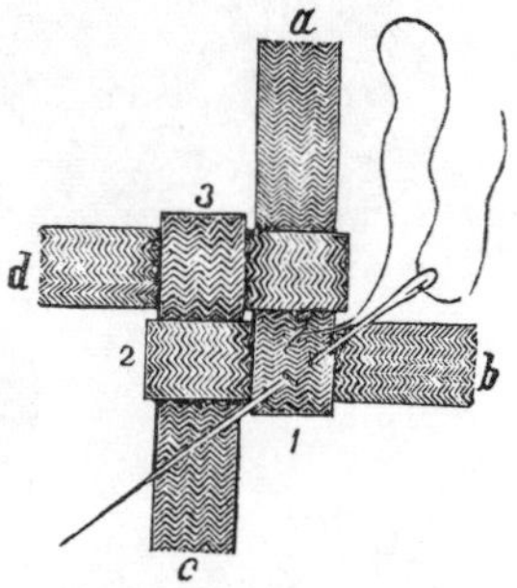

is now a favorite exercise with ladies, we trust the model will be acceptable. Our model is of *toile cirée*, and is lined with canvas. The entire length of the bag is cut both front and back, being in one piece; the latter turns over with a flap. This is now covered with a trelliswork of crimson braid, each diamond being fastened

Fig. 4.

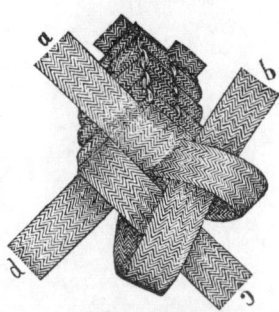

it over with button-hole stitches and a few beads. These rings are for the handle, so that when the bag is filled, the metal rings prevent the cloth breaking. Both sides are alike, and both are bound with braid, and ornamented

Fig. 5.

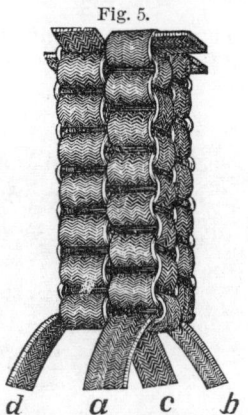

down with fine chalk-white beads. When this is completed, proceed to cut the sides, which are made of the same material. Before joining them to the front and back, cut a round hole at the top and three parts down, as shown in the illustration, put a ring into hole, and work

with beads. The handle, which is forty inches long, is made of braid, plaited according to the details, Figs. 2, 3, and 4. Commence with four pieces, and loop them together according to detail Fig. 2; make these loops firm by stitching, according to detail Fig. 3 (this is only done to start with); fasten off the thread, and continue working as in detail Fig. 4. Fig. 5 shows a portion of the completed handle full working size. It is lastly stitched to the bottom of the side of the bag, the fastening being concealed with beads. It passes through the ring, and is again brought to the outside at the top. The same proceeding is observed on the opposite side, working downwards instead of upwards.

EMBROIDERED CLOTHES-RACK.

THIS rack is to hang up on the wall, and is

wool and knit with both threads 1 row plain; before knitting each stitch, the wool must be wound round a mesh measuring two-fifths of an inch round. Then knit 1 row with the gray thread only, without forming loops; after this draw the mesh out of the row of loops; repeat these 2 rows constantly till the strip is sufficiently long. Before working each row of loops, the wool must be begun afresh. When the strip is sufficiently long, cast off, cut the loops open, comb them out, and clip them. The strips are fastened on the muff as seen in illustration.

made of oiled walnut. The piece in the back is embroidered on canvas.

MUFF OF VELVET AND KNITTED STRIPS.

THIS muff is eight and four-fifth inches long, and measures nineteen inches round. It is

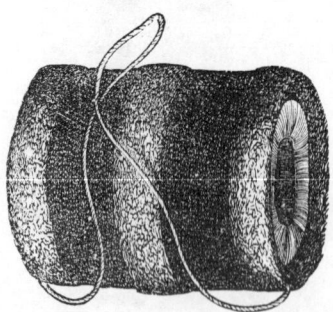

made of black velvet, with a quilted blue silk lining, and trimmed with 3 knitted strips, which imitate fur, as can be seen in illustration. The latter are worked with gray thread and gray fleecy, with fine steel knitting needles, in the following manner: Cast on 20 stitches with the gray thread, then take up the gray

BRUSH FOR SILK DRESSES AND MANTLES.

THIS brush is very useful for cleaning silk clothes. It consists of colored flannel strips

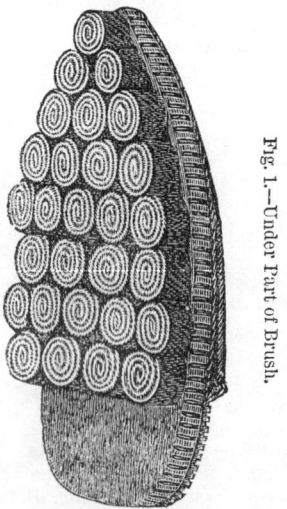

Fig. 1.—Under Part of Brush.

two-fifths of an inch wide, rolled up as seen on illustration, and sewn together; they are then

Fig. 2.—Brush for Silk, Etc.

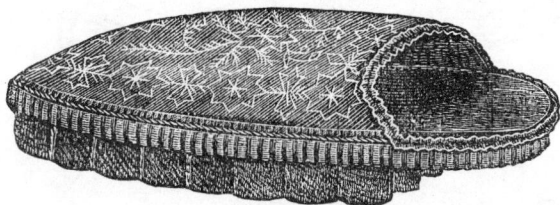

Fig. 3.—Roll of Flannel for Brush.

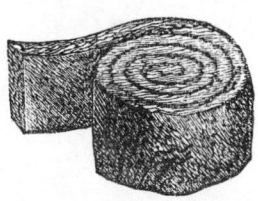

sewn on to a thick piece of felt, six and two-fifths inches long, three and three-fifths inches wide, rounded off at one end, and pointed at the other. At the edge, the felt part is covered with even stitches of red wool taken double; on the top sew a piece of red cloth, which covers the stitches with which the flannel strips have been sewn on. Another piece of cloth, forming a sort of bag, is sewn on the top of the brush; it is ornamented with point russe embroidery of black silk. Into this bag the hand is inserted while brushing.

BELL-ROPE OF CORD PLAITING.

THIS bell-rope consists of a plait of cord. Take 4 pieces of cord (taken double), over 2

Fig. 1.

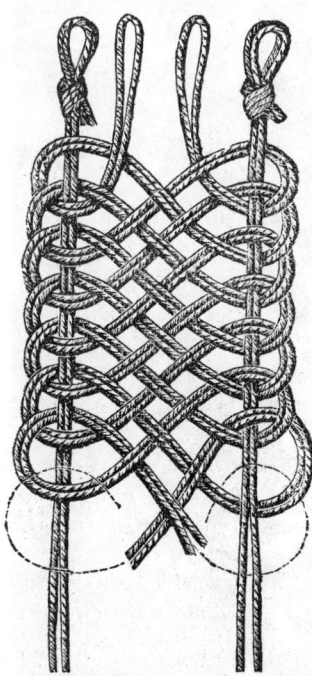

of which you work, and with the 2 others of which you work the plait. The 2 pieces over which you work must be as long as you wish

the bell-rope to be; they are knotted together at one end, and form a loop, which is fastened on a lead cushion. The 2 other pieces of cord (taken double likewise) must be 6 times as long as the others, and are wound in a ball.

Fig. 2.

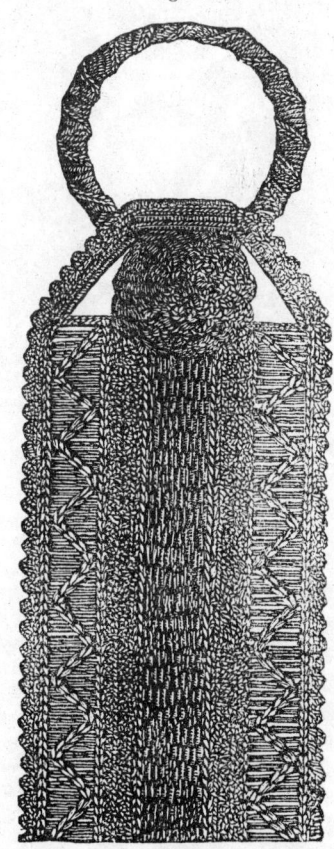

Fasten these cords on the lead cushion, and work the plait from Fig. 2. When it is sufficiently long, draw the cords over which you have worked through a wooden handle covered with thread, and fasten them round a circle from Fig. 1. This circle, which completes the handle, is also covered with thread. The other cords are also drawn through the handle, and fastened on the circle.

CORNERS FOR POCKET-HANDKERCHIEFS

𝕮𝖗𝖔𝖈𝖍𝖊𝖙 𝕬𝖓𝖙𝖎𝖒𝖆𝖈𝖆𝖘𝖘𝖆𝖗.

CAMEO-PATTERN.

(*See Instructions, Page* 121.)

CAMEO PATTERN.
(*See Illustration, Page* 120.)

Materials.—Crochet cotton No. 12; one ounce of colored Berlin wool: twelve yards of mohair braid, about three-quarters of an inch wide; and needles Nos. 1 and 2½. The braid and wool should either match in color, or be a direct contrast. Or the braid may be dark green or mauve, and the wool a light shade of these new colors.

THE CAMEO.

1st Leaf. Commence with the cotton and No. 2½ needle, work 22 chain, turn, and down the chain miss 1, 2 plain, 2 treble, 3 long, 2 treble, 2 plain, 2 single, leaving 8 chain for the stem; and for

THE FLOWER.—Make 16 chain, turn, miss the last 8 and work 1 single in the 8th stitch of the chain to form a round loop; turn, so as to cross, and in the round loop work 1 plain.

1st round. Make (5 chain and 1 plain in the round loop, 6 times); 1 single on the 1st plain stitch.

2d. Turn the loops of the 1st round down under the thumb, put the needle in the round loop at the back, between the two 1st plain of the 1st round, and work 1 plain; then make 5 chain, join to the 1st long stitch of the leaf; and on the 5 chain, miss 1, 1 plain, 2 treble which leaves 1 chain; make 1 chain and work 1 plain in the round loop, between the two next plain stitches of the 1st round, that is, at the back of the second loop of chain; then * 6 chain, turn, and on these 6 chain, miss 2, 1 plain and 2 treble; then 1 chain and 1 plain in the round loop at the back of the next loop of chain; repeat from * 3 times more, forming in all 5 divisions; then on the 7 chain, work 3 plain and 4 single; and on the 8 chain, 2 single.

2d Leaf. Make 6 chain, join to the last division of the flower; 6 chain, turn, miss 1, 2 plain, 3 treble; and on the next 6 chain work 3 long, 1 treble, 1 plain, and 1 single; then on the stem 5 plain, 1 single.

THE OVAL, *1st round.* Make 6 chain, and up the stem and 1st leaf, miss 10, and work 1 long, 6 chain, miss 5, 1 treble on the leaf—6 chain, 1 plain at the point of the leaf, then (6 chain and 1 plain on each of the 3 divisions of the flower); 6 chain, 1 plain on the point of the 2d leaf—6 chain, miss 5, 1 treble on the leaf; 6 chain, miss 4, 1 treble; 6 chain, 1 single on the last stitch of the stem. Fasten off.

2d. Use the wool and No. 1 needle, and commencing in one of the loops of 6 chain in the 1st round, work 1 plain in it; then * for the 1st point make 5 chain, and work 1 plain in the 1st stitch of these 5 chain, then 2 plain more in the same 6 chain as before; for the 2d point make 5 chain and 1 plain in the 1st stitch of these 5

chain; then miss 1 and work 2 plain in the next 6 chain. Repeat from * all round, when there will be 20 small points; end with 1 single on the 1st stitch. Fasten off.

3d. Use the cotton and needles as before, and commence in the point of the last round which is over the end of the stem, make 6 chain, and work 1 plain in each point; repeat all round.

4th. Miss 1 and work 7 plain in each loop of the last round, so as to form 20 little scallops. Fasten off.

THE SECOND CAMEO.—Repeat the whole of the direction of the first cameo to the last 7 plain of the 4th round, then work 4 plain in the last loop, join to the centre of the 11th scallop in the 1st cameo, then 3 plain in the same loop, and 3 single on the 1st 3 plain of the round, join to the next scallop of the 1st cameo, 1 single, and fasten off.

Repeat this cameo until sufficient are made for one stripe.

THE JOINING PATTERN.

1st row. Commence with the cotton, make 4 chain. Take the left side of the first cameo, and join to the centre of the 6th scallop, counting from where the two are attached; then 3 chain, 1 single in the 1st stitch of the 4 chain, which forms a small loop; * make 8 chain, join to the 5th or next scallop to the right, miss 1 and 1 single on the 8 chain; 8 chain again, join to the 4th scallop, miss 1 and 1 single on the 8 chain; then 10 chain, join to the 3d scallop; 3 chain and 1 single in the 7th stitch of the 10 chain; then 17 chain, join to the 2d scallop; 7 chain and 1 single in the 10th stitch of the 17 chain; then 10 chain, join to the 1st scallop; 9 chain and 1 single in the 1st stitch of the 10 chain; make 10 chain again, join to the 1st scallop of the next cameo; 9 chain and 1 single in the 1st stitch of the 10 chain; then 8 chain, join to the next scallop; 7 chain and 1 single in the 1st stitch of the 8 chain; then 13 chain, join to the next scallop; 3 chain and 1 single in the 10th stitch of the 13 chain; repeat from *, ending with the small loop attached to the 6th scallop of the last cameo; then turn so as to work along the chain stitch.

2d. For the dot make 5 chain and work 1 single in the 1st stitch of these 5 chain; then 3 single on the last 6 chain of the 1st row; then make a dot and 3 more single. Work the same on the other two loops of 6 chain, then on the 9 chain make a dot and 3 single 3 times; make a 10th dot; then 7 chain and 1 single in the third stitch of the 7 chain, to form the 11th dot; and on the next 9 chain work 3 single; then a dot and 3 single twice. Repeat from the commencement of the row.

For the right side, commence at the 6th scallop of the last cameo, and repeat as before.

THE WREATH.

1st Leaf. With the cotton make 12 chain, turn, miss 2, 1 plain, 2 treble, 1 plain, and 1 single, leaving 5 chain for the centre stem. Repeat the leaf until sufficient is made for the stripe; and for

The leaves on the other side. Work 1 single more on the last 5 chain; and for the leaf make 7 chain, turn, miss 2, 1 plain, 2 treble, 1 plain, and 1 single; then 4 single on the 4 chain of the stem. Repeat to the end.

THE DOTS.—Commence in the point of the

loops on the braid, two on the insertion, three on the next braid, and one loop on each scallop of the cameo. Repeat all round.

2d. Make 5 chain, and work 3 treble in each loop of chain. Repeat all round.

3d. Use the wool. Make 7 chain, and work 1 plain on the centre of each 3 treble. Repeat, and fasten off.

BED POCKET.

THIS pocket is to hang on the wall at the side of the bed, to hold handkerchief, brush and comb, etc. It is composed of fine white

1st leaf, make 6 chain, and work 1 single in the 2d stitch of these 6 chain; 6 chain again, 1 single in the 2d stitch; then 1 chain and 1 single on the point of the next leaf; repeat to the end. Work the other side the same.

THE BRAID.—Take a length of the braid, and with a needle and thread secure the ends by stitching them in a slanting direction, as in the engraving; then commencing at the point of it, sew the dots of the insertion to the side of the braid, placing the tops of them a trifle over the braid and stitching them to it; then take another length of braid and attach the other side of the insertion to it. The dots of the cameos are to be joined in the same manner.

THE BORDER, *1st round.* Use the cotton, and commence on the stripe of braid which forms one side of the antimacassar; work a row of 7 chain and 1 plain, putting the needle in the braid and using it for the foundation; the stitches should be three-eighths of an inch apart; then along the end of the pattern work three

muslin lined with pink and plaited, trimmed all around with a pink satin ribbon quilled. The pockets are trimmed the same. A rosette of ribbon is in the centre of back, to which a hook is attached to fasten to wall.

WASTE-PAPER BASKET.

THIS waste-paper basket consists of six parts of deal canvas pointed off at the top, each about thirteen inches long, six inches and a fifth wide at the top, and four inches and two-fifths wide at the bottom. These parts are fastened on to a card-board centre, which is mounted upon a bamboo stand. The deal canvas consists of small pieces of deal fastened on to one another. The different parts of the basket are bound with ribbon and embroidered in gobelin stitch with purple wool. For each square row of the pattern insert the needle between the strips of deal and work two stitches close to one another. Before beginning to work, always fasten the

Fig. 1.

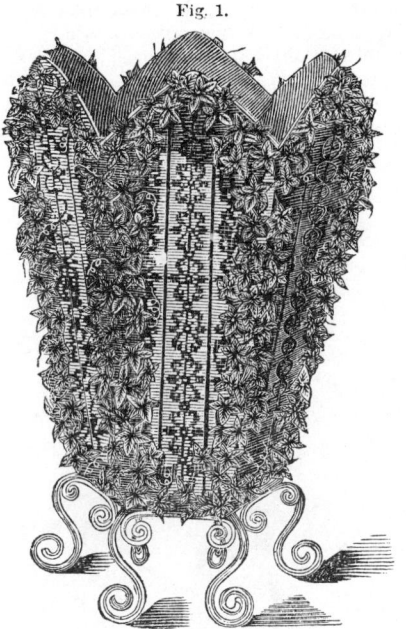

Fig. 2.

Fig. 3.

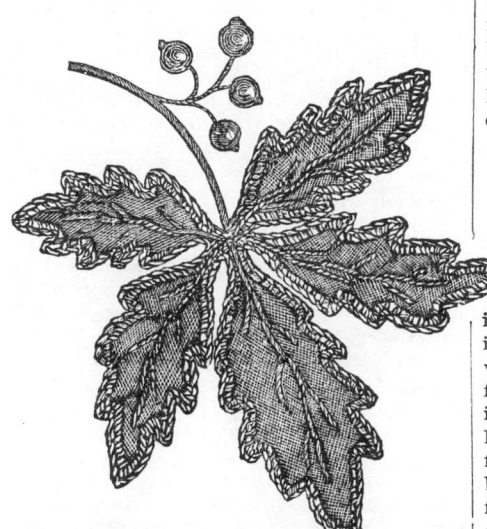

wool on to the thread which joins the strips of deal together; when the wool is to be carried from one place to the other, always fasten it in a straight line above the place where the needle is to be drawn out. The ornaments of the basket consist of leaves or green wool of four shades, arranged into a garland on a strip of card-board an inch and four-fifths wide, covered with some material. Before working these leaves, trace the outlines of each leaf separately on stiff linen, and work them in satin stitch in the manner seen in Fig. 2, which shows such a leaf full size. Each leaf is worked in several shades. Then cut the leaves out, fasten a piece of wire in the centre, which forms at the same time the veining and the stem; cover the stem with green wool and the veining with overcast stitch, the side veinings of the leaf are also worked in overcast stitches, but not over wire. Fig. 3 shows another kind of leaf full size. It is made of green or red-brown crape, taken several times double, which is worked round with buttonhole stitch round the edges, over wire; the veinings are worked in coral stitch. These leaves are also suitable for bell-ropes or Vandyke trimmings.

CIGAR ASH STAND.

THIS curious little stand for containing cigar ashes is easy to make, and that with materials easily procured. An oyster-shell is meant to hold the cigar ashes, and this shell is supported by two crawfish. The under part is formed of a round piece of black varnished wood, measuring three inches across, and two-fifths of an inch in thickness. A piece of Spanish bamboo three inches long is fastened into a hole in the centre of this wooden circle, and fastened at the top under the shell. At the bottom of the bamboo fasten long narrow green feathers, which imitate reeds. Two boiled crawfish (the meat being of course taken out), gummed together, and made yet brighter with vermilion and gum, are gummed on to the stand and oyster-shell from illustration. At the bottom of the tail they are nailed upon the wooden circle. The head of a dried pike is nailed on close to the crawfish; the open mouth of this fish is meant to hold the matches, and for lighting these a small ribbed shell is also nailed on to the stand. The arrangement of the whole can easily be copied from illustra-

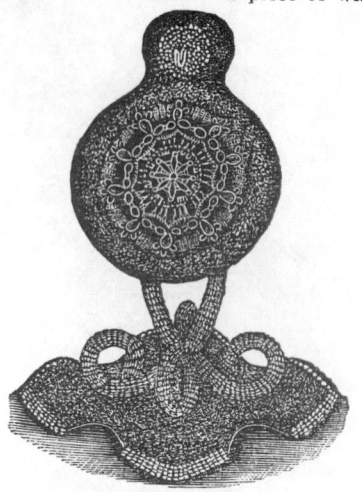

tion. In Paris, one sees some wondrous little articles made of lobster-shell—its bright color giving a glow and bestowing an effect quite astonishing to those who have not seen them.

WATCH-STAND.

Materials.—Dark red velvet, gold beads, card-board, wire.

THIS watch-stand is made of card-board, dark red velvet, and gold beads. The top is ornamented with a silk cushion, covered with a tatted rosette. First make the bottom part of the stand in card-board. It is four inches and three-fifths long, and three inches and two-fifths wide, cut out in four scallops in the manner seen in illustration, and covered with velvet on the top. Round the edge sew on a row of gold beads close to one another with overcast stitch, threading on three or four gold beads for every stitch, thus imitating a metal border. For the upper part of the watch-stand cut two pieces of card-board, each four inches long, two inches and four-fifths wide, and curve them in the manner seen in illustration. One of the pieces of card-board is covered on one side with velvet. Work a small bead rosette from illustration, and fasten it at the upper edge with a brass hook; fasten likewise on this part a small

silk quilted cushion. This cushion is edged with a piece of wire covered with beads, and ornamented with a tatted rosette. The other piece of card-board is covered on one side with black silk. The frame of the watch-stand consists of a piece of wire twelve inches long. Bend the six inches in the middle into a loop, which measures one inch and three-fifths across at the place where it is widest; both the ends of this piece of wire are bent into circles. Then take two pieces of wire, each thirteen inches and three-fifths long, wind them round the first piece of wire, binding them also into loops four-fifths of an inch long in the middle of the completed loop; one of these loops must be turned upwards, the other downwards. Fasten another piece of overspun wire five inches and three-fifths long underneath the large loop, at the place where the pieces of wire cross each other; the ends are likewise bent into loops, and must be placed opposite the first circles. The frame is then closely covered with gold beads, then fasten it from illustration on the watch-stand with the two short loops, bending them so as to give them a slanting shape. Lastly, fasten on the stand the part covered with the cushion, and cover the bottom part of the stand with black silk or glazed paper.

PAPER FLOWERS.
FULL-BLOWN MALLOWS ARRANGED AS A BOUQUET FOR A VASE.

Materials.—Colored and white tissue paper, several shades of water color paints, fine yellow sand, flower wire, thick dissolved gum, pincers.

FIG. 1 represents a branch of mallow in reduced size, with graduated buds and flowers. About twelve such branches are required for a vase. Fig. 2 gives a flower in full size. For a shaded flower, white tissue paper, covered with carmine, or any other color suitable to the

Fig. 1.

Fig. 2.

flower, may be used. For the colored flowers, tissue paper of the proper color must be selected.

Circles of paper of two sizes may be cut out for each flower. The flowers look more natural not cut too much of a size; these must be folded together from the middle to form a triangle, and then, having folded the flower part so that the paper is threefold, cut so that scallops are formed. Then take the under part of the triangle with the left hand between a piece of thin old linen, lay it with its contents upon a corner of a table, hold it firmly, and push with a twisting movement, pressing the ball of the right hand with great force over it several times, which gives the necessary folds for the circle of petals. Afterwards the triangle of

Fig. 3.   Fig. 5.

Fig. 4.

white tissue paper must be painted and dipped in clean water, and then laid upon the edge of a plate that the color may gradually run; and, lastly, the separate circles of petals are laid out to dry.

For the large flowers, the sizes for the circles

of petals are placed in regular order; sometimes, also, two of the smallest are first pushed on the wire stalk, and pressed on to it, which must have a pistil of wadding and colored sand (see Fig. 3).

The smaller the corolla the fewer the number of petal circles; the smallest have no pistils. The bud represented in Fig. 4 is composed of wadding wetted with gum, and painted green; the point is squeezed with the pincers crosswise, according to Fig. 5. All the stalks have light green tissue paper twisted round them.

The green leaves may be purchased at very little expense.

INITIAL MEDALLION.

SUITABLE for a pocket-handkerchief. These are worked partly in *appliqué*, partly in satin stitch. The open-work parts are worked in straight and slanting ladder stitches.

HAND MIRROR.

Materials.—Thick card-board, brown velvet, goose feathers, white silk, a small mirror, etc.

THIS mirror is very prettily ornamented; the material used for the purpose is cheap and imitates ivory carving. It is made of the feathers of the wings of geese. The flowers and leaves are made of the fringe of the feathers; the stems and the framework on the handle of

silk. The velvet covering is edged outside and inside with chenille. The pattern is sewn on the velvet before fastening the latter on the frame. The mirror is fastened between the velvet and the card-board. For the pattern, cut off the fringy part a certain number of feathers, some of which must be shaved and some not. (The feathers are shaved by holding them a few minutes in hot ashes, and then rubbing

Fig. 1.

Fig. 2.

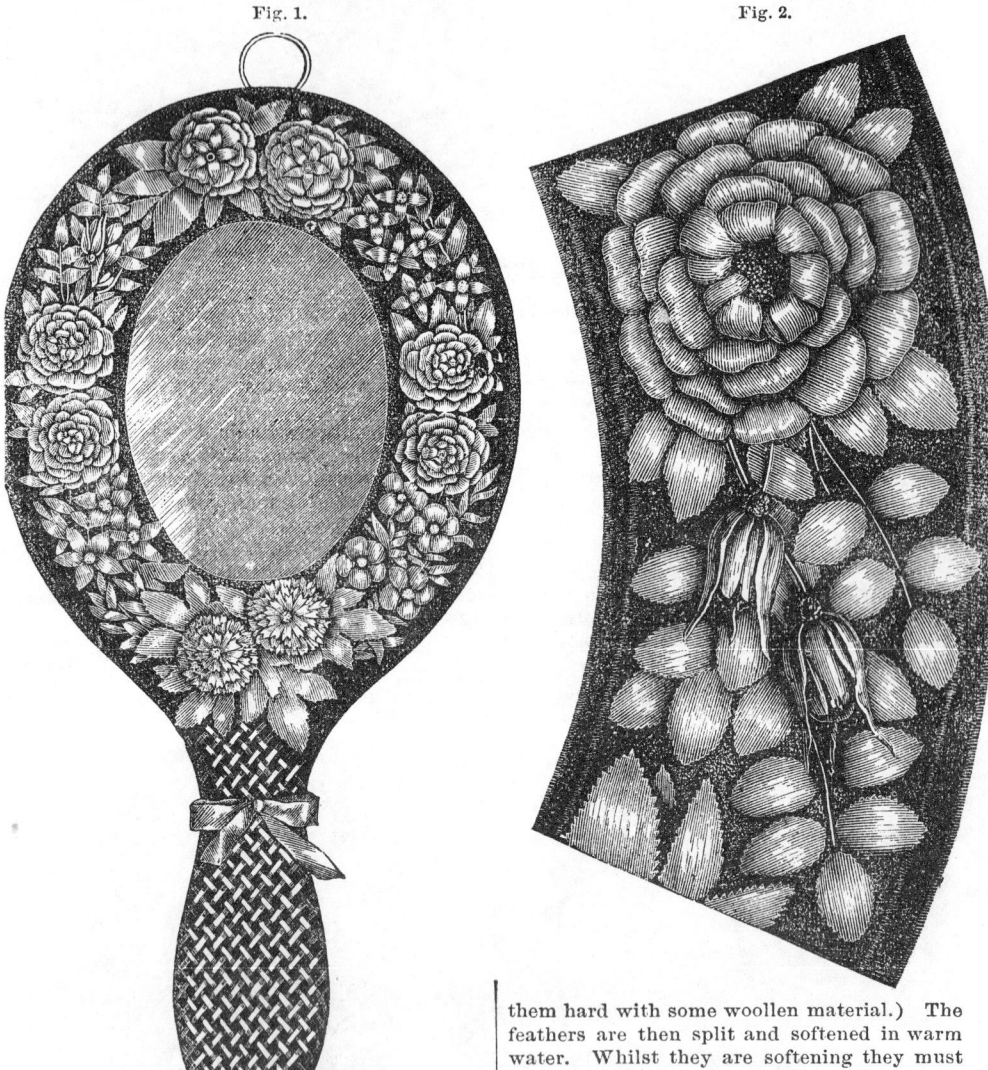

the mirror are made of the quills, Fig. 1. The shape of the mirror is made of thick card-board, over which a thin, flat, fork-shaped wooden frame is fastened so as to render the shape stronger. This frame is covered on the upper side with velvet, on the wrong side with *glacé*

them hard with some woollen material.) The feathers are then split and softened in warm water. Whilst they are softening they must be arranged in the shapes seen on illustrations, and bent accordingly. The separate leaves are then arranged from Fig. 2. The larger flowers are sewn on with silk thickly covered with wax; they are fastened on a card-board foundation of corresponding shape. For the roses, take the leaves made with the feathers from which the fringe has not been shaved off; the leaves, buds, and small blossoms are made separately with the other feathers. The stems of the leaves and buds are made of the upper part of the quills which have been split into narrow pieces. For the cores and stamens paste on a sufficient quantity of liquid gum, which must be scraped off with a knife. The framework on the handle of the mirror is made with the inner part of the feather, and sewn on in the manner seen in illustration.

LADY'S COMPANION IN SHAPE OF A PARASOL.

THIS companion is in the shape of a parasol (see Fig. 1). The lower part of the parasol, which simulates the lining, and forms the bot-

Fig. 1.

tom of the case, is made of card-board, on to which the handle is fastened—on one side only, to the upper part of the parasol—and is buttoned on to it by means of an elastic loop. Cut first for the parasol eight similar parts of thick card-board, cover them on both sides with green silk, and sew them together with overcast stitches. Then cut eight similar parts of green watered silk, draw the pattern seen in illustration on them. Then work the embroidering. The outer lines are formed of fine gold braid, sewn on with black silk; the inner fine lines of green silk braid, sewn on with silk of the same color. Between the lines work point russe with

green purse silk. Then sew the watered silk parts over those of card-board, carefully turning in the edges, and sewing them together with overcast stitches. Sew on inside the parasol a small cushion (see Fig. 2), edge it with gold braid, and fasten strips of elastic over it. Fasten a small metal button in the middle of the embroidered part, and a similar one at the lower edge of the parasol, which fastens at the same time an elastic loop one inch and a quarter long. Then cut an eight-cornered piece of card-board, which must fit

Fig. 2.

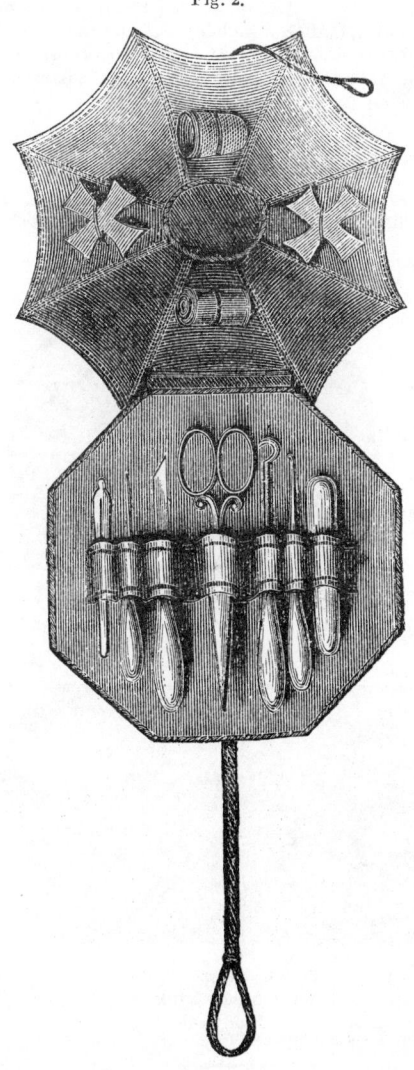

exactly into the upper part of the parasol; cover it on one side with green silk, so that it forms a border of one-fifth of an inch on the other side. On the side covered with silk sew on a ribbon four-fifths of an inch wide, stitched across at different intervals, into which the sewing implements are to be placed. Then fasten at the edge of this part several pieces of wire about three inches and three-quarters long for the handle ; these are twisted and bent into a loop at bottom, and wound round with dark brown beads. On the opposite side of the same part fasten a piece of green ribbon four inches long and four-fifths of an inch wide ; it forms the hinge, and is stitched down at the other end on the lining of the upper part of the parasol. The lower part of the parasol is covered on the wrong side with green silk, sewn on in plaits. Then cut a long straight strip of green silk, eighteen inches long, two inches and two-fifths wide. Sew the ends together, and gather it on the green silk binding of the parasol.

TATTING CASE, OPEN AND SHUT.

THE case is made of pieces of card-board of the shape seen in illustration. The pieces are

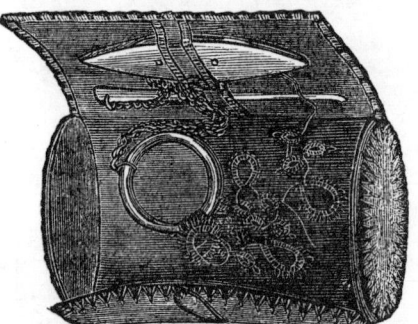

then covered with scarlet merino. After they are joined together, they are worked around the edge with black silk. The inside of case has

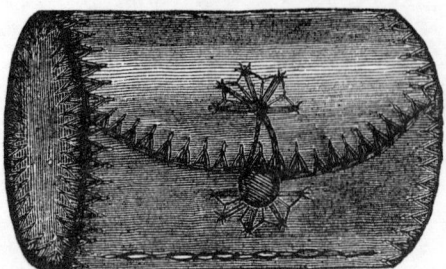

pieces sewed on for the tatting implements. It is fastened when closed with a button and loop, worked around in fancy stitch in black silk.

EMBROIDERED SCISSOR SHEATH.

Materials.—Gray kid, gold thread, gold lace, card-board, white kid, gray sewing silk.

THIS scissor case can be made of gray kid,

cloth, watered silk, or velvet of any color preferred. Instead of embroidering with gold thread, purse silk of different colors may be chosen. The embroidery is worked in raised satin stitch and overcast. The case is made of white card-board, which is covered outside with the embroidered material, and inside with

white kid ; the different parts are sewn together with overcast stitch. On the outlines of the case sew on a gold lace, a silk cord, or some chenille.

LETTER FOR MARKING.

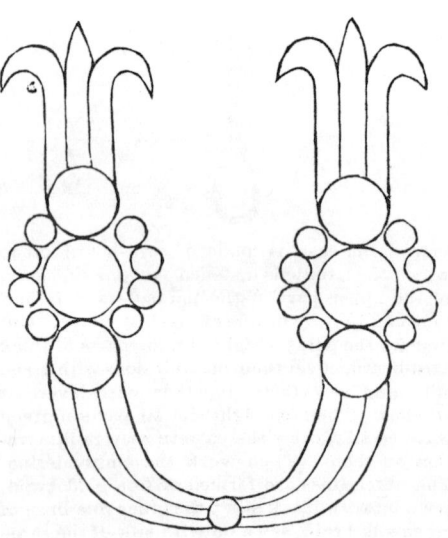

INSTRUCTIONS FOR MAKING MISS LAMBERT'S REGISTERED CROCHET FLOWERS.

Miss Lambert, having seen the very beautiful vase of flowers, worked in Berlin wool, that obtained the honorable mention prize in the Great Exhibition, was struck with its simplicity and beauty; and being convinced that, were it generally known, it would become universally popular, she purchased the idea of the inventor, and now begs to lay it before the public; feeling assured that her opinion was well founded that this species of artistic work is likely to become one of the most popular amusements of the ladies of the present day; and the worker may be prepared for finding it as pleasant and as delicate an employment as any branch of needle-work. In its occupation, ladies can spend their leisure hours delightfully in the garden, the drawing-room, or the seaside, as neither tints nor gum are required, but merely the wool and the crochet-hook.

It may be turned to as many useful as ornamental purposes; dresses may be worked, and wreaths for the head, to supersede the present Berlin wool cap, besides numerous other applications.

The only materials required are Berlin wool of the best quality, which may be had of all colors, a small quantity of the finest iron wire, about the thickness of "30" cotton, and the common crochet hook.

Fig. 1.

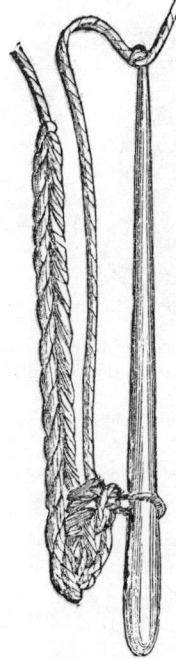

To form the Leaf.

Take a leaf that you intend to copy, or its pattern; make a chain of the proper green tint, of the length required for the centre vein; retain the last chain stitch upon the hook, insert the hook into the next stitch, draw the wool through, and there will be found three loops upon the hook; the wool must be drawn through again and repeated.

The foundation of every leaf is formed exactly the same, Fig. 1 showing the length of chain required to form the Camilla leaf, from nineteen to twenty-six stitches, according to the size the worker may think proper to select.

Having completed the three stitches, the next engraving shows that the single trebles (meaning once round the hook) are continued four times, and then, to

Fig. 2.

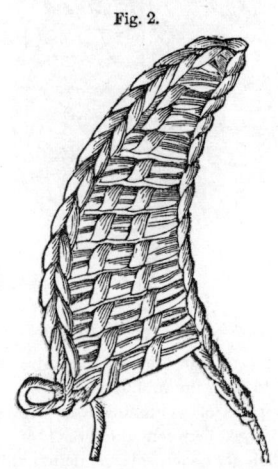

widen it, double trebles (or twice round the hook) are used seven times.

The third figure shows that to decrease the leaf at its junction with the stem, two single trebles must

Fig. 3.

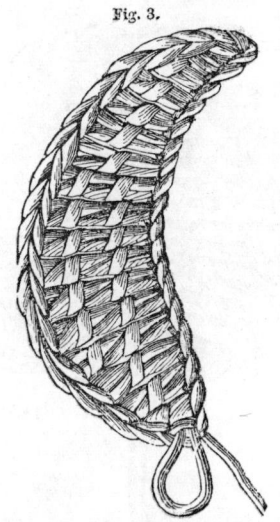

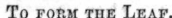

be worked and two plain ones: this forms one-half of the leaf.

The fourth figure shows the leaf completed, by working the last side in precisely the same manner as the first, beginning at the stem and finishing at the point; the wool is then drawn through the last

Fig. 4.

loop and the end run down the centre, upon the upper side, to form the middle vein.

Insert a piece of your fine iron wire carefully round the edge, between the twists of the wool, leaving sufficient at each side to mount: this is done by twisting it round the stem, which is formed of another piece of the same kind. It is then to be damped and hotpressed.

The fifth figure shows the geranium leaf, which is

Fig. 5.

commenced in the same way as the camilla: but, in order to obtain the notches around the edge, three

chain stitches must be made between every three trebles.

TO MAKE THE FLOWERS.

For convenience in making, we divide flowers into three classes. The petalled, viz., those like Camillas, Roses, &c.; the Lilied class, viz., those that have petals which taper to a point; and Bell Flowers, as the Convolvulus, &c.

CLASS I.—PETALLED FLOWERS.

Under the head of Petalled Flowers are included the Rose, Dahlia, Pansy, Poppy, Geranium, Forget-me-not, Orange-Blossom, Camilla, Sweet Pea, Verbena, &c. The directions given to complete the Camilla apply to all these flowers, except the mounting and arrangement of the petals, which must be done according to nature.

TO MAKE THE PETAL.—Take a flower that you intend to copy—the camilla, for instance; pull off a petal for a pattern, then form a loop for the base, thus ○, and work from it four chains, passing the wool twice round the hook, and working two trebles, repeating it three times round the hook, working *four* trebles; and to decrease, passing the wool round the hook twice, working two trebles, break off the wool and run the end in.

In the camilla there will be required about thirty-two of these, decreased in size according to nature, and then properly mounted.

The petal of the tulip is rather different. It is formed by working in rows of plain crochet the size required; the ends are run down to form a point, the shaded frame and feathered stripe being worked in with a needle.

The rose, dahlia, and other flowers of the same

Fig. 6.

sort, are worked in a similar manner, increasing or decreasing the stitches according to the pattern required.

FOR MOUNTING.—Cut a round piece of paper

Fig. 7.

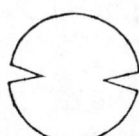

rather less than the size of the flower, to tack the leaves to; cut a triangular piece out of each side, and then sew the edges together, so as to form a shallow saucer; cover one side, the centre half with green, and the outer circles with white plain crochet work. Then with needle and thread tack the petals in the proper places upon the paper base, and so complete the flower.

The pistil and stamens are merely pieces of the fine wire covered with wool of a proper tint.

CLASS II.—FOR MAKING THE LILY CLASS.

Lilies, including lilies of the valley, the water, yellow, African lily, passion flower, fuchsia, Turk's cap, jessamine, iris, &c. &c.

In consequence of their shape, the petals of these flowers are worked in their natural tints, precisely the same way as the "GREEN" leaf of the camilla; according to the flower and the size required, the length of chain must be made, and the single and double trebles worked with judgment, to be increased and decreased according to pattern: they must be carefully wired and mounted with their respective stamens, leaves, and buds.

CLASS III.—TO MAKE BELL FLOWERS.

All bell flowers are formed according to these directions, including the daffodil, gentian, blue bell, &c.

The convolvulus is formed by making a white petal, the size of the camilla, in Fig. 6, then tying on the purple wool at the top of the petal, and working six chains, casting the wool around the hook, and working three trebles in each chain of the white petal to the end; recommencing and working a plain row, inserting the hook twice in every chain; the indentations are formed by working two chains between every eighth treble, the variegated vein being run down with a needle; it is then damped and hotpressed, and joined neatly together with fine cotton.

Wreaths for the head, &c., are formed by making a frame of ribbon wire, and covering it with thin green silk. The roses and leaves are made according to the former directions, and tacked round the foundation. This wreath is adapted for an opera-cap, but is exceedingly neat and novel for an evening party or ball.

KNITTED ARTIFICIAL FLOWERS.

NARCISSUS.

ONE or two flowers only will be needed to form a branch, neither buds nor leaves being required.

Six petals and three stamens for each flower.

Cast on one stitch in white split Berlin wool.

2*d row*.—Make one, and knit rest of row.

3*d*.—Make one, purl the row.

4*th*.—Knit plain row.

5*th*.—Purl plain row.

6*th*.—Make one, knit row.

7*th*.—Make one, purl row.

8*th*.—Knit plain row.

9*th*.—Purl plain row.

10*th*.—Make one, knit row.

11*th*.—Make one, purl row.

12*th*.—Knit row. 13*th*.—Purl row.

14*th*.—Make one, knit row.

15*th*.—Make one, purl row.

You must now knit and purl alternately 10 rows without increase, and then begin to decrease one in the next knitted and purled rows; knit and purl one row plain; decrease one in the next two rows; knit two plain, and thus continue till you have but three stitches left, gather these with a rug-needle and fasten the wool.

The next most important part of this flower is the Nectarius, which looks like a little yellow cup, edged with scarlet.

The petals first made must have a wire sewn

neatly round them, and, like all the white flowers, will look better if washed and slightly blued, before the wire is put on.

FOR NECTARIUS.

Cast on six stitches in very pale yellow wool, split.

1*st row*.—Knit plain. 2*d*.—Purl.

3*d*.—Make one, knit one, repeat through the row.

4*th*.—Purl one row. 5*th*.—Knit one row.

6*th*.—Purl one row.

7*th*.—Make one, knit two, repeat through the row.

8*th*.—Purl one row. 9*th*.—Knit one row.

10*th*.—Purl one row.

Take scarlet wool (or scarlet China silk), knit one row, and cast off very loosely. Sew up the open side. Make a little tuft of pale green, or yellow wool, to fill the bottom of the little cup and preserve its shape; place at the top of these three stamens, each formed by a knot of yellow wool, fixed on a bit of wire. Then take green wool. Cast on six stitches; knit a piece about half an inch long, increasing irregularly about six stitches before you reach the top. Sew this piece under the flower, closing the open side.

The stem should be made of a piece of thin whalebone, about a quarter of an inch in width, which is better covered first, with a strip of green tissue paper, and then with green wool as usual; the flowers must be fixed to the top of this, according to their natural appearance.

BRUSSELS EMBROIDERY ON NET.

We present to our subscribers a new style of ornamental embroidery, which is especially pretty for many purposes. It is worked on a clear Brussels net, not too fine. The diamonds, which appear crossed, are darned with a fine soft cotton. These can be worked with the greatest regularity by counting the threads of the net, and keeping them exactly the same size. Leaving one hole of the net between each short length of the darning, as will be seen in our illustration, gives it a much lighter appearance. The alternate diamonds are filled in with a sprig, embroidered in satin stitch, which shows to great advantage on the light net ground.

CROCHET PURSE.

THE materials are half an ounce of scarlet purse-silk, quarter of an ounce of green ditto, quarter of an ounce of maize-colored ditto, and a quarter of an ounce of black ditto. A steel crochet needle. Begin to work at the bottom of the purse. Make a foundation-chain of 5

Fig, 1.

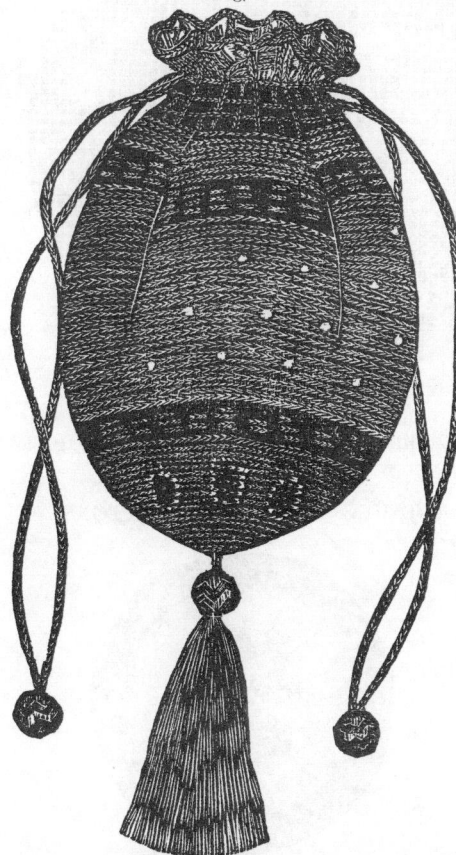

stitches, join them into a circle, and work 7 rounds with scarlet in double crochet, increasing regularly so as to keep the work flat. Then take the maize-colored silk, and work on in rounds, alternately 1 maize colored stitch and 4 scarlet ones. Over these work 3 maize-colored stitches and 2 red stitches; in the following round take the black silk and work the black diamonds edged with maize color. Above the diamonds work 4 scarlet rounds, and leave off increasing. Then begin to work the border seen in Fig. 2; work first 1 maize-colored round, then a black round. Then work the spotted pattern in green and red on a black ground; it

is 4 rounds wide; finish the border with a black and maize-colored round. Then work from illustration 25 rounds in red silk, with black and maize-colored pattern, repeat the border, and

Fig. 2.

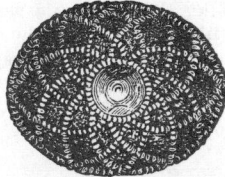

work 3 red rounds; finish off the purse with 5 rounds of open treble stitch in red, and a maize-colored border. Draw a red cord through the first open work round to close the purse. At each end of the cord fasten a black and red grelot, as can be seen in illustration.

BUTTONS FOR DRESSES, ETC.

FIG. 1.—The mould is covered with velvet, a

Fig. 1.

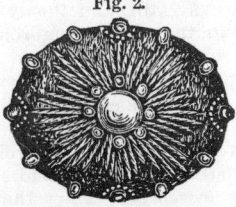

large jet button ornaments the centre, and smaller ones cover the button in a sort of network. Fig. 2 has a velvet covering, and, like

Fig. 2.

Fig. 1, is ornamented with a large bead in the centre, surrounded by smaller ones, and finished with long stitches in purse-silk.

PINCUSHION AND WATCHSTAND IN THE SHAPE OF A CHAIR.

THIS pretty little chair of ebony is six inches high. The seat forms a pincushion, and the watch is hung upon a small gilt hook fastened to the back of the chair. The seat is covered

Fig. 1.

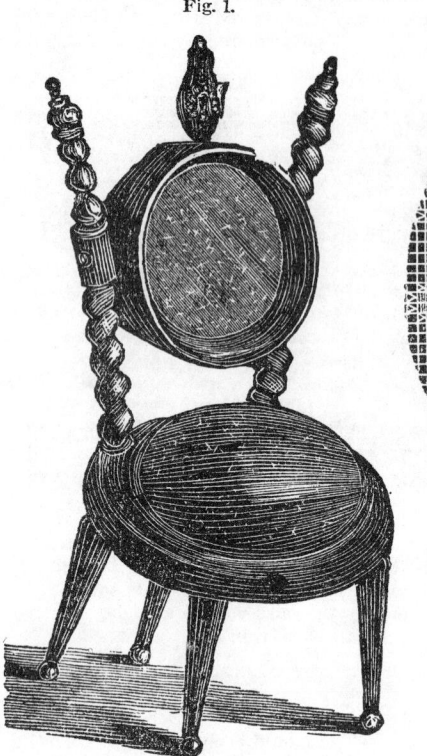

with double crochet; the ground is worked with green silk; the pattern is worked from illustration without cutting off the silk, which is drawn along on the wrong side. One of the spots has six yellow stitches and four black ones in the centre; the second spot is red, and the third purple.

EMBROIDERED KNITTING BAG.
(*See Engraving, Page* 135.)

THIS bag is made of card-board, covered outside with brown satin, and lined with white silk. A design in flowers is embroidered with sewing silk of various colors on the satin. Cut out six pieces of card-board from illustration. Then cut out the pieces of satin and silk, allowing for turnings, observing that the satin should be on the cross; then embroider on the satin with small flowers, the middle flower being in *point de reprise.* Trace the outline as well as the middle vein of the leaves in silk, and sew these threads over in *point de réprise.* When the embroidery is finished, sew all the

pieces together on the right side, leaving only one seam open. Cover the seams with a fine silk cord. Make the handle of brown silk cord, and fasten it in the middle and at the sides with bows of brown satin ribbon. Two wooden acorns joined by an elastic serve to

Fig. 2.

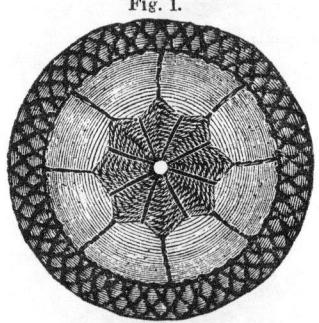

hold the knitting-needle. The elastic is fastened in the middle to the inside of the bag.

DESIGNS FOR FANCY BUTTONS.
Fig. 1.

Fig. 2.

FIG. 1 gives a design in embroidery from which fancy buttons can easily be worked. Fig. 2 is ornamented with cord and bugles.

Embroidered Knitting Bag. See Page 134.

FANCY MAT FOR SMELLING-BOTTLES,

This little mat is made of thin gray cardboard, embroidered in *point russe* with red cotton, and finished around the edge with a plaited frill of colored paper. The mat is seven inches square, and when the work is finished, it is lined with white paper. Fig. 2 represents the border in full size.

Fig. 1.

Fig. 2.

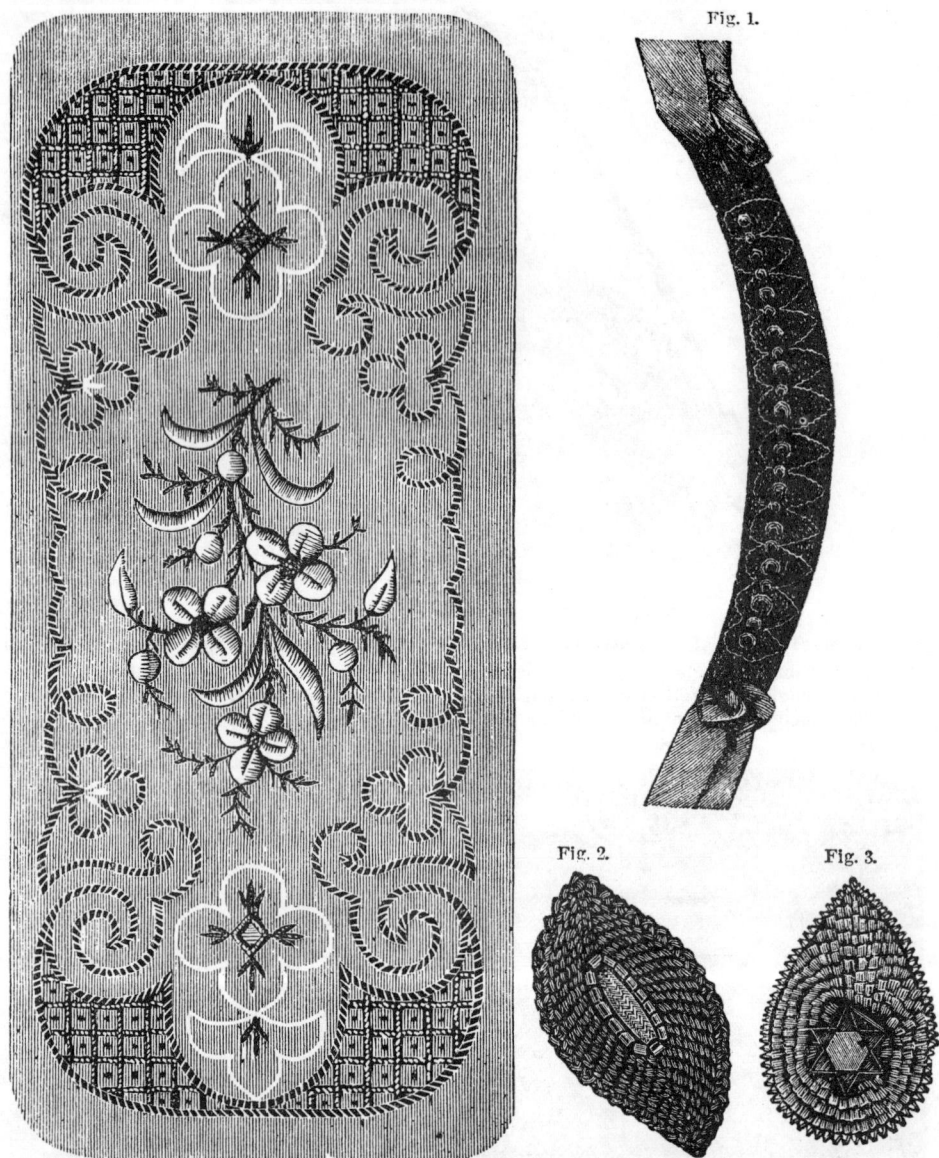

Fig. 1.

Fig. 2.

Fig. 3.

COVER FOR CIGAR-CASE.

EMBROIDERED in gay-colored silks, on gray kid or Russia leather. It is made up on a frame of gilt or steel. The revers side has a monogram worked on it in different colors.

BANDEAU OR NECKLET.

THE foundation is of velvet, cut to the shape and size required, and tied with a bow of ribbon. The bandeau has a piece of ribbon wire, top and bottom, to make it stand up. Either of the leaves can be used.

Fig. 2 is of crochet in silk, with a long button sewn on the middle.

Fig. 3 is of beads threaded on thin wire, with a fancy button in the middle.

IT is best to mark linen on a dry day.

LINEN of all descriptions should be marked with permanent ink.

FINE plain muslin articles ought to be ironed on a clean, soft woolen cloth.

CLEAR-STARCHING to be well done requires very careful previous washing.

BACHELIK PELERINE (KNITTING).

Materials.—Two ounces of white Shetland wool, five steel knitting needles No. 14.

OUR model is composed of two parts; the pelerine, short and open at the back, and prolonged in shawl-like ends in front (as seen in Fig. 1), and the hood (which, when thrown

Fig. 1.

back, forms a kind of cape), the edge of which lies in plaits round the face. The whole bachelik, with the exception of the lace, may be lined with colored sarcenet or llama, and thus converted into a warmer evening wrap if intended for winter use.

The knitting for the pelerine itself is done in two parts, and when completed the slope at the back is sewn together. The pelerine is commenced at the outer edge of the longest side, and the curve for the throat is given to

the knitting after it is completed by pinning the entire piece of knitting out over the pattern (cut in stiffer paper) on an ironing-board or a table with a woollen cover, putting a clean cloth under the work, and damping it with a sponge dipped in very weak gum water. Of course it is the wrong side of the knitting that

is to be damped, and, in pinning it out, this side must be kept uppermost. 218 stitches loosely cast on (divided on the four needles) are required for the length of one-half of the pelerine, and are to be knitted in the pattern shown in detail, and of its real size at Fig. 2*a*.

1st row. Slip 1, * 1 plain, over, knit 2 together, 3 plain, knit two together, over; repeat from *. 2*d*. And all the even-numbered rows. Purl. 3*d*. Slip 1, 2 plain, * over, knit 2 together, 1 plain, knit 2 together, over, 3 plain;

repeat from *. *5th*. Slip 1, 3 plain, * over, slip 1, knit 2 together, pass slipped stitch over, over, 5 plain ; repeat from *. *7th*. Slip 1, 2 plain, * knit 2 together, over, 1 plain, over, knit 2 together, 3 plain ; repeat from *. *9th*. Slip 1, * 1 plain, knit 2 together, over, 3 plain over, knit 2 together ; repeat from *. *11th*.

at that end, and in the next 10 rows, 4 stitches each time. During these same 60 rows, the end towards the back is also to be sloped by taking off the 1st stitch, purling the next, and passing the slipped stitch over at the beginning of each purl row, and in addition at intervals of 6 rows, by knitting 2 together also,

Fig. 2a.—Detail.

Slip 1, knit 2 together, * over, 5 plain, over, slip 1, knit 2 together, pass slipped stitch over ; repeat from *. *13th*. Like 1st, and repeat the pattern. The end of the knitting intended for the back is kept straight for some time, whilst, to give roundness to the front end, a stitch is to be added at the beginning of every row at that end, by bringing the thread over before commencing, until by two repetitions of the pattern 24 rows have been knitted.

at the conclusion of the rows ending at the back. There will then remain 33 stitches for the neck, which are to be cast off. The second half of the pelerine is to be knitted in exactly the same way, but care must be taken to reverse the ends for the back and front, so that the two halves may correspond when joined together. For the width of the hood cast on 82 stitches, and knit the first 32 rows quite straight in the pattern before given ; 112 more

Fig. 3b.—Border.

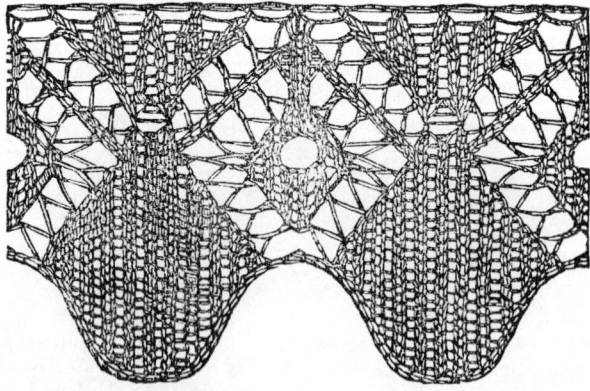

In the next 24 rows, the 12 stitches that have thus been gained are to be decreased by knitting 2 together at the commencement of each row at the front end. In the next 60 rows the front is to have the complement of stitches reduced by two-thirds ; this is done by casting off loosely 5 stitches at the beginning of every row

rows then follow, in which, at intervals of 3 rows, that is every 4th row (being the 33d, 37th, 41st, 45th, etc.), 1 stitch is to be taken in at the beginning and end of the row, so that at the conclusion of the 144 rows 26 stitches only will remain, which are to be cast off.

The lace or edging shown in detail at Fig.

3*b* is knitted separately, and sewn round the pelerine and hood. It is done in pieces, and joined together afterwards, as many stitches being cast on at once as a needle will conveniently hold, but their number must be divisible by 13. *1st row.* * over, knit 2 together; repeat from *. *2d.* And all even-numbered rows, purl. *3d.* * 5 plain, over, knit 3 together, over, 5 plain; repeat from *. *5th.* * 3 plain, knit 2 together, over, 3 plain, over, knit 2 together, 3 plain; repeat from *. *7th.* * 2 plain, knit 2 together, over, 5 plain, over, knit 2 together, 2 plain; repeat from *. *9th.* * 1 plain, knit 2 together, over, 2 plain, over, knit 3 together, over, 2 plain, over, knit 2 together, 1 plain; repeat from *. *11th.* * 1 plain, knit 2 together, over, knit 2 together, over, 3 plain, over, knit 2 together, over, knit 2 together, 1 plain; repeat from *. *13th.* * Knit 3 together, over, 1 plain, over, 5 plain, over, 1 plain, over, knit 3 together; repeat from *. *15th.* * 1 plain, knit 2 together, over, 1 plain, knit 2 together, over three times (these three overs are to be knitted as 3 stitches, purl, plain, and purl in the next row), knit 3 together, 1 plain, over, knit 2 together, 1 plain; repeat from *. *17th.* * 1 plain, knit 2 together, over, 1 plain, over, knit 2 together, 1 plain; repeat from *. *19th.* * 3 plain, over, knit 2 together, 3 plain, knit 2 together, over, 3 plain; repeat from *. *21st.* * 4 plain, over, knit 2 together, 1 plain, knit 2 together, over, 4 plain; repeat from *. *23d.* * 5 plain, over, knit 3 together, over, 5 plain; repeat from *. After the end of this row turn the work, and purl the first 21 stitches; turn and † knit back 13 of these plain; turn again, and purl the first 12 of these last plain stitches, passing the 1st stitch over the 2d, so that the stitches on the wrong or purl side of the work are cast off as you proceed, whilst those on the right or plain side are not cast off till the top of the scallop is reached. * Turn again, and knit the same 11 stitches plain; turn, purl the next 10, passing the 1st over the 2d, so that in each of the purl rows one stitch more is left unknitted at the end every time. Continue repeating from *, but each time the number of stitches is reduced by 1, till you come to only 1 stitch. Then the stitches that have been left on the right or plain side are cast off, which brings you to the commencement of another scallop, for which purl the next 13 stitches, and repeat from †. The stitches remaining from the first 21 stitches knitted of course serve to complete a neighboring scallop on the other side; when another portion of lace is finished, 6 stitches will be found left at the other end, and the first 7, being taken up with them, must be knitted in the same manner as has been described to make a complete scallop, the lace being sewn together on the wrong side as far as the 23d row, where the thick scallops commence. It may sometimes be more convenient for the length required to knit these stitches as a half scallop, which can be done. It is best to sew the lace to the pelerine and hood before they are pinned out; it must also be damped like the rest, and a pin put in the centre of each scallop.

The work, having been damped with gum water, must be allowed to become thoroughly dry before it is taken off the board or table; then the hood is to be sewn round the neck of the pelerine, and the front edge of it plaited in 12 or 14 plaits. The first of these plaits begins five inches above the join at the neck. The hook is either to be tied at the throat with ribbon, or fastened with a middle-sized hook and eye.

BOY'S GAITER.

Materials.—One ounce of white and one-quarter ounce of colored Berlin wool, four knitting-pins No. 15 (bell-gauge.)

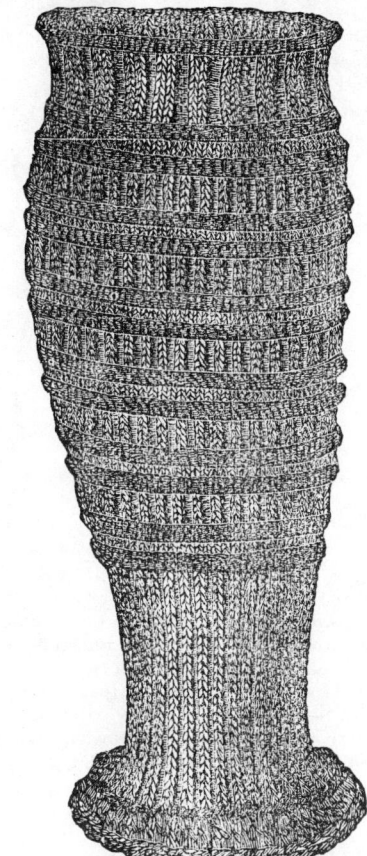

BEGIN at the upper edge with white wool. Cast on sixty-three stitches—twenty on each of two pins, and twenty-three on the third. The twelfth stitch on the third pin is knitted to form the seam at the back.

Knit eighteen rows as for a stocking, alternately two plain, two purled; then, with colored wool, one row plain, two rows purled; then, with white, three rows plain; then colored one row plain, and two purled. For the broad white stripe alternately as follows: Purl one, knit one (the back part of this stitch is knitted in each instance), so as to form a narrow perpendicular stripe. The whole stripe contains seven rows; then the colored is repeated, then the plain white stripe, and so on until, according to design, there are twelve

Fig. 1.

FUR FOR THE NECK.

THIS fur is made of feathers or down. You require a piece of linen, fifteen inches long by one wide; some poultry feathers or down, which should be prepared. As this is a very useful as well as fashionable work, we will describe a good method of preparing feathers for the benefit of those who keep poultry. Feather trimming is much worn, and it is not difficult to make; and, if sold, would prove far

Fig. 2a.--Detail of Fur for the Neck.

Fig. 3b.--Detail of Fur for the Neck.

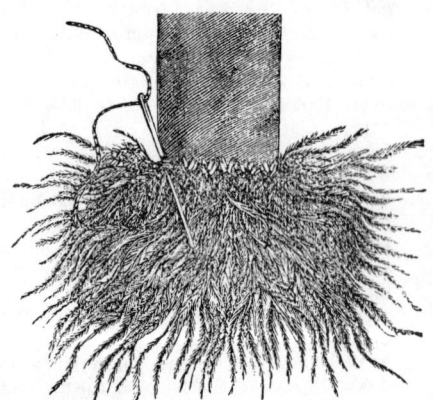

narrow colored stripes. Between them there must, however, be a decrease in the same manner as for the calf of a stocking, and this begins from the seventh stripe in each colored one, so that when the last of these stripes is finished, the number is reduced twelve stitches. Now knit without decreasing forty rows all white of alternately one purled stitch and one plain stitch, then cast off loosely. For the under conclusion, work a few rows of crochet with white wool as follows: In each of the knitted stitches work five double-treble.

In the following row, work one single and one chain between every fifth treble. This raises the trebles into little flutings. At the top and bottom of these flutings, work little scallops of three chain and one single, and work a line of three chain and one single at the top of the gaiter.

more profitable than disposing of the feathers to upholsterers or drapers.

As soon as your feathers are taken from the bird, put them into brown paper bags, which tie close—coarse calico bags would do as well—and put them into a moderate oven, where they should be kept for some hours; this kills all vermin. When you take them out, put on a cloth, and shake them well; then pick each feather out, and cut off the little hard piece of quill at the top. If you intend to make trimming of the feathers, before your birds are plucked they should be gently washed in lukewarm water and soapsuds, with a little whiskey or gin in it; by this means the plumage is rendered perfectly clean and free from all dirt and dust, and, if the birds are left in a *clean* warm place to dry, they can receive no harm. Nearly all birds are washed in this manner before exhibition, on account of the gloss and lustre it gives to the feathers.

Fig. 2*a* shows how each feather should be cut. Prepare a large quantity before you commence working.

Fig. 3*b* shows the manner of sewing on. You take for the first row three or four feathers, and sew them in a row at the extreme end of the linen. They must be sewn on with sewing silk, at about the distance from each other shown in the figure. The stitch used for sewing on is made by working over each feather twice on each side the quill. The figure shows the stitch and the position of the needle so clearly that further explanation is unnecessary.

In the 2d and all other rows the feathers are put close together, and on each side the linen —that is, for this boa for the neck; in making a trimming, they must not be put so close that they fall over each other, but be carefully arranged. Sew the feathers on the linen till about one inch from the middle, then commence the other half, working to the same distance from the middle; then sew the feathers on in a slanting direction, by which means the turning, or rather meeting of the feathers, will not be so visible. When the piece is finished, sew ribbon strings to the extreme ends of the linen to tie it with. When you mount feathers as a trimming, it is well to mount them on material as nearly the color of the feathers as possible. The feathers of the golden-pencilled or spangled Hamburg fowls form a beautiful rich trimming, and a good gray one well marked can be had from the silver-pencilled birds of the same breeds, also from the Brahma Pootra fowls.

BIB WITH CROCHET LACE, FOR BABIES ONE YEAR OLD.

THIS bib is made of calico taken double, inside which skeins of white knitting cotton have

Fig. 1.—Front.

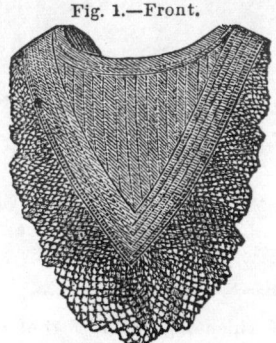

been stitched. The shape of the bib is seen on illustration. The bib is bound with a double strip of calico, with skeins of cotton stitched in. This strip continues on the shoulders about six inches long; a buttonhole is worked

in the end of each shoulder-piece. The bib is fastened by means of these buttonholes, with button on the waistband, made like the bib. Then edge the bib with a crochet border, which is narrower round the slope of the neck. This lace is gathered and worked in the following

Fig. 2.—Back.

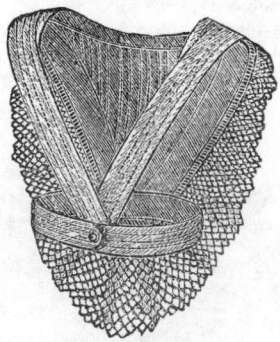

manner: Make a foundation chain the length required, and work on this always alternately 1 treble, 1 chain, missing one stitch of the foundation chain under the latter. *2d row* *: 2 double, divided by 3 chain; on the next chain stitch 7 chain, missing 1 treble, 1 chain, 1 treble, under them repeat from *. The following rows are worked in the same manner, only work the two double, divided by three chain, round the chain stitch scallop of the preceding row.

MATCH-BOX IN SHAPE OF A DRUM.

THIS match-box consists of a strip of cardboard eighteen inches and three-fifths long, two inches and three-fifths wide, rolled up in such

a manner as to leave an opening in the middle measuring two inches and three-fifths across; it is then gummed so as to remain in this shape. The case is then bound on both edges with light brown *glacé* silk, and covered on the inside with silver paper, and on the outside with a strip of embroidery consisting of alternate red and white cloth Vandykes; these Vandykes are fastened on a strip of calico, and edged with gold braid; the white Vandykes are embroidered with point russe stitches of different colored purse silk, the red ones are ornamented with a colored spot worked in satin stitch and with gold beads. On both sides of the strip of embroidery paste on a strip of card-

and on the outside with sand-paper. The cover consists likewise of a round piece of card-board covered on the top with white leather, and underneath with sand-paper; fasten two sticks of wood on the upper surface to imitate the sticks of a drum.

LAMP SHADE.

THIS lamp shade is made of glass paper, and imitates glass mosaic. It consists of six parts,

Fig. 1.—Lamp Shade.

Fig. 1.—Shoe-Bag Closed.

Fig. 2.—Rosette of Lamp Shade.

Fig. 2.—Shoe-Bag Open.

board three-fifths of an inch wide, covered with light brown silk, ornamented with Vandyked lines of gold braid, fastened down with small black stitches. These strips must come slightly beyond the edges of the case. Then fasten a card-board bottom into the case, which must be covered on the inside with silver paper,

the size of which depends on that of the lamp. For each part cut two pieces of the same size, one of white transparent paper, the other of white glass paper. The pattern is traced on the transparent paper; the pieces and strips of the colored glass paper are pasted on it with gum, following the outlines of the pattern. On our pattern the divisions are ornamented alternately with a mosaic rosette and with mosaic patterns. Fig. 2 shows the rosette and a part of the mosaic pattern full size with the manner of working them. The choice of colors depends on personal taste.

When the mosaic patterns are completed, the ornamented parts must be pasted on the white glass paper thus :—

The different parts are joined together with strips of thick white paper pasted on the outer and inner sides of the divisions wherever they meet. On the outer side these strips are ornamented with leaves; a similar ornament is fastened round the upper and lower edge of the shade. These leaves are made of different colored crape; they must be pasted on in such a manner that the edge of one leaf overlaps the next. Instead of glass paper pieces of *glacé* silk can be used.

EMBROIDERY SHOE-BAG.
(*See Instructions, Page* 42.)

THIS shoe-bag is made of brown cloth. It is ten inches and one-fifth long, eight inches and two-fifths wide, and fitted up with division and flaps, so as to form two pockets. The outer parts, the lower lappets, and the revers are cut in one piece, taking for the same a piece of double cloth, thirty-two inches long, eight inches and two-fifths wide. Between the double folds of the cloth fasten a piece of cardboard for the back and front part of the bag, leaving the revers and the lower flap free. Then cut a piece of card-board for the division of the bag; cover it on both sides with cloth, and fasten it with overcast stitch on to the part of the leather cloth which is to form the lower flaps. Then join the front and back parts of the bag on to strips of cloth four and four-fifths inches wide with overcast stitch. The flaps at the sides and at the back of the bag are slanted off at the corners, and fastened with overcast stitch. Then work the embroidery on the outer part of the bag; it consists partly of brown silk braid, sewn on with hemstitch of light brown silk, and partly of loose buttonhole stitch of light brown silk. Lastly, fasten a thick handle of cord and elastic, for fastening the bag.

BABY'S GLOVE.

Materials.—Four needles No. 15, four No. 13 required. Care must be taken to use the needles as directed. Half an ounce of white German wool, a quarter of an ounce of colored.

WITH white wool cast 40 stitches on one needle, knit them off on three needles, 12 on two, 16 on the third. Use needles No. 13. Knit 3, seam 1 alternately for 2 rounds.

Take colored wool. Knit 1 round plain. Seam 3 rounds. With white wool. Knit 1 round plain. Knit 3, seam 1 alternately for 3 rounds. Take colored wool. Knit 1 round plain. Seam 3 rounds. With white wool knit 1 round plain. Knit 3, seam 1 alternately for 7 rounds.

You are now to take needles No. 15 and colored wool. Knit 2 rounds plain. Next round * Knit 2, make 1, knit two together; repeat from *. Knit 2 rounds plain. You may break off the colored wool. Take needles No. 13 and white wool. Knit 2 rounds plain.

3d round. Knit 1, seam 1 alternately all round.

4th and *5th.* Knit plain. Observe 2 rounds plain knitting are to be repeated between each increasing round.

6th. Knit 1, seam 1, raise 1. This is done this first time in the round by, when you come to the 3d stitch, before working it, putting your needle through the loop below, in reality the stitch of the last row, and drawing the wool through it; the second time you raise it is done after you have knitted or seamed a stitch by, before you let the loop down, putting your needle in at the back of the same loop and drawing the wool through. Knit 1, seam 1, raise 1. Knit 1, seam 1 alternately rest of round.

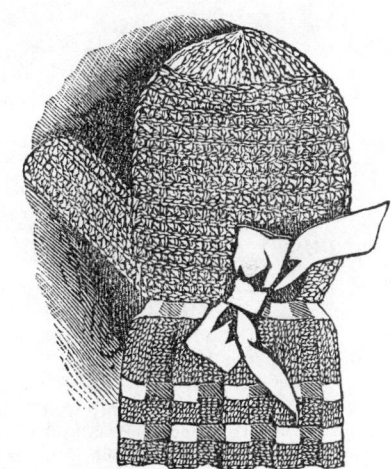

9th. Knit 1, seam 1, raise 1. Seam 1, knit 1 twice (this means repeat the seam 1, knit 1 alternately so many times between the raisings), raise 1. Knit 1, seam 1 alternately rest of round.

12th. Knit 1, seam 1, raise 1. Knit 1, seam 1 three times. Raise 1. Knit 1, seam 1 alternately rest of round.

15th. Knit 1, seam 1, raise 1. Seam 1, knit 1 four times. Raise 1. Knit 1, seam 1 alternately rest of round.

18th. Knit 1, seam 1, raise 1. Knit 1, seam 1 five times. Raise 1. Knit 1, seam 1 alternately rest of round.

21st. Knit 1, seam 1, raise 1. Seam 1, knit 1

six times. Raise 1. Knit 1, seam 1 alternately rest of round.

22d. Knit 3, slip on a piece of wool the next 12 stitches, and secure it to prevent their slipping off. These stitches are afterwards taken up for the thumb. Rest of round knit plain.

23d. Knit plain.

* 24th. Knit 1, seam 1 alternately. Knit 2 rounds plain. Repeat from * five times more.

You now use the smaller needles to reduce the size at the top of the glove. 1st round.

MAT WITH FOOT MUFF.

THIS pretty mat forms a foot muff in the shape of a shell. It is made of fine brown cloth, ornamented with a rich pattern of brown soutache. The mat is edged all round with a deep worsted fringe of two shades. The mat measures thirty-four inches long and twenty-eight inches wide. It must be lined with brown Holland, and slightly quilted. The foot muff is worked separately, lined and quilted, and bound with brown worsted braid. It should be

Knit 1, seam 1 alternately. Two rounds plain knitting. 4th. Knit 3, knit 2 together alternately. Knit 2 rounds plain. 7th. Knit 2, knit 2 together alternately. Knit 2 rounds plain. Take the larger-sized needles, and knit one round plain with them. Break off a sufficient length of wool, slip all the stitches on it, and draw together.

THUMB.—Use needles No. 13. Take up thumb-stitches thus: 4 on each of three needles, adding two more on the 3d by taking up two where there is the opening. * Knit 2 rounds plain. One round seaming 1 and knitting 1 alternately. Repeat from * three times more. Take needles No. 15, knit 2 rounds plain. 3d round. Knit 2 together, knit 3 alternately, end with knit 2. Knit one round plain. Knit another plain round, but with the larger needles. Draw wool through the loops, and fasten off.

To make a left-hand glove, form the thumb at the end of the third needle, instead of at the beginning of the first. Make the 1st, raising when within four loops of the end of the round.

stitched through in such a manner as to imitate the ribs of the shell. The muff can be lined with fur or with crochet in imitation of the same.

DIRECTIONS FOR RICE WORK.

BY far the best thing for sticking rice to cardboard is white of egg, as it does not discolor the rice, and is more effectual than any gum. The card-board must first be wetted with the white of egg (a small paint brush is the best thing to use), and then a thick layer of rice be sprinkled indiscriminately over the part wetted; this must be allowed to dry on (which will take some little time), and then the loose rice which has not stuck shaken off; then more white of egg, and another layer of rice, and so on until the required thickness is obtained. It requires patience, as it is useless to put more rice until the first layer is dry and has firmly stuck. Any little interstices can easily be filled up afterwards.

WHAT-NOT.—BRAIDED IN A NEW STYLE.

Materials.—A piece of fine green cloth, stamped according to the engraving, for the back and front of the What-not; one piece of gold-colored Russia silk braid, one piece of crimson purse silk, four yards cord (gold and green), and four tassels to match.

THERE are two novelties in this pretty what-not : one is the shape, which is extremely elegant ; the other is the mode of braiding, which is done, not by taking the stitches through the soutache, but across it at regular distances, with silk of a contrasting color. It is thus possible to harmonize three colors in the same article ; and, indeed, the work quite loses the appearances of ordinary braiding. The ends of the braid must be drawn through to the wrong side of the cloth as usual.

It is afterwards to be made up, over stout card-board, and lined with crimson or gold-colored silk. There is a plain piece at each end, the back and front being about two inches apart. The lining should be set on in plaits here and there. The bottom has a layer of wadding under the silk, and the edges are finished with silk cord. One pair of tassels hang from the cord by which it is suspended ; the other two are placed at the corners in front.

The colors selected should be such as will suit the room. Brown cloth with gold-colored braid will always look well, whether crossed with green, crimson, scarlet, or blue.

This style of braiding may be employed for any other purpose with excellent effect.

COLLAR IN IMITATION OF HONITON LACE.

IF, very fine cotton is used for this crochet you will find it closely resembles Honiton lace. When all the sprays and leaves are worked, cut a piece of paper the shape you wish the collar, join them together upon the paper, and

THE ROSE.—Make a chain of 12, unite, then 7 ch, 1 dc in the 2d chain in the ring, * 4 ch, 1 dc in the 2d ch, repeat from * 3 times, then 4 ch, 1 dc 6 long, or the thread once round the needle, 1 dc, take the cotton to the back of the round, 1 single in the 1st dc in the 1st round, 5 ch, 1 single in the next dc, repeat all round;

work a row of long and treble stitches for the neck; the longest of these are double treble or the thread 3 times round the needle; upon this row for the neck work a row of plain double crochet, then a row of 2 ch, 1 long in the 3d dc underneath.

then over every 5 ch work 1 dc, 8 long, 1 dc. For the 3d round of leaves work 6 ch, 1 single upon the single at the back in the 2d round of leaves; repeat 5 times, then over every 6 ch work 1 dc 10 long, 1 dc. For the 4th round of leaves, 7 ch, 1 single on the next single at the back; repeat

5 times ; over each 7 ch work 1 dc, 4 long, 4 treble (or the thread twice round the needle), 4 long, 1 dc, then fasten off. Work double the number of rows given in the engraving.

THE LEAVES.—You work 6 sprays of 3 leaves each, and 6 odd leaves ; they are worked in ribbed crochet. Commence with 8 ch, work back on it 7 dc, 2 ch, turn, 7 dc, working the first on the first of the 2 ch, * 1 ch, turn ; work

miss the first dc on the round and work 2 dc in each stitch until you come to the other side ; then fasten off.

BUTTERFLY PINCUSHION.

THIS cushion is made of fine white cashmere, embroidered in colored silks. The shape must first be cut in card-board, and both sides

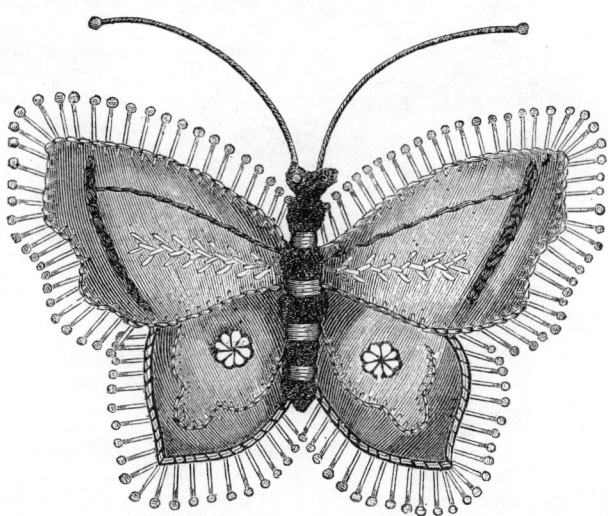

dc to the end, then 3 ch, turn, 1 dc on the 2 ch and each of the next dc, excepting the last, which is left unworked ; repeat from * until you have 7 little ribs, then work to the outside again, 3 ch, turn, dc on each stitch excepting the last 3, 1 ch, turn, dc to the end, 3 ch, turn, 1 dc on each stitch excepting the last 6, turn, dc to the end, 3 ch, turn, dc on each stitch of last row, then on each stitch left in all the preceding rows, and on the edge of the rows also ; when you come to the first row of ch, turn, work 6 ch, 1 long on the 3d dc, * 2 ch, 1 long on the 3d dc ; repeat from * to the end, turn, and work dc on each stitch ; then work the other half the leaf like the first, joining the inside of each row to the 2d dc on the vein, and therefore leaving out the ch stitch at the turn.

THE BUDS.—18 of these small buds are required for the collar. Commence with 2 ch, work 5 dc in the first ch, join, work a round of dc on this 5 dc, working 2 in each stitch of last round, then 13 ch, work back dc on the chain, then 2 dc in each stitch on the round ; now 4 ch, 1 long on the 5th of the 13 ch, 3 ch, 1 treble in the 9th ch, 4 ch, draw through the last chain on the left side of the bud ; then turn and work dc on the last little row as far as the round, on which work 4 single, missing the first dc ; turn, 1 dc, 2 long, 12 treble, 4 long, then 1 dc on the join at the top of the buds, the 9 ch, 1 single on the first 3 times, 1 single on the last dc, 4 long, 12 treble, 2 long, 1 dc on the left side of the bud ;

covered, the edge being finished with buttonhole stitch. The body and head are made of fine white cotton, with gold braid over it. The feelers are of gilt wire. The pins are allowed to stand up around the edge.

LETTER FOR MARKING.

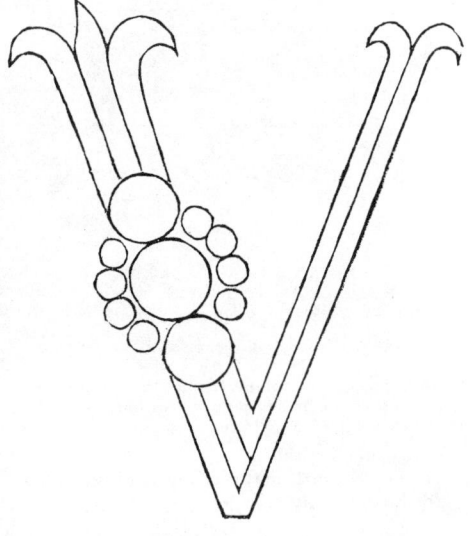

PINCUSHION.

THIS is a good design for a showy pincushion, likely to prove saleable at a fair. A round box must first be procured, and the lid well stuffed with sawdust, and covered with red cloth, worked all round with a row of herringbone stitches in black silk. In the centre of the lid there is a small octagon cushion covered

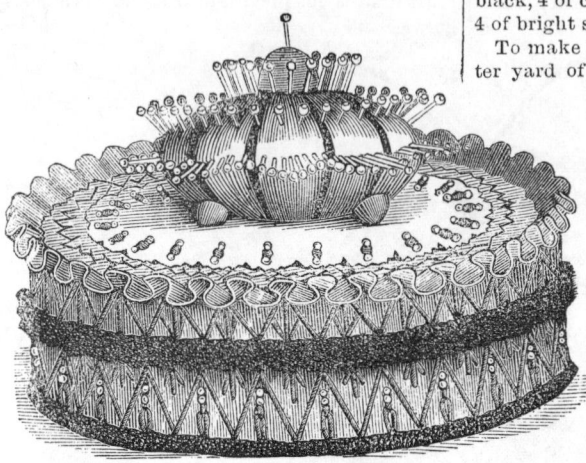

with white cloth, and standing on a flat frill of the same pinked out at the edge, and decorated with crystal beads. This small cushion is for black pins. The sides of the box are decorated with a ruche and point russe, worked with black silk.

KNITTED WORKBASKET.

Materials.—This is done in filoselle. 4 skeins of deep maize, 6 of bright scarlet, 6 of dark scarlet or claret, and 3 of black, are required.

CAST on 37 stitches.

1st row. Seam 1, make 1, slip 1, repeat.
2d. Seam 2, slip 1, repeat.

3d. Seam 2 together, slip 1, make 1, repeat, at the end of the row seam 1, instead of 2 together.

4th. Seam 1, * slip 1, seam 2, repeat from *.

5th. Slip 1, make 1, seam 2 together, repeat at the end of the row. Seam 1 after seaming 2 together, repeat from 2d row till you have worked the colors 14 times. Knit 4 rows of black, 4 of claret, 4 of bright scarlet, 6 of maize, 4 of bright scarlet, 4 of claret, and repeat.

To make up the basket—one and three-quarter yard of rose-colored satin and 14 yards of satin ribbon, three-quarters of an inch wide, with an edge to it, will be required. Join the knitting round, and quilt a piece of satin, the same depth and length as the knitting, then hem a stiff wire in at the top and bottom, and 8 pieces of wire the depth of the satin, at equal distances, 1 piece at each end and each side, and 1 piece between each of these. For the bottom of the basket, cover a piece of cardboard, 11 inches long by 8 wide, with the corners rounded off, with quilted satin, stitch a strap across the centre of it, with divisions run in for scissors, stiletto, etc. For the pockets, cut a piece of satin on the cross, one and a half yard long and 7 inches deep, double it and run a tuck a quarter of an inch deep, and put a prepared whalebone through it. For the pincushions at the end, cover a piece of cardboard, about 4 inches long and 3 deep; double the corners back and cover the top, then stuff them with bran, and place one at each end, then put the pockets round the basket, 4 on each side of the pincushions, with one small one about the size for a thimble, then put a quilling of ribbon round each pincushion. For the cover, quilt a piece of satin, the same size as the bottom, and line it with sarcenet, with a stiff muslin between, then edge it round with a quilled ribbon. For the handles, take two pieces of prepared whalebone, the length you wish them, then place them together, and wind a thread tightly over them, then cover them with swan's-down calico, and wind a ribbon firmly over it, giving it here and there a stitch to prevent its slipping.

This very useful basket has been much admired, and is very easy to make.

SHIRT BUTTONS.

THESE are very easy to make and pleasant work, and by the help of some linen thread and a sewing needle you need never be without a button, which sometimes does happen; for wear we cannot recommend them. Thread your needle with a long length of thread, then wind it twelve times round the end of a thick lead pencil; loop the first end of the thread with the second after having wound it round; now slip it off the pencil, and work over this ring of 12 threads with embroidery buttonhole stitch. The detail 2a gives you the position of

Fig. 1.—2a.

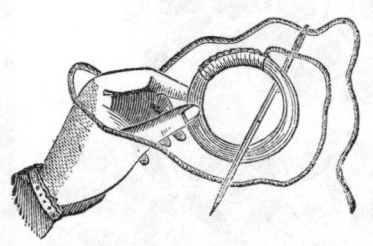

the needle and cotton exactly. When this is finished pass your thread through the inner thread again, and make the cross line. (See detail 2b). Bring the needle out at a, cross

Fig. 2.—2b.

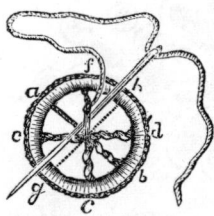

over to b, pass the thread over this cross, line once, and then insert in the ring at c, pass under the line into the middle again, and catch the needle through the half loop just made in leaving b. Then cross to d. Work in this

Fig. 3.—2c.

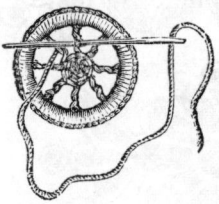

manner regularly from letter to letter, always taking through the middle in the half loop last made; it will leave one-half bar, a to b, plain; this does not matter. When all are crossed over work round and round, as in detail 2c, putting the needle under each little bar as you see it there, until the whole of the centre is filled in. It is then very much the same size as the engraving, and will be far better than no button at all.

FRINGE FOR COUVRETTES, ETC.

THIS fringe is made of white cotton cord the strands are knotted a short distance from

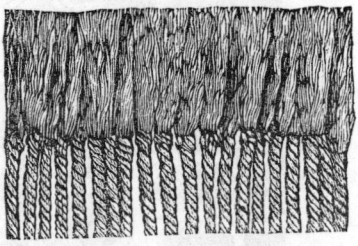

the bottom, and then fringed out. This fringe can be used for a variety of purposes where cotton fringe is used.

FOR A SOFA CUSHION.

Materials.—1 ounce each of 4 shades of violet, 4 of green, and 2 ounces of black, 1 ounce of carmine filoselle.

MAKE a chain of 20 inches.

1st row. Take up the wool on the needle, insert the needle in the first loop, draw the wool through; draw the wool through 2 loops on the needle, repeat this in every loop.

2d. Draw the wool through 1 loop, then through 2 at a time, to the end of the row.

Repeat these two rows alternately; in the 3d row the needle be inserted in the long stitch in front; work 2 rows of each shade, from the dark violet to the lightest; 4 of the lightest, 2 of each back to the darkest, 2 of black, 2 of filoselle, 2 black; this completes one stripe; work a green stripe in the same way, and repeat the violet and green alternately. The cushion looks well with both sides worked, and it should then be lined with deep maize gold satin or silk, and made up with tassels and cord to match; if both sides are worked, the chain must be 36 inches.

PEARL NECKLACE.

THE mode of making this pretty-shaped necklace is too clearly shown in the design to need

description. The beads should be strung on round white elastic, and fastened by satin bows.

BRODERIE ANGLAISE FLOUNCING.

(See Instructions, Page 151.)

PETTICOAT TRIMMING.—IN BRODERIE ANGLAISE.

Materials.—French muslin, with royal embroidery cotton, No. 30, and Moravian, No. 24.

THIS engraving is on a scale just half the size of the original pattern. It is so strong that it is peculiarly adapted for jupons, which are worn, generally, most elaborately trimmed. The edge, which consists of a single scallop, is considerably raised; the Moravian cotton is to be used for this purpose. The wheels are all worked round in button-hole stitch, over a tracing of three threads, a rosette being in the centre of each. Indeed, if the entire pattern be overcast, instead of being sewed in the usual way, it will contribute much to the durability as well as the appearance of the work.

BRODERIE ANGLAISE FOR FLOUNCING.

(*See Illustration, Page* 150.)

Material.—French embroidery cotton, No. 20.

THIS description of work, now so extremely fashionable for every description of dress, is usually done on fine jacconet muslin; and, to prepare the pattern, either of the following methods may be used : Place the muslin over the pattern, taking care to keep it even and tight; then, with a fine camel-hair brush, and a solution of indigo or powder blue, mixed with gum-water, copy the outline of the pattern, and, to continue it, take care, after one length of the design is drawn, to place the muslin so that the pattern joins correctly. The other method, which is useful for thicker material—take the design, and, with a fine penknife or scissors, cut out the blue parts of the pattern, place it over the material to be used, and trace it round the cut-out parts as above directed ; pierce the small eyelet-hole with a stiletto. When the pattern is prepared, tack the muslin on a piece of oil-cloth (green is the best color to work on for all descriptions of embroidery) ; run twice round the outline of the pattern with the cotton used double, and join the open spaces, cut a small piece out of the centre of the rounds and ovals, and, with the single cotton, work the edges in overcast stitch—the cotton run round, and the edges cut, forming the foundation. In the parts between the ovals and rounds, when there is only a small division of muslin, the whole should be overcast so as to form one bar between the open spaces. Repeat the same for the ovals which form the scallop round the outer edge, the diamonds of twelve ovals, and the rounds which form the Vandykes. The remainder of the pattern is worked in the same manner; but, instead of the overcast stitch, the open spaces are to be sewn thickly over. A small portion only of the pattern should be cut out at a time; and, should the design be worked on a fine material, use cotton No. 24 or 30,

---

EMBROIDERED COLLAR.

Materials.—French muslin, with embroidery cottons, Nos. 70 and 50; and boar's head sewing cotton, No. 90.

As the popularity of embroidery in muslin has become greater during the past year than it had been for a long period previous to it, so the skill of the majority of lady-workers has greatly increased; and we can now venture on presenting them with designs of a more elaborate nature than we have hitherto done, in the hope that our friends will be tempted, by the novel style of the pattern, to try the effect of a blending of the open work with satin-stitch.

The medallions are given of the full size, and any number may be used for a collar, according to the taste of the wearer. One half must fall in one direction, and the other half in the opposite one. Perhaps the design may appear hardly deep enough to those who are accustomed to the outrageous size of some of the mousquetaire collars; but very large collars are entirely exploded, and the dimensions of this now given are quite in accordance with the mode.

The design is so clearly seen in the engraving that no description of it is required. The finest embroidery cotton is to be used for the satin-stitch, and for sewing round the eyelet-holes; the coarser for the button-hole stitch; the boar's head cotton for the herring-bone.

ROSE AND PANSY: CONE-WORK.

THE materials are pine and larch cones, beech-nuts and shells, acorns, lime-tree blossoms, etc.; moss, thin and thick flower-wire, card-board, brown tissue-paper, amber varnish, to make the hard rind soft, so as to enable a needle or wire stalk to be put through. The shapes must often be sharpened with the scissors for the different flowers.

A dwarf pine-cone gives the inner petal part

Handkerchief Case, with Scent Bottles. See next page.

a small paint-brush, a small fine brush, thick gum or glue.

To collect the materials found in wood and grove, autumn is the best time. We will venture to believe that most of our readers who have from time to time had their attention and interest taken up by our patterns and directions for using the treasures of the wood, will have a sufficient quantity of collected material in store, and those who have not, we hope to arouse to exertion and trial of this pretty and useful work.

The cones must be cleaned with a brush so as to remove the dust, and laid in river water, of a rose; around this are grouped cone-leaves curved flat to the outside (of single leaves cut off a large pine cone) in reversed rows, till you have the required size; the two last leaf-circles must be bent over to the outside. Beech-nuts, pasted over with brown dyed moss, are used for the rosebuds.

For the pansy, the two upper petals are cut off larch cones, the three lower ones of pine cones, and then tied on the wire stock around a small fruit knot, taken from the lime tree; the black streaks coming out from the middle of the pansy petals are made with ink.

Pretty bell-flowers are obtained from acorns

hollowed out, which, cut off to the half, are slit up and rounded off in four curves. A very pretty small sprig is of beech-nuts; every three and three glued together, and held by pieces of wire.

HANDKERCHIEF CASE, WITH SCENT BOTTLES.

(See Engraving, Opposite Page.)

MADE of card-board, covered with blue satin,

semble natural flowers. Fine flower-wire, green tissue-paper, water-colors, gum, and cotton, are the materials needed. The feathers must be cut to the shape of the petals shown in Figs. 9, 11, 12, 13, 14, and 17, gummed at the lower parts, and neatly fixed to the wire stalks with cotton; then the stalks are covered with paper. The stamens in Fig. 15 are of cut feathers; but the centre must be of cotton, first tied up into a little bunch, next gummed, then dipped into silver-sand, and afterwards into

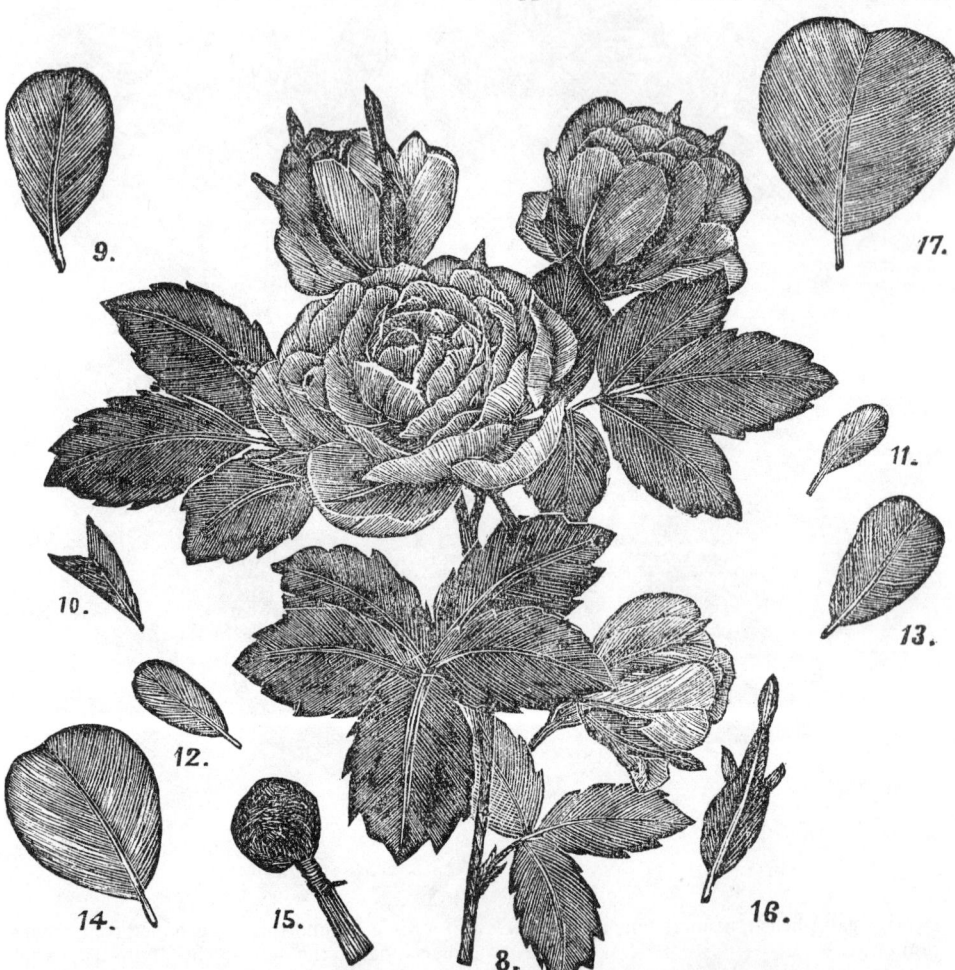

quilted on the inside, plain on the outside, and edged with a silk cord. The bottles are in the corners. The covers turn back. When closed, make a complete cover.

FEATHER FLOWERS: ROSES.

THE feathers of which these pretty flowers are made are those of common poultry. White are preferable, as, with water-colors and a camel-hair pencil, they may be painted to re-

yellow ochre. The leaves and calyces must be painted in two shades of green. Judson's dyes will be found suitable for coloring purposes.

WATCH CASE.

THE engraving represents a watch stand; the back is made with a box to hold the watch; the front is made of wood; the design on it is etched in lamp-black and Indian ink; the initials are worked in silk and put at the back.

We have seen book stands made in this manner, but to save the expense of good wood and workmanship for etching on wood, the design was etched on card-board; the groundwork

Fig. 1.—Veil.

was filled in with lampblack, and then varnished in imitation of ebony. This watch stand might be made in the same manner.

WORK-BASKET FOR THE TABLE.

Two dozen skeins of each of two shades of light violet wool; seven-eighths of a yard of

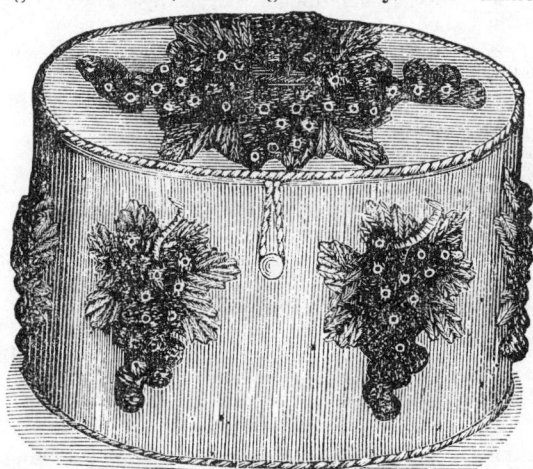

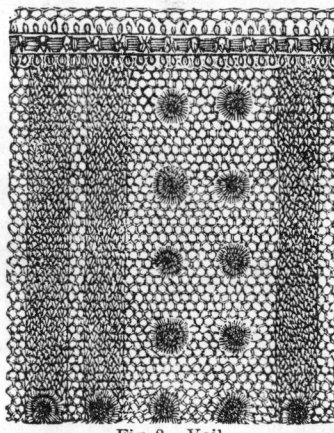

Fig. 2.—Veil.

very fine Cashmere, of a pretty French gray; two or three sheets of thin card-board; one yard of silk to match the Cashmere as nearly as possible, if not violet or rose-color to contrast with it; about one-fourth of thin cloth of a

beautiful light shade, and the same quantity of a rich dark shade of the green cloth; four skeins of shaded green silk. Cut out six large leaves and four smaller ones, but leave the centres of them (natural leaves are the best to copy for the shape); mark the veins of the leaves and stitch them in chain stitch with shaded green embroidery silk (they need only be stitched as far as the work will show), place the leaves two in front, two behind, and one at each end, and the larger one on the top of the basket. To make the grapes, cut a thick piece of mill-board the size given, and wind into the hole as much German wool as you can of one of the shades of violet, then cut it along the outer edge, and pass a strong string along the inner edge; when all is cut tie the wool as tightly as it is possible to do, or, when combing the wool, a great deal of it will come out. Comb just the surface only with a large comb, then take a finer and a still finer, till the wool is quite soft and fluffy; cut it with a sharp pair of scissors into the shape of a grape, some larger and some smaller. A great many grapes will be required. Sew them on as shown in the engraving; but first of all cut two pieces of card-board eight inches wide by thirty inches long, and three ovals eight and

chenille are gummed on. It is finished with two rows of pearl edge, with a line of beads in the middle.

UMBRELLA CASE.

The case, which is intended to contain four umbrellas or parasols for travelling, is made of strips of Holland joined together, and orna-

Fig. 1.

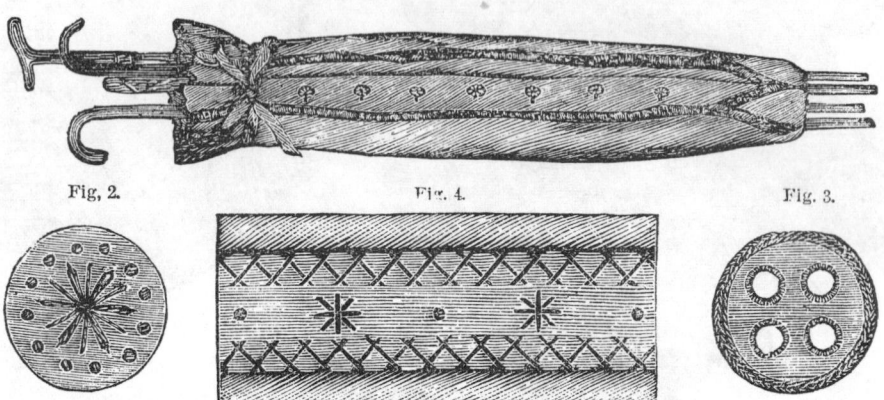

Fig, 2.　　　　　　Fig. 4.　　　　　　Fig. 3.

half inches wide by eleven inches long; cover the long piece neatly with the Cashmere, and measure the distances where the grapes are to come. The leaves will require a great deal of neat sewing at the edge; then make a stem to each bunch of grapes with a thin stiff cord, place it on as shown in the engraving, and stitch it over with brown embroidery silk, sew on the grapes as shown in the engraving, line the top with gray or violet silk and trim with violet cord; the oval at the bottom to be covered inside with silk, and outside with cloth and sewed into the band.

mented over the joins with a small pattern in embroidery, the design for which is shown in the full size in Fig. 4. Fig. 2 shows the embroidery for the buttons; Fig. 3 the mode of making and binding the bottom of the case. This, of course, is in a greatly reduced size. The pointed pieces joined to the bottom will be easily copied from design Fig. 1. The top of the case is buttonholed in small scallops. The slide, into which a piece of sarcenet ribbon is run, is covered with a strip of the border shown in Fig. 4.

VEIL,
WITH BORDER OF TUCKED NET, ORNAMENTED WITH CHENILLE AND BEADS.

(*See Engravings, Page* 155.)

The shape of the veil is shown in Fig. 1; a small piece of the border in the full size in Fig. 2. The thick part of the border is formed by running tucks in the net. The little dots of

GLOVE-BOX.

A card-board box will serve for the foundation. This is covered outside with puffed satin, and inside with scented wadding, covered with quilted satin. The top may be of velvet or satin, embroidered with purse silk. The top is finished with a ruche of quilled ribbon.

FRINGE.

MADE of wool, with netted heading, and balls at the end. It is suitable for mantles or overdresses.

with pockets, in which to put tubes of color, paper of different sizes, etc. Elastic bands hold the brushes. The case is fastened by a band of broad elastic.

Fig. 1.

Fig. 2.

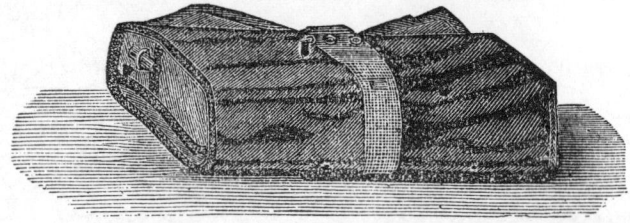

ARTIST'S CASE.

FIG. 1 shows the case open; Fig. 2 closed. The outside is of American cloth, bound at the edges with braid, and fastened by a band of elastic. The inside is of Holland; it is fitted

THEY who are in the greatest spiritual danger seldom manifest any spiritual anxiety. If a man exhibits the slightest solicitude about his soul's welfare, he certainly has not outlived his day of grace.

CORNER FOR A POCKET HANDKERCHIEF

FOR MARKING A LADY'S WARDROBE.

SOFA PILLOW IN LONG-HOOK CROCHET.

Materials.—Two colors of 8 thread or double Berlin wool (these colors should be adapted to the tint of hangings of the room) ; one skein of shaded double wool, either scarlet or any other hue which will harmonize. The cushion from whence the engraving is taken is composed of stone-color and light emerald green (not grass green). The scroll work is scarlet ; one skein of the darkest claret is necessary for dividing the pieces. A cushion of calico, the size of the crochet, cut in the same shaped pieces, then joined together, then well waxed by rubbing a lump of beeswax on the inside to prevent the feathers from coming through, and then filled with four pounds of feathers, will make a handsome cushion. A crochet-hook nine inches long, and, on measuring round with a piece of tape, it should measure half an inch and one-eighth over, or, in other words, five-eighths of an inch.

Explanation of Stitch, which it were well to practise first on a foundation of ten stitches, and decrease every other row :—

Foundation row.—Make 21 chain as in ordinary crochet ; miss the 1st chain or loop ; place the hook through the next ; catch hold of the wool at the back ; pull it through as a loop on the hook, *still* keeping it on the hook. Repeat the same to the end of the chains, *still keeping all the loops on the hook, till there are 20 loops on the hook.*

1st row.—Twist the wool over the hook ; pull it through the two loops nearest the point of the hook, thus working it backwards. Twist the wool over again, pulling it through the next two, and continue working backwards till there is only one loop on the hook.

2d.—On examining the work, a row of un-twisted loops will be found in *front*, not *on the edge;* miss the first long loop; place the hook through the next; draw the wool through as a loop on the hook, still keep it there, and con-tinue till there are as many loops on the hook as was commenced with. Count this row every time to see there is no diminution of stitches till the decrease. Make 21 loops; * now work 10 rows on, till 5 long loops in front can be counted; then decrease at the end of next row on left-hand side, by taking the two last of the front loops together. Now work the row back, and take the last three loops together on the right-hand side; repeat from * until there are only four loops on the work. *But observe that, after the decrease on the right-hand side* IN THE NEXT ROW, *the hook must be inserted in the* THIRD LONG STITCH, *or there will be no decrease; and be sure to take up the last loop on the left-hand side in every row that is not decreased.* Now, with 4 loops on the hook, twist the wool over the hook; draw it through two loops again; twist over; draw through 2; then again through 2; now

place the hook through 2d long in front; pull the wool through, then again through next long, and pull the wool through; now through 2 loops backwards; and again through 2; then 1 chain, and fasten off. Now there are 43 long loops on the surface, from the point to the commencement, reckoning from the centre. Now join on the wool to the broad end of the point, and at the right-hand side insert the hook in the 1st loop of the foundation; twist the wool over the hook, and pull it through; repeat this till there are 20 loops on the hook; then finish this point as the first. Now observe that on one side of the piece, at the edge, a perfect chain stitch appears, and on the other side only a slight loop. Now, with the darkest claret wool, work a row of single crochet all round the piece, taking up the two loops of the chain on one side, and only one on the side of the single edge. Now, with same wool, sew the pieces together, making one stitch in every loop. There must be sixteen of these divisions, which will make a handsome cushion.

INSERTION.

EMBROIDERY.

HEART-SHAPED SCENT SACHET.

THESE pretty little sachets should be made by every lady, to be scattered through her drawers, so as to impart a general fragrance to the various articles of her wardrobe. The trouble is very slight, and the material no more than any trifling remnant of silk of the size shown in our illustration, and three-quarters of a yard of ribbon to form the bow. The little group of flowers which we have given is to be embroidered on the sides as slightly as possible ; the two parts are to be laid face to face and stitched together, with accuracy, to their shape, leaving an opening at the top ; after this they are to be turned and filled with fine cotton wool, impregnated with any perfume most agreeable to taste ; after which the aperture is to be closed, and the rosette of ribbon laid upon the place. Ladies who are not inclined to undertake the embroidery may take any piece of fancy silk, or even such as are quite plain, and make them up in the same way, without this decoration. These little sachets make pretty presents, and it has been with reference to this that the "Forget-me-not" has been selected for its embellishment.

CHILD'S BRAIDED GAITER BOOT.

The toe and heel are to be tipped with patent leather.

SCENT CASE FOR NOTE PAPER.

THE material on which the cover of the Scent Case is worked is satin, which may be of any rich color; royal blue, purple, ruby color, or, in short, any that may be preferred. The medallion in the centre is of white watered silk, but to avoid trouble this may also be left of the satin which has been chosen. The medallion is surrounded by a double row of gold beads, of which the interval between may be filled up with either clear white or black beads. When the medallion is in white silk, this margin effectually conceals the line of its insertion. The scalloped pattern is worked in chain-stitch, in double lines; of the first row, the inner one is in light maize-color, and the outer one of dark maize. The second row of scallops is in either two crimsons or two blues, according to the color of the satin. The two straight lines of the margin are in the two shades of maize, while the zigzag line between is simply a herring-bone of violet color. The group in the centre is worked in maize color.

When the ornamental needle-work part has thus been completed, it will of course be less trouble to send it to the repository to be made up; but as we think some ladies may feel inclined to finish it themselves, and as we think that with ordinary care it is one of those things which come within their own power, we will go on to offer them a few further instructions. A blotting-book of the required size must be taken; within each cover must be laid a piece of wadding exactly fitting its dimensions, and sufficiently impregnated with whatever perfume the lady worker may prefer. This being neatly squared round its edges, the satin cover must be laid on the outside, brought over, and carefully tacked down, having been so arranged as to leave a margin of about half an inch all round of the plain satin beyond the needle-work pattern. This being done, two pieces of perforated card-board are to be placed inside, just within the margin, which having been first bound with narrow ribbon, is then fastened down. Through the apertures of this perforated card-board exudes the scent which impregnates the note paper of which the scent case is the receptacle.

COTTON WAGON.

THIS useful and tidy little article for the work-table, capable of holding five different sized reels of cotton, is made of card-board,

bound with narrow satin ribbon, and sewn together in the form shown in our illustration. A small piece of card-board, three yards of ribbon,

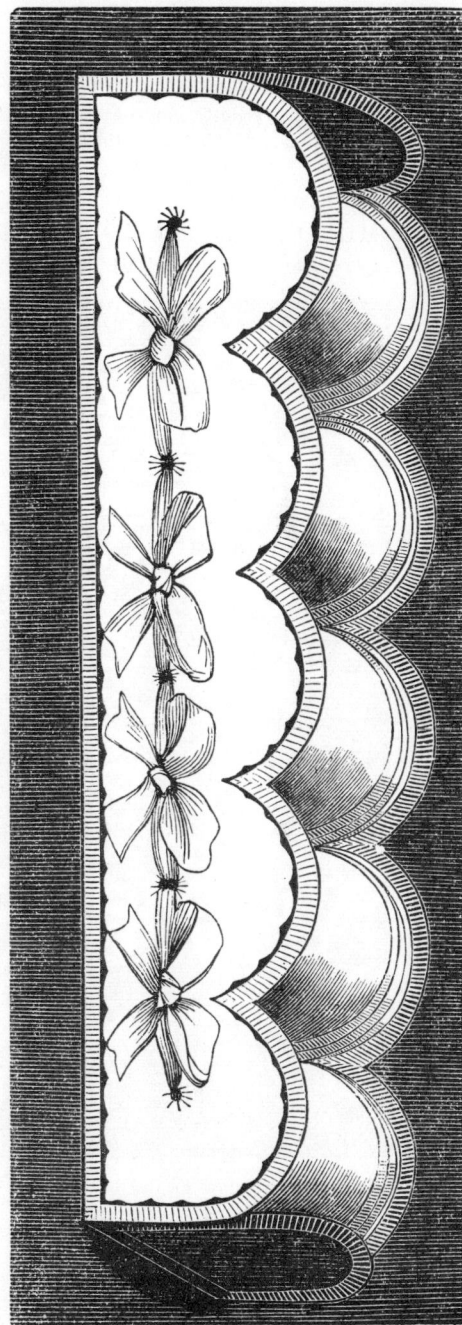

and five reels of cotton, will be required to make it. Cut out of card-board five pieces the exact size of the diagrams above, one piece for the bottom, one each for the two ends, and two scalloped pieces for the sides. Bind these pieces all round with narrow satin ribbon of any bright color, as mauve, scarlet, pink, or blue; then sew them together on the outside to the proper shape. Previously to putting the wagon together, the two scalloped pieces must have five holes pierced with a stiletto, for the ribbon to pass through to tie in the reels; these holes should be slightly overcast with silk, to keep them from breaking out. Place the cotton in the wagon, the coarsest at the top, and tie it in by drawing the ribbon through the first reel and back again through the second, and tie it in a bow; then pass it through the second reel and back again through the third, and tie another bow; proceed in this manner until all the reels are tied in.

EMBROIDERY BORDER FOR THE DOUBLE SKIRT OF A LITTLE GIRL'S DRESS.

THE pattern we are now giving has a very rich effect worked on the edges of an upper and under skirt of a little girl's dress. It is formed of heart-shaped parts, which are linked within each other, and appear as interlacing; these are of two kinds, and alternate. The one has a row of open holes at each edge, the branching lines to which they are attached in the interior being sewn over. The other is filled in with leaves in the cut-out work. The flowers in the centres of the hearts may be either in well raised satin-stitch or in the cut-out work. The scallop is in clear distinct button-hole stitch. This border should be worked over a tolerably wide hem, instead of being cut out to the scallop, as the effect is better, and firmness and durability are more secure.

BEAD MAT.

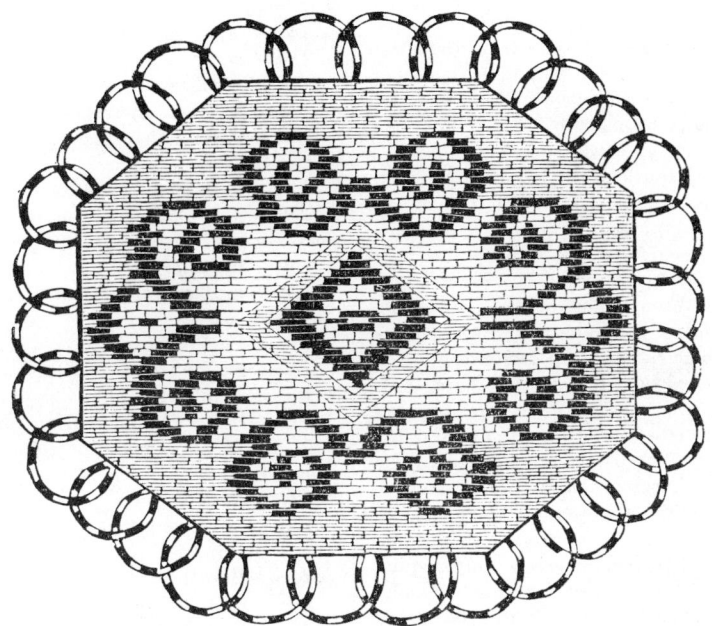

It is quickly made, and very pretty. The beads are large, and of glass, white and red, strung on purse silk of a deep crimson. Make the pattern of the beads, the dark ones red, the light white, and fill up the canvas in black tapestry stitch. Take a piece of card, the shape of pattern, and sew the canvas down to it; line with crimson silk. The fringe is made of the beads fastened down in loops crossing each other.

LADY'S COMPANION.

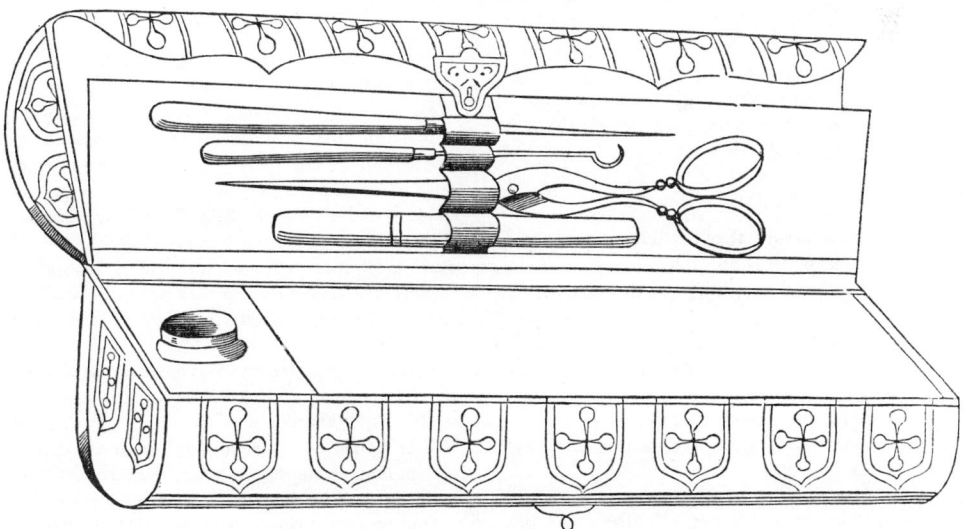

To be made of pasteboard, and covered with fancy velvet.

KNITTED ARTIFICIAL FLOWERS.

HEART'S-EASE.

THIS flower requires five petals to form it, two violet and three yellow; one of the latter must be larger than the rest, and of a deeper color. All the wool must be split.

For the violet petals, cast on ten stitches on two needles, five on each; fold the two needles so as to bring the last stitch behind the first, and *double knit* a piece of rather more than half an inch in length, taking one stitch from one needle, and one from the other throughout each row. When you take the needles out, run the wool through them with a rug needle, and pass a piece of double wire through the little bag which the knitting has formed, catch it at the top and sides to keep it in form, draw up the other end, and twist the wires together after having shaped the wire to the form of the petal. The yellow petals are knitted in the same way, the largest requires twelve stitches, and the last four or six rows must be done with violet wool, to form the dark spot at the top. The two smaller yellow petals only require eight stitches, with two or four rows of violet at the top; twist the wires of the five petals together, and cover the stem with green wool; a cross stitch, like herring-bone, should be made with green wool, where the petals join in the middle of the flower.

For the calyx, thread a needle with whole green wool, fasten this on the stem, at the back of the flower, and take a herring stitch at the back of each petal, making the stitch rather long, and leaving the wool loose. The bud is formed by making a little tuft of yellow, violet, and green wool, mixed together; fix it on a piece of wire by crossing the wool over, and twisting the wire very tight, turn the ends of the wool down the wire, and fasten them at about a quarter of an inch down, by twisting some green split wool round, with which the little stem must be also covered.

LEAVES.—Cast on three stitches.

Knit one row, purl one row, then

1st row.—Make one, knit one throughout the row.

2d.—Make one, purl the row.

3d.—Make one, knit three, make one, knit one, make one, knit two.

4th.—Make one, purl the row.

5th.—Make one, knit five, make one, knit one, make one, knit six.

6th.—Make one, purl the row.

7th.—Cast off, or fasten off, three stitches, knit three, make one, knit one.

8th.—Cast off three stitches, purl the row.

9th.—Make one, knit five, make one, knit one, make one, knit four.

10th.—Make one, purl the row.

11th.—Make one, knit seven, make one, knit one, make one, knit six.

12th.—Make one, purl the row.

13th.—Fasten off three stitches, knit the remainder.

14th.—Fasten off three stitches, purl the rest.

15th.—Knit six, make one, knit one, make one, knit six.

16th.—Purl the row.

17th.—Knit seven, make one, knit one, make one, knit six.

18th.—Purl the row.

19th.—Fasten off three stitches, knit four, make one, knit one, make one, knit seven.

20th.—Cast off three stitches, purl the row.

21st.—Knit six, make one, knit one, make one, knit five

22d.—Purl the row.

23d.—Knit seven, make one, knit one, make one, knit six.

24th.—Purl the row.

25th.—Cast off three stitches, knit remainder.

26th.—Cast off three stitches, purl remainder.

27th.—Knit row plain.

28th.—Purl the row plain.

29th.—Knit row plain.

30th.—Purl row plain.

31st.—Cast off two, knit remainder.

32d.—Cast off two, purl remainder.

33d.—Knit row plain.

34th.—Purl row.

35th.—Knit row plain.

36th.—Purl row plain.

37th.—Cast off two, knit remainder.

38th.—Cast off two, purl remainder.

Fasten off the two last stitches.

It is on this principle that all kinds of indented leaves are made; by knitting more rows with increase between the castings off, they are made broader: by working more rows between the castings off, they are made longer; and by casting off more stitches at a time, the indentations are made deeper; so that the endless variety of natural leaves may be copied without difficulty.

Having completed the leaves, some wire must be sewn neatly round, following the turnings of the leaf exactly; and for the larger ones, it will be better to sew a double wire in the centre of the leaf at the back, which will conceal the openings left by the increase of stitches.

One or two flowers, with a bud, and two or three leaves, are sufficient for a small branch.

ALPHABET OF FANCY LETTERS.

CORNER FOR A POCKET HANDKERCHIEF.

EMBROIDERY PATTERNS.

FOR PILLOW AND BOLSTER CASES.

FOR A DRESS OR CLOAK.

INSERTION.

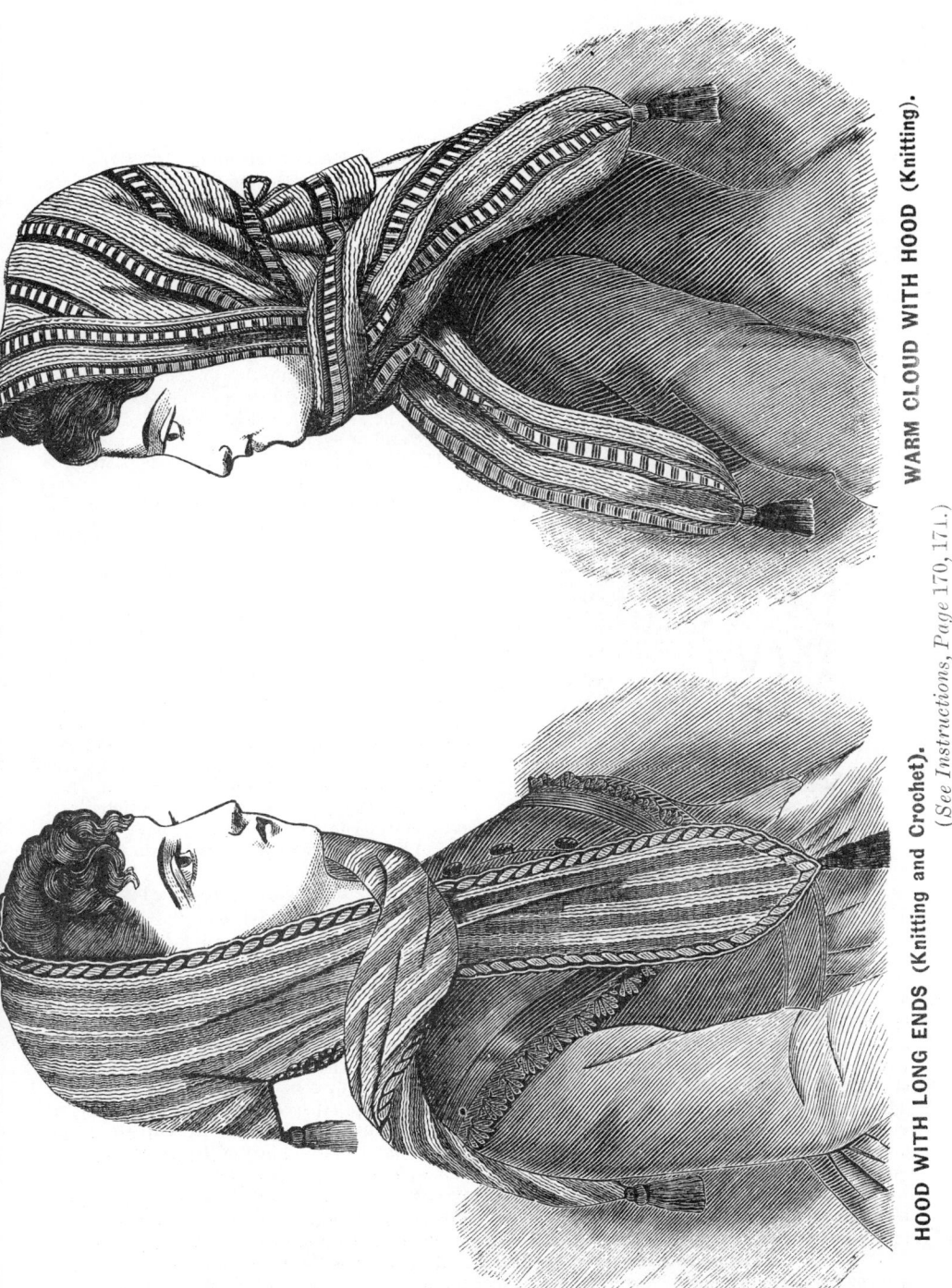

WARM CLOUD WITH HOOD (Knitting).

(See Instructions, Page 170, 171.)

HOOD WITH LONG ENDS (Knitting and Crochet).

HOOD WITH LONG ENDS, KNITTING AND CROCHET.
(*See Engraving, Page* 169.)

Materials.—Three and a half ounces of white single Berlin wool in long skeins, one ounce of blue Shetland wool, half an ounce of black single Berlin, three long wooden needles, No. 10, without knobs, three ditto, ditto, No. 5, and a bone crochet hook, No. 11.

THIS hood, which partakes somewhat of the nature of a cloud, is very easy of execution, being all done in plain knitting. It is worked, as will be seen from detail Fig. 1a, lengthwise,

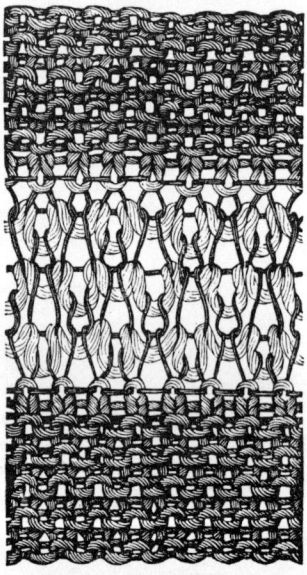

Fig. 1a.—Detail of Hood.

and for the front edge, on which afterwards a crochet edging is laid down, such a number of stitches must be cast on the No. 10 needles, with white wool, as will measure, when knitted, 60 inches. Usually on this sized needles 6 stitches may be reckoned to the inch, which would give 360 to be cast on for the whole length; but, as scarcely any two people knit quite alike, it is better to work 12 or 18 stitches for a few rows, and compare them with the inch measure, so as to be able to calculate the exact number required. In our model, close white stripes, knitted with the fine needles, alternate with more open ones of mixed blue and white, for which the larger needles are to be used. If preferred, pink or Ponceau Shetland wool may be substituted for blue.

The stripes are all knitted plain, backwards and forwards, each white stripe consisting of 14 rows, and every mixed one of 7 rows, of which the 1st, 3d, 5th, and 7th are knitted with the Shetland wool, and the three intervening ones with the white Berlin.

The hood is commenced by a white stripe, and in order to form the shape of the ends, as shown in engraving, for the first half of the depth a stitch must be increased at the end of every row, either by knitting twice in the last stitch, first from the front and then from the back, or by taking up the loop under the last stitch, and knitting it before the stitch itself; and in the last half, a stitch must be decreased at the end of every row by knitting 2 together.

The whole depth of the hood consists of 9 white and 8 mixed stripes.

At the conclusion of the 6th white stripe, to form the pointed part of the hood which hangs down in the neck, the 80 centre stitches must alone be knitted backwards and forwards, continuing the stripes as before, and decreasing a stitch at the beginning of every row, so that in 80 rows they will all be used up and the piece brought to a point. The sloped sides must then be sewn together on the wrong side, and the point finished with a white wool tassel three and a half inches in length. The 3 white and 2 mixed stripes still wanting to complete the depth of the hood at the sides, are to be knitted with the remaining stitches, on each side separately, and after being completed and cast off, the edges of these pieces next the back are to be sewn together, for a certain distance, to close the neck.

The entire outer edge of the hood is to have a flat crochet trimming laid down upon it, which will conceal the joins and fastenings off. For this, make a chain with the white wool of the necessary length (it will be seen by the illustration that the trimming goes up to meet the hanging part of the hood behind); about the same number of chain as of knitting stitches may be reckoned to the inch, but a trial should first be made. For the 1st row, work a treble (thread once over the needle) in every stitch. For the 2d row, with the black wool, * make a dc., putting the needle through the middle of a treble (not *between* two of them), 2 ch., miss 2 trebles, and repeat from * the whole length. A similar row is to be worked on the other side of the chain stitches, and completes the trimming. In case one of the brighter colors is used instead of gray, the same in single Berlin must be substituted for black in these edgings. After the trimming is tacked on, the lower ends of the hood are finished with white wool tassels five inches long.

WARM CLOUD WITH HOOD (KNITTING).

(See Engraving, Page 169.)

Materials.—Four ounces of white single Berlin wool in long skeins, one ounce of Ponçeau ditto, three long wooden needles No. 10, without knobs.

THIS wrap consists of a straight scarf, one end of which, after encircling the face, is thrown over the shoulder, as seen in the illustration, and, for greater warmth and protection to the head and throat, it is drawn in at the back by means of a cord.

The scarf is knitted lengthwise, according to detail Fig. 1, in close white stripes of plain

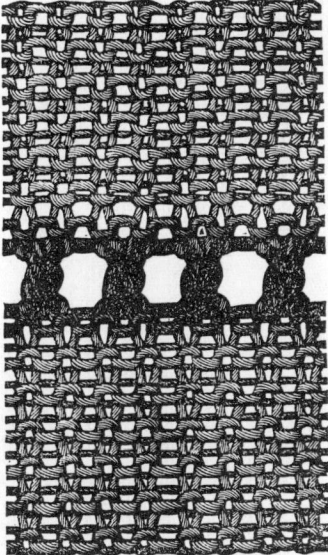

Fig. 1.—Detail of Hood.

knitting, separated by narrow open ones of Ponçeau. Such a number of stitches must be cast on as will measure, when knitted, fifty-five inches; the exact number cannot be given, as it depends on whether the worker knits tightly or loosely; the best way is to try twelve or eighteen stitches, knitting them backwards and forwards for a few rows, and then comparing them with the inch measure, as recommended for the hood with long ends.

The scarf is begun and ended with a white stripe of 23 rows of plain knitting, and 9 of these stripes form the width of it. Each white stripe is separated by a narrow open Ponçeau one, worked as follows: 1*st row.* Purl. 2*d.* * Over, slip 1, knit 1, pass slipped stitch over, repeat from *. 3*d.* Purl. Then re-commence the 23 plain rows with white wool. The ends of the scarf are gathered up together and finished with white wool tassels five inches long. For the drawing-string of the hood, make two lengths of chain stitches, each measuring half a yard, and run them through the second open Ponçeau stripe from the edge, so that they can

be tied together in a bow at the back. The ends of these strings, which hang down behind, are also to be finished with white wool tassels.

ETAGERE.

WITH lambrequins done in crochet and ornamented with worsted ball fringe. This consists of two three-cornered brackets, ornamented with lambrequins in crochet, and balls made of red wool. The straight sides of the brackets are eight inches long; the front part, which is rounded off, measures thirteen inches from corner to corner. To make the lambrequins, cast on a foundation thirteen inches long in cro-

chet of unbleached netting cotton. 1*st row.* Treble stitches, instead of the 1st treble stitch, 3 chain stitches. 2*d.* To return scallops in chain stitch of 17 stitches and 1 plain stitch, caught into the 10th stitch of the preceding row. 3*d.* 1 chain stitch, turn the work, go on with plain stitches, observing to put 3 plain stitches into the middle stitch of each scallop, and to pass over the stitch at the bottom of the scallop. There should be 15 scallops. From this point, carry each succeeding row as far as complete the point by crocheting backwards and forwards, and then take up the loose stitches on the one side, and crochet plain stitches into them. For the next point, fasten

Fig. 1.—Candle Screen.

the middle of the last scallop, then turn the work and proceed. *4th.* Like 3d row. *5th.* Like 3d row. Then finish off each point of the lambrequin separately. Fasten the thread on to the middle stitch of the 4th scallop, and the thread on to the middle stitch of the 10th scallop, crochet 5 scallops in chain stitch, and finish off the point like the former one. Crochet the 3d point like the first. Make the balls of Berlin wool, and attach them to the lambrequins and along the edge, as indicated in the plate. Fasten the work to the brackets; pass 3 red cords through the wood, making a knot underneath each bracket; tie the cords together at the top, and make a bow with a tassel of worsted balls as a finish.

CANDLE SCREEN.
(*See Engraving, Page* 172.)

THE frame is of walnut, gilt, bronze, or any white wood. The banner is given in full working size in Fig. 1. It is worked in *appliqué* on

Fig. 2.

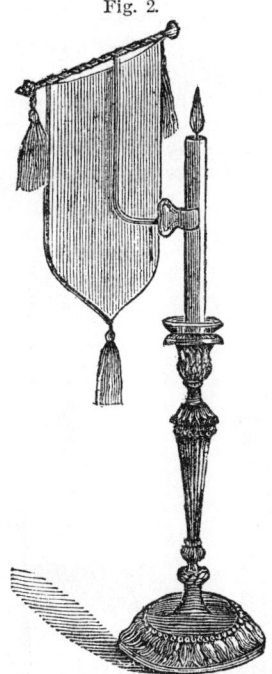

scarlet cloth. A frame can be made without a place for light, to be used as a screen between the gas and a person sitting at a table.

FLOWERS AND FLOWER BASKET.

Materials.—Middle-sized gold thread; crystal and gold beads; Roman pearls in two different sizes; silk paper in three shades of pink, dark red, gold yellow, two shades of violet, etc.; fine flower wire, etc. It materially assists workers to have the natural flowers to copy from.

THE flowers are arranged in the basket in natural moss. The foliage, calix, seed pods, stamina, etc., are better bought at an artificial florist's, as they are sold by the dozen, do not cost much, and are much neater made by experienced hands than they can be by amateurs.

Figs. 1 and 11. White Verbena.—The little petals are of white paper, cut out to the size

and form of Fig. 11, and must have a line marked with a crochet hook in the centre of each petal. The middle of the flower is composed of a little knot of yellow silk, twisted round the top of the wire, which should be the fine green-covered wire sold by florists. Fig. 1 shows the grouping of the flowers.

Fig. 2. Scarlet Verbena.—The detail of this flower is the same as that of the white verbena. It is cut out of paper, sold under the name of Dahlia paper. Each little blossom is finished with a yellow knot.

Figs. 3 and 8. Syringa.—The half of the bloom is shown in Fig. 8. The whole four leaves are cut out together in white letter paper. The bloom should be double, and pasted together. The points for the open blooms are bent outwards, those of the half-open blooms are bent inwards. The stamens are of white cotton, touched at the top with a little gum, sand, and yellow powdered ochre. The flowers are easily arranged over the twisted wire stalks.

Fig. 4. Marigold.—A brown stamp pistil is required for the flat middle of the flower. Two rounds of yellow paper, graduated in size, are cut up like fringe for the flower, and pointed at each tip, then a fine knitting needle must be drawn along the centre of each petal.

Figs. 5, 9, and 10.—A knot of yellow silk paper, taken double, is fastened as the inner part of the flower calix on a wire stalk, and this is then inclosed by a strip of yellow paper, half an inch wide, folded in quite small folds, which must have on one side a narrow edge painted over with scarlet; also the centre is touched with red. The flower-leaf parts of the narcissus—of which Fig. 10 gives one in the full size, after the small Fig. 9—hang together in the round, and are to be cut out in a flower circle of good white silk paper; each flower-leaf is then to be folded together sharp along the middle at the back, and then opened; the side edges are drawn over the scissors to give them a slight curve towards the outside. A little gum and a small calix hold together the flower-leaf circle.

Figs. 6 and 13. Forget-me-not.—Thick blue paper is used for cutting out this flower to the size shown in Fig. 13. It is slipped over the wire, and fastened like the verbena with a yellow knot.

Figs. 7, 14, and 15. Myrtle Blossom.—The blooms, in graduated sizes, are cut out of white paper, and put over stamens of cotton, just tinged at the top with gum and yellow ochre; a few of the little green buds, which can be purchased ready-made, will give an excellent effect.

Figs. 17, 18, and 19. Flower Basket.—This pretty and tasteful basket will do as well for a card as for a flower basket. The entire basket is shown from the bottom, flattened out, in Fig. 19. The framework must be made by a tinman. The outer ring of the bottom, to which three little feet are attached, is four inches and a quarter in circumference. On the cross middle rod is a ring two inches and three-quarters in circumference. Round the four and a quarter inch ring are placed seven other rings rather larger than the centre ring on the cross lines. These rings are bound together with an outer ring, to which the handle, shown in a reduced size in Fig. 18, is attached. All the foundation is worked over with beads; one gold and three crystal are threaded together, and twisted over the wire very evenly. The centre of the basket is filled up by two pearl beads threaded on the gold cord; these must be fastened over the foundation wire before covering it with beads. The opening at the edge of the seven rings is filled in a similar way. The two wire rods of the curved handle are seventeen inches long; the three rings of the handle are three-quarters of an inch apart in the middle. The filling-in of beads and gold

stitched over with black thread, makes the middle of the flower; long stamens of black cotton, gummed at the tips, and touched with poppy seed, go along the same. Round these are placed the leaves, cut out of scarlet paper, and twisted in a cloth, as described for the carnation. These leaves must be gummed with the side edges over each other. The upper part of the stalk should be twisted over with green wool.

Figs. 12, 23, *and* 24. *Rose.*—Fig. 24 shows the way the centre part of the rose is made; Fig. 12 the outer leaves, which are gummed on the outside.

TEA CADDY OR TOBACCO BOX.

THIS is a convenient little thing to make for a fancy bazaar. We should recommend its being made for a tobacco box. You require a frame of cane (any upholsterer can make the frame by the engraving if you are unable to do

Fig. 1.

Fig. 3.

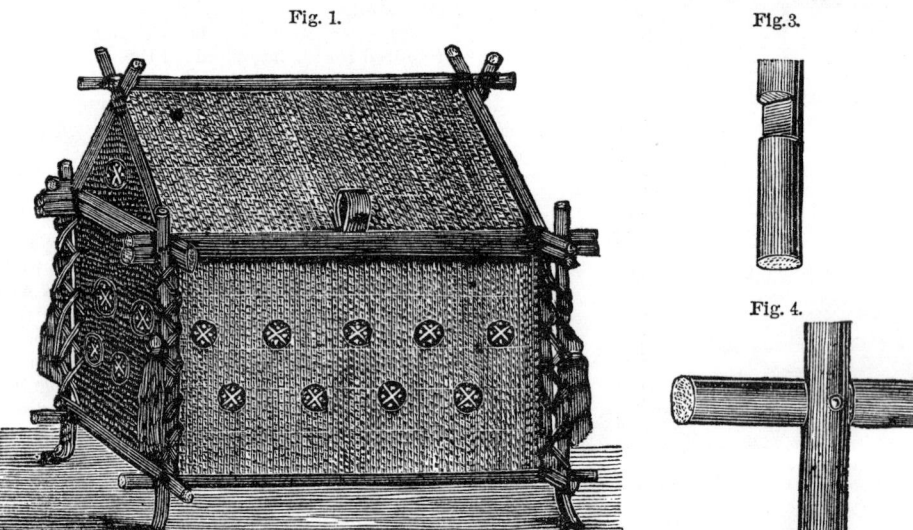

wire will be easily seen in the design; the seven side rings of the basket are filled up with crochet. The pattern is so simple, and every stitch is shown in Fig. 19, so that there will be no need to explain the way it is worked.

Figs. 16 *and* 20. *Pink.*—Two parts, cut to Fig. 16, are required for this flower, which is folded in eight folds, and cut into tiny points at the edges. Each part must then be laid in a piece of soft rag, and twisted tightly, so as to get all the stiffness out of the paper, and give it a natural appearance. A green calix is drawn over the outer part of the flower when it is fastened to the wire stalk. It should be cut down as far as the opening shown in Fig. 16, and the folds mark the other part.

Figs. 21 *and* 22. *Scarlet Poppy.*—A little wadding, covered with yellowish-green paper, and

it, though a sharp strong knife and some brass tacks are all that are required). The three engravings (Figs. 3, 4, and 5) illustrate very clearly the manner in which the frame is put together. The top is made quite separately from the bottom, and pieces of ribbon are fast-

Fig. 2.

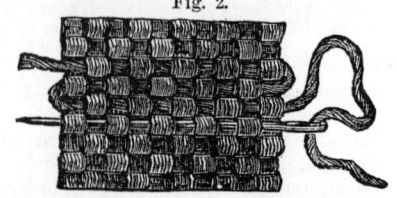

ened to the two parts to form hinges. Our model is nine inches and a half long, seven inches wide, including the frame work and the corners, and about six inches high, *without* the lid. The other materials required are four green tassels, card-board, plain white canvas, or gold canvas (which is coarse gold perforated card-board), some black and any shades of wool; also red and green crochet silk, gold beads, some fine silk cord. Fig. 2 illustrates the manner of working the canvas; it is worked entirely with loops of wool, then darned through with the different colored silks, working several rows of each color to form a stripe. The mode

Fig. 5.

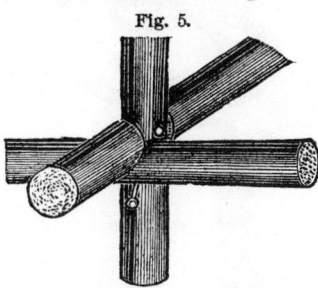

of working is simply plain darning with the wool, this must go up the canvas, then cross the canvas by darning with silk and taking up the wool. It would save much trouble and look better to work a plain star or stripe in one or two colors upon the gold canvas. When the work is finished, mount it on card-board, line through with black silk. If meant for a tobacco box, you must line through with thin sheet gutta percha, which will prevent the tobacco becoming too dry. The pattern on the sides of the box is composed of medallions in black; the pattern on the medallion is a large cross-stitch and knots all round. It is the best plan to cut these medallions in black velvet, and gum them on to the work, then embroider the edge with silk.

KNITTED WOOLLEN UNDERSLEEVES.

Materials.—Two and a half ounces of pearl-gray or violet single Berlin wool in long skeins, and a little black ditto, five steel needles, No. 14, and two ounces of black seed beads, as large as will pass through the stitches of the knitting.

THESE sleeves are warm and comfortable to wear under a *paletôt* or mantle, or with the open bell sleeves when out of doors. They

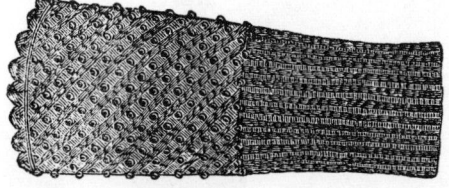

may be knitted in a pretty shade of pearl-gray, bright violet, or, indeed, in any color preferred. The part next the hand is plain, that is, with-

out beads, knitted in ribs of 1 plain, 1 purl, and, if greater warmth around the wrist be desired, can be turned in to half its depth, thus making it double. Begin by casting on 52 stitches, equally divided on the four needles, and knit as before directed for 60 rounds, but after the 30th, increase as follows at the under part or seam of the sleeve. In the 31st round

Waistband Hook for a Fan. (See page 177.)

knit the 1st stitch again from the back, and do the same in the last stitch of the round. Then follow 5 rounds without increase, purling 2 stitches instead of 1, between the original two first plain stitches of the round, and the same at the other end. *37th round.* Increase at the beginning and end again, in the same manner as before, and now you will be able to knit the second stitch of former round plain, and purl the next, thus carrying on the rib, and the same at the end. Five rounds without increase. Increase again as before in the 43d, 49th, 55th, and 60th rounds, the last two having only 4 rounds between them; and whenever the number of stitches will admit of it, beginning additional ribs next the seam on both sides. You will now have increased 12 stitches in all, and should have 64 on your needles. The pattern with the beads now commences. They should be chosen as large as will conveniently pass through the stitch of the knitting, and must be threaded on the wool. For greater convenience, this should be done on a second ball, and the remainder of the first kept for the lower part of the other sleeve. Having joined on the wool with the beads, proceed thus: *1st round.* * 1 purl, 3 plain, in the centre stitch of which

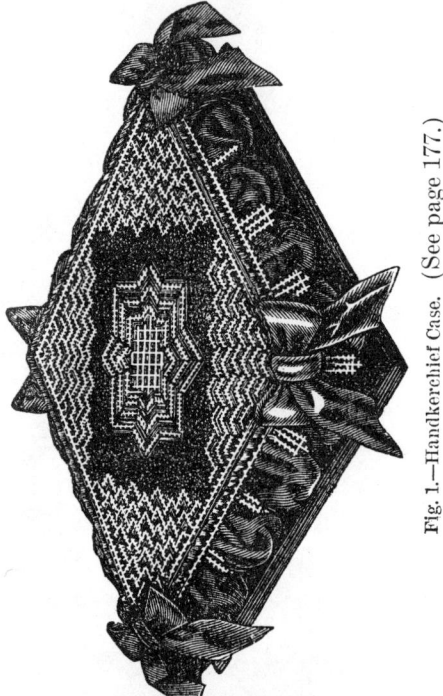

Fig. 1.—Handkerchief Case. (See page 177.)

pass down a bead, and bring it through to the front of the stitch when knitting it; repeat from *. *2d* (without beads). * 1 plain, 1 purl, repeat from *. A plain stitch will, throughout the pattern, come over the bead, and care must be taken not to allow it to slip to the back. *3d.* 2 plain, putting a bead on the 1st, * 1 purl, 3 plain, with a bead as before on the middle stitch; repeat from *. *4th.* Like 2d. Then recommence at the 1st round, and repeat these four rounds 18 times for the depth of the sleeve, making 72 rounds and 36 rows of beads. Cast off loosely, and at the upper and lower edge of the sleeve, with black wool, crochet the following as a finish: * 1 dc. in the 1st

stitch, 4 ch., 1 dc. in the 2d of these 4 ch., pass over 2 stitches of the foundation, and repeat from *.

CORD AND TASSELS.

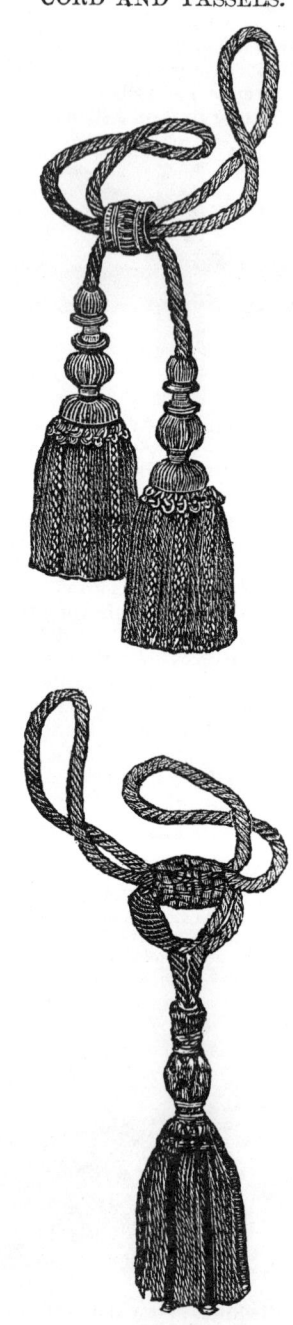

For looping back curtains of silk, of the same color as the curtains.

WAISTBAND HOOK FOR A FAN.
(*See Engraving, Page 175.*)

THIS hook for a fan is quite a new invention, which will be found very useful for balls and theatres. It is worn on the waistband of the

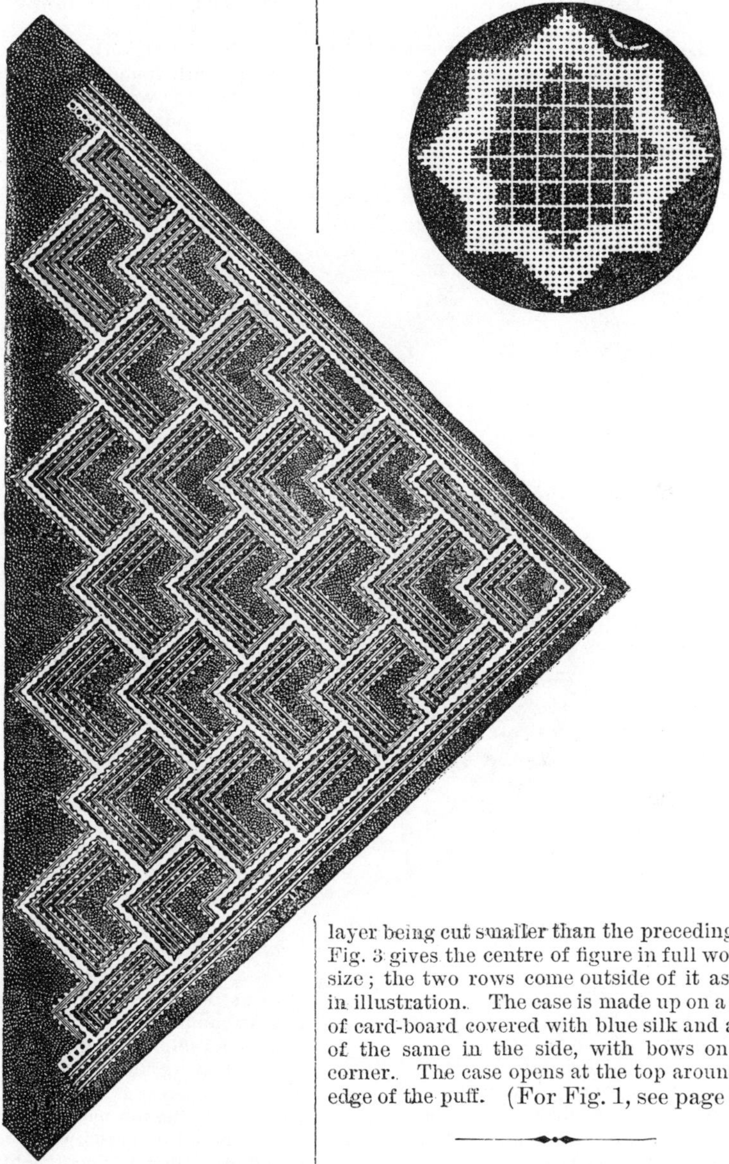

HANDKERCHIEF CASE.

THIS case is made of perforated card-board. Fig. 2 gives one of the corners in full working size. The card is put on as there shown, each

Fig. 3.

Fig. 2.

layer being cut smaller than the preceding one. Fig. 3 gives the centre of figure in full working size; the two rows come outside of it as seen in illustration. The case is made up on a piece of card-board covered with blue silk and a puff of the same in the side, with bows on each corner. The case opens at the top around the edge of the puff. (For Fig. 1, see page 176.)

dress; the fan is drawn through the metal loop of the hook by means of the circle fastened at the lower end. Our pattern is made of open work silver, with the initials M. S.

CLEAN paper, torn into small pieces, and put in a case, makes excellent sofa cushions.

NETTED SPONGE BAG.—Net twelve stitches with coarse crochet cotton on a piece of the cotton, with mesh about three-eighths of an inch wide. Net twelve rows to form a square. Run a piece of cotton into the centre stitches, and continue netting round twenty-four rows. Run a piece of tape through the last row. Tie the ends in a knot.

LADY'S WATCH-POCKET IN NETTED EMBROIDERY.

Materials.—One reel crochet cotton No. 16; two meshes, one flat, nearly half an inch wide; and the other round, steel No. 16; a netting needle; one skein of colored wool, of any color to suit the drapery of the room; a yard of inch wide sarcenet ribbon; a round of card-board; and a small piece of silk the same color as the wool.

12th. Small mesh, one in each.

13th, 14th, 15th, and 16th. Small mesh, one stitch in each.

Fasten off and work the edge as before.

In the 14th round darn every alternate diamond with the wool.

On a foundation of 18 stitches, with wide mesh, net one round.

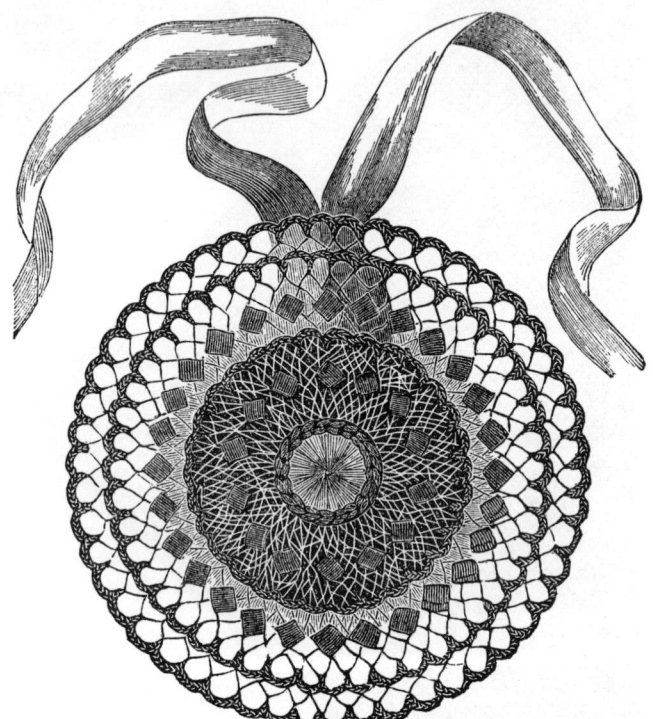

ON a foundation of 28 stitches net one round with wide mesh.

2d round. Small mesh, one in each.

3d, 4th, 5th, and 6th. Same as 2d.

7th. Large mesh, two in each.

8th. Small mesh, one in each.

9th and 10th. Same as 8th.

Fasten the thread, and with the wool cover the entire outside round of meshes with loosely-wrought buttonhole stitches. This forms the first round of the pocket.

On the same foundation, with wide mesh, net one plain round.

2d round. Wide meshes, two stitches in each.

3d. Small mesh, net two stitches together all round.

4th. Small mesh, one in each.

Do 6 more rounds the same.

11th. Small mesh, two stitches in each.

2d. Small mesh, two in each.

3d. Small mesh, one in each.

Do 5 more rounds the same, and work the edge as before; darn every alternate diamond in 6th round.

Take a round of card-board the size of a *large* watch, leaving about an inch above the round at the top, cover it with the silk, lay the first piece of netting flat on it, and stitch it round.

Now take the second piece and stitch the 5th round of diamonds down tightly, rather more than half round, so as to make the edge come to the 7th round of the first piece. This will leave it loose in the centre to form the pocket. Stitch the other piece of netting to the middle of this, and finish with a knot of ribbon in the centre. Attach a piece double, about three inches long, to the top, and add a rosette and ends.

PAPER FLOWER.
POMEGRANATE.
(See Engravings, Page 180.)

Materials.—Dark red and brownish tissue-paper (the latter for twisting round the stalk); dark red and yellow-green glazed paper; wire, etc.

LAYING the paper eightfold, cut six circles of petals, according to the design, Fig. 2, which, when unfolded, gives the form represented in Fig. 3. Inclose it in a piece of old linen, and twist it between the thumb and forefinger of the right hand, so that the circle appears as shown as required. A straight rib in the middle of the leaves is made with the help of a needle without a point (a fine knitting-needle), and the whole is completed with a fine wire stalk.

WASH-STAND.

THIS stand is both elegant and useful. We offer it to the attention of our readers as being well worthy of imitation, and especially suitable for a pretty dressing-room; it is made at

in Fig. 4. Then unfold it very carefully, so that the petals are crumpled like the real flower. In fastening the separate circles firmly to a covered wire stalk, the flower is drawn several times through the hollow of the hand, in order to arrange the petals close together. Calix leaves and buds may be purchased ready made, or for the calix a piece of dark-red glazed paper may be cut with the points turned outwards, according to Fig. 5, which gives the half of the open shape. This must be covered at the back with loose wadding, which must be gummed on before the side edges are gummed over each other. The shape of the yellowish-green leaves is shown in Fig 1, and must be arranged larger and smaller, small expense and little trouble. The table itself, with a plain bracket part attached, and square frame for the looking-glass, is constructed in any kind of wood—even deal looks very well. The top and bracket must be painted to imitate marble. The draped part consists of spotted white muslin over a colored foundation (glazed calico or silk), with muslin and silk bows; any kind of stuff, such as used for furniture, etc., can, however, be taken. The curtains in front closed by a bow, are made to draw by putting on brass rods and rings underneath the frill at the top, so that the lower board of the table can be used with advantage for the foot-bath.

Fig. 1.

Fig. 2.

Fig. 3.

Fig. 5.

Fig. 4.

Fig. 6.

COFFEE-MILL OF PERFORATED CARD-BOARD FOR A YARD MEASURE.

THE four outer walls are made of medium-sized perforated card-board, lined with white paper, ornamented with silk stitches, and sewn together at the corners. The bottom and cover must have the card-board double, and must project two ribs beyond the wall part. Only

BAG FOR BATHING COSTUME.

THIS bag is made of black leather-cloth, lined with the same and bound with red worsted braid. First cut out the bottom part from illustration, bind it with red worsted braid, and sew in from Fig. 2 the bag, which must be ten inches deep and sufficiently wide. The bag is ornamented all round with red woollen sou-

Fig. 1.

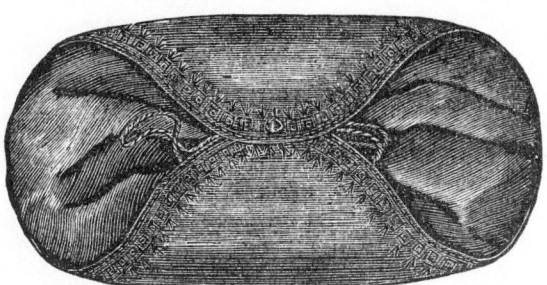

Fig. 2.

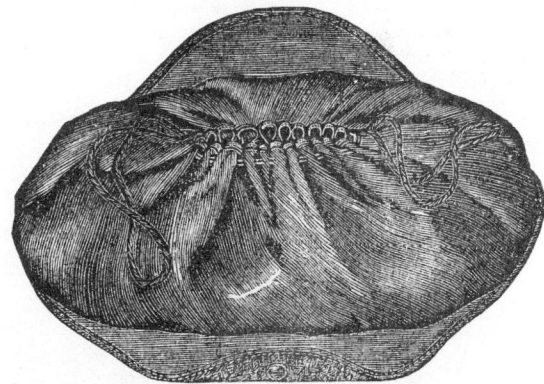

one part, however, of the perforated card-board is joined to the wall, then a rather smaller layer of card-board is gummed over, and then the outer layer is placed to complete them. A hole is bored in the middle of the bottom and cover for the winding peg, upon which the ribbon, introduced through an opening in the side wall, must roll easily. A piece of thin wood will answer this purpose. It must be exactly the height of the mill, and the measure firmly sewn on in the centre. The wood will be strengthened by passing three fine wires half an inch long over the bottom, and one inch and three-quarters long at the top. The under end of the peg is wound separately, and the whole of the rest with red silk. At the end of the handle a knob of black sealing-wax is placed. When the winder is carefully pushed in, the three ends upon the bottom of the card-board are placed out in the form of a wheel, and covered with another layer of card-board, and finished with the outer part of the bottom. The ribbons are placed to hang it up by if desired.

tache; the lappets are fastened with button and buttonhole.

FOOTSTOOL AND CROCHET COVERING.

THIS footstool is very practical; it is of a slanting shape, and covered with crochet, as can be seen on illustration. The framework of the footstool is made of wood. The bottom is twelve and four-fifths inches long, nine and three-fifths inches wide; the front and back parts are each twelve and four-fifths inches long, the back part is four and four-fifths inches high, the front part only two and two-fifths inches high. The sides are each nine and three-fifths inches long, and must correspond in height to the back and front parts, being, therefore, slanted off. The different parts are then covered with gray or brown glazed calico. The wooden shape is then filled up with horsehair; the top part, which must be slightly curved, is then likewise covered with calico taken double. The crochet cover is worked with fleecy wool in two shades of one color (light and dark green on our pattern), in double crochet; always work on the same side, and insert the needle into both upper chain, the ground being worked with dark wool. The pattern is worked with light wool in the following manner: Work with the dark wool over the light wool, making for each square of the pattern a loop of the light

two places where the thread has been fastened, taking care not to cut the thread through, so that the balls hang all in a row. Then draw the balls through hot water, and clip them so as to make them smooth. The under part of the footstool is covered with black cloth. At the upper edge fasten a handle formed of two cords worked in double crochet.

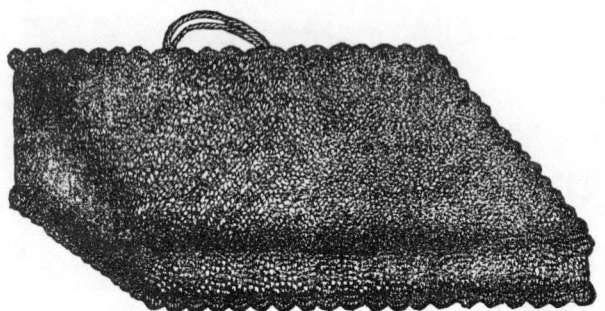

wool on the right side. When the crochet cover is completed, it is sewn on to the footstool; the latter is ornamented all round the edge with small worsted balls of the same color as the

NEWSPAPER-CASE.

THIS case is intended to hang up against the wall to put paper and pamphlets in. It is made of thick card-board, covered with scarlet

NEWSPAPER-CASE.

covering. For the balls, take a skein of wool twenty times double; fasten some black thread round it at distances of four-fifths of an inch; then cut the skein open in the middle, between

cloth, embroidered in colors, and *appliqué* of black velvet. It is made with a gore of scarlet leather in the sides, to allow room for the contents.

PAPER-WEIGHT.

Materials.—Green cloth, muslin, cherry-colored crape, green purse-silk, cherry-colored filoselle, some quilting, moss and dried grasses, emery, and card-board.

FOR this paper-weight, take first a piece of card-board four and four-fifths inches long, three and one-fifth inches wide, and three-fifths of an inch high (a flat square bag will do very well, if filled with lead, and covered with calico); the upper surface is covered with moss and fine dried ferns and grasses, which are gummed on. The ornament on our pattern consists of leaves of green cloth, into which the veinings have previously been worked with green silk; a piece of wire is sewn in along the middle veining; the leaves are sewn on to a piece of tape two-fifths of an inch wide. This tape is pasted on the outer edge of the card-board, and the leaves are bent upwards. Then cut also out of green cloth a vine leaf of middle size, work the veining sewing in wires. The strawberries consist of tufts of wadding, covered with cherry-colored crape taken double; in the middle of the tuft fasten the end of a piece of wire one inch and one-fifth long: the end which comes beyond is meant for the stem, and is

covered with green silk. The berry is then ornamented with short stitches of cherry-colored filoselle; fasten the buds, consisting of five leaves of green cloth, and paste on a few bits of moss, as seen on illustration. Lastly, fasten the bunch on the cloth. The paper-weight is covered on the wrong side with green glazed paper.

LETTER FOR MARKING.

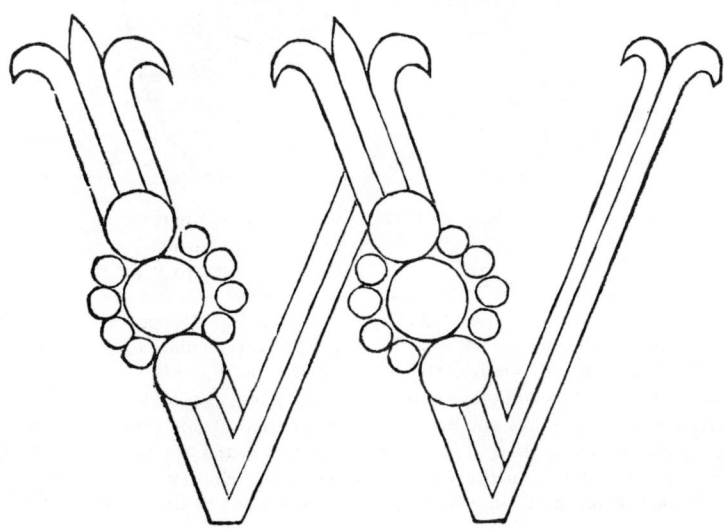

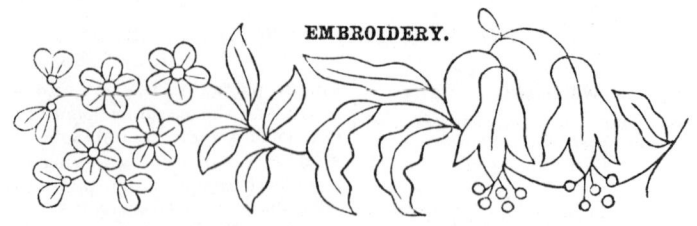

SONTAG, OR WOOLLEN HABIT-SHIRT.

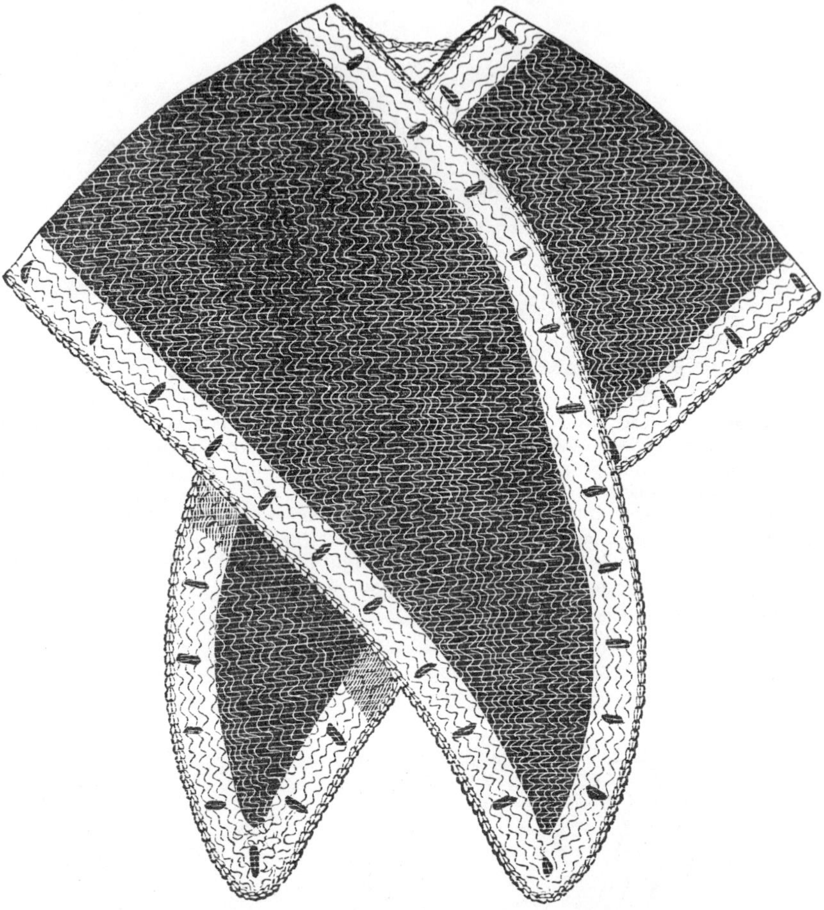

Materials.—Two ounces of double Berlin wool, of any dark color, and one ounce of white ditto. Knitting needles, No. 10.

This very pretty and comfortable habit-shirt is intended to be worn under a mantle or cloak; and as it gives great additional warmth, without making the figure at all clumsy, it has many advantages over shawls and other wraps.

With the dark wool cast on five stitches, and knit, increasing one stitch at the end of every row, until eighty stitches are on the needles. This is the back. Then knit only half the stitches, the others being left on the needle (which will be found much more convenient than slipping them on a separate one). Still increase one at the *outer* edge, in every alternate row, but decrease one at the inner edge, in the intermediate rows, so that forty remain on the needle, until you have done seventy rows, when cast off loosely. Do the other half the same. Then take up on one needle the stitches round the neck, and along these cast off ends. Knit, with white wool, ten rows, increasing one at the end of every row. Cast off loosely. Take up the stitches along the outer edge, and do the same, increasing, and joining to the inner border at the ends, and increasing also at each side of the five original stitches, that it may set square. Cast off loosely, and work small spots at intervals with the dark wool. The ends cross over the bosom.

KNITTED OPERA HOOD.

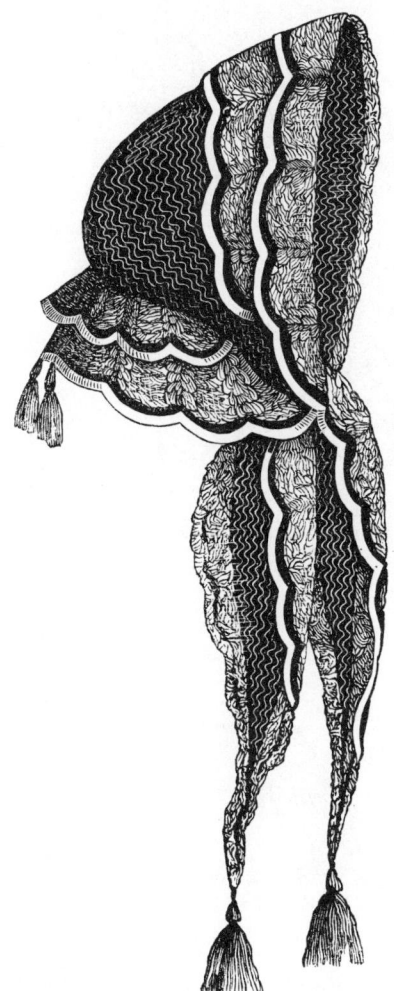

Materials.—Two ounces four-thread Berlin wool, of any color that may be preferred; one ounce gray-and-white pearl wool, half an ounce black, and ditto white; ivory needles, No. 9 and No. 7.

BEGIN with the colored wool and No. 9 needles, casting on two hundred and fifty stitches. Knit two plain rows, and, after that, cast off four stitches at the beginning of every needle

for thirty rows; then cast off two only at the beginning of every row for fifty-four rows, when cast off altogether.

THE CURTAIN.—Cast on seventy stitches, and knit eighteen rows, increasing *one* at the end of every row. Cast off loosely.

Sew this piece along the back, in the centre, slightly holding the hood in, and sewing on the ends as well as the length, as the border is carried from the points, along the sides where stitches were cast off, and along the outer edge of the curtain, in one continuous piece. For this purpose take up the stitches on the entire length; and knit with the pearl wool (No. 7 needles) twelve rows of ordinary shell pattern; then two rows with black wool, to be followed by a single plain row with white wool; after which, cast off loosely with the same.

Do another frill of ten shells, exactly the same, to sew on above the curtain, so as to cover it; and make end and tassels, which you run in along the back of the neck, to draw it in. They are put along the seam below the upper frill, which is a few rows above that seam.

A similar border is carried along the front, from point to point, and laid back; and the second (under) frill is put on a cape, sewed about six rows within the edge, so that it turns over easily, the upper frill border just covering this cape. It has seventy-two stitches cast on; and fourteen rows are knitted, with one stitch increase at the end of every row.

The second border just goes the length of the head, and does not extend to the barbes.

No combination of colors is prettier for this hood than *mauve*, with the gray, black, and white borders.

EMBROIDERY.

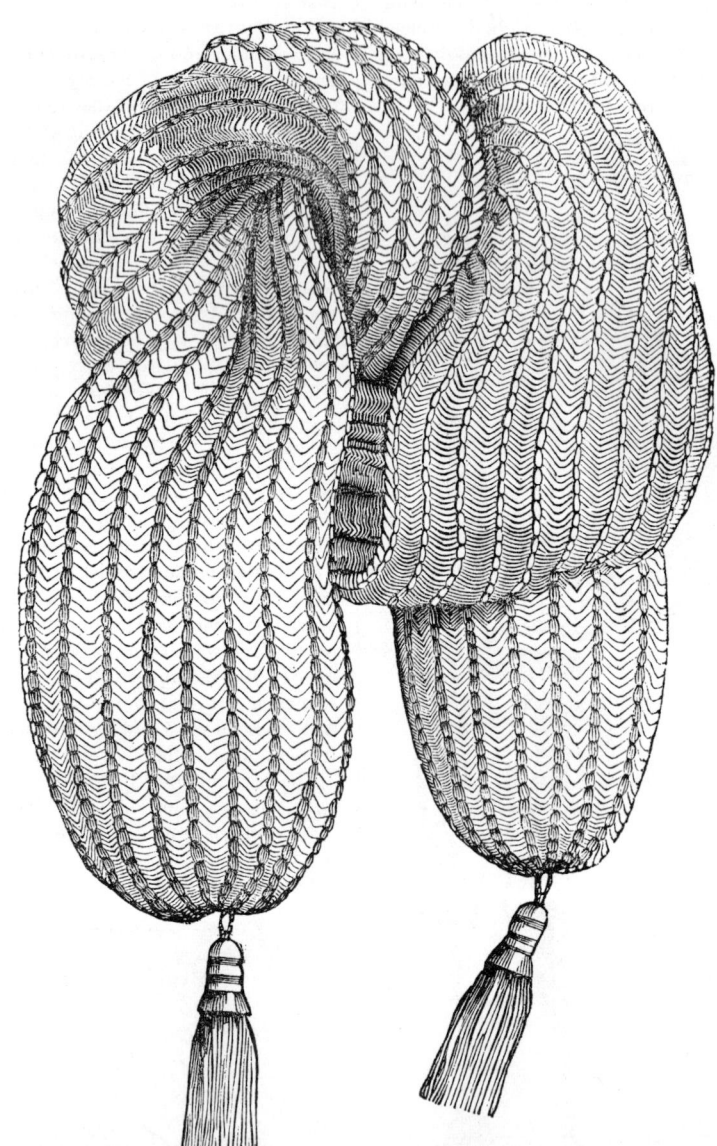

NECKTIE.

Materials—Half an ounce of blue and half an ounce of white Shetland wool, pins No. 10, and two mixed blue and white silk tassels.

Cast on 40 loops with blue; knit the first three rows alternately, pearl and plain.

4th row.—Fasten on the white, slip 1, *a*, thread forward, slip 1, knit 1; repeat from *a*.

5th row (blue).—Slip 1, *a*, thread forward, slip 1, knit 2 together; repeat from *a*.

Every row is knit like *5th*, but alternately with blue and white, changing the wool at the beginning of each row. Knit until you have one yard and an eighth completed; then knit one row 2 loops together, and 4 rows of plain knitting with blue; cast off. Join the two edges together on the wrong side; draw up the ends, and sew on the tassels.

CROCHET CURTAIN-HOLDER.

THIS curtain-holder is worked with crochet cotton. Begin to work that part of the holder which is fastened round the curtain. Make a sufficiently long foundation chain for the string on which the circles are drawn, and work on this chain, over thick soft cotton, 7 rows of double stitch. After the 2d row always insert

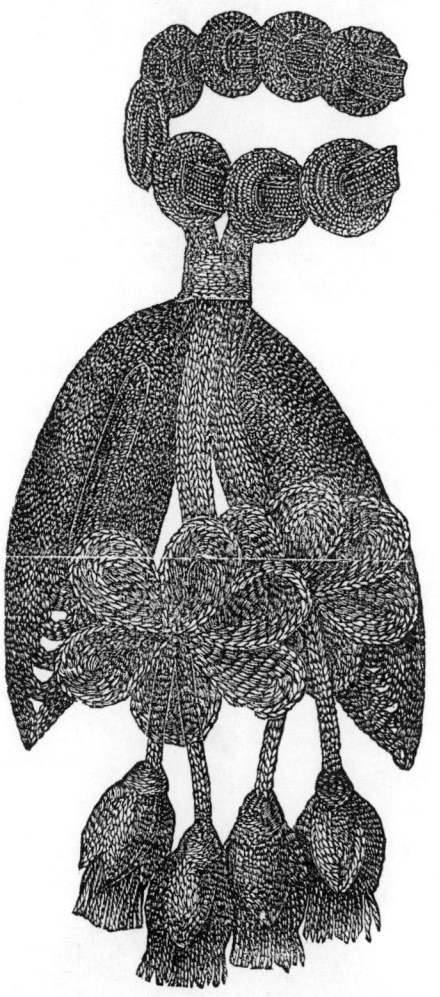

the needle into the 2 upper chain. For each circle work as in the 1st round over cotton 42 double stitches, join the stitches into a circle; draw the cotton over which you have worked a little tight, so that the stitches lie close to each other, and that the size of the circle corresponds to the width of the crochet string. On this round work 4 rounds of double stitch, al-

ways inserting the needle into both upper chain. Increase in such a manner that the circles keep perfectly flat. They are then drawn on the crochet strip, and sewn fast. The branch of the curtain-holder consists of crochet flowers and leaves. Begin with one of the long leaves in the centre, make a foundation chain of 20 stitches, miss the last, and work on both sides of the foundation chain—that is, in rounds—2 rounds of double stitch over cotton. Increase sufficiently at both ends of the leaf. When the 2d round of double stitch is completed, cut off the cotton over which you work, turn the work so that the wrong side of the leaf lies uppermost, and work from left to right 4 rounds of slip stitch, always inserting the needle into back chain. At both ends, stem and point of the leaf, work twice 1 chain in the first 3 rounds on each side of the middle stitch after a space of 2 slip stitches between; in the middle stitch work 2 slip stitches divided by 1 chain. For the 4th round of slip stitch work 3 chain at that end of the leaf which is meant for the point, miss the middle stitch, and increase at the upper end, as has just been described. The increasings at this end take place in the same manner till the leaf is completed. At the point of the leaf work an extra row, which is worked on the 8 stitches of each side of the middle stitch; then work 1 round all round the leaf, working 5 chain into the point, and missing under the same 2 stitches of the preceding round; then work again an extra row like the preceding one; then another one, which begins and finishes at about 12 stitches from the upper end. At the point of the leaf work 5 chain, missing under them the 3 middle stitches of the preceding round. Work another extra row on the 6 stitches on both sides of the middle stitch of the last extra row. Work 6 chain at the point, missing the 3 middle stitches of the preceding row. The next extra row is worked on the 4th stitch from the beginning of the last longest extra row; then work 1 round all round the leaf, working 2 double divided by 2 chain in the middle stitch at the point of the leaf. Begin the stem in this round at about 3 stitches from the upper end of the leaf. For this make a foundation chain of 16 stitches after the last stitch; work backwards and forwards 7 rows of slip stitches, always fastening one stitch at the end of one row on to the upper end of the leaf, and turning the work. Work one round of stitches all round the leaf and the stem; the leaf is then completed. The wrong side of the leaf is the right side of the work. The 2d leaf is worked in the same manner. For the flowers work each of the petals separately. Begin in the centre of one petal with a foundation chain of 5 stitches; miss the last, and work all round the foundation chain from right to left 7 rounds of slip stitches; at the lower pointed end of the petal work in the middle stitch of every round 2 slip stitches divided by 1 chain; at the other round end work 2 or 3 times 1 chain, leaving spaces of 1 or 2 stitches between. The middle one of the 3 upper petals, as well as the middle one of the 3 lower ones, is slanted off at the lower side. To obtain this work in the 5th round of slip stitches always 1 chain at the place of the 2 slip stitches, divided by 1 chain stitch worked on both sides of the middle stitch at the lower point. These chain stitches come forward in the next 2 rounds, and are placed, therefore, before the chain stitch of the preceding round, where a slip stitch must be worked. All the petals forming one flower are then sewn together from illustration; the stem of each flower consists of a double foundation chain, on the lower side of which work a row of slip stitches. The stems of the blossoms are worked in the same manner. These blossoms consist of a thick bunch of thread, which is surrounded by 4 leaves, forming a cup. Each leaf begins in the centre with 7 chain; miss the last, and work all round the foundation chain 6 rounds of slip stitches, increasing sufficiently to keep the leaf flat. For the pointed end of the leaf work here also 2 slip stitches divided by 1 chain stitch in 1 stitch; at the lower end, where the leaf is square, work in every round 1 chain stitch before and after the middle stitch. In the following round these chain stitches are worked before and after those of the preceding round, working 1 slip stitch in the chain stitch of the preceding round. When 4 such leaves are completed, join them together by a row of double stitch worked on the edges of the leaves. Then work 4 rounds on these, closing the cup by decreasing gradually. The different parts and branches are sewn together from illustration, and joined on to the crochet cord and circles.

JEWEL-STAND.

THIS jewel-stand consists of a cup made of card-board, covered with maize-colored silk, which latter is ornamented with point russe embroidery of brown silk. The stand on which the cup is fastened is made of wire, covered with crystal beads; it forms a circle and three feet. For the circle take a piece of wire six and two-fifths inches long joined into a circle; cover it closely with cotton, fastening at the same time the feet, which must be placed at equal distances from each other; each foot consists of a piece of wire six and two-fifths inches long, the ends of which, on which small crystal buttons are fastened, are turned back two-fifths of an inch; then cover the circle and feet with crystal beads, threaded on cotton. The cup consists of six pieces of card-board; each part

is covered on both sides with maize-colored *glacé* silk; the outer side of each part is previously worked in point russe embroidery with brown silk; the different parts are then sewn

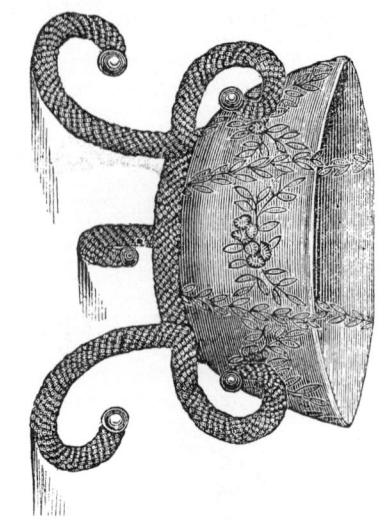

together on the wrong side with overcast stitch; along the seams work an embroidery pattern in point russe, as can be seen in illustration; lastly, fasten the cup on the stand.

EMBROIDERED PEN-WIPER.

THIS pen-wiper consists of a piece of white cloth, of the shape seen in illustration, to be

lined with card-board. The cloth is ornamented with embroidery. The card-board must be covered on the other side with black cloth. A pinked-out strip of black cloth is box-plaited and sewn on the inside of the card-board, as can be seen in illustration. The handle of the pen-wiper is made of wire, covered with crystal beads, threaded on wool or silk. Lastly, edge the white cloth all round with a strip of red cloth, pinked out on both sides; this strip is fastened down at intervals of one-fifth of an inch always with two steel beads.

WHAT-NOT OF SILK AND BEADS.

THIS what-not is meant for keeping odd articles lying about the room, or also for a duster, which it is always convenient to have at hand. Our pattern is made of blue silk; both the circles and the bars between are made of perforated card-board, crystal beads, and filoselle. The back part is made of thick card-board; it is ten inches high, ten and two-fifths inches wide; it is slanted off towards the bottom, and pointed at the top, as seen in illustration. The bottom part is six and four-fifths inches wide; its length must correspond to the width of the back part. It is rounded off according to the shape of the what-not. For the front part cut a piece of card-board four inches high, fourteen and two-fifths inches wide; it must be slanted off towards the lower edge, so as to be only twelve and four-fifths inches wide. All these pieces are first covered with gauze; the back and bottom part are covered on the outside with blue glazed calico, and on the inside with

back part. Then cut the different parts for ornamenting the front in perforated card-board. The Vandykes at the upper and lower edge are cut in one piece with the circles and bars. In our pattern each circle is one inch and one-fifth wide, each bar one inch and three-fifths high, and three-fifths of an inch wide. The bars are edged at the sides with buttonhole stitch of blue filoselle, and then covered in the long way with six rows of crystal beads. The circles are likewise covered with a plaited pattern of crystal beads. The bars between the circle consist of three rows of beads lying close to each other, and crossing each other in the manner seen in illustration. The space between the bars is covered with cross-stitches of blue filoselle. The circles are also edged with buttonhole stitch of blue silk on the inner edge; the remaining Vandykes of the perforated card-board are likewise covered with buttonhole stitch. When the trimming is completed, sew on a bouillon of blue silk, letting the upper and lower Vandykes come beyond it. Sew on loops, by means of which the what-not is hung on the wall.

WORK-CASE.

THIS small work-case is one of those German inventions that demonstrate how natty and neat-fingered the ladies of that country show themselves to be, even in trifling matters. It

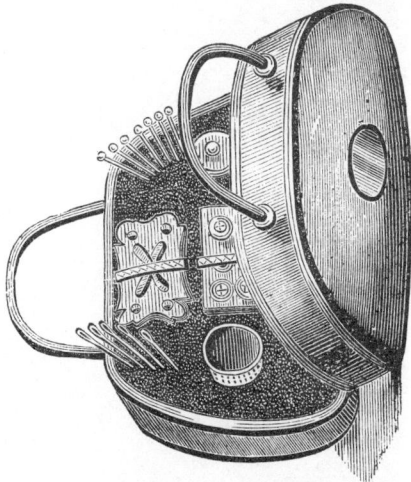

blue silk. The front part is covered on the inside with plain silk; on the upper edge of the same fasten a piece of silk six inches deep, sixteen and four-fifths inches wide, through the top of which an elastic eight inches long is drawn. Then sew the different parts of the what-not together, bind the back part at the upper edge with blue silk braid, and ornament the same with a three-skeined plait of crystal beads, covering the sewing on of the bag on the

is called a ball work-case, as it is home-made, and only intended to carry pins, needles, a little silk, hooks and eyes, and any small matter that will temporarily serve to mend a ball toilet. The case is cut the size required in strong card-board, and the different pieces are covered with brown Holland, and lined with blue silk; the handles are blue silk cord. Small receptacles are then made to contain the necessary implements.

DOLLS' FURNITURE.

Materials.—Card-board, pasteboard, wire, wood, knitting-pins, wadding, woollen reps, colored sewing silk, Berlin wool, gold beads, canvas, gimp, plush or Utrecht velvet, mahogany cloth.

in. The size of the carpet should be made in accordance with the doll's house. The squares, which are eight cross-stitches high, are all worked in lines of one color, and lie in two lines over each other, filling a square of four

THE middle of the carpet is of plush or Utrecht velvet, the border is in wool work. The work is in long cross-stitch—that is, over two threads of canvas one way, and four the other. For the fringe, fleecy wool is knotted canvas crosses. In our model there are, alternately, two lines in red and green, violet and gray, so that always gray and red, violet and green meet together. A loose black stitch marks the middle of each square; the corners are ornamented with little crosses of yellow silk.

THE TABLE.—The framework of which is shown in Figs. 2 and 3; strong card-board must be used at the outer edge. It is made firm by sewing wire round it. The frame of the top measures five and a half inches in

Fig. 2.

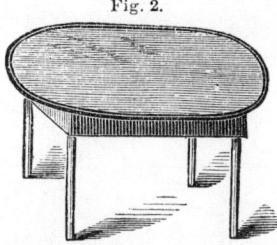

length and three inches and three-quarters in width; the edge is three-quarters of an inch broad. The edge and top are covered with brown cloth, which is gummed on. The legs, made of wood knitting-needles, are glued in; they are four inches high. The oval top is eight inches long and five inches wide. After it is covered with the cloth, and bound with black worsted braid, it is glued to the frame. The cover may be of woollen reps or velvet embroidered. Round the edge of the table-

Fig. 3.

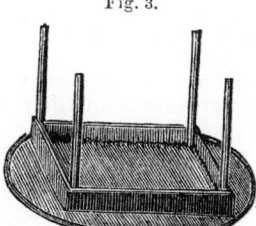

cover a woollen or silk fringe is put. The centre ornament consists of a small piece of white cloth, put on in *appliqué*, with blue coral stitch; round it are some little tatted rosettes of red silk.

THE OVAL FOOTSTOOL is two inches and a half long, and two inches and a quarter wide, and about an inch high; the cushion is stuffed with wadding—any small embroidery or *appliqué* pattern is suitable for the centre. The edge is a small piece of plaited red cloth, with a gold bead at intervals.

The round foot cushion is about an inch across. Any colored velvet will be suitable; it has a fringe of gold beads, and a few beads are sewn on at intervals. (See design.)

FOR THE SOFA, a piece of card-board nine and a half inches long is required. The middle of the back is six and a quarter inches high, sloped off for the arms, so that the front is only three and a quarter inches high. The two and a quarter inches high and nine inches long front part, together with the seat, which is rounded at the back, and three and three-quar-

ters deep in the middle, form the shape of the sofa. A wire is sewn round the back, on which the lines for the placing of the seats are marked, as well as the square divisions of the wadded back. The seat is also thinly wadded, and the material is fastened with separate beads, by which means the wadded squares are a little raised. The covering of the front and wadded seat is all in one piece, and the whole is joined to the back. Lastly, the back, the joining seam of the seat, etc., are covered with the reps; a braid border is placed in front of the seat, which is sewn on with gold beads and cord all round, and completes the whole except the feet. For these a part of a wooden knitting-needle an inch and a quarter high is fastened at the front corners and middle of back; about an inch of the needle is split off, then a hole is bored, and the flat side is laid upon the stuff, and each foot is fastened with very strong thread. The arm-chair is exactly like the sofa; the under part of the back wall is six and a half inches, and five and a half inches high in the middle of the back, waved off to two and a quarter inches at the front straight part. The straight front stripe is one inch and three-quarters broad and three inches long; the seat is two inches and a quarter deep in the middle.

The other chair requires a seat of card-board two inches and a quarter square sewn on. The back is four inches high, rounded at the upper part. When the seat and back are wadded, the reps cover is drawn over all in one piece, and the chair is completed in the same manner as the arm-chair and sofa. The feet are two inches high, cut from the pointed end of a wooden knitting-needle, and fastened on with good glue.

The back cushion is of white alpaca, about three inches square, and has also a middle piece and corners. The cushion is ornamented with fish-bone stitch upon yellow silk braid, and a narrow red ribbon ruche round the outer edge.

THE BOLSTER HANGING over the chair is three inches and a half long, covered with white alpaca, upon which are diagonal stripes of bright-colored herring-bone stitch.

The little circular Antimacassars are made of small tatted rosettes.

WATCH-POCKET IN PERFORATED CARD-BOARD.

THIS watch-pocket is embroidered with fine silk on perforated card-board. Our pattern consists of two parts, the back and the pocket. The pattern on each is a spray of rosebuds and forget-me-nots, embroidered in natural colors with two shades of pink and two shades of blue for the flowers, two shades of green for the foliage, and two shades of brown for the stems. The embroidery is worked in long stitch. The border is of brown stamped leather, sewn on with brown silk. The pocket is lined first with wadding, and then with silk; it is edged all

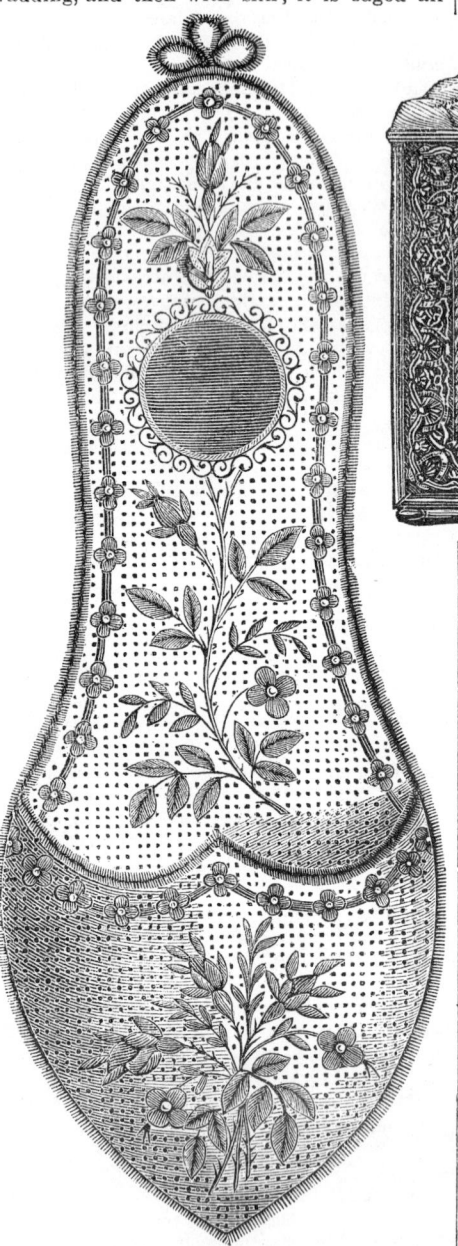

round with white chenille, which is arranged in loops at the top. The lining of the pocket must be slightly quilted. The hook is gilt.

BOX OTTOMAN WITH EMBROIDERY.

THIS elegant ottoman will be very useful in a sitting-room for holding newspapers, books,

work, etc. It is square, covered on the outside with purple cashmere; the cover is fitted up with a cushion. On each of the four sides of the case a piece of cashmere is plaited and arranged in the manner seen in illustration; it is gathered in the middle, and fastened with a rosette. Round this plaited part work a border of embroidery in *appliqué*. The arabesque patterns of purple *glacé* silk are sewn on in *appliqué* on the purple cashmere ground, and fastened with purple silk cord; the other figures of the pattern are worked in chain stitch with purple silk. The seams are covered with purple worsted braid. Any other color may be chosen for the covering of the ottoman, according to the furniture of the room.

WORK-CASE MADE OF A PUMPKIN.

Materials.—A yellow pumpkin measuring four and four-fifths inches across, some brown *glacé* silk, thick brown silk braid, round brown transparent beads, gold-colored purse silk, fine gold-colored silk cord and ribbon three-quarters of an inch wide, nine round brown glass buttons, some wadding.

THE pumpkin to be used for this case must be quite dry when gathered. Then hang it up to be dried. After some weeks cut it into halves, empty each half carefully as far as the skin, and bind each half round the edge with a strip of brown silk a quarter of an inch wide. This binding is covered on the outside with gold-colored ribbon, which is folded as seen on Fig. 2, then cover it with brown transparent beads from the same illustration, always drawing the yellow thread through the back of the pumpkin. The half destined for the lower part of the case is ornamented from illustration with eight round buttons, which form the feet, and are placed at intervals of one inch from each other, and at a distance of one inch and two-fifths from the centre. The loops of these buttons are drawn through the bark, a cord is drawn through these loops inside the bark so as to fasten them; the two ends of the cord are carefully knotted together. Each half is lined with card-board and brown *glacé* silk. The card-board lining is made of a strip of card-board three and three-fifths inches wide; its length must correspond to the width of the pumpkin; this strip has been gored seven times on one side at regular intervals, so as to have the shape of the pumpkin. The lining is then covered with a similar one of brown silk. The

cord. The lining of the upper half is not ornamented. Sew a round flat piece of card-board, covered with brown silk, in the top half at a distance of four-fifths of an inch; a double cross-strip of brown silk three-fifths of an inch wide is sewn on across this piece of card-board; it is stitched down along the edges, ornamented in the middle with coral stitches of yellow silk, and stitched on the bottom in such a manner as to form loops, in which the scissors, thimble, cotton, etc., are to be placed. The seams are covered with silk cord and beads wound round

Fig. 1.

Fig. 2.

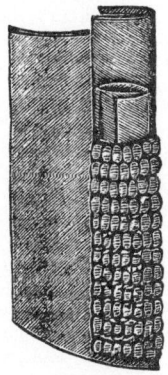

Fig. 3.

silk lining for the lower part of the case is turned back four-fifths of an inch on the card-board, which latter must be about two fifths of an inch higher than the pumpkin bark. On the inside the silk lining is edged along the top with two rows of yellow buttonhole stitches at a distance of three-fifths of an inch from each other; between these two rows work a row of coral stitches. Similar rows of coral stitches cover the seams of the lining. At the bottom of the case fasten a small round silk quilted cushion; the seam is covered with gold-colored silk

it. Both halves of the necessaire are varnished on the outside, and ornamented with bead borders worked from Fig. 1. In the middle of the upper half the ends of the bead borders are joined to a bead circle, in the middle of which a glass button is fastened. Two bead loops are fastened from illustration on the opposite sides of the case, through which two thick brown cords are drawn for the handle. The cords are plaited together in the middle; the lower ends are sewn together, and fastened on a button of the necessaire, as can be seen on illustration.

EMBROIDERY.

CARDINAL CAPE (TRICOT).

Materials.—Eight ounces of violet, two ounces of black, and one and a half of white 4-thread fleecy wool, a few small skeins of black wool twisted with while silk, eighteen medium-sized black beads, two or three wooden tricot hooks No. 8 (Bell gauge), of the same length.

THE violet foundation of this pelerine is worked in tricot. The under border is worked separately, and sewn on afterwards.

Begin at the under part of the foundation with 279 stitches for the width, and work the first 11 rows plain; in the 12th row commence the requisite decrease, by which the pelerine gradually becomes narrower over the shoul-

ders, and fits close at the throat. For this the 5th and 6th stitches on each side in the 12th row must be worked up together; then always after 13 stitches the two following must be worked up together. Upon this always after every 4 rows the 5th and 6th stitches are worked up together, and again decrease, as in the 12th row. By this means the spaces between are gradually reduced to 1 stitch, and from the 2d decreasing line care must be taken that the stitches knitted together from the middle of the back (with regard to the right and left front part) go in opposite directions. Therefore, in the first half, as far as the middle of the back, work always the stitch standing after, and in the last half the stitch standing before, with the stitches rising in straight lines from the under decreasing stitches. Continue this until 43 rows are worked, and in the 44th row leave the

10 end stitches untouched. In working off leave the 10 front stitches on the hook.

45th row. Work up and off the worked-off stitches of the preceding row.

46th. Besides the 10 end stitches previously left leave 3 more, and retain also 3 more at the beginning upon the hook. Work these 2 last rows alternately as far as the 52d row, and in the 48th row continue the decrease as far as possible.

53d. With this row work up and off all the end stitches as far as the end of the 44th row. Draw a violet wool cord of chain stitch, one and a half yard long, through the front perpendicular stitch threads of this row, and to the ends of this cord fasten woollen tassels of the same color 6 inches long, and twice bound round at the upper part with black wool twisted with white silk.

For the under border begin with 19 stitches for the breadth. For this crochet 20 single with black wool, and now work so that the under scallops represented in the design go towards the right hand obliquely, as before mentioned.

1st row. In tricot work the first 6 stitches with black wool, then, take a white reel and work up the following 6 stitches with white, then take a second black reel and work up the 6 following stitches with black, and take a second white reel and work the remaining stitches with white. All four reels remain on the work, and the stitches are always worked up and off with the same reel.

2d. Like the 1st, that is, the loop remaining upon the hook from the last stitch of the preceding row forms the first stitch of the new row; then work through the 2d perpendicular stitch thread lying in front, and so on.

3d to the 7th. In these five rows the scallop advances outwardly 1 stitch downwards; therefore, always at the beginning of this row, instead of working through the second, work through the front stitch thread standing outwards. There remain, however, as shown in the design, 6 stitches of each color, and the scallop gradually widens at the end from 1 to 6 white stitches.

8th and 9th. Plain, namely, working through the 2d stitch thread, and always 6 stitches of each color.

10th to the 14*th.* As the scallop must be again worked back in this row, work through the third instead of the second perpendicular stitch thread. For this the end stitch must be reversed at the first 3 times, 6 stitches always upon the first stitch of the other colors; and the white stitches at the end are reduced to 1 stitch.

15th and 16th rows like the 1st and 2d, and so on for the whole width of the bottom of the pelerine, which contains 18 scallops; then crochet on the scallop side of this a row of double stitches with violet, and over these little scallops with white wool * 1; double in the nearest 3 chain, passing over one under stitch; repeat from *; into the top of the white work little scallops with black wool twisted with white silk; * draw 1 loop through in front of the nearest double, and work off both by putting the thread round a fresh 3 chain, and repeat from the last *.

In the middle white scollops work according to the design a running pattern in feather stitch with black wool twisted with white silk; with the latter work also the little feather sprigs with a black bead in the middle in the upper white scallop; sew the border to the pelerine, and then crochet up the front 5 rows of double stitch—the 1st violet, 2d white, 3d black, 4th white, 5th violet. In working these double, inclose both the horizontal stitch threads upon the hook. The trimming for the throat is also worked separately, and sewn on. For this make a chain of 80 stitches with white wool and tricot, 1 plain row over it. In the next row work up with white wool, and work off with black twisted with white silk. In working off these stitches draw 3 loops always through the front before the following stitch of the hook is worked off with it. Work a similar pattern on the under side; for this turn the work, and crochet again through the front perpendicular stitch threads of the 1st row with white wool, and work off as before with black twisted with white.

GAITER FOR LITTLE GIRL.

Materials.—One ounce and a quarter of white Berlin wool, one skein of rose-colored filoselle, crochet hook No. 13, bell gauge.

WORK in rows forwards and backwards. The upper part is ornamented with little shells, increasing in number towards the front of the gaiter.

Commence with fifty stitches. The chain should be loose. Work the first row plain in double stitch, increasing one stitch in the last, sticking always in the back thread. The first pattern is worked at the end of the second row. For this lay the thread round the needle, stick over the first row into the last stitch but three —the forty-sixth stitch of the first row—and draw a loop through. When there are four of these double loops formed by sticking in the

same stitch upon the needle, take them from the needle all together with one chain, then crochet another chain, and conclude the row with three plain stitches. The upper edge is in straight lines. At the under edge as far as the middle, increase one stitch at the conclusion of each row.

At the end of the fourth row, work two shell patterns in reversed order, and afterwards the

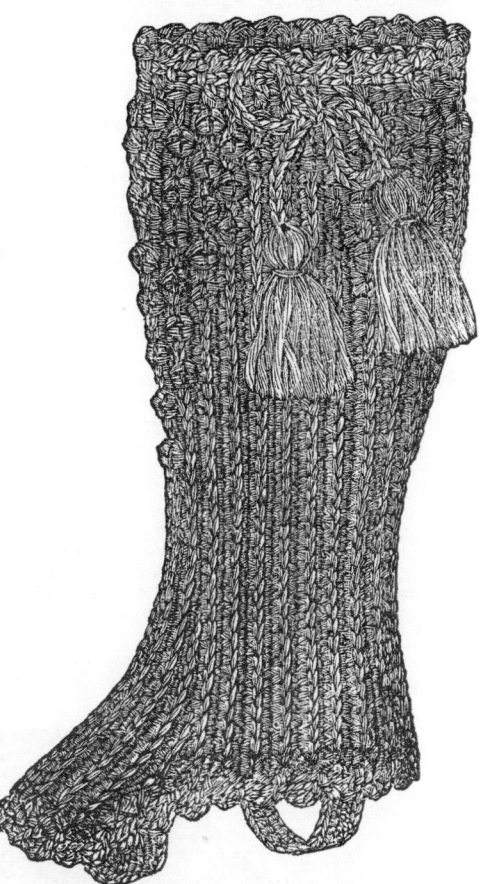

remainder in the same manner. The first of these two patterns commences in the sixth stitch, reckoning backwards from the edge; the latter must meet the last edge stitch but one.

6th row contains three shell patterns separated by three double.

8th. Work six double to form the beginning of the gore, work back upon these six stitches, and at the end make thirteen chain to begin the front of the foot; upon this chain work thirteen double, then six double upon the six stitches of the gore, and six stitches further on to lengthen it. Work back again to the end of the foot.

From here work as far as the front middle of the gaiter three entire rows forward and two back. In the first of these three rows forward, work five shell patterns, six in the second, and eight in the third; then continue the work in the same manner in the opposite direction until you have reached the row with one shell.

The back of the gaiter requires twenty-two rows with the patterns arranged in two little scallops. Each scallop begins like the front with one shell. The longest pattern row contains five patterns. All the rows are worked in straight lines except the eleventh and twelfth. In order to widen the upper part, turn the work in the eleventh row after thirty-eight stitches; and in working back upon these, crochet a shell pattern in the last stitch but one.

When these rows are finished, sew the gaiter up lengthwise on the wrong side. Then work one row of double round the upper and under edge. For the under conclusion, crochet picots containing five chain with one double in the first chain. At the upper edge work an interrupted treble row. Make a chain with two little tassels at the ends to run into this row. Above the interrupted treble work a line of picots as before described. Then crochet two narrow straps, consisting of four rows of double, and fasten them under the foot. Each shell pattern has a cross stitch of filoselle in the middle, and a line of cross stitch round the edge of the foot (see design.)

WRITING-CASE.—EMBROIDERY.

Materials.—Brown woollen reps, silk flat braid in two corresponding shades of brown, silk cordon, also in suitable colors; card-board, black silk cord, brown ribbon, etc.

are arranged in the same manner, the outer square of which is five inches and a half high, four inches and a half broad. It will be easy to work the scallop ornamented with light silk braid. A large flower fills the middle space (Fig. 1) like the corner flower, or initials may be worked in raised embroidery, surrounded with a kind of foliage in fish-bone stitch, worked with shaded brown silk.

Fig. 2.—Writing-Case—Open.

Our model is embroidered with maize silk, with black stalk stitch and black knots; the fish-bone stitch is of brown silk. Between the two sides of the cover a space is left for two lines of stitching, which forms the back of the book; but these lines must not be stitched until the entire cover is lined with the same material, and a piece of card-board pushed in, which is fastened at the same time.

The inner arrangement of the case shown in Fig. 2 is also of brown reps, and is sixteen and a half inches long and six and a quarter inches broad. A flat piece of card-board, ten inches

Fig. 1.—Writing-Case—Closed.

Both the outer cover sides are worked upon brown reps, measuring sixteen inches in length and eleven inches and a half in breadth.

The pattern is braided in black, while stitches of maize silk, three together, ornament the outer edge of the dark braid, and light brown buttonhole stitch the inner edge. The corner flower consists of leaves of raised embroidery, between which are fish-bone stitches of brown shaded silk; the veins and calix knots are maize color. The colors for the middle pattern

and a half long and six inches broad, is gummed underneath exactly in the middle.

The narrow stuff part that turns over is fastened with fish-bone stitch in maize color, and, with the piece of the material that turns over at the sides, forms a pocket for sheets of paper, envelopes, etc. The outer edge of the case is ornamented with silk cord; a narrow ribbon is placed in the middle of the case. For holding the blotting-paper, white moire paper is put in as a cover for the blotting-paper. Little elastic straps are placed for the pens, etc. The nibs of the pens are put in a little pocket of cloth and pasteboard, which forms the pen-wiper also, see design. At the other end is a pocket for steel pens.

TOILET CUSHION.
(*See Illustration, Page* 201.)

Materials.—A piece of very fine white Swiss muslin nine inches square, a little rose-colored Shetland wool, a very fine rug needle, a half yard of narrow white braid, and one yard of white silk fringe.

THE design (which consists of sprays of leaves in the centre, surrounded by Vandykes, having a single leaf in each), must first be drawn on paper thus :—

Draw a circle 5 inches in diameter, in which draw four sprays of three leaves, each spray occupying the space of one-quarter of the circle. Let the stems incline towards the centre, as seen in the engraving. Now draw eight Vandykes round the circle, in each of which draw a single leaf to corespond with those in the sprays—the leaf running to the point of the Vandyke, which should be about two inches deep.

The design being thus prepared, place it under the muslin, on which trace it with a fine black lead-pencil or a brush, and indigo mixed with thin gum-water.

Now remove the paper, and with the Shetland wool chain stitch the sprays and single leaves in the Vandykes very finely. Take a piece of white braid sufficient to go round the circle, and with the wool slightly and loosely work a row of open buttonhole stitches on one edge of it, and run it neatly round the circle, taking the two ends through the muslin, as it is difficult to fasten braid invisibly. Cut away the muslin between the Vandykes, leaving sufficient outside each to form a narrow turning which must be made on the right side of the cushion. On this turning lay the white silk fringe, and run it neatly round each Vandyke, making the edge exactly cover the mark forming the outline of the Vandykes. Now make a cushion of strong white linen, sufficiently high to allow the fringed points to touch the table ; the bottom of it may be covered with rose-colored silk, and the top and sides with white silk or satin. Fill it tightly, but not too hard, and tack the circle round which the braid is sewn to the top of the cushion, allowing the points to fall over. Make a pretty knot of rose-colored and white ribbon mixed, tack in the centre, and the cushion is complete.

It is impossible to describe the chaste and elegant appearance of this simple cushion when made ; and we feel sure our fair young friends will acknowledge it to be a pretty specimen of the many ornamental and useful articles which may be made at very trifling expense both of money and time.

The cushion may, of course, be made to suit the drapery of any room by substituting any other colored wool, ribbon, etc.

WORK-BASKET.

Materials.—Silver glazed perforated card-board (canvas *à la* jardinière), green chenille, green satin ribbon, four-fifths of an inch wide, green sewing silk, thin card-board ; white calico, narrow green ribbon.

THIS work-basket, in the shape of a star, is covered with silver glazed perforated card-

board, which is embroidered with green chenille in the manner seen in the illustration. Cut first the bottom and the cover of the basket of both plain and of perforated card-board ; and the border, which must be four inches deep, and long enough to correspond to the outer edge of the star parts, which forms the cover. All the different pieces of card-board must then be covered with calico. Then join the border with overcast stitches on to the bottom of the basket, and ornament the pieces of perforated card-board with embroidery, as seen in illustration. When the different parts are completed, fasten them on to the pieces of card-board with overcast stitches, bind the upper edge of the basket with green silk ribbon, and join the seam by a ruche of green satin ribbon ; a similar ruche is sewn on the edge of the cover. The basket fastens with a crystal button and a loop of white elastic. Lastly, sew on the handles, which consist of strips of perforated card-board, trimmed with ruches of green ribbon.

SHIRT-BOX.

Materials.--Leather or cashmere, either green or brown, silk cordon to match, curled cord, gold cord. If the case be made at home, card-board, white glazed paper, and stiff linen must be added.

Fig. 1.—Shirt-Box (Closed).

THE box should be just large enough to hold the number of dress shirts required for packing.

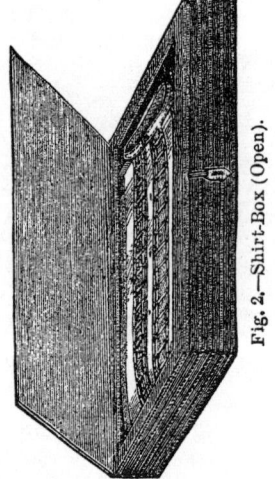

Fig. 2.—Shirt-Box (Open).

It may be made by a lady, but is better purchased of a portmanteau-maker.

It may then be covered with cashmere, leather, or velvet, embroidered. The initials of the owner should be in the middle of the box cover.

ORIENTAL TABLE-COVER.

(See Instructions, Page 201.)

Materials,—Knitting cotton No. 4, three meshes, two flat, one-half an inch wide, the other an inch and a half, and one round mesh No. 14, twenty-seven skeins of Berlin wool, three of each of the following colors: peach, green, plum, yellow, claret, dark blue, pink, light blue, and scarlet, a large rug needle, and a netting needle.

ON a round foundation of 23 stitches with the half inch mesh, net 2 plain rounds.

3d round. Round mesh, plain netting.

4th, 5th, and 6th. The same.

7th. Half-inch mesh, 2 stitches in each.

8th. Same mesh, 1 stitch in each, missing the first, netting the next stitch, and returning to the missed one all round.

9th. Round mesh, 1 stitch in each.

10th, 11th, 12th, and 13th. The same.

14th. Half-inch mesh, 3 stitches in each.

15th and 21 succeeding rounds. Round mesh, 1 stitch in each.

37th. Wide flat mesh, 3 stitches in each.

38th. Round mesh. Net 3 stitches together missing the first 3, netting the 3 next, and returning to the missed 3, continue all round.

39th. Round mesh, 1 stitch in each.

40th and 4 succeeding rounds The same.

The top part of the cover is now netted, and there remain but the points to net.

With round mesh net 13 stitches, and instead of continuing the round, return on the 13 stitches, missing the last. Continue backwards and forwards on these, always missing the last till you have but one stitch left on the mesh. Cut the cotton and fasten the end; take up the next 13 stitches, and make another point, and continue the same all round the cover.

Now commence the darning. Thread the rug needle with green wool, and insert it in the 5th mesh from the centre (which is where the two knots are visible in one mesh), and darn 3 meshes upwards to the right, filling the meshes closely with wool; then in a line with the first of these 3 and upwards to the left darn 2 meshes, each separately, in order that all the darning may lean to the right.

Having done this there will be one mesh left in the middle of the green Vandyke, which darn in plum color. Darn 6 of these round the centre of the cover. Between the lower points of each Vandyke there will be three diamonds, darn the middle one in dark blue.

Now in the 12th mesh (where the 3 knots are seen in one mesh), with scarlet darn a diamond of 4 meshes to the right; do the same in every 5th mesh all round.

As before, there will be 3 vacant meshes between the lower points of each scarlet diamond, the centre one of which fill with dark blue, and above the dark blue spot darn a Vandyke of 4 meshes in claret.

In the 36th round of netting darn close diamonds of 9 meshes (leaving a space of 3 meshes between the lower points of each), of different colors, in the following order: peach, green, plum, yellow, claret, dark blue, pink, light blue. There are 33 diamonds required in the round; it will therefore be necessary to work these 8 colors 4 times, which will leave one still vacant; this one may be darned in scarlet.

Miss 3 meshes upwards from one of these closely-darned diamonds, and darn 6 meshes to the right, then 4 meshes in an opposite direction from each point of the 6 already darned, thus three sides of a diamond are formed; complete the 4th side by darning 6 meshes.

There will be 17 diamonds, which may be darned thus: yellow, dark blue, scarlet, green, peach, claret, light blue, pink. Repeat these colors twice, which will leave one to do; this may be done in plum-color.

This will leave an open diamond of 16 meshes (4 each way), the centre 4 of which darn in 2 colors, the two opposite each other in one, and the other two in a good contrasting color.

There is always a slight irregularity in round netting, which will cause the first diamond to appear scarcely even with the last. This, however, cannot be avoided, and is not discernible except on very close examination, and does not at all affect its appearance when on the table. It will also be found necessary to lessen the space between the open diamonds, one mesh in two instances, as if there were two more meshes it would cause an irregularity in the close diamonds.

The top part of the cover is now finished, and the points only remain to be darned.

Between each point darn a close diamond of 9 meshes, the lower point of which will hide the fastening of cotton at the commencement of the netted point.

At the end of every point darn an open diamond of 4 meshes, and knot a tassel in the last mesh of each point composed of 4 strands of each color used in darning.

This cover is quickly done, and has a very foreign and elegant appearance.

NEEDLE CASE WITH EMERY CUSHION.

THIS pretty little case is very practical; it can be carried in the pocket. It is made of card-board of a square shape, about two inches and two-fifths high, with a well-fitting cover, and ornamented with point russe embroidery on glacé silk. The top of the case is cut out on the four sides, as seen in Fig. 1, which shows the case without the cover. Inside the case place a smaller card-board box filled with emery; the top of this box is covered with glacé silk. Between the box filled with emery and the needle case, place four papers filled with needles, as can be seen in Fig. 1. On the

Fig. 1.—Needle Case with Emery Cushion—Open.

outside the case is covered with colored glacé silk, embroidered with point russe, see Fig. 2.

Fig. 2.—Needle Case with Emery Cushion—Closed.

The pieces of silk are joined together at the corners of the case with fine buttonhole stitch.

LETTER FOR MARKING.

SKIPPING-ROPE OF GRAY COTTON, COVERED WITH RED WOOL.

Materials.—Spanish bamboo or cord, red fleecy wool, gray cotton.

Fig. 2 shows one end of the skipping-rope. It consists of a piece of Spanish bamboo or cord, one yard and thirty-two inches long. The ends must be covered with cotton, so as to form the handle, which are then covered with thick gray cotton, drawn on very tight, and

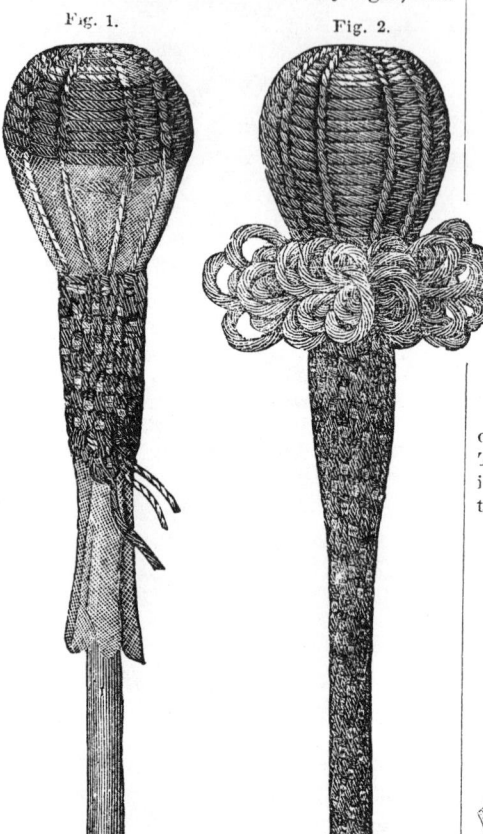

Fig. 1.   Fig. 2.

fastened underneath the knob. Then begin to darn the handles, from Fig. 1, with gray cotton, beginning in the middle of the top, and then work on with red wool. When the handle is completed, cover the bamboo or cord with buttonhole stitch of red wool, working over one double gray thread, always working two buttonhole stitches in every other button stitch; loop; these two stitches must be alternated in every round, as can be seen on Fig. 1. Loops of red wool finish off each handle at the bottom.

KNITTED OVERSHOE.

This is intended to be drawn over a boot or slipper for evening parties. A pattern should

first be cut of the boot worn, and the shoe knitted from that, in double rip of any plain

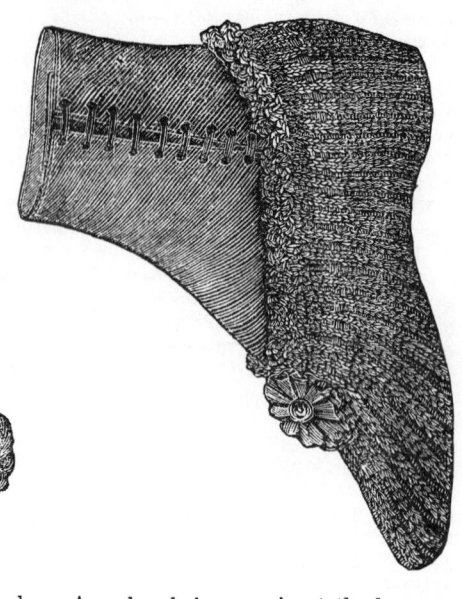

color. A cork sole is sewn in at the bottom. The border around the top is of open crochet, in scarlet wool, and a rosette of scarlet on the toe.

INFANT'S BIB.

Made of quilted *piqué;* the edge finished with narrow points, made of the *piqué.*

TOILET CUSHION.
(See Instructions, Page 197.)

ORIENTAL TABLE-COVER.
(See Instructions, Page 198.)

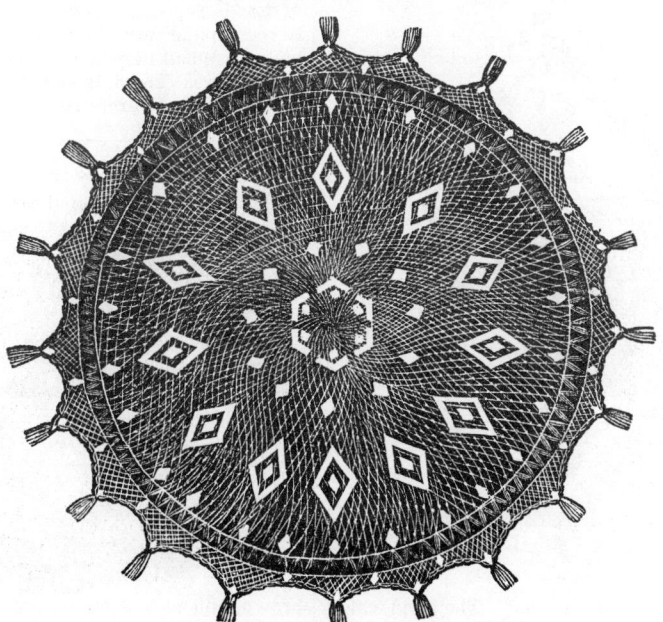

WORK-BASKET.

FIG. 1 shows the finished basket, the framework of which is of cane. The basket is of fine

Fig. 1.

white cloth, pinked at the edges. This is shown in the full size in Fig. 2. A blue trimming is sewn down upon it with maize and gold-colored

Fig. 3.

wicker-work. This is covered nearly to the edge with crimson silk, lined and fitted with

Fig. 2.

purse-silk. The lace-like stitches are of crimson silk. The forget-me-nots are worked in the natural colors.

Fig. 3 gives the design for top of basket. This design is repeated eight times, and is worked to correspond with the band going around the basket. Small buttons covered with silk finish the corners. The dots may be beads or a knot-stitch of silk, as preferred.

———◆◆———

PENWIPER.

THE materials required for this are black,

pockets of the same material. The band which goes around the outside of the basket is of fine

brown, and cinnamon-colored cloth, and light blue satin ribbon; blue, brown, and gold silk;

a brown and gold handle. The foundation of the penwiper is a piece of card-board, circular in shape, and measuring in diameter four inches. This should be covered with a little black silk, and under it place several folds of black cloth neatly pinked at the edges; the top of the penwiper is formed of frills of the colored cloth pinked at the edges, and embroidered with the different colored silks. First of all it is a black frill, worked with gold; then a brown frill, worked with gold, and on this lies the cinnamon-colored frill, worked with stars of gold, and edged with blue silk; the centre has a rosette of blue ribbon, on which is placed the handle, which is of turned wood, and should be painted brown and gold. Of course any other handle could be substituted.

FAN.—EMBROIDERED NET.

THE design is shown in the full size in Fig. 2. It may be of black or white net, embroidered with silk or gold thread, according to taste.

FRINGED BORDER

FOR COUNTERPANES, ETC., IN POINTED BRAID AND CROCHET.

THIS fringe border is worked with white linen pointed braid and white crochet cotton No. 30, commencing with the centre rosette inside a scallop in the following manner: For the outer circle of the rosette of braid, cut a piece of braid 10 points in length, sew the 2 end points over each other, so as to form a circle of 9 points, and crochet on one side of the braid into each point 1 double stitch, after each double 2 chain. The inner circle of braid of 7 points is worked in the same way, but this is joined to the one already made by being laid on the centre and by working in with every double stitch 1 stitch of the crocheted edge inside the first circle; after every double stitch, only 1 chain stitch. Then the thread is cut off and secured. Around the edge 5 rows are now crocheted as follows: 1st row. Into each point of the outer circle of the rosette 1 double, then

Fig. 1.

Fig. 2.

The design must be traced upon paper to the required shape and size, and the net tacked over the work. The fan has a lace trimming sewn on at the upper edge.

always 5 chain, 1 treble between 2 points, 5 chain, at the end of the row 1 slip-stitch into the 1st double of this row. 2d. 3 slip-stitches into the 3 first chain stitches of the last row,

then alternately 5 chain, 1 double into the centre stitch of each loop of chain stitches of the
last row. 3d. 3 slip stitches into the first 3
chain stitches of the last row, then alternately
7 chain, 1 double into the centre stitch of each

points are required for the top and 20 points
for the bottom edge; they are joined in the
next row, as shown in the illustration, to the
work. 5th. 5 slip stitches into the first 5 chain
stitches of the last row, *, 4 chain, 1 double

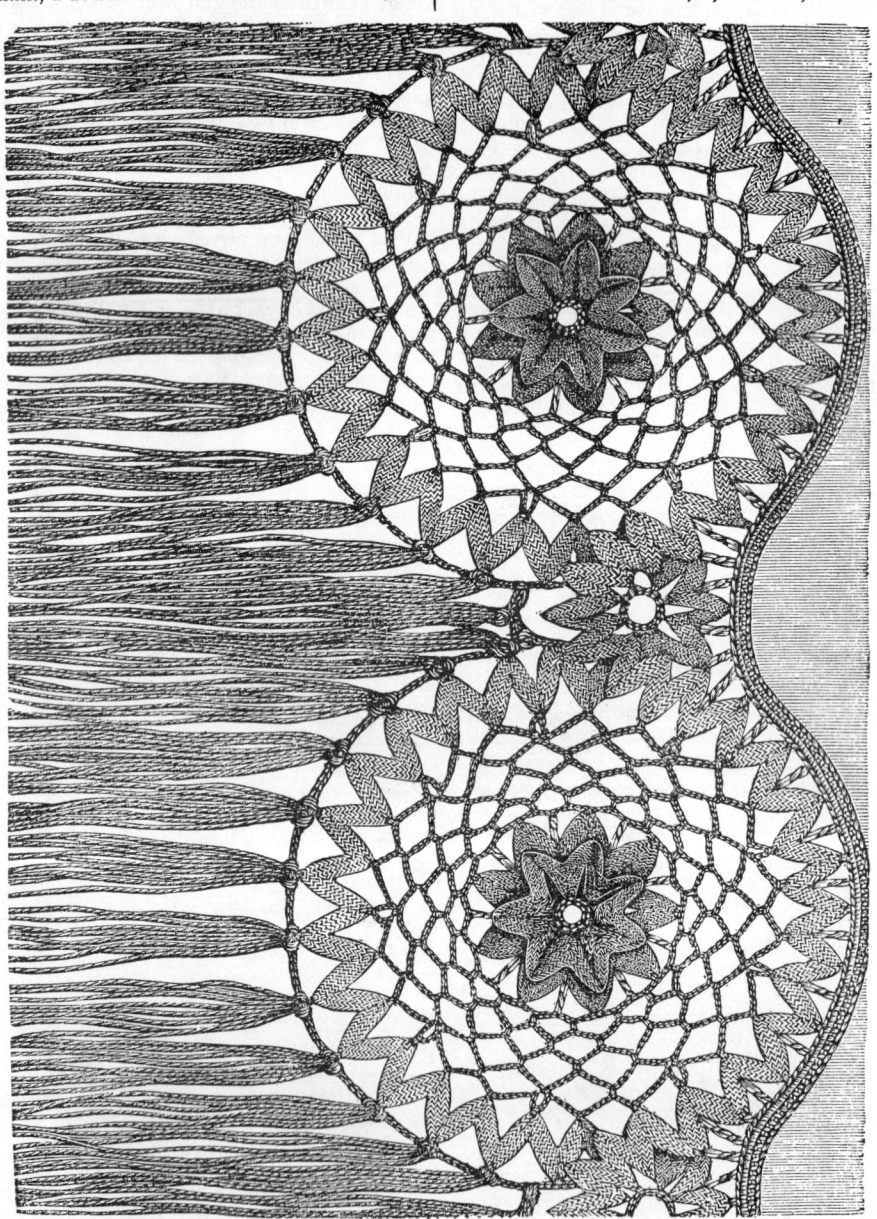

loop of chain stitches of the last row. 4th. 4
slip-stitches into the first 4 chain stitches of the
last row, then alternately 9 chain stitches, 1
double into the centre stitch of each loop of
chain stitches. Then 2 more rows of braid are
arranged according to the illustration; for each
of these, till the repetition of the pattern, 18

into the point of the first row of braid marked
with a cross (†) (see illustration), 4 chain, 1
double into the centre stitch of the next loop
of chain stitches of the last row, 4 chain, 1
double into the next point of the braid, 4 chain,
1 double into the centre stitch of the same loop
of chain stitches of the last row into which 1

double has been already worked, 4 chain, 1 double into the next point of the braid, 4 chain, 1 double into the centre stitch of the next loop of chain stitches of the last row; repeat according to the illustration 8 times from *, but at the commencement of the 5th repetition from * the 1st double stitch after the 4 chain stitches is crocheted into the 18th point of the 2d row of braid. The last double stitch of this row is joined to the last of the 4 slip stitches which were crocheted at the commencement of this row. Then the thread is cut off and secured. Of the 5 points of both rows of braid hitherto disregarded at the commencement of the border (and for the future between all the scallops), and which cross each other twice, the 4 centre points of both rows are joined to a circle, according to the illustration. When the border is the requisite length, it is edged at the bottom with a row of alternately 1 double into each point of the braid, then 7 chain stitches. Now the fringe of fine cotton is tied in according to the illustration. The top of the border is edged with 2 rows as follows : 1st row. *, 1 double into the centre point between 2 scallops, 2 chain, 1 treble between the 2 next points of the braid, 2 chain, 1 treble, according to the illustration, into the next 2 points, 2 chain, 1 long treble between the next 2 points, 2 chain, 8 times alternately 1 double into the next point, 3 chain, 1 treble between the next 2 points, 3 chain ; then 1 double into the next point, 2 chain, 1 long treble between the next 2 points, 2 chain, 1 treble, according to the illustration, into the next 2 points, 2 chain, 1 treble between the 2 next points, 2 chain, repeat from *. 2d. Into every stitch of the last row 1 double. This border is attached to the article for which it is intended by means of buttonhole stitches.

TRAVELLING-BOX FOR COLLARS, CUFFS, ETC.

The materials are black cloth, buttons, and

Fig. 1.

scarlet braid, scarlet and gray drill, a wicker-basket or tin box.

The basket or box should be about twelve inches in diameter, and nine inches deep. The cover must be cut just large enough to pass over it, and to allow for turnings. The outside is of good black cloth, bound with scarlet braid, about three-quarters of an inch deep, ornamented at distances of an inch, with white porcelain buttons.

Fig. 1 shows the outside of the finished box, with the place for handles and straps. The straps are made of cloth, lined with Holland, and bound with scarlet braid. The straps are one inch wide.

Fig. 2.

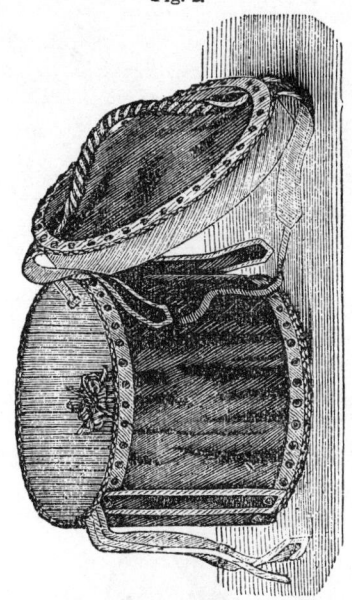

Figs. 2 and 3 show the different arrangements for the inside of the box, which is neatly lined with the drill.

In Fig. 3 a bag, the size of the bottom of the box, is put in and is drawn up with a double

Fig. 3.

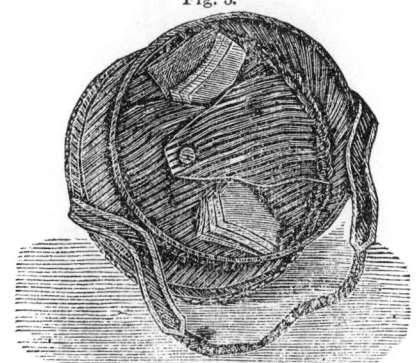

slide at the top. The edge of the box is finished by a cord.

Fig. 3 shows flaps put in, which fasten over the contents with a button and buttonhole.

CIGAR-CASE.

THE materials are cardboard, fawn-colored kid, leather strap, crimson purse-silk, and silk braid of the same color for binding. Fig. 2

Fig. 1.

shows the cigar-case open. Fig. 1 half the design for embroidery. Cut two pieces of cardboard six inches long, and three and a half

Fig. 2.

inches wide, rounded at the top, and sloped at the bottom (see design).

The sides and tops are cut in one piece; for this a strip measuring one inch wide, and fifteen inches long, is needed. The embroidery must be first worked, then put on the cardboard foundation, which is covered with it, and neatly lined with silk and bound with braid. Loops of braid are sewn on at the side to pass the strap through. The inner part to hold the cigars is cut to the same shape, just small enough to go into the outer part, and fits it closely; this has a loop of braid at the bottom, to pass the strap through; a simple design may be embroidered at the top of the outer part of the case.

NOTE-BOOK WITH LOOSE LEAVES.

THIS note-book is made of card-board, and covered with Russian leather. The inside of the upper cover is ornamented with a medallion of taffetas, in which initials are worked

in gold thread and crimson silk, and flowers in shaded gray silk. At the side of the under cover there is a small clasp or strap to hold the pencil. The leaves are loosely fastened at one end, and can be taken out singly.

SMALL CROCHET ROSETTE.

To be made of fine cotton. These can be joined together to form a tidy.

DESIGNS FOR BED-ROOM ANTIMACASSARS.

THESE designs may be worked upon Java canvas or honeycomb cotton material. Red and black ingrain Andalusian wool is generally used for the work. The edge of the material frayed out forms the fringe.

Fig. 1.

FANCY STITCH FOR KNITTING.

EMBROIDERED CROSS FOR CHURCH MARKERS.

To be embroidered in gold-colored silk. A pretty design.

Fig. 2.

PATCHWORK DESIGNS.

THREAD FRAMES.

THE frames are cut out in card-board and covered with paper of the requisite color, which is cut large enough to turn over the edges and be pasted down at the back. The card-board for Fig. 3 is best cut by a stationer. That for Fig. 1 is cut each side separately.

in the filoselle, passing it through the overcasting to secure it, and slipping it from one to the other at the back, bringing the needle out at the upper edge. Both stitches may be caught at once. Each oval has a separate back, secured by strips of paper, and the support is fastened to the upper one.

Fig. 1

Cover the foundation of Fig. 3 with blue paper. Take a skein of gold-colored filoselle, and divide it into threads of three strands each, with which work the pattern over and over the foundation in buttonhole stitch, keeping the filoselle quite smooth and even. When the gold has been worked, take black purse silk and work a stitch at each edge of the divisions

Cover the separate sides for Fig. 1 with wood-brown paper, measure the crossings, and carefully cut away their width for half the thickness of the frame, doing this underneath for the two side pieces, and on the upper side for the top and bottom, so that the frame may be put together. Take the slip for the top, and make a slit for a third of its width half an inch from

Fig. 2.

Fig. 3.

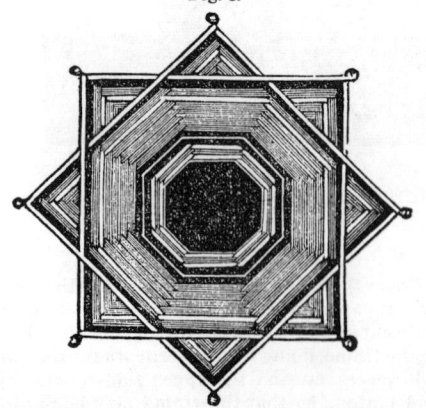

the end. Take a reel of machine thread, and cut from it seven strands rather more than twice the length of the slip of card, double them, pass the doubled end through the slit, and secure it there by a small pin passed through the loop; proceed in this way with all the seven strands, and pull them quite tight around the pin, let them lie on the card quite straight, and be careful that the central two are exactly in the middle. Take a reel of wood-brown *glacé* thread, tie it around the slip of card, as near as possible to the end, and wind it around perfectly smoothly and evenly fifteen times, which will bring you to the beginning of the strands. Keeping the others flat and smooth, turn back the two middle strands, wind the brown thread three times, turn back the two strands on each side, wind the thread three times more, the two next in the same way, and finally the two outer ones. Wind the brown thread three times, turn the two outer ones on each side down again, wind three times, and so on until the diamond is complete. Wind the brown thread over all fifteen times, lay the strands quite smooth along the part cut away for the crossing, securing them by a turn or two of the brown thread. Wind the brown thread twelve times after the crossing has passed, and make another diamond; wind six brown, and make the pattern again, continuing it for six diamonds, with six brown threads between each, and before you come to the crossing wind the brown twelve times. Finish the end as you began, only pulling the strands smooth and flat, and putting the diamonds into shape with a needle, cutting them off before the end is quite reached. Wind the brown thread as near as possible to the end, and fasten it by a knot on the wrong side. If the diamonds are too large or too small, the brown

fore the last one, but only six brown threads are wound between the thirteen others, as directed for the top and bottom. Gum the upper and under sides of the crossings strongly, and fitting them exactly put the frame under a heavy weight, not disturbing it until it is dry. Put red paper at the back, and cover the back of the frame and the support with it also.

BOX FOR CIGARS.

THIS cigar box, seen open at Fig. 1 and closed at Fig. 4, which can be manufactured with little trouble, is prepared of a proper size

Fig. 1.

Fig. 3.

Fig. 2.

Fig. 4.

thread may be slipped backwards or forwards, but it must be perfectly smooth and even, and the strands close together. Make the bottom of the frame in the same way, and then the sides, but the whole of these are covered with the pattern, as they come outside in the crossing. After the first diamond the brown thread is wound twenty times, and this is repeated be-

and depth, either in stout card-board or thin wood, and lined with tin foil. The outside is covered with Havannah brown fine cloth or Cashmere, a strip of which, in one piece (the length and depth required to go around the sides), is worked with a design in chain stitch, dots, and picot stitch, according to detail shown at Fig. 2, and the centre of the piece for the top with a corresponding one seen at Fig. 3. Having pasted some dark brown colored paper over the bottom of the box, proceed to cover the sides and top with the embroidered material, the former being finished at the corners and around the top edge with gold-colored sarsnet ribbon. Two lengths of the same ribbon, sufficient to go around the box and make a bow at the top, are sewn by the centre at a

row you work, 5 dc over the ring, * 5 ch, 5 dc over the next ring; repeat from *.

FEATHER ROSE.

FIG. 2 shows the shape and size for cutting the feathers to form the rose. The stamens and leaves may be made as described for carnations in our last number.

Fig. 1.

short distance from the side of the upper edge in front, and serve to tie the box together when closed, in the manner shown in the illustration Fig. 4. Three shades of Havannah brown *mi-torse* silk are to be used for the embroidery.

CROCHET EDGING.

THIS edging is crocheted the short way. Commence with * a chain of 9, 1 single in the first ch. The 2d of these 9 chain should be cro-

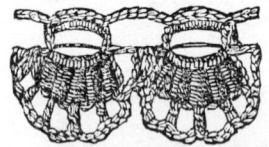

cheted very loosely, as all the long stitches have to be worked in it; 3 ch, 6 twisted long in the 2d ch. Each twisted long is worked with the thread 12 times around the needle, then 3 ch, 1 single on the next stitch in the ring, 5 ch, and repeat from *. *The 2d row.* Commence with a treble on the 1st long, * 3 ch, a treble on the next long, 3 ch, a treble on the next long, 3 ch, a treble on the next long, 3 ch, a treble on the last long, 2 ch, a treble on the 2d of the 5 ch, a treble on the 4th of the 5 ch, 2 ch, a treble on the next long; repeat from *. The under

Fig. 2.

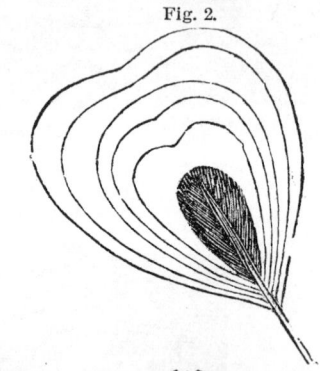

GIMP EDGING FOR UNDER-LINEN.

CROCHET cotton, No. 24, metal pin, and crochet needle. Prepare a gimp according to illustration, 1 double in the 2d loop which has been placed over the 1st loop, 7 chain; repeat. For the upper side, alternately twist the loop once around the needle, 1 crochet, 1 double, 2 chain.

CROCHET BOLSTER CUSHION COVER.

THE material chosen in the original is gray wool of two shades, with which four stripes twenty-three inches long is worked in a kind of raised crochet. Two stripes are worked of the darker, and two of the lighter shade. Crochet along a chain of 16 stitches as follows: *1st row.* Miss 1, 1 double in every stitch, 1 chain. *2d and 3d.* 1 double in both parts of every stitch, 1 chain at the end of each row. *4th.* * 3 double, 1 spot in the upper part of the next stitch of the *second* row. The spot is made by winding the thread around the needle, and drawing it through the above-named stitch as a loop

into a circle, and crochet 4 rounds of double crochet, increasing as required by the shape. Cut off and fasten the thread. Then take a length of white wool. *5th round.* * 1 slip stitch in the upper *front* part of the next double; 6 chain, going back along these 6 chain 1 double in the 2d, 5 double, 1 slip stitch where the last stitch was worked, repeat from *. *6th.* Like the 5th, only the stitches must be worked in the upper *back* parts of the same stitches of the 4th row, and the leaves must be lengthened by one stitch each; the wrong side of the work is the right side of the flower, see Fig. 2. The flowers and leaves on the paler stripes are cro-

Fig. 1.

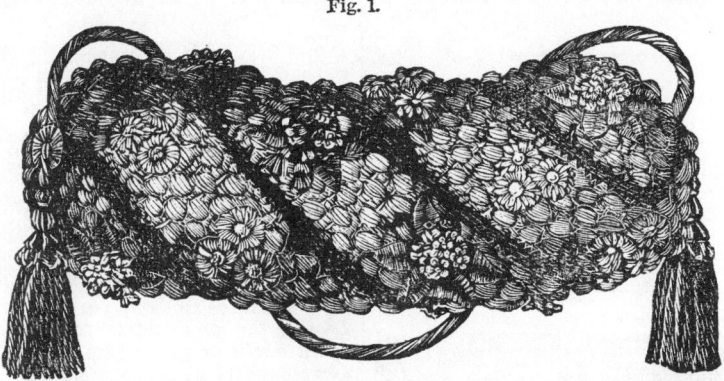

half an inch long, this is repeated four times, then 1 slip stitch in the next stitch of the 3d row. The slip stitch must hold together all the loops and the working threads, repeat twice from *, then 3 double. *5th.* double crochet. *6th.* 5 double, 1 spot in the next stitch of the 4th row, and 1 slip stitch in the next stitch of the 5th row, 3 double, 1 spot, and slip stitch as before, 5 double, repeat the 3d to the 6th rows 26 times, then 1 row double crochet. Now edge

cheted partly in scarlet, partly in violet, and partly in green (3 shades grass, and 2 olive green) wool. *1st petal.* 8 chain, 1 double in

Fig. 3.

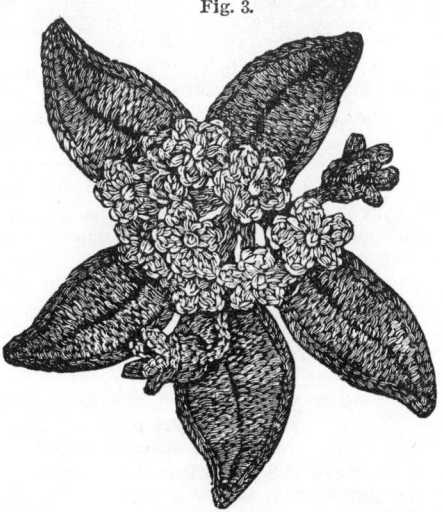

Fig. 2.

each stripe with a row of double crochet, taking in alternately first 1 and then 2 of the marginal stitches. The stripes are joined together with a row of double crochet of black single Berlin wool, and ornamented by flowers and leaves arranged in sprays, and worked in single wool. The flowers which are arranged on the dark stripes in groups of three are crocheted as follows: Make a chain of yellow wool, close

the first chain stitch, then for the following 4 petals 4 times alternately 7 chain, 1 double where the first double was worked; the wrong side of the crochet is the right side of the flower; and the centre is finished by 1 knotted stitch of white wool. On the wrong side of the flower, 1 double of green wool in the first chain, then 5 or 6 chain to form the stem. There are nine similar flowers in each spray, and two more are formed into buds by crocheting around them several treble stitches of green wool (see Fig. 3). For the leaves crochet back along a chain of 20 stitches, as follows: miss 1, 1 treble, 2 long treble, 4 double long treble, 3 treble long treble, 4 double long treble, 7 long treble, 1 treble, 1 double, 1 slip stitch, then 1 chain. The other half of the leaf is worked in the same way along the other side of the foundation chain. Then arrange the flowers and leaves according to Fig. 3. The violet with the olive, and the scarlet with the grass green leaves. The cover is then fitted on to a horse-hair bolster, and finished with a cord and tassel, see Fig. 1.

DIFFERENT METHODS OF MENDING STOCKINGS.

Fig. 1 shows the ordinary way, which consists of simple darning.

Fig. 2 gives another method which imitates the stitch of the stocking, so as to make the repairs scarcely perceptible. First, cut carefully along the whole till you have a straight margin on all sides, then fill up the space with

Fig. 1.   Fig. 2.

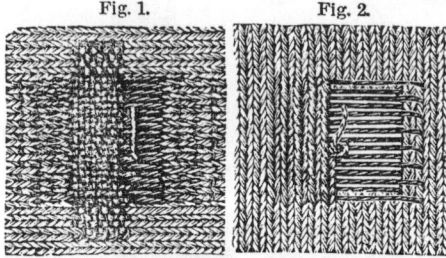

threads drawn across in a straight line from side to side. Thread a sewing or darning needle, let the thread lie to the left, put the needle in the lowest of the crosswise threads, and draw it up carefully till it has made a half stitch; continue till the upper edge of the opening is reached; then turn the work, pass the needle through the next upper stitch, let the thread lie to the right, put the needle in the next crosswise thread and draw it to a loop, which completes the first stitch; continue till the opening is filled up.

Fig. 3.—This is only another way of working this stitch, as the repair is only perceptible the wrong side. Prepare the opening as before, then draw the threads across from the upper to the lower edge, on the wrong side of the stocking, and continue then for about four stitches beyond the opening; then turn the stocking, and fill up across and across. Great

care is required in the transition from the firm edge to the opening itself.

Fig. 3.

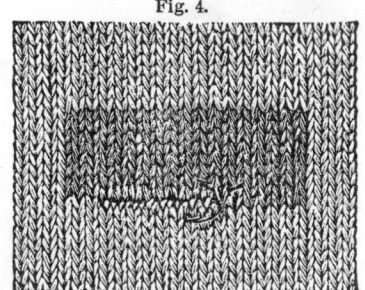

Fig. 4 shows how the sound stitches of the margin are joined to the repairing thread.

Fig. 4.

Lastly, the stocking is turned, the turned down edges of the opening are carefully cut away, and the threads are cut off.

CHILD'S KNITTED CAP.

Cast on 7 stitches, close them into a circle, and knit as follows: *1st round.* Knitted. *2d.* Alternately cotton forward, knit 1. *3d.* Knit-

Fig. 1.

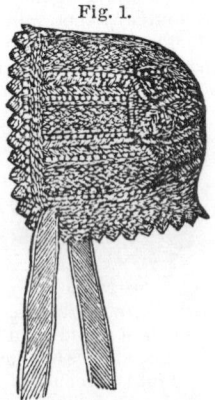

ted. All the rounds with uneven numbers up to 57 (inclusive) are knitted plain. *4th.* Alternately cotton forward, knit 2 together. *6th, 8th, 10th, and 12th* are like the 4th, only the number of knitted stitches is increased by 1 in each round. 14*th*. * Cotton forward, knit 1, cotton forward, knit 4, knit 2 together; repeat. 16*th*. * Twice alternately cotton forward, knit 3, then knit 2 together. 18*th*. * Cotton forward, knit 5, cotton forward, knit 2, knit 2 together. 20*th*. * Cotton forward, knit 2, knit 2 together, cotton forward, knit 3, cottton forward, knit 1, knit 2 together. 22*d*. * Cotton forward, knit 2, twice alternately knit 2 together, cotton forward, then knit 3, cotton forward, knit 2 together. 24*th*. * Twice alternately cotton forward, knit 1, then 3 times alternately knit 2 together, cotton forward, then knit 2, knit 2 together. 26*th*. * Cotton forward, knit 3, cotton forward, knit 2, twice alternately knit 2 together, cotton forward, then knit 2, knit 2 together. 28*th*. * Cotton forward, knit 5, cotton forward, knit 1, twice alternately knit 2 together, cotton forward, then knit 2, knit 2 together. 30*th*. * Cotton forward, knit 2, knit 2 together. 32*d*. * Cotton forward, knit 9, cotton forward, knit 1, knit 2 together, cotton forward, knit 2, knit 2 together. 34*th*. * Cotton forward, knit 11, cotton forward, knit 4, knit 2 together. 36*th*. * Cotton forward, knit 13, cotton forward, knit 3, knit 2 together. 38*th*. * Cotton forward, knit 15, cotton forward, knit 2, knit 2 together. 40*th*. * Cotton forward, knit 17, cotton forward, knit 1, knit 2 together. 42*d*. * Cotton forward, knit 19, cotton forward, knit 2 together. 44*th*. * Cotton forward, knit 21, cotton forward, knit 1. 46*th*. Now consult Fig. 2, which represents in the original size a part of the square; * knit 2, 4 times alternately cotton forward, knit 2 together, then knit 1, cotton forward, knit 1, cotton forward, 5 times knit 2 together, cotton forward, knit 1, cotton forward; repeat from * 6 times. At the end of the round knit 2, twice alternately cotton forward, knit 2 together, then knit 1. 48*th*. * Knit 1, 4 times alternately knit 2 together, cot-

twice 46*th* and 48*th rounds*, and once again the 46*th;* then pass the first 36 stitches on to a fresh needle to form the back of the cap, and knit backwards and forwards along the remaining stitches as follows: 1 row purled, 62 rows in the same pattern as the square just knitted, only that the rows with uneven numbers must now be purled instead of knitted, and two stitches must be knitted at the beginning of each pattern row. Then take up the side marginal stitches on to needles, and knit in the round, with the 36 stitches for the back, as follows: 4 rounds purled, then 1 round twice cotton forward, knit 3 together. In the following round knit off the made stitches as 1 knitted, 1 purled, and 1 knitted stitch, then 3 rounds purled, and cast off. For the knitted edging cast on 8 stitches, and knit a plain row. Then, 1*st row*. Slip 1, knit 1, twice cotton forward, knit 6. 2*d*. Slip 1, purl 4, knit 2, purl 1, knit 2. 3*d*. Slip 1, knit 8. 4*th*. Slip 1, purl 4, knit 5. 5*th*. Slip 1, knit 1, twice cotton forward, knit 2 together, twice cotton forward, knit 6. 6*th*. Slip 1, purl 4, twice alternately knit 2, purl 1, then knit 2. 7*th*. Slip 1, knit 12. 8*th*. Cast off 5, knit 7. Repeat till the required length has been obtained, and then sew the edging to the cap.

WHITE EMBROIDERY.—JULIE.

EMBROIDERED PEN-WIPER.

THE central part is of black cloth, around which are twelve separate pieces, six scarlet

Fig. 1.

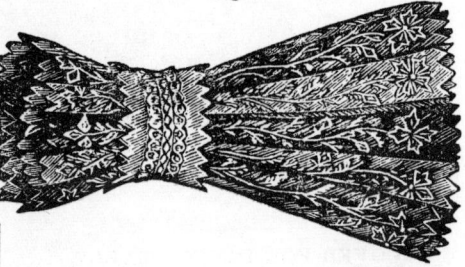

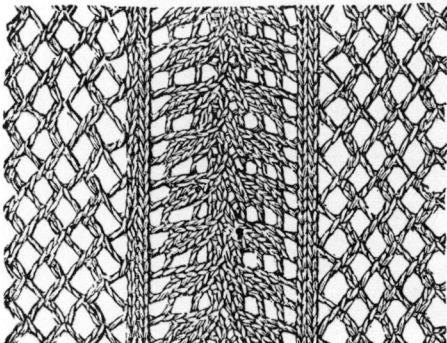

Fig. 2.—Detail of Cap.

ton forward, then knit 2, cotton forward, knit 3, cotton forward, knit 2 together, knit 3 together, cotton forward, knit 3, cotton forward; repeat from * 6 times. At the end of the round knit 1, twice alternately knit 2 together, knit 2 together, cotton forward, then knit 2. Repeat

and six black, cut from the pattern given in Figs. 2 or 3. Each of these pieces is embroid-

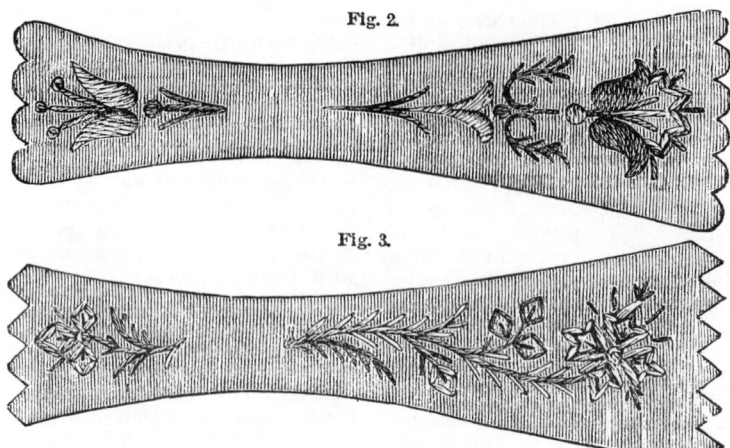

Fig. 2.

Fig. 3.

ered in *point russe*, with purse silk of various colors; they are then joined together on the wrong side with overcast stitches, and held in place by a strip of cloth ornamented with gold braid and beads. The strip and the separate pieces are vandyked, and the latter are arranged around the black cloth centre in alternate colors of black and scarlet.

vals. The strips of canvas are embroidered with brown single Berlin wool in *point russe*. Fig. 2 gives the original size of this embroidery; the cover is lined with brown oil baize, and bound with sarsnet ribbon to match.

Fig. 1.

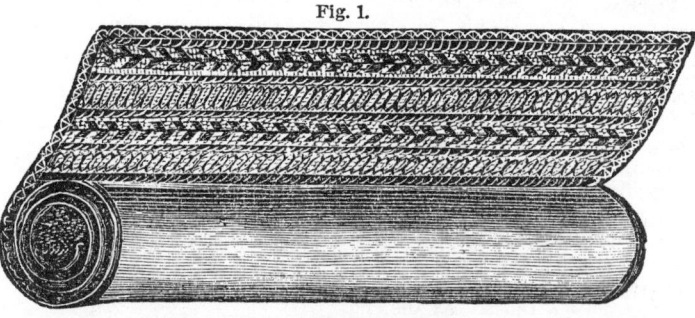

Fig. 2.

COVER FOR DINING TABLE.

THIS cover is worked on canvas, into which black cane has been woven at regular inter-

EMBROIDERY.

KNITTED PELISSE, WITH JACKET.

(*See Instructions, Page 222.*)

INFANT'S SWATHE IN KNITTING AND CROCHET.

This is worked with coarse knitting cotton crosswise backwards and forwards, and is commenced at the straight end with a foundation of 37 chain stitches missing the last 7 of which the following rows are worked back on the remainder. *1st row.* Alternately 2 double into the 2 next stitches, 2 chain, miss 2 stitches, at the end of the row 2 double into the 2 last stitches. Then 7 chain and turn the work. *2d.* Join to the last stitch of the preceding row (by dropping the stitch from the needle, inserting the needle into the stitch to which you

Fig. 1.

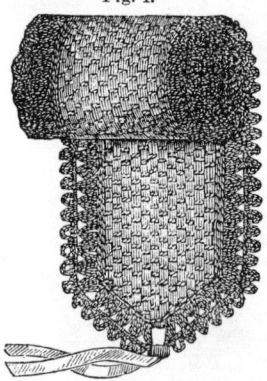

are to join and drawing the dropped stitch through), 30 chain, join to the 1st stitch of the last row; then 7 chain, turn. *3d.* 2 double into the 2 next stitches of the 1st row, working in the chain stitches of the last row, then alternately 2 double into the 2 next foundation

Fig. 2.

stitches, working in the bottom stitches of the 2d and 1st rows, 2 chain, miss 2 stitches. At the end of the row 2 double into the last 2 stitches of the 1st row. Then 7 chain, turn. These last two rows are repeated till the band is the required length, but the long stitches with which 2 rows are worked in must not be

one above another (see Fig. 2, which represents part of the crochet work the original size). In the last 10 rows the band is formed into a point by shortening the rows of chain stitches, and instead of joining to the 1st and last stitch joining to the 2d and last but one of the preceding row, and in each of the following rows miss 2 stitches at the commencement and end. Then the band is edged with 2 rows of crochet (not including the straight end) as follows: *1st row.* Alternately 1 double working in the two next loops of chain stitches, 2 chain; at the sloping side of the pointed end 1 double is worked into each of the loops of chain stitches. *2d.* 2 double into the chain stitches between the double stitches of the last row, after the 2 double, 1 purl (of 5 chain and 1 slip stitch into the last double). At the point of the band a tape is sewed on.

ORNAMENTAL BOX FOR CARDS.

This box with a cover is made of pasteboard, and covered with Russia leather The interior

Fig. 1.

is divided by card-board partitions into four compartments, which serve to contain the different packs. The cover is ornamented at the

Fig. 2.

top with a medallion of gray silk embroidered with chenille of various colors (see Fig. 2), also in front; in the manner of the illustration with small China cards.

CIGAR CASE.

THE work for the cigar case is shown in the full size in Fig. 2. The foundation is fine drill. Ribbon or velvet of three colors is required, as seen in Fig. 1, where the proper width is shown. The herring-bone stitch is worked with purse-silk in blue, gold, yellow,

Fig. 1.

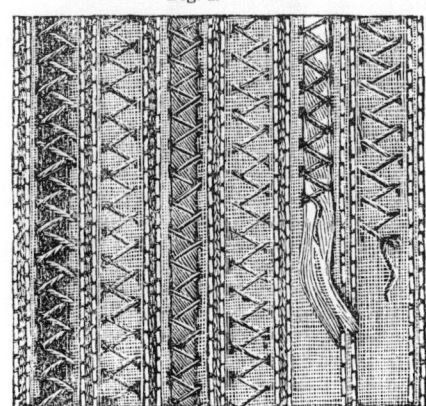

scarlet, and green, with a row of gold cord sewn down at the edge of the chain-stitch line running between the herring-bone stitch. A thin piece of card-board is required for the outer part, four inches wide, and eleven inches long; for the inner, three and a half inches wide, and thirteen and a half long. These are folded exactly in half, covered with the drill, and lined with silk, sewn together at the sides, and bound with ribbon at the sides and open ends.

INFANT'S CAP IN CROCHET AND KNITTING.

THIS cap is knitted with fine knitting cotton and steel needles. It is commenced in the centre of the crown with a foundation of 8

stitches, joined to a circle, on which the following rows are worked: 1st *row*. Entirely

knitted. 2d and 3d. Entirely purled. 4th. Knitted. 5th. Alternately the thread brought forward, knit 1. 6th. Knitted into every thread brought forward in the last row, knit 1, purl 1. 7th, 8th, and 9th. Purled. 10th. Knitted. 11th. Alternately bring the threads forward, knit 2 stitches together. 12th. Knitted into every thread brought forward in the last

Fig. 2.

row, knit 1, purl 1, knit 1. 13th—16th. Purled. 17th. Knitted. 18th. Alternately bring the wool forward, knit 3 stitches together. 19th. Knitted, but into each thread brought forward in the last row knit 1, purl 1, knit 1. 20th—23d. Purled. 24th. Knitted. The 18th to the 24th rows are repeated three times. Now the crown of the cap is finished, with the next row the other part is commenced. The number of stitches must be divisible by 5, therefore the requisite number of stitches are increased at regular intervals. 4th. Alternately purl 2 stitches together, purl 1, purl 2 together, bring the thread forward. 47th—53d. Knitted. In the 47th row knit 1 and purl 1 into the thread brought forward in the preceding row. 54th. Alternately knit 3, the 2 stitches which were knitted into the thread brought forward, and in the next rows are knitted and are dropped from the needle and undone up to the 47th row, then the upper thread is brought forward, into all the threads of the preceding rows, put on the needle in the left hand, and knitted as a stitch. 55th. Knitted, into the stitch which was knitted into the 8 loose threads, always knit 1, purl 1; repeat the 46th to the 55th rows once, then the 46th and 47th rows once again. Now take 31 stitches on another needle, leave them for the present, and knit the 68th to the 159th rows, backwards and forwards in the same pattern, in the 159th row always knit 1, purl 1, knit 1 into the threads brought forward in the last row. Care must be taken that each row begins and ends with a stitch of the stripe of the pattern. When the 159th row is finished, the stitches of the edge on both sides are put on needles, and all the stitches, including those which were left aside, are knitted around as follows: 160*th row*. Knitted. 161*st* to 164*th*. Purled. 165*th*. Alternately bring the wool forward, knit 3 stitches together. 166*th*. Knitted; into every thread brought forward knit 1, purl 1. 167*th* to the 170*th*. Purled. 171*st*. Knitted. Then take a crochet hook and crochet with the same cotton alternately: 1 double with which three stitches of the knitting are worked in, 3 chain. For the edging of the cap two rows are worked with crochet cotton No. 40. 1*st row*. Into each double of the last row, 1 treble, after each treble 3 chain. 2*d*. *, into the next chain stitches between 2 treble, 1 scallop, consisting of 4 treble, 1 purl (consisting of 5 chain, 1 double into the 1st chain), 2 long treble, 1 purl, 2 long treble, 1 purl, 4 treble, 2 treble divided by 3 chain; repeat from *. Through the row of holes at the edge of the cap, a narrow colored satin ribbon is passed, and strings the same color are attached.

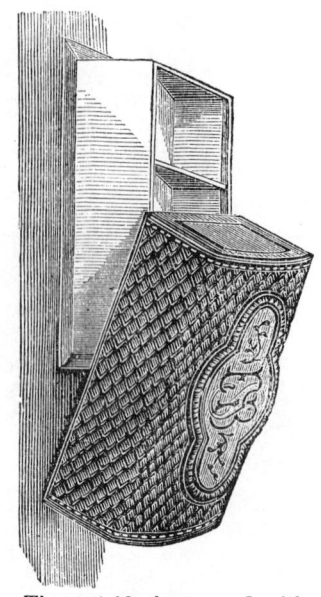

EMBROIDERED MAT FOR SCENT-BOTTLES, ETC.

MATERIAL, light gray cloth. The embroidery is given in illustrations 1 and 2, the latter

Fig. 1.

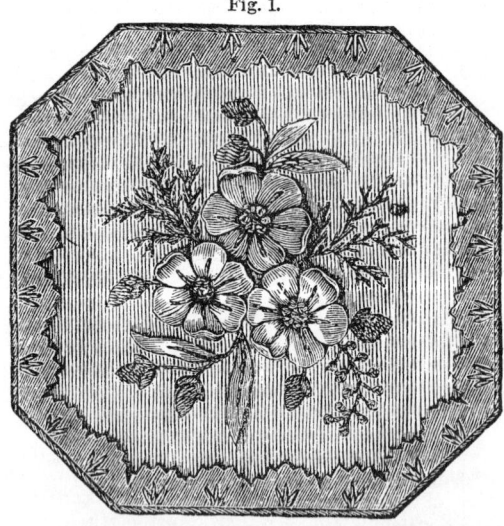

paper. The outside is covered with reddish-brown stamped Russia leather; in the centre of the lid is a medallion of gray silk rep, on

Fig. 2.

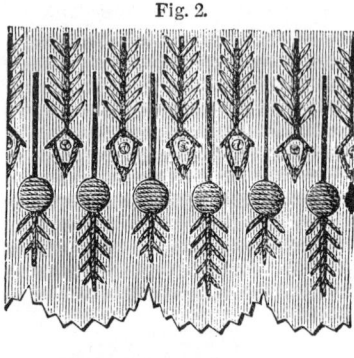

representing a part of the border in the original size. It is worked partly in satin and overcast stitch, and partly in Russian point, with different shades of gray silk cord, white silk, and gold thread. The mat is lined with white card-board and gray lining, and edged with fine gray silk cord.

POSTAGE-STAMP BOX.

THIS box is of card-board, divided into three compartments, and lined with white *moiré*

which either the monagram or a small satin-stitch embroidery is worked with reddish-brown silk and gold thread.

ORNAMENTAL FRAME FOR A THERMOMETER.

PARTLY of black polished, partly of green bronzed wood, about 11 inches in height, and covered at the bottom with black velvet, which is edged with button-hole stitches of green filoselle, and ornamented with an embroidery of green filoselle and beads on canvas cut in the Greek pattern. Fig. 2 gives the pattern of the

Fig. 1.

embroidery and indicates the materials used. The embroidery is sewn on to the velvet with

Fig. 2.

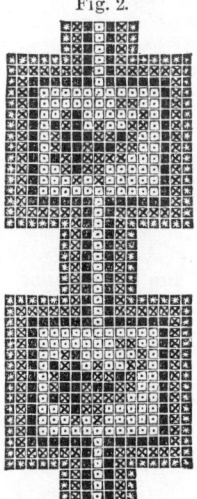

Steel Beads.

□ Alabaster.   ⊡ Crystal.   ⊠ Green Filoselle.

long stitches of green filoselle, so that the same stitches also form the outline of the design.

NET FOR BOILING EGGS, IN NETTING AND CROCHET.

THIS is partly netted with coarse knitting cotton, partly crocheted with white and gray crochet cotton. First work the bottom by netting over a mesh about four-fifths of an inch round into a foundation loop 31 stitches, drawing them into a circle, and then working 9 rounds over the same mesh; in the 5th at every third stitch one stitch is increased. The stitches of the 1st round are drawn closely together, and the commencement and end of the foundation thread tied. Then for the top part, which forms a bag, work over the same mesh 41 stitches, draw them into a circle, and continue netting with the same number of stitches 30 rounds. Now crochet for the side which joins the bottom to the top part of the net, alternately with gray and white crochet cotton, 17 rounds as follows: 1*st round*. With gray cotton, alternately 4 double into the next stitch of the last round of the bottom, 8 chain. 2*d*. This and the two following rounds with white cotton, into each stitch of the last round, 1 double. 3*d*.

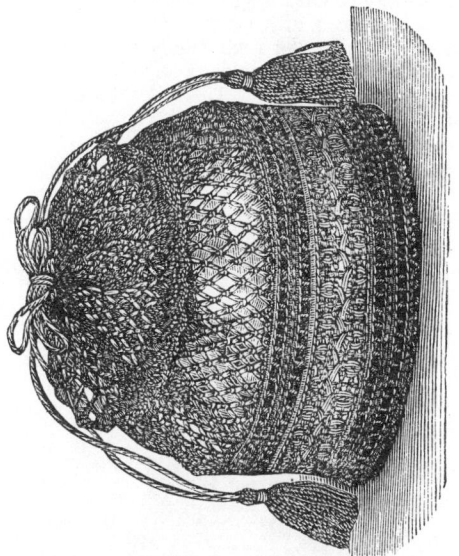

1 long treble into each alternate stitch, after each long treble 1 chain. 4*th*. Into each stitch 1 double. 5*th to the* 10*th round*. With gray cotton alternately, 1 treble, 2 chain, missing two stitches. The treble stitches of these 6 rounds must be always one above another. 11*th*. This and the next round with white cotton, into each stitch 1 double. 12*th*. Like the 3d. 13*th*. With gray cotton, into every stitch 1 double. 14*th*. This and the next round with white cotton, into every stitch 1 double, crocheting in with every 4 stitch 1 foundation stitch of the netting for the bag. 15*th*. Like the 3d. 16*th*. With gray cotton, alternately 3 double into the next 3 stitches, 1 purl (of 5 chain, and 1 slip-stitch

into the 1st), missing 1 stitch. The 17th round is crocheted on the other side into the lower part of the stitches of the 1st round in the same way as the 14th round; then the 18th and 19th rounds like the 15th and 16th. These rounds must, both top and bottom, overlap the netting. The 6 treble rounds in the centre, worked with gray cotton, have, as shown in the Illustration, white knitting cotton drawn through them. The top part of the net is now edged with scallops of chain stitches, crocheted with gray cotton, as follows: Into each netted stitch 5 double, 7 chain, 1 double 3 times alternately, 11 chain, 1 double, then 7 chain and 5 double; in each succeeding scallop the first loop of 7 chain is joined to the last loop of the preceding scallop. Now the last 8 rounds of this netting are turned over, so as to form a kind of frill on the outside, and two rounds are then crocheted into the 21st and 22d rounds of netting together at the top for the cord. 1st round: *, 2 double before, 2 double behind, the next netted knots with two chain between, then 3 chain, repeat from *; second round: into each loop of chain stitches of the last round 2 long treble, after which always 2 chain. 2 gray cords are passed through this last round, and a whalebone through each round of treble stitches worked with white cotton of the side parts. The ends of the latter are carefully fastened together.

SLIPPER WATCH-STAND.

This stand is in the form of a pretty slipper

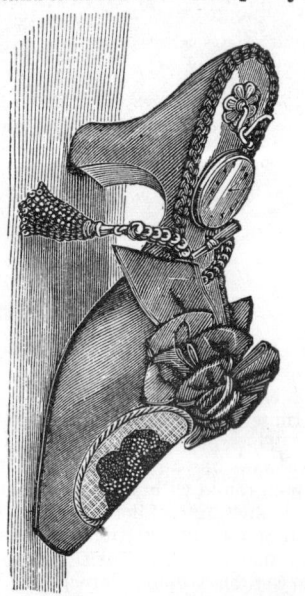

in card-board, covered outside, including the heel, with blue satin, and lined with gray silk rep. The centre of the front part of the slipper is ornamented with bead embroidery. Blue silk gimp and bows of the same colored ribbon form the trimming.

KNITTED PELISSE WITH JACKET.
(See Illustration, Page 217.)

The materials required are 4 bone needles, No. 8, with points at each end; 2 needles, same size, with knobs. *A loose knitter must take smaller-sized needles.* About half a dozen silk buttons, for down the front, to match the colored wool used. This pelisse or frock is knitted in white Berlin fingering, with rolls of colored wool. About eight ounces of white and two and a half ounces of colored wool will be necessary. The waist should be made of white cashmere or merino, as knitting is too thick to go under the jacket. The jacket will fit a child of from one to two years old, and can be easily made larger or smaller. The skirt you knit to any length required.

Skirt.—This is knitted in one piece, and sewn up afterwards; it should measure about a yard and a half in width. Take the needles with knobs, *white* wool, and cast on 300 stitches. Knit plain a length of three and a half inches; this makes the hem for bottom of frock. Observe always to slip the first stitch of each row, except when you begin with a fresh color. You next knit the 1st roll.

Colored wool.—*1st row.* Knit plain. *2d.* Purl all. Repeat these two rows *twice* more; then cast off evenly, but not too tightly, all the stitches.

White wool.—Take up, and as you take up knit 300 stitches, being particular to begin to take up at the side where you *commenced* with the colored roll. In taking up, you put your needle into the *same* stitches as you did the *first* row of color, to make the knitting roll over. This may *sound* puzzling, but, with the work in your hand, you easily see which stitches are meant, as the colored wool marks them. Knit, in plain knitting, about an inch and a quarter for distance between the rolls.

Colored wool.—The 2d roll. Mind you begin this at the same side as the 1st. It is knitted exactly the same as that, and the stitches cast off.

White wool.—Take up 300 stitches as before, and plain knit the depth of one and a quarter inch.

Colored wool.—Knit a 3d roll, exactly like the others; this is the last roll. No more colored wool is required.

White wool.—Take up 300 stitches as before. The skirt is now knitted in a fancy stitch, which rather draws it in. You must slip the 1st stitch in *each* row, though the directions may be to knit or purl. For example: in the 1st row slip the 1st stitch, instead of knitting it, purl the 2d; but the rest of the row it is knit 1, purl 1 alternately. This is a rule in nearly all knitting.

1st row. Knit 1, purl 1 alternately. *2d.* Knit 3, purl 1 alternately. *3d.* All plain knitting. *4th.* Knit 3, purl 1 alternately. Repeat these 4 rows until your skirt is the length you require. Instead of casting off the stitches, run a narrow soft braid through them, and sew the waist to it. Sew up the skirt, leaving a vent and turn-up hem at the bottom, slightly catching it down, not to show the stitches. The rolls are sewn together last, to make them turn over nicely.

JACKET.—*White wool.*—Take the needles with knobs, and cast on 136 stitches. *1st row.* Knit 3, purl 1 alternately. *2d.* Knit 1, purl 1 alternately. *3d.* Knit 3, purl 1 alternately. *4th.* All plain knitting. Repeat these four rows *five* times more. *25th.* Knit 3, purl 1 alternately. *26th.* Knit 1, purl 1 alternately. *27th.* Knit 3, purl 1 alternately. *28th.* In this row you divide for the sides and back. Work thus: Knit 32 stitches, knit the next 2 stitches, and pull the first of these over the second; knit a third stitch, and do the same. Continue knitting and pulling over until you have cast off 8 stitches. Knit 55 stitches, cast off 8 more, and end with knitting 31. You next knit the first side.

First side.—This is formed by knitting backwards and forwards as far as the cast-off loops. Repeat the 4 rows which form the pattern until you have done 32 rows or 8 patterns. If you count up the ribs or plain knitted rows you have knitted, you will find you have 15.

Narrowing for shoulder and shaping neck.— Knit 3 patterns of the 4 rows, but *at the shoulder side* knit 2 together at the *end* of each row to slant it. After you begin the reducing, the commencement of each row will vary. Always slip the 1st stitch, knit or purl the next according to the pattern.

After these 3 patterns, to slant for neck as well as shoulder, you must knit 2 together at the *end* of *each* row, working the pattern in the middle as regular as you can. The pattern is to be repeated until you have only 2 stitches left on your needle. Knit these together, and draw the wool through.

Back.—Begin this at armhole nearest the side that is knitted. Knit a straight piece same length as you did for side, that is, 8 patterns. Afterwards shape for shoulders by knitting 2 together at *end* of *each* row, repeating the pattern until you have worked as many ribs and rows as at the side. Then cast off the stitches remaining on the needle.

The second side is knitted exactly like the first.

This completes the centre of the jacket. It must not be sewn or knitted up at the shoulders *before* commencing the roll.

Colored roll.—To form this you must use the 4 needles without knobs. Observe the sketch of the jacket, and where the letter A is marked

begin there to take up the stitches. Along the bottom of jacket, from A to B, take up, and as you take up knit 136 stitches. With a second needle take up, and as you take up knit all the stitches from B to C. It is impossible to give the exact number of stitches, but be careful to

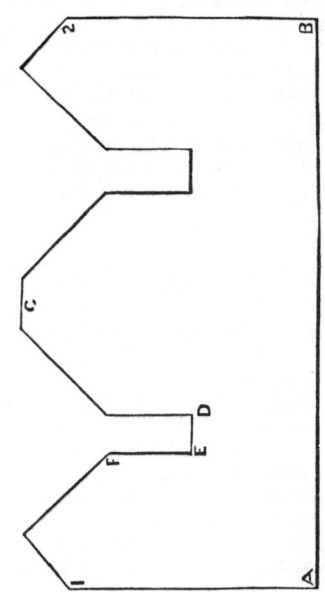

avoid dragging the jacket by taking up too few. With a third needle, take up all the stitches from C to A where you first commenced. Knit plain 4 rounds, and then cast off. This roll, as you will see, is knitted all around the jacket. Some people find it easier to work by using five instead of four needles. If you use five place half of the 136 stitches on the extra needle. Hold your work as if it was a stocking you were knitting.

White edging below roll at the bottom of jacket.— Take up, on same stitches as you did the colored roll, with white wool 136 stitches. Knit backwards and forwards 4 rows plain knitting; cast off. Begin to take up at A.

The jacket buttons down the front. You have to knit a sufficient width on each side for this with white wool.

For the left side.—Take up on the same stitches as you did the colored roll, beginning where marked 1 in the sketch down to A, all the stitches there are *about* 44. Knit plain 11 rows, then cast off.

Right side.—Take up, beginning at B to 2, on same stitches as colored roll, all the stitches there are. Knit 5 rows plain. *6th row.* Knit 4 stitches, make 1, knit 2 together. See how many stitches you have left on your needle, and divide for equal distances between the button holes which are formed by the make 1, knit 2 together, plain knitting so many stitches between each button hole; 6 button holes are enough.

The top one should be made on the 2 last stitches. Plain knit 4 rows, and cast off.

Neck.—With white wool, along the neck, take up about 52 stiches. Rib—that is, knit 2, purl 2 alternately—4 or 5 rows. Cast off.

SLEEVE.—*Colored roll round armhole.*—Use the 4 needles for this. Look at sketch, and take up with colored wool, knitting as you take up, from D to E 12 stitches. You must take up stitches in the corners to get this number. With a second needle, take up all the stitches from E to F, where the knitting has been sewn together for the shoulder seam ; there should be *about* 17. With a third needle, take up all the stitches from F to D. Knit 4 rounds plain ; then cast off.

Sleeve.—With white wool, cast on 40 stitches. Repeat the 4 rows that form the pattern 17 times. Cast off, and sew up all the sleeve but half an inch. This half inch, when you put in the sleeve, you sew along the cast-off stitches at bottom of armhole ; the seam goes directly in the centre, and it gives more room for the arm. Observe the stripes go *across* the arm.

Roll round sleeve.—With colored wool, and 4 needles, take up stitches at bottom of sleeve. Knit a roll of 4 rounds ; then cast off.

Ribbed cuff.—With white wool, and 4 needles, take up same stitches as for colored roll, and rib 4 rounds. Rib 4 rounds in colored wool.

End with ribbing 4 more white rounds, and cast off.

TOWEL RACK.

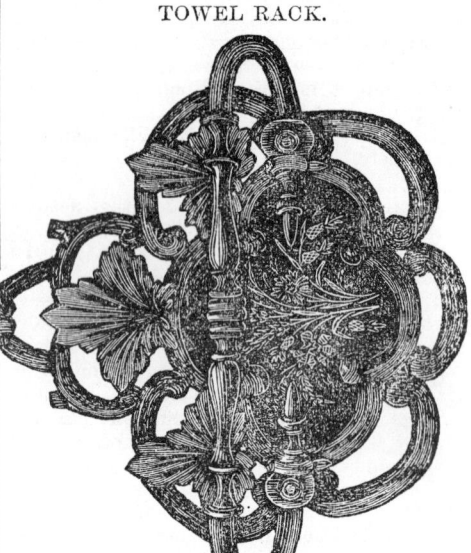

MADE of oiled walnut, with a piece in the centre of blue satin embroidered with flowers in gay colored silks.

DESIGN IN EMBROIDERY.

MONOGRAM DESIGN.

SCENT BOTTLE CASE.

Materials.—Black velvet, lilac satin, purse silk the same color, fifteen inches of plain sarcenet ribbon half an inch wide, middle-sized steel beads, thick card-board, and wire.

THIS case, seen in Figs. 1 and 2, closed and open, is intended for three bottles, but can also be used for a work-box. The foundation is of a box made of thick card-board, with double sides throughout. The covering for the outer

Fig. 1.

sides is of black velvet, which is worked over with beads and silk.

Fig. 3 gives the trimming which is used for the case when open. This is mostly, as seen, of silk stitches, and in two shades.

The crocheted cord is made in a very simple

Fig. 2.

manner of four double crochet worked from the inside in the round.

Fig. 3.

The **four-cornered bottom**, covered on both sides with lilac satin, measures five inches and a quarter in length and four inches in breadth. The two outer long sides are each cut three inches and a quarter, the two inner ones two inches and three-quarters high and five inches and a quarter long.

The two inner end parts are to be made somewhat narrower and shorter. All the inner end parts are lined with lilac satin, and seamed to the box. The outer end parts are joined together and to the bottom. The inner box, on the contrary, is only seamed to this at the upper edge—as thus the inner smaller box part touches the bottom without being fastened, the outer sides come further out, and the curved shape is made.

The lid, made with velvet and satin, like the largest part of the box, requires a straight card-board surface four inches and three-quarters long and four inches and a half wide. For the hollow part, a piece of wire is set under all round at the back. Then the upper rounded card-board side, an inch and a quarter high and two inches and a quarter wide, covered with satin on both sides, is joined to the box after the side wall of the box. A thin layer of wadding is put in between the card-board and the satin lining. The lid parts are set together, as in the box, by the buttonhole edge, and that of the lid, when finished, by five ribbon straps, each an inch and a quarter long, which, at the ends of the upper edge of the box, and at the inner lid space, are to be stretched tight.

When taken for a work-box, these straps serve to hold the knitting cotton, when for a scent bottle case they can be put on underneath the lining. The close of the lid is hidden by a narrow sarcenet ribbon, sewn on only at the ends, and this can be taken for the hinges. The cord, crocheted with purse silk, covers the outer joins of the case, and makes the bordering of the lid and the two loops put on to each long side, the two being at the back each three inches and a quarter long, and those on the front side each six inches long.

The long, loose, hanging loops are drawn through the shorter ones, fastened an inch and a quarter long on the lid, and the case is thus closed, the first making the strap for the handle. The tassels hanging on the cord loop at the top, as also the imitation lock, the settings and the knob on the lid, are, according to Fig. 2, partly made of twisted strings of beads.

Should this case be used for a work-box, a small bag for a thimble, three-quarters of an inch long, of double crochet, is fastened on one of the short sides, and on the other a strap of single crochet to hold the scissors.

VASE OF PERFORATED CARD FOR CIGARS.

THE ground layers for the various parts are given in a reduced size, but exactly agreeing in the number of the holes with the full-size parts.

Begin with the bottom, which is to be cut in an octagon form; four and three quarters inches in size, a quarter of an inch thick; this is to be covered with rose-colored sarcenet.

A small star pattern, three types large, made in a perforated paper stripe nine types high, make, as seen, the border round; an edge one type wide, beyond which all round one type of the first layer stands out; borders in relief the open-work pattern of the border part.

Fig. 2, in the whole (but reduced in size as foundation), serves not only as a hold all round for the relief edge, but gives also the ground

Fig. 2.

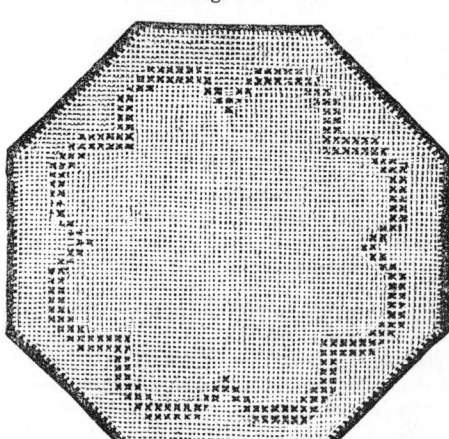

plan (line) for the foot, which is in eight curves, becoming narrower towards the top. Of the twelve paper layers, making the relief edge of the bottom the seventh, counted from below in answer to the thick edge, the six layers going before this are widened at the sloping outer edges always by one type; the graduation of the straight outer edges, on account of the corners, cannot be quite regular. Upwards, the width of the outer edge, catching in with points, gradually decreases, till at last the sloping sides are two, the straight ones one, type wide. We now come to the building up the curved-out layers of the foot, the particulars of which can be taken from the description, but requiring a clear head and hand, as also an idea of form and shape. As already stated, Fig. 2 can be taken as the outline for the first layer; rising gently, fifty-two layers go gradually up to a circumference of three quarters of an inch, being double and treble at the sloping edges, and at the straight ones treble and fourfold, piled up on each other in

a very regular manner. The small smooth surface is then covered by an eight-cornered piece the same size, to which follow thirteen for the little square finish of the foot, which, only in double layers on all sides, are always enlarged by one type. The next five layers of the same size have a cover of the same colored silk as the bottom edge, and, as a decoration, an open-work perforated paper stripe, as seen in Fig. 1. The eight-cornered shape is now graduated down again to the original size of three-quarters of an inch; the twenty-one layers are piled double-treble and fourfold on each other. To complete the foot and hold the cup (at the same time the bottom) a six-cornered piece two and three-quarters inches round, with side-edges, each an inch and a half long, is to be made. A little over half an inch high, the paper-layers for the outer relief covering of this are gradually reduced to the size answering to the eight-cornered shape; later only, when the cup is finished and united to the sexagon, both parts are joined.

The cup is of six single pieces of card-board, each five inches high, two and one-quarter inches wide above, and an inch and a quarter wide below, which are to be pasted on a piece of lining, hanging together on the straight, lying close together. To make the round they are joined and pasted over with lead paper in the inside, with which also at the top the turned-over edges are covered; this frame must then have a sexagon-shaped piece of card-board, covered with silver paper, as a bottom part; the folds in the stuff at the lower edge of the sloped card-board parts are to be neatly turned over and pasted down. The ground layers of two different designs of the relief decoration of these cup parts are seen in Figs. 3 and 4. The other layers of the outer edge, alike in every part, are graduated off at the top and sides always by one type; but below, on the side across the third, fourth, fifth, sixth, seventh, and eighth paper layers, meet always in piles on each other. The deeper-lying middle shapes, the edges of which (not including the lowest point seven layers high) are everywhere evenly (either towards the inside or outside) shortened by always one type, contain on the whole only five layers; according to the way the relief-shape is graduated, these hang together with the first or sixth paper layer of the outer edge. Each separate part of the cup is next to be sewn down with fine thread at the cross standing-out type row below, at about the third row of holes in the before-mentioned sexagon shape, before pasting the parts in the whole on the silk foundation of the card-board frame. Thirteen paper-layers belong to each shield, with which the lower part of the cup is decorated; the last layer but three, with open-work edge, gives, as Fig. 2, for the relief-edge of the bottom, the hold for the relief-edge of the shield. The proper pattern is seen in Fig.

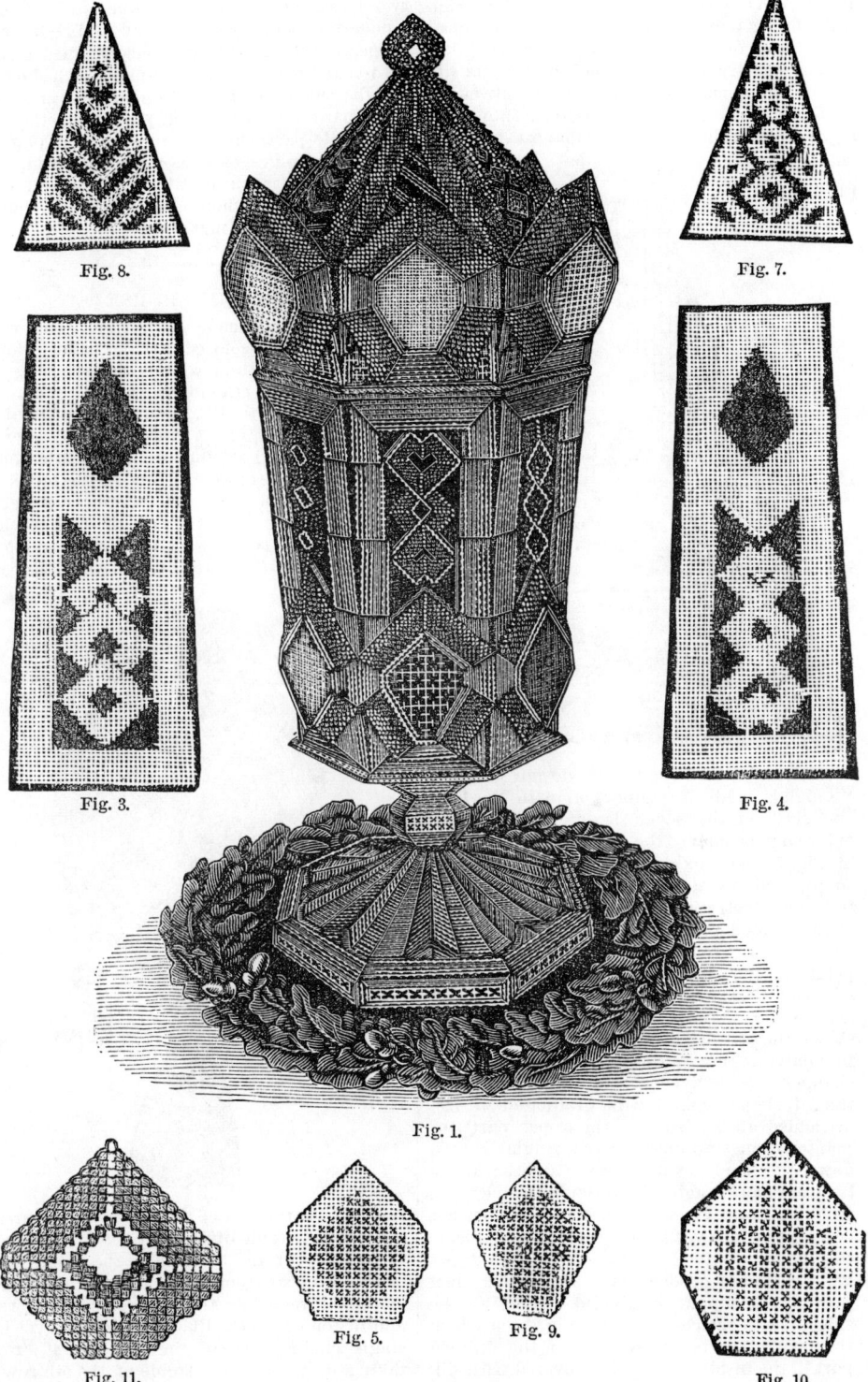

Fig. 8.

Fig. 7.

Fig. 3.

Fig. 4.

Fig. 1.

Fig. 11.

Fig. 5.

Fig. 9.

Fig. 10.

5. The inner open-work pattern can easily be altered. After the full-sized illustration, Fig. 6, the upper pointed part of the lid made separately, and of lead-paper, and covered with silk, is constructed next, each of the six divisions being marked by a sharp break made on the outside. The relief-pattern shown in Fig. 6, in the full size, is easily made, especially

Fig. 6.

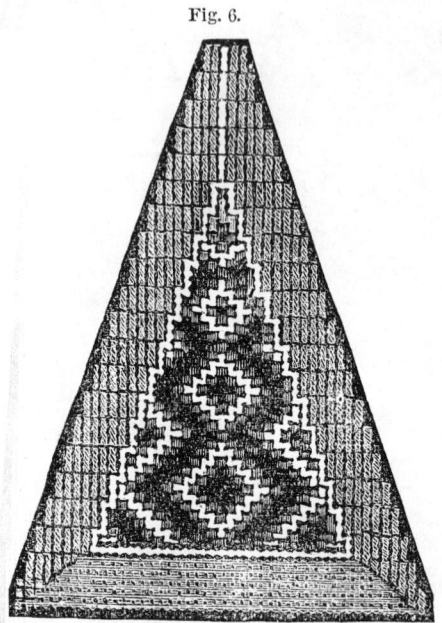

when we add, that the middle design two layers high is made in connection with the fifth and sixth of the seven layers of which the outer-edge is made; the ground layer is seen in Fig. 7. The explanation of the two other simpler middle designs is seen very clearly from the illustrations; Fig. 8 is the foundation of the pointed pattern. It is advisable, before pasting on the foundation, to fasten the upper points of the single relief parts with a few stitches. The shields complete the lid of fifteen layers, Figs. 9 and 10 (shown in different sizes), the last layer but four with open-work foundation, the running pattern of which changes in each division. In order to complete the full shape, eight layers, graduated in size, are added at the back to the upper parts, of pointed form, standing out as a triangle. Fasten down the shields with small stitches; and a hoop cut in a sexagon shape ten or twelve types wide, and four layers high, which reaches out two types wide over the edge of the cup; inside this hoop are two layers, each three types wide, a kind of groove round, which last must prevent the slipping of the lid. After all the shields, with the corners after Fig. 1, on which the pointed parts are sewn firm, the unlined part in the inside of the lid is covered with silk

and lead-paper. The lid point (Fig. 11) is of two halves, each of eight graduated layers. Under the point is secured by a six-cornered shape, answering to the space slipped in, of card-board covered with lead-paper. The holder for the cigars is a sexagon-shaped piece of card-board, and lead-paper pasted together to the middle part, cut out an inch and a quarter large; a cup-like piece is added, to hold, besides the cigars placed all round, some spills for lighting these when required. Fig. 1 shows the goblet put on a mat.

CROCHET PURSE

THIS purse is made with rings, and red, black, and gold-colored netting silk. Commence at the bottom with covering a ring an inch and a half in circumference, with 32 double stitches in yellow silk, then 1 row of double stitches in black, and 1 row of red silk over a ring two and a half inches in circumference, making 2 stitches into each one of the previous rows; fasten off. 4th row, yellow. * 4 treble stitches into the first stitch on the ring, with 3 chain between the 2d and 3d of the 4 treble, 1 chain, missing 7 stitches of the ring. Repeat

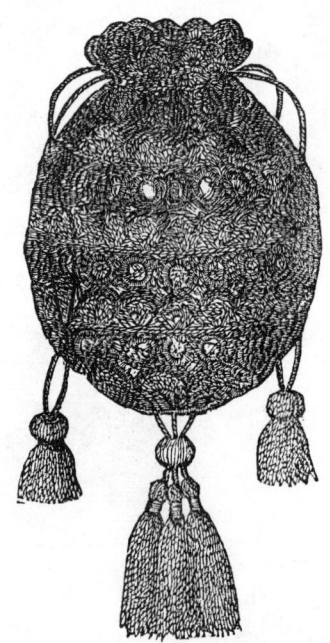

from *. At the end of the row loop the thread into the 1st treble of the row. 5th. 1 chain, * 14 treble over the 3 chain of the last row, 1 chain. Repeat from *. At the end of the row loop the thread into the 1st treble of the row and fasten off. 6th. Black * 1 double over the single chain stitch of the 5th and 4th row, taking up both, miss 1 treble of the 5th row, 1 double into the next 12 treble, miss the last treble. Repeat from *. On to this row work over 16 rings 1 inch in circumference with red silk as follows: 8 double round a ring, *, loop the thread into the back thread of the 4th of the 12 double of the former row, 8 double round the ring (this covers half of the ring), work 8 double round another ring, loop the thread into the 11th of the 12 double, 8 double round the ring, 8 double round another ring, and repeat from * till all the 16 rings are worked half over, and the row completed. Then cover the other half of the rings with 17 double in red, work 3 double in yellow into the 3 middle stitches of the 17, and 5 chain after each 3 double. Now make another row of spots as above, observing to work the 4 treble of row 4 into the middle stitch of the 3 double of the previous row. Make another row of 16 rings with red silk as above, but in this row make the rings closer together than in the lower ones; then another row of spots, then two rows of open crochet for the cord, and finish with a scallop around the top. Finish with a cord and small tassels, with three larger tassels at the bottom.

LIST BRUSH FOR CLEANING SILKS.

THIS brush will be found very useful for taking the dust off silk dresses and mantles.

It consists of rows of cloth list about an inch wide, plaited on very thickly to a piece of cardboard the shape of an oval clothes brush, covered with gray calico. On the top of this brush glue a piece of pasteboard, and over this again another piece a very little larger than the former, and covered with gray calico. Cover this with cloth, and sew a rim of pasteboard covered with cloth round it, adding a brown silk cord at the edge. Ornament the top as well as the rim of the brush with figures, cut out of dark brown cloth, according to illustration.

LOW CHAIR FOR BEDROOM.

THE cover of this pretty and comfortable chair is of chintz; the stuffing of the back and

wide seat is fastened down in rows with covered buttons; the wide edge is gathered on each side, and finished with a plaited ruche. The flounce round the legs is put on in broad box-plaits.

UMBRELLA-STAND, ORNAMENTED WITH DRAPERY.

Materials.—Reddish-brown cloth or ribbed woollen material for the ground: cloth in two shades of brown for the applique; purse silk in three shades of the same color, completing the shading and black; silk braid of the lightest shade: narrow gold braid and cord.

THE brown shades of this embroidery, enlivened by gold braid and cord with a dark reddish-brown ground, would be just as effective with green, violet, or white. The two leaf halves of the applique in dark and light cloth, and fastened on by a row of gold braid, going all round, and overcast with black, come close together in the middle under a row of cross-bars, worked in the darkest silk. Herring-bone stitches in the two light shades give the leaf veins; the other light sprigs of single stitches have stalks of gold cord, overcast with black. The latter goes round the dark outlines of the pattern, worked in twisted, over chain stitch; the decoration at the upper leaf point made in the same stitch, and the

fancy stitches between the light braid, are in the middle color. The arabesque shapes of this pattern would also make a setting for any other centre shape than the leaf before us; for instance, a colored group in flat-stitch embroidery.

This pretty stand, intended for a summer-house or hall, is of carved black-polished wood, with a china holder below for wet umbrellas; the wide embroidered drapings going round make it especially suitable for a present.

WORK BASKET.

OUR model is of a brown basket work stand twenty-eight inches high, inside of which are two yellow open-work cane baskets of a graduated size. The upper basket has a lid with hinges and brown handle; this, as well as the two baskets, the bottom of each being wadded thickly, is lined with lilac silk. On the outer side of the lid is a round pincushion of wadding and silk somewhat flat in shape, and four and three-quarters inches large, the place where it is put on being hidden by a pinked silk quill-

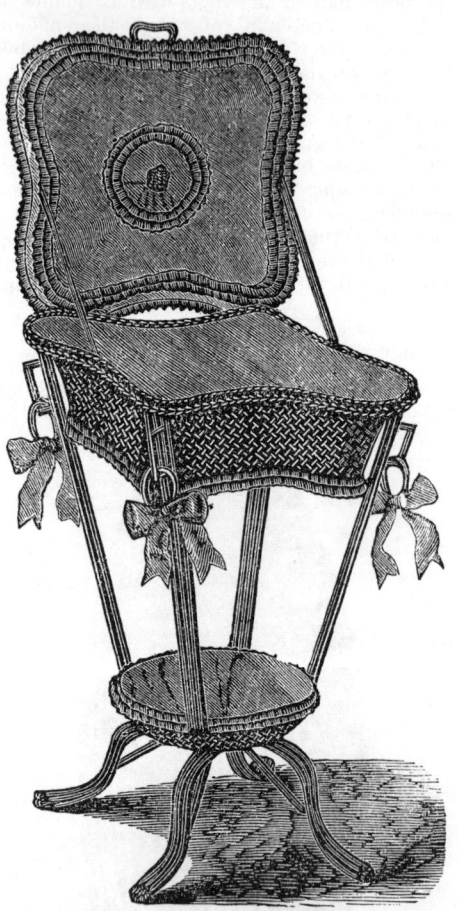

ing an inch and a quarter wide. The same finish is seen on the lid round the inside, which is of a straight piece of lilac silk drawn full over a round of card-board. Pinked silk quilling is also put around the in and outside of the lid, and the outer edges of both baskets; the bottom parts, of a like quilled setting, stand out in a curve-like way. Four bows of the stuff complete the trimming of this pretty basket.

an *appliqué* of gray cloth laid over card-board, and sewn on with gold cord and yellow silk

Fig. 7.

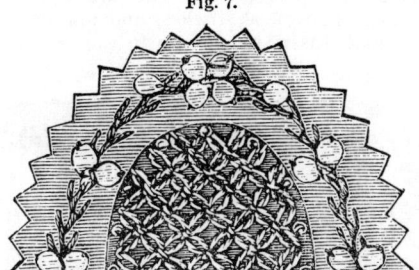

(see Fig. 7). Underneath this oval is a box-plaiting of several strips of cloth, also vandyked around the edge.

TRAVELLING BAG.
(*See Engraving, Page* 234, 235.)

THE bag itself is of Russian leather, with straps and metal lock. On each side is an embroidery worked on canvas ground, with wool and filoselle.

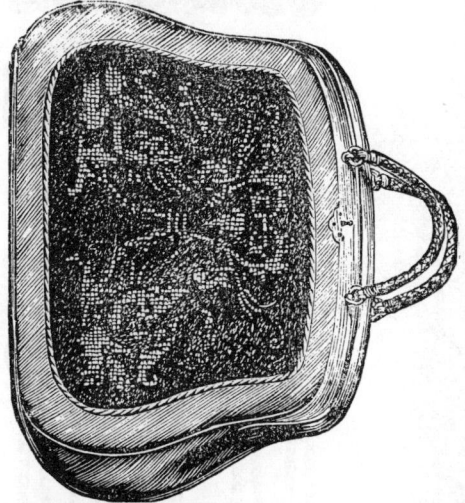

First Side.—■ Dark red. □ 2d shade. ▣ 3d shade.
Second Side.— I Yellow. ▪ Scarlet. ▤ 2d shade. ▨ Green. ▢ Blue.

FRINGE: CROCHET AND MIGNARDISE.

CHOOSE mignardise of the size shown in design. For the upper part, work one double into two picots of mignardise together, five chain. Repeat for the entire length. For the fringe side, * one double into two picots of mignardise together, twelve chain, one roll picot into the third stitch of chain (a roll picot is made by winding the thread seven or eight

times around the hook, inserting the hook into the stitch the roll picot is to be worked into, and drawing the thread through it and all the

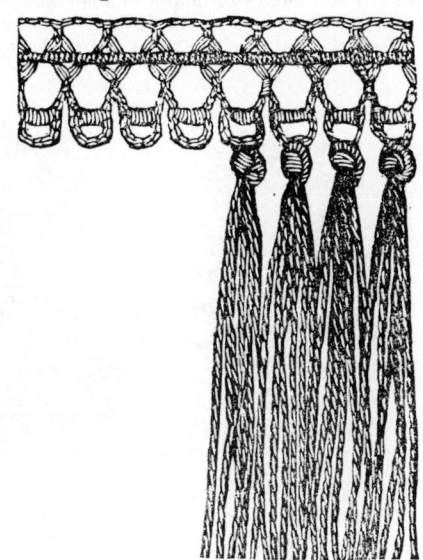

stitches on the hook together, then work one single to make the picot firm), two chain. Repeat from * for the entire length. Finish by tying in the fringe.

EMBROIDERED MATCH-BOX.

THE box is made of card-board, covered with black leather, and ornamented with an embroi-

dery, worked on black satin, with purse-silk of various colors.

CASE FOR KNITTING-NEEDLES.
(*See Engraving, Page* 233.)

THE foundation may be of Cashmere or Holland. The embroidery may be worked in silk or Andalusian wool. A piece of the centre stripe is given in the full size in Fig. 1, and two-thirds of it must be repeated on each side. The case must measure twenty-two inches in length; it is intended for steel knitting-needles, and is lined with flannel. The sides, about half an inch in breadth without turnings, are let in, and the flap at the top turns over four and a quarter inches, and is fastened by a strap and bow of ribbon. The case is shown made up in Fig. 2.

FASHIONABLE TRIMMINGS FOR MANTLES, ETC.

BEADS and bugles form a prominent portion of the popular trimmings on both mantles and dresses. Not only are black and white jet seen,

BABY'S GLOVE (CROCHET).

ONE ounce of white 4-thread German wool and an ivory crochet needle are required. Make a chain of 36 stitches, and unite them. *1st round.* Insert the needle in the first loop,

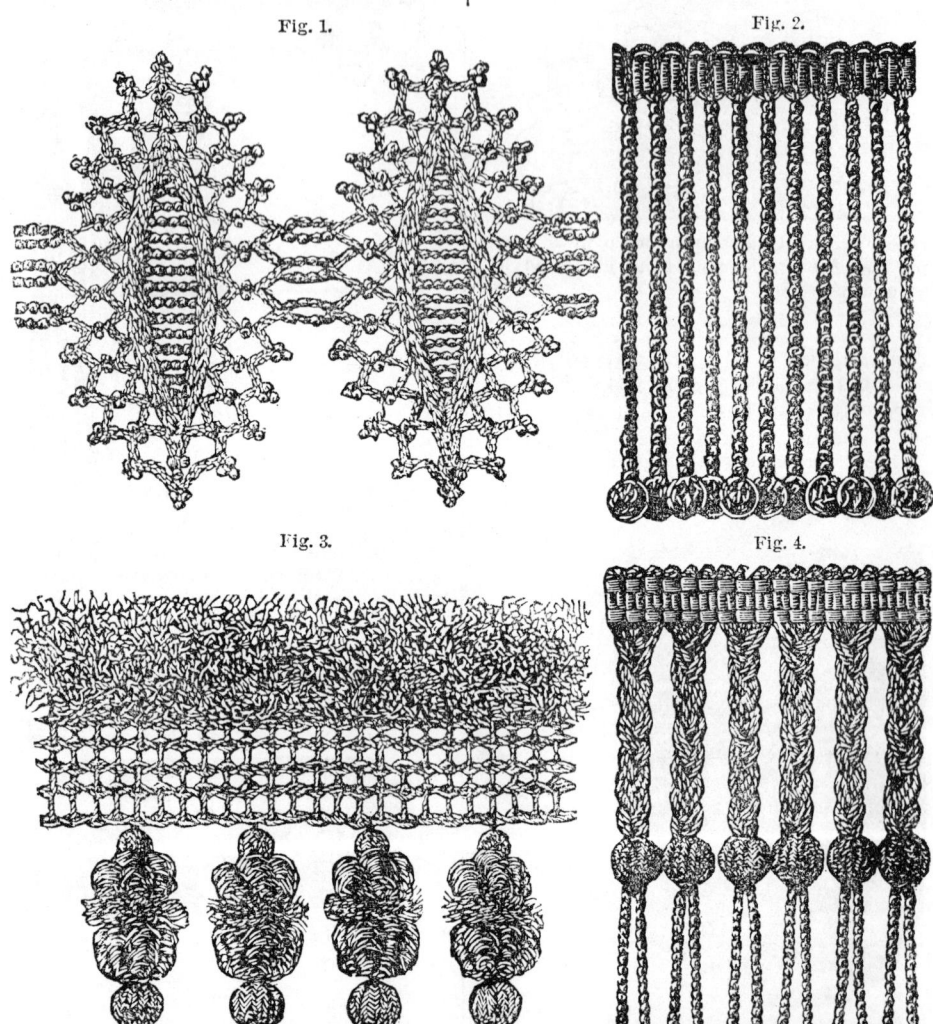

Fig. 1.

Fig. 2.

Fig. 3.

Fig. 4.

but blue beads and steel beads are both mixed with the finest makes of passementerie. These engravings will serve as a guide for the style of pattern most in vogue in Paris for trimming garments of all sorts.

All these passementeries are intended for trimming dresses, etc. Fig. 1 is entirely composed of gimp and beads; Fig. 2 is jet fringes, with a fancy satin galoon heading; Fig. 3 consists of floss silk tassels with a heather heading; Fig. 4 is a fringe with satin heading—every strand is a plait, terminating with a ball from which jet drops escape.

draw the wool through that and the loop on the needle; repeat this in every loop. *2d.* Insert the needle in the first loop, taking the upper part of the chain, draw the wool through that and the loop on the needle; repeat; this is called single crochet. *3d.* The same as 2d. *4th.* Take the wool on the needle, insert the needle in the first loop, taking the upper part of the chain, draw the wool through that and the two loops on the needle; repeat. *5th.* Take the wool on the needle, take up both the loops of chain, draw the wool through these and the 2 loops on the needle; repeat till 16 stitches are done, take the wool on the needle, take up the 17th and 18th stitches together, taking only the front loops, draw the wool through these and the 2 loops on the needle; repeat the stitch as at the beginning of the round till within 2 stitches of the end, take up these 2 together. *6th.* The same as the 5th, but without decreasing; repeat the 5th and 6th rounds 3 times more the round the decreasing is made in, it

tween the two worked into one loop of the row before, this will have increased 12 stitches for the thumb; unite these into a round, and work 4 rounds the same as 5th without increasing or decreasing, then decrease a stitch at the beginning of the next 3 rounds, decrease a stitch at the beginning and middle of each of the next 3 rounds, gather up the stitches that remain, and fasten off the end. Return to the hand part,

Fig. 1.

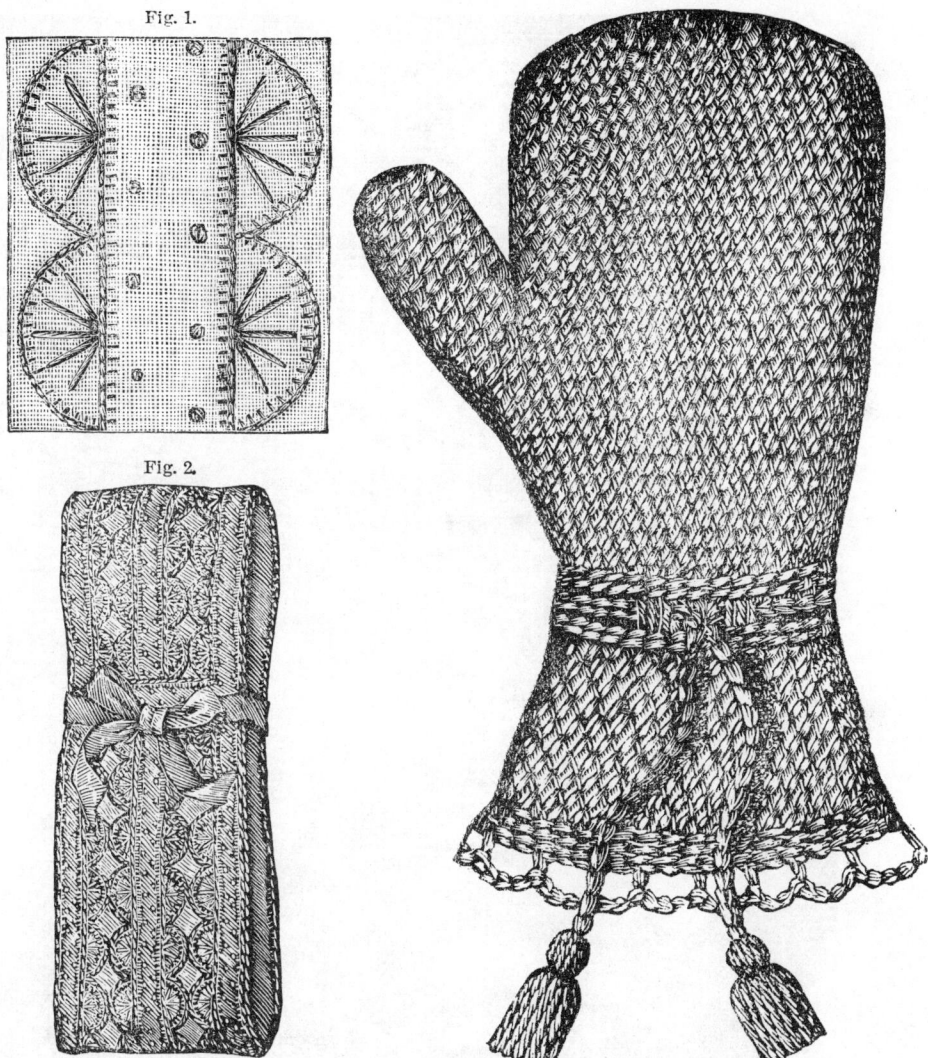

Fig. 2.

must be in the middle and at the end. *13th* and *14th* rounds the same as 2d. *15th.* Work 3 long stitches into successive loops, make 1 chain, miss 1 loop; repeat. *16th* round the same as 4th. *17th* round the same as 5th, till you come to the centre stitch; work twice into that, work the remainder of the round the same as 5th. *18th* and 11 succeeding rounds, the same as 17th, the increased stitch to come be-

and work with the remaining stitches 14 rounds, then decrease in the middle, and at the end of each of the next 4 rounds; turn the glove inside out, and sew up the remaining stitches. Work into the 1st row around the wrist a stitch of double crochet, make 3 chain, miss 1 loop, repeat a cord and tassels made of the wool, or a colored ribbon run into the 15th round completes the glove.

(*See Instructions, Page* 231.)

TRAVELLING BAG.

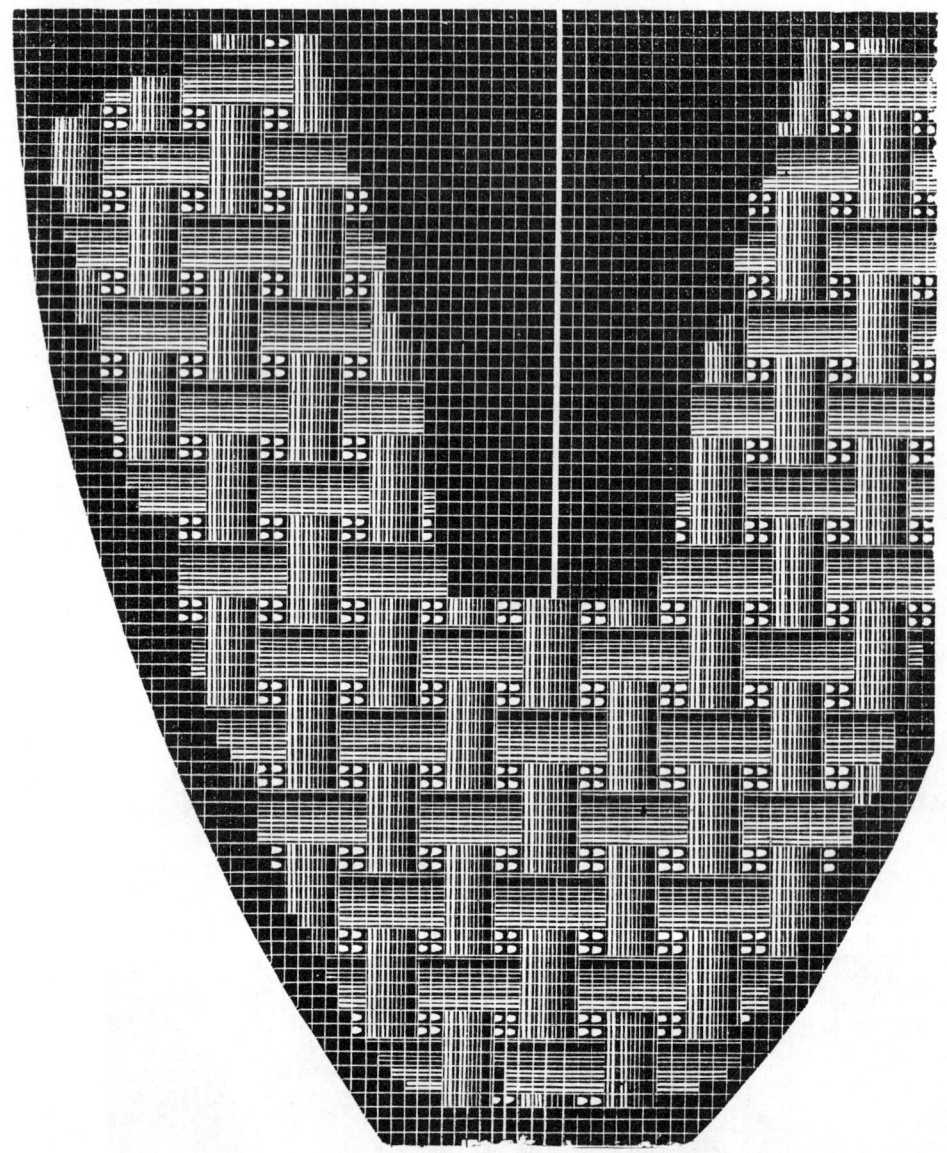

THE CINDERELLA SLIPPER,

Material.—Two skeins, each of four shades, of scarlet wool, the darkest to be the color of a dark clove pink.

Figs. 1 and 2.—Night-caps for a bridal wardrobe; the most tasteful, and at the same time becoming and serviceable styles that we have given in years.

Fig. 1 is particularly comfortable; it is cut

THIS pretty slipper is adapted for a child four years old, but may be made either larger or smaller. Its glittering appearance, which sparkles with every movement of the foot, has an exquisite effect. As a morning slipper for young ladies, it cannot fail to please; for fancy fairs it would also prove a very salable article.

First pencil from the engraving the outline of the slipper in thin writing or other paper;

then cut it exactly in the pencil marks ; pin or tack it on the canvas ; then, with needle and black cotton, tack an outline on the canvas, outside the paper all round, but observe to have only 16 stitches across the instep ; fasten the cotton off securely, and run a black thread through the centre between the 16 stitches. Now, with the darkest wool, cross-stitch over this outline of cotton. Then commence to work the slipper thus : Begin first stripe close to the line of instep, but two stitches of the canvas from the centre thread of black, and having the *heel of the slipper at the right hand ;* with the lightest shade on the 2d row of canvas from the centre work 8 cross-stitches ; then slip the needle under four threads of canvas, and work 8 more stitches on same row ; then slip 4 ; 8 more stitches ; slip 4 ; work any that may be left in same row. Take the 3 next shades, and work exactly the same. Thus there will be two rows of wool stitches on each the dividing line of black thread.

2d stripe.—Miss 2 rows of canvas ; with lightest shade work 2 stitches ; miss 4 ; work 8 ; miss 4 ; work 8 ; miss 4 ; work the remainder with the remaining three shades exactly the same.

3d stripe.—Miss 2 rows of the canvas ; work 8 ; miss 4 ; work 8 ; miss 4 ; work 8 ; miss the remainder, and finish the stripe towards the heel in similar manner.

It will be scarcely necessary to give any further directions for this pattern, which latter must be worked entirely over the slipper before proceeding to work the bars across, which are worked exactly in the same way ; but, instead of slipping the needle under the canvas, the needle will be slipped under the 4 worked rows ; but observe that all the stitches are crossed in the same direction. The intersection of these bars will cause 4 stitches of canvas to be left between each bar (*see engraving*), and these 4 stitches are filled up with steel beads, thus : Take No. 30 cotton, *doubled,* and fine needle ; fasten the cotton into back of slipper ; thread two beads ; cross these over the stitch of canvas the same way as the wool stitches are crossed ; then 2 more over next stitch, and the same over the other 2 stitches of canvas. Thus there are 8 beads in each 4 stitches of canvas ; but, as the beads would wear off round the sole, and round the edge of the slipper where the binding comes, fill these squares in with steel colored twist, or silk used double. The slipper should be trimmed with a rosette of scarlet or cerise color satin ribbon, of a tint not to obscure the brightness of the wool.

THE RAILWAY STOCKING.

TO BE WORKED IN COTTON THREAD OR WORSTED.

Cast on the needles as many stitches as would be required for an ordinary stocking for a child. Knit it once around, then rib it until an inch long, then bind off. Take up the stitches and commence knitting straight around plain stocking stitch until you have a finger and a half done ; then knit once around, dropping every other stitch off the needle ; then stretch out the stocking, and the stitches will run down until it reaches the ribbed piece, and no farther, forming a beautiful open worked stocking. Having kept the remaining stitches on the needles, finish off the toe by knitting straight around, narrowing every time on each needle. It will shape itself on the

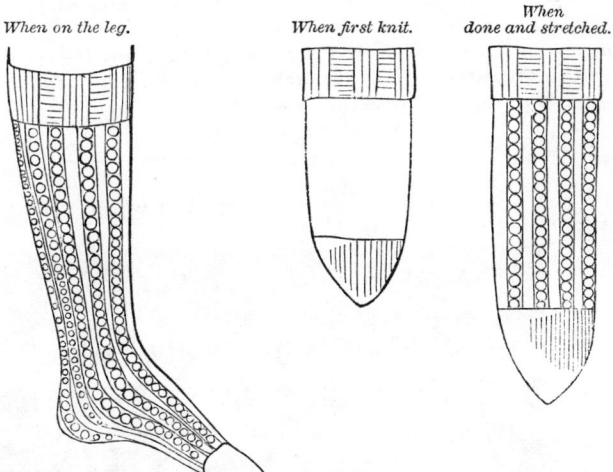

When on the leg.   *When first knit.*   *When done and stretched.*

leg, and will be sufficiently long, as it only requires two fingers in length for a lady's stocking.

BAG TO BE BRAIDED ON VELVET OR CASHMERE.

GOLD braid on velvet, or cerise on black cashmere, are both pretty.

To those who are unacquainted with the method of transferring the designs to velvet, or any dark material, it would be as well to say that the pattern should be drawn on thick paper, then carefully pricked. Then the pattern should be laid over the material to be worked, and some powdered starch or whitening rubbed over it; on removing the pattern, the design will be traced in white spots, which are then to be followed out with a camel's-hair pencil and white lead.

INSERTION.

CURTAIN BAND.

THE band is made of course mignardise and crochet, the ends of which are edged with the trimming shown in Fig. 2. The band may be made of a length to suit the curtains it is intended to loop. From half to three-quarters of a yard is the usual length of the finished band.

For the edge of ends, take a fresh piece of mignardise, and work 1 double in the first point up each previous worked single; this brings the stitch to the last 7 chain; repeat from *.

This trimming may be sewn or joined with single stitches in working to the loops of the mignardise.

------◆------

NEEDLE-BOOK.

THE outside is of card-board, covered with silk, and edged with a little crochet or tatted

of mignardise, * 13 chain, pass over 2 picots of mignardise, 4 chain, 2 treble in the same picot as last worked in, 4 chain, 2 treble in the last of four chain, 1 single in 12 successive picots of mignardise, 4 chain, 2 treble in the same picot as last worked in, 1 double in the centre of the 2 leaves, 4 chain, 2 treble in the same

Fig. 2.

stitch as last double was worked in, pass over two picots of mignardise, 1 double in the next, 6 chain, 1 single in the 7th of 13 chain, 7 chain, pass over 2 picots of mignardise, 1 double in the next. Turn the mignardise, and for the pattern between the scallop work 6 single up the back in successive picots of mignardise; then, on the other side, work 6 single, taking

lace. Take a square measuring four inches; fold it corner to corner, so as to form a triangle. Fold again, forming another triangle half the size. Fold in the same way once more. Fold

again, and cut off the long corner; now cut the rounded scallop (see design). The leaves forming the inside are of white Cashmere, worked with buttonhole stitch in colored silk. Any number of folds may be placed inside the covers. The cord ties the needle-book together when not in use.

DINNER MAT OF PLAITED TWINE.

THE twine should be fine, and of a pretty shade of gray; It is twisted into a Russian plait. This is simply a plait of five strands, the left-hand strand being placed over the two next

row of three rings are worked first, then the next three joined to them, and so on until the length required is completed. Commence with 12 ch, which join into a ring, * work 4 dc on the ring, a picot of 5 ch, 1 single on the last dc, 1 dc over the ring, a picot, 1 dc, a picot, 4 dc, 12 ch again, join in the first, and put the thread over and work over the same side of this ring as the last, repeating from * once;

strands, and then the right-hand strand over the two next to the left; the completed plait is sewn together with fine gray thread, beginning from the centre, until the mat measures ten inches in diameter. It is edged with red braid, and a border consisting of two Russian plaits, arranged as in the illustration. Lastly, the mat is ornamented with an embroidery of scarlet single Berlin wool in *point russe*, and a design, worked with fine gray cord, sewn on with buttonhole stitches of scarlet wool.

then over the last ring work 4 dc, a picot, then 1 dc, a picot, three times, 2 dc, a picot, three times, 1 dc, a picot, three times, * 4 dc; now work over the next ring 4 dc, a picot, then 1 dc, a picot, twice, 4 dc; repeat from the last * in the next ring, then 1 single in the first dc, 11 ch for the foundation between the rings, and then commence with the first 12 ch in the pattern. Join the rings together by the three first picots on each.

BORDER CROCHET.

THIS pattern is worked across the design, not in one long length, so that the first little

CROCHET EDGING, WITH LITTLE FLOWERS.

SIX reels of cotton, No. 16, and a fine crochet needle, are required. Make a chain the length

required. *1st row.* Work a stitch of double crochet into 1 loop, make 15 chain, miss 5 loops; repeat. *2d.* Take up the 1st and 2d of the 15 chain together, and work them as one stitch, work 5 stitches of double crochet into successive loops, work 3 stitches into the next loop, work 6 stitches of double crochet in successive loops, * miss the last loop of this 15 and the first of the next, work 6 stitches of double crochet into successive loops, work 3 into the next, work 6 stitches of double crochet into successive loops ; repeat from * to the end. Work 5 more rows on the same plan. 8th. Work a stitch of double crochet into the first point, make 5 chain ; repeat. 9th. Work a stitch of single crochet into the centre one of the 5 chain, make 5 chain, take up the 5th loop from the needle, draw the

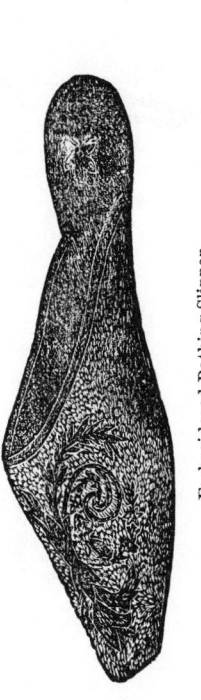

Embroidered Bathing Slipper.

different colored wools in satin stitch. The sole is of cork, covered inside with a lining of linen. Embroider the Baden-Baden cloth according to the illustration, bind the slipper with scarlet braid, and join it to the sole.

GYPSY JEWEL BASKET.

PRETTY little gilt or Berlin wire stands for these little baskets are sold at most fancy-work shops. In our model, the basket is lined with blue satin over scented wadding. A ruche of satin ribbon hides where the lining is put in, and drapes of brown kid ornament the inside

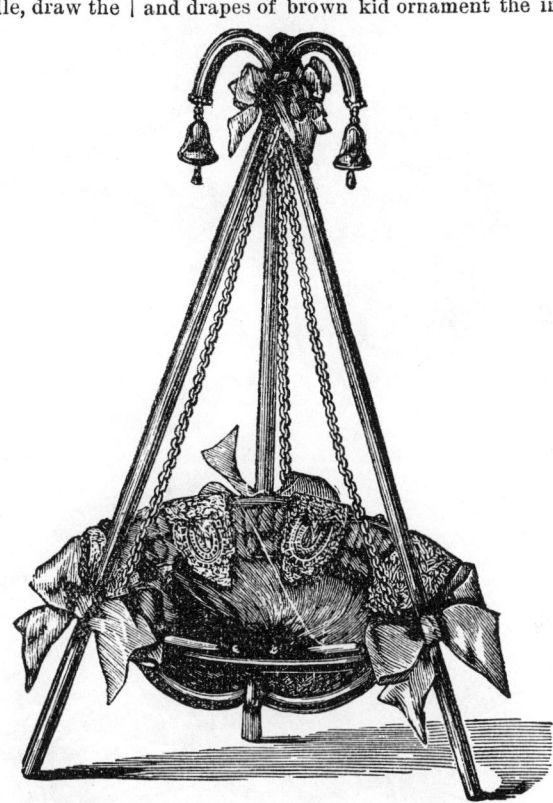

cotton through that and the loop on the needle, make 11 chain, form the last 6 of these into a circle, * work a stitch of double crochet into it, make 6 chain, take up the 6th from the needle, draw the cotton through that and the loop on the needle ; repeat from * 4 times more. Make 3 chain, unite to centre of next 5 chain in last row, make 3 chain, work a stitch of single crochet into the first of double crochet, make 5 chain ; repeat from the beginning of the 8th row.

EMBROIDERED BATHING SLIPPER.

THIS slipper is made of Baden-Baden cloth, bound with scarlet braid, and embroidered with

of the basket. These are worked with blue and crimson purse-silk and gold cord.

LACE PATTERN FOR CROCHET EDGING.

ONE piece of fine braid, six reels of cotton No. 16, and a steel crochet needle are required.

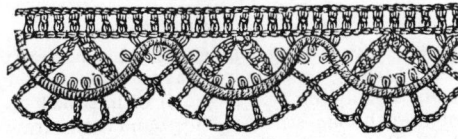

Make a chain 4 or 5 yards in length. 1st row. Work 1 long stitch and 1 chain stitch alternately. missing 1 loop between till 4 of each are done, then with another reel of cotton make a chain of 18, take 'up a loop of the braid about an inch from the end, work a stitch of single crochet to unite it, work a stitch of double cro-

chain, work a stitch of double crochet into the last chain, miss 4 loops of braid, and unite to the 5th with a stitch of single crochet, fasten the end securely with a sewing needle, return to the foundation row, and make 1 chain stitch

Carnation Feather Flower.   See page 85.

Carnation Feather Flower.   See page 85.

chet into the 2d of the 18 chain, * make 1 chain, miss 1 loop, work a long stitch into the next; repeat from * twice more, make 1 chain, miss 1 loop, take up the next loop and with it the loop of the 4th long stitch of the foundation, draw the cotton through, and then through the 2 on the needle; repeat from first * 3 times, make 1

and 1 long stitch alternately, missing 1 loop between each till 4 chain stitches are done, with the next long stitch, unite the 2d loop of the braid, * make 1 chain, miss 1 loop, work a long stitch with the next loop of braid; repeat from * twice more, every scallop to be done in the same way.   For the outer edge * work a long stitch into the third loop from the centre of scallop, make 5 chain, repeat from * into each of the next 6 loops of braid, miss 3 loops of braid; repeat.

FEATHER FLOWERS.
(See Engravings, Page 242.)

THE feathers are cut to the shapes shown in Figs. 2, 3, and 6, and the petals may be dipped in Judson's dyes, or covered with a camel-hair pencil and water colors. Peacock's or parrot's feathers form the foliage. The wire stalks may be covered with green paper. If preferred, the petals may be made with white feathers. For the pistils and stamens, white cotton is tied in little bunches; the ends are dipped first in dissolved gum-arabic, next in fine silver-sand, and then in yellow ochre.

BRUSH RACK AND BRACKET.

THIS is a most useful addition to a toilet table. The bracket is made of wood; our engraving is a sufficient guide for either an amateur or

a skilled workman. These brackets may be made to hang on the back of a table, or be fastened to the wall. The bottom shelf is ornamented with a valance, worked in beads on canvas, with a fringe of the same.

CROCHET AND TATTED LACE.

THE materials are cotton, tatting shuttle, and crochet needle. The tatting is first worked as follows, only one shuttle being required : * 9 double, 1 purl, 9 double, close into a circle, and tat at a short distance twice alternately a circle like the one just described, only that the circles must of course be joined at the purl, then close to this circle repeat from *. When a sufficient length has been tatted, crochet along it as follows : *1st row.* * 1 long treble in the purl, 8 chain, 1 double long treble in the thread be-

tween 2 circles, 8 chain; repeat. *2d.* 1 long treble in every stitch; then along the other side of the work crochet the 3d row : * 4 times alternately 1 double, 1 purl of 5 chain and 1 double in the first chain stitch in the next interval of thread; then 1 double in the same interval, 4 times alternately 1 double, 1 purl in the next interval of thread; then 1 double in the same interval, 1 double in the lower part of the next double long treble of the 1st row; repeat from *.

GARDEN MITTENS.

THESE mittens may be made in wash-leather or in a soft cotton material. Fig. 3 shows the

Fig. 1.

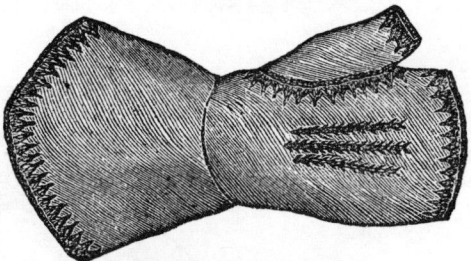

Fig. 3.

Fig. 2.

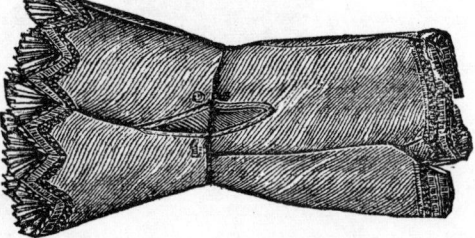

stitch for the back. Fig. 2 is edged with a frill of white muslin.

BRIDE'S SACHET.

(See Instructions, Page 249.)

Fig. 1.

Fig. 2.

CROCHET SQUARE FOR ANTIMA-CASSAR.

For this square, cotton No. 12 and a fine crochet needle are required. Make 4 ch and join. *1st round.* 2 dc in each of the 4 ch. *2d.* * 3 dc in one stitch, dc in next, repeat from * three times more. The 3 dc in one stitch form the corners of the square, and in each round they must be repeated on the centre stitch of the 3 in one in the previous one, thus forming the square, pulling it into shape occasionally to keep it square and make the corners sharp. Proceed in the same manner for the *3d,* *4th,* and *5th* rounds. After the 5th round there should

on the next stitch, when finished and closed, work 3 dc, to centre of next corner stitch; repeat from * 3 times more, and fasten off. Cut off a piece of cotton (a yard will be sufficient), bring it through from the back, in a centre corner stitch of the 2d round, make 9 ch, pass the loop on the needle, through the top of centre stitch of the opposite corner of same round, in a diagonal direction, and, drawing the thread through it, make 9 ch, and pass the loop to the back, through the 1st ch that was made; draw the thread through at the back as if fastening off, and bring it out again on the right side in a loop, at the centre stitch of opposite corner

12 stitches on each side of the square. *6th.* From the centre corner stitch * make 12 ch for the foundation of a long leaf, turn back and work a single on the last ch, dc on the next, 7 treble on the next 7 ch, then dc and a single on the 2 first ch, and a single taken through the corner stitch of square, from whence the 12 ch began, dc into the same stitch of previous round (to make up the 3) 2 dc on square, a single on next, 9 ch for a leaf, turn back down the ch, 1 single, dc, 4 treble, dc, a single through the same stitch of square, from which the 9 ch began, 5 dc on side of square; repeat the last small leaf

of same round, make 9 ch, pass the last loop of them through top of centre stitch of the 4th corner, make 9 ch, pass to the back, through the 1st of the 9 ch previously made, and fasten off. This forms the cross in centre of square, which is quite raised and detached from the work, only being united to it by a stitch at each of the corners.

For Frame.—1st round. Commence on point of one of the long leaves at the corner, 3 dc into it (for corner), * 7 ch, 5 ch for a picot, close it by a single in the 1st of the 5 ch, turning the work in the fingers, taking out the needle, inserting it again in the same loop, but in the opposite direction, so that the picot may turn downwards towards the centre, 5 ch for a 2d picot, closed in the same manner in the same stitch as the first, 5 ch for a 3d picot, to be closed still in the same stitch, 3 ch, dc on point of 1st smaller leaf; 3 ch, a group of 3 picots make exactly as before, 3 ch, dc on point of 2d smaller leaf; 3 ch, a group of 3 picots as before, 7 ch, 3 dc on point of long leaf at next corner; repeat from * 3 times more. 2d. 3 dc in centre one of each corner, and dc in all the other stitches. 3d. Like 2d. 4th. † from 2d dc of centre corner stitch, take 4 treble into top of centre corner of dc of 2d round (passing over the round between), take out the needle, insert it in first of these treble, take up the last of the 4 just left, and draw the thread through both so as to close them, another dc in the same corner stitch to complete the 3, then 6 dc in following stitches of 3d round, * a similar knob of 4 treble over next stitch, all taken into top of corresponding one of 2d round, after closing

still in the same, to make up the 3 corner stitches, then a shorter treble and dc in the next 2 ch, and a single on the dc between the scallops; * then on the 5 ch of last round, dc, 3 treble, on the 2d of which make a group of 3 picots of 5 ch each, all closed in this same 2d treble, after the 3d 1 dc, and a single on the dc between the scallops; repeat from *, for each of the 7 other scallops to complete that side of square; and the whole from † three times more for the other 3 sides, ending with a single to join to the first corner, and fasten off. In working another square pass the centre stitch of centre picot of each group of 3, at the edge, through the corresponding stitch of those on the previous square, to join them.

REEL-WAGON.

THE foundation is of card-board; it is cut in one piece, and turned up to form the sides. The whole is covered and lined with silk. A simple pattern is worked at the edges, which are neatly

the knob miss 1 stitch directly behind it, and word 5 dc on following stitches of last round; repeat from * 5 times more, working the last time 6 dc instead of 5 after the knob; and repeat the whole from † 3 times more for the other three sides of the square. 5th. Like 3d.

For Open Edge.—1st round. † from centre corner stitch, make 11 ch, a single in the same stitch, turn the work to the back, and make a single and 2 dc on the 3 last of the 11 ch, turn to the right side again, 8 ch, miss 5 stitches of last round of frame, a single into the 6th, * turn to the wrong side, work a single and 2 dc on the 3 last of the 8 ch, turn to the right side of work again, made 8 ch, miss 5 stitches, a single into the 6th, and repeat from * 6 times more (making 8 open scallops, besides the corner one), last time taking the single into the corner stitch, and repeat the whole from † at the beginning, 3 times more for the other 3 sides of the square, but the last time to join at the end, make only 5 ch instead of 8, turn the work to the back, and make 2 dc and a single on the 3 first of the 11 ch at the beginning. 2d. Pass the thread up at the back, and continue upon the free stitches of the 11 ch, 1 dc, a treble worked short, a longer treble, along (thread twice over) in the 6th or centre stitch of the 11 ch, a group of 3 picots of 5, 6, and 5 ch each, all closed in this same centre stitch, and another long treble

bound with ribbon; eyelet-holes are pierced to pass the ribbon through, and a little star is worked around each. Ribbon is passed through the reels to keep them in place.

BOX-PATTERN RUG FOR THE BEDSIDE OR PIANO—KNITTING.

THE materials are black, green, scarlet, and white double Berlin wool; wooden needles, No. 9. Each diamond is knitted separately, and sewn together as shown in designs. For the diamond, cast on two stitches. *1st row.* Knit 1, knit 1 at the front, 1 at the back of same stitch. *2d.* Slip 1 as if for purling (each slipped stitch is the same), knit 1 at the front, 1 at the back in the same stitch, knit 1. (The increase is made in this manner in each row.) *3d.* Slip 1, knit 3. *4th.* Slip 1, knit 2, increase 1, knit 1. *5th.* Slip 1, knit 3, increase 1, knit 1. *6th.* Slip 1, knit 4, increase 1, knit 1. *7th.* Plain knitting. *8th.* Slip 1, knit 5, increase 1, knit 1. *9th.* Slip 1, knit 6, increase 1, knit 1. *10th.* Slip 1, knit 7, increase 1, knit 1. *11th.* Plain knitting. *12th.* Slip 1, knit 8, increase 1, knit 1. *13th.* Slip 1, knit 9, increase 1, knit 1. *14th.* Slip 1, knit 10, increase 1, knit 1. *15th.* Plain knitting. *16th.* Slip 1, knit 11, increase 1, knit 1. *17th.* Slip 1, knit 12, increase 1, knit 1. *18th.* Slip 1, knit 13, increase 1, knit 1. *19th.*

Plain knitting. 20th. Slip 1, knit 14, increase 1, knit 1. 21st. Slip 1, knit 15, increase 1, knit 1. 22d. Slip 1, knit 16, increase 1, knit 1. 23d. Plain knitting. 24th. Slip 1, knit 17, increase 1, knit 1. 25th. Slip 1, knit 18, increase 1, knit 1. 26th. Slip 1, knit 19, increase 1, knit 1. 27th. Plain knitting. (This is the exact half.) 28th. Slip 1, knit 18, knit 2 together, knit 1. 29th. Slip 1, knit 17, knit 2 together, knit 1.

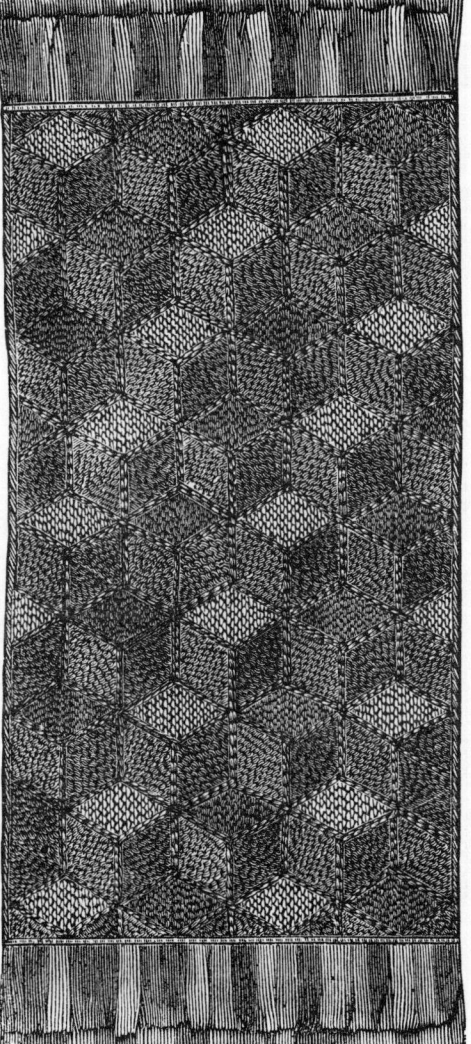

30th. Slip 1, knit 16, knit 2 together, knit 1. 31st. Plain knitting. 32d. Slip 1, knit 15, knit 2 together, knit 1. 33d. Slip 1, knit 14, knit 2 together, knit 1. 34th. Slip 1, knit 13, knit 2 together, knit 1. 35th. Plain knitting. 36th. Slip 1, knit 12, knit 2 together, knit 1. 37th. Slip 1, knit 11, knit 2 together, knit 1. 38th. Slip 1, knit 10, knit 2 together, knit 1. 39th. Plain knitting. 40th. Slip 1, knit 9, knit 2 together, knit 1. 41st. Slip 1, knit 8 knit 2 to-

gether, knit 1. 42d. Slip 1, knit 7, knit 2 together, knit 1. 43d. Plain knitting. 44th. Slip 1, knit 6, knit 2 together, knit 1. 45th. Slip 1, knit 5, knit 2 together, knit 1. 46th. Slip 1, knit 4, knit 2 together, knit 1. 47th. Plain knitting. 48th. Slip 1, knit 3, knit 2 together, knit 1. 49th. Slip 1, knit 2, knit 2 together, knit 1. 50th. Slip 1, knit 1, knit 2 together, knit 1. 51st. Plain knitting. 52d. Slip 1, knit 2 together, knit 1. 53d. Slip 1, knit 2 together. 54th. Knit 2 together, knit 1. 55th. Knit 2 together; fasten off. When the whole of the squares are joined together, the rug is lined. A thick worsted cord is sewn around. The fringe made of the four different colors can be bought at any fancy store.

DISPATCH-CASE.

THIS case, which is made without any firm foundation, may be made of any material at hand. The outside is quite straight. It is ornamented with silhouettes cut out of black velvet, and gummed on to the foundation.

Fig. 1.

Fig. 2

Two rows of braid are sewn down with cording-stitch, and the edge is neatly bound with silk braid. The pockets of the inside are cut according to Fig. 2, and ornamented with little branches of coral-stitch. These little pockets are the receptacles for letters, etc.

FANCHON—KNITTING.

THIS fanchon, being knitted in Shetland wool, will be found light and convenient for throwing over the head on leaving the theatre or any public place. It is knitted plain, in rows throughout, with Shetland wool of white and contrasting color, such as blue or ponceau.

Two steel needles, No. 15 or 16, and two long wooden ones, No. 10, will be required. Cast on 20 stitches with the blue on the steel needles, and knit 6 rows; then cut off the wool, leaving a short end; with a weaver's or other secure knot join on the white wool, and knit 18 plain rows with the No. 10 needles, increasing a stitch at the end of every alternate one, so that the increase should always come at the same end. After these 18 rows, join on the

blue wool again, and knit 6 rows with the steel needles without any increase. In half the fanchon there will be 8 white stripes, which look full, and in each of which the increasing is to be continued as directed for the 1st, and the same number of blue ones, knitted without increase, the 9th blue one forming the centre stripe. From this work regularly back 8 white and 8 blue stripes, now decreasing a stitch at the end of every alternate row in the white ones, so that the last blue stripe will have only 20 stitches, as at the commencement, which are to be cast off. Tassels of the blue wool, five and a half inches long, and not thick, are placed at the two corners of each of the front ends of the fanchon, and at the termination of the three centre blue stripes at the back.

SILK-WINDER.

THE winder may be cut in wood or stiff card, and painted according to design.

SHOE CASE.

Fig. 1.

FIGS. 1, 2, and 3. Fig. 1 shows the shoe case open; the boots are laid in, and the

Fig. 2.

straight flaps then button down over them. Figs. 2 and 3 show both sides of it when closed.

Fig. 3.

It is made of gray linen, braided with scarlet, and trimmed with a narrow plaited ruffle. It can be made of Cashmere, if preferred.

BRIDE'S SACHET.
(*See Engravings, Page* 244.)

THE materials are white or colored sarcenet, or satin; ribbon to correspond, one and a half inch broad; lace or blond, two inches broad; crystal beads; wadding; scent powder.

The firm foundation is of card-board ten inches square. The inner ground consists of a piece of stuff of the same size, covered with wadding sprinkled with violet or some other scent-powder, and quilted in squares measuring half an inch. The initials must be worked upon the silk intended for the outer covering in silk, gold, or silver thread. This had better be worked in a frame.

The corners are quilted in squares measuring half an inch. The corners of the squares are ornamented with crystal beads, as represented in the design. The ruche inclosing the middle field is of ribbon to match the sachet, one and a half inch broad, arranged in a kind of rose quilling, joined in the middle by a bead. The inclosed inner part consists of a piece of scented wadding or flannel the size of the flat ground, covered on both sides with silk, and quilted all over in slanting squares measuring half an inch. By cutting this part in a slanting direction from one point to another there will be four parts exactly meeting each other, which must be bound on the sloped sides, and ornamented with beads, Fig. 2. The point of one of the flaps is ornamented with a flat rosette, which keeps the four together in the middle. The straight sides of these four flaps must be sewn to the ground covering, and the puffings measuring about two inches in breadth are put around these. At the joining of the inner and outer covering the upper edge of the puffings must be joined with the large cover pieces. The separate parts of the square cut through in a slanting direction must be all ornamented with beads in squares. The scented wadding is only necessary in the upper covering; the middle of each square is ornamented with a bead. The under side is then covered plain of the same material; and at a narrow point, about two inches long, a piece of card-board is laid in, behind which, to make it firm, the stuff is stitched through with the wadding without taking in the upper covering. The sloped and straight side of each part which touch the card-board must be bound like the inner flaps, and ornamented at the outer edge with beads.

Each of the remaining straight sides takes up one of the upper edges of the puffing, and the edge is ornamented with two rows of beads to hide the place where it is joined. The corners are ornamented with bows of ribbon.

For closing the sachet, these three large three-cornered parts must be laid over each other in such a manner that one straight side at the right lies over the slope along the middle. The fourth with the card board point must be pushed under the first. The whole is ornamented with broad lace, myrtle leaves, and flowers at the corners.

ORNAMENT FOR A HEADDRESS.

A LEAF cut out of black stiff net, edged with two rows of cylindrically-shaped bugles. The

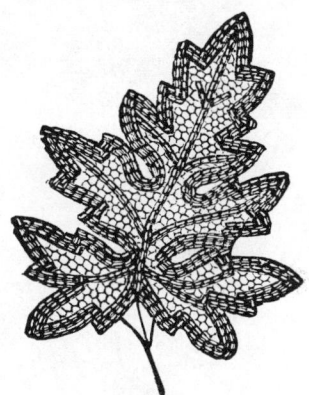

veinings are traced by one row of the same bugles.

WHITE EMBROIDERY. BETTY.

FICHU FOR THE HEAD OR NECK
(CROCHET).

Materials.—Two colors are required, or one color and white, in Pyrenees wool, and half an ounce of each color in Andalusian; No. 12 crochet hook.

IF worn on the head, it should be so folded that the fichu is 3 doubles in the centre, with a small point formed by the corner on each side; the other corners then hang down in the shape of lappets. It is placed on the head in the same manner as the little morning caps so much in vogue. It can be used square, as a neckhandkerchief, and we recommend the stitch most strongly, working in eider yarn or Shetland wool for a shawl.

(this is to form the increase for the corner), 7 ch, 1 dc in the 4th ch of 4th lp, 7 ch, 1 dc in 4th ch of 5th lp, 7 ch, 1 dc in same ch as the last dc, 7 ch 1 dc in 4th ch of 6th loop, 7 ch, 1 dc in 4th ch of 7th loop. Work another loop of 7 and dc in the same chain as last dc, 7 ch, 1 dc in 4th ch of 8th loop, 7 ch, 1 dc in the 4th single at the commencement of the round, 7 ch, 1 dc in same loop again.

Continue the work in this manner, always increasing each round on the corner loops by making an extra loop. Work 15 more rounds in gold.

17th. Join the dark shade, and work 4 rounds.
21st. Join the gold; work 2 rounds.

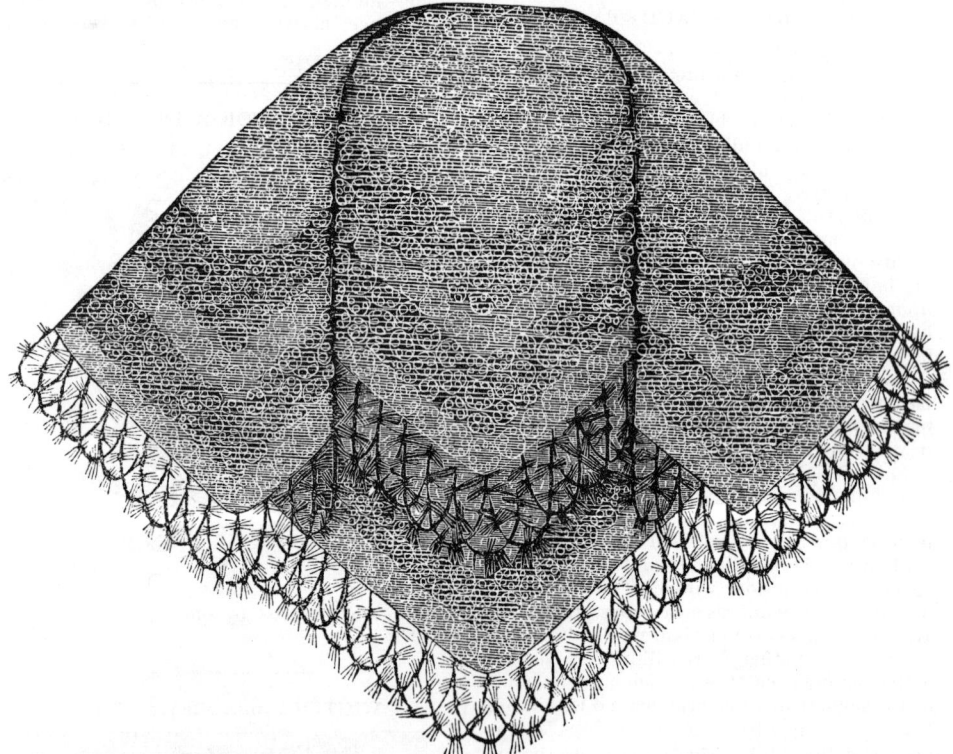

The pattern is worked in gold and maroon; 2 skeins of gold, 1 of maroon.

Make a chain of 12, unite (with gold), 7 chain or ch, 1 plain or double crochet dc in first of the 12 ch, 7 ch, 1 dc in the 3d of 12 ch, 7 ch, 1 dc in 4th of 12 ch, 7 ch, 1 dc in 6th of 12 ch, 7 ch, 1 dc in 7th of 12 ch, 7 ch, 1 dc in 9th of 12 ch, 7 ch, 1 dc in 10th of 12 ch, 7 ch, 1 dc in 12th of 12 ch.

2d round. Work 4 single crochet on the 1st 4 ch of the first loop of 7, then 7 ch, 1 dc in 4th ch of 2d lp of 7, 7 ch, 1 dc in 4th ch in next lp of 7, 7 ch, 1 dc in the same chain as the last dc

23d. Join the dark shade, and work 4 rounds.
27th. Join the gold and work 2 rounds. Fasten off neatly.

THE FRINGE.—Take 6 very long lengths of both shades of Andalusian wool, 5 or 6 yards each length. Fasten the ends together. Wind off on a ball one longer length of the dark color. Tie the 12 lengths together tightly with this ball, without cutting the wool on the ball every half inch. Leave the wool rather easy between each tie; then there will be no fear of cutting the wrong thread. When the whole length is tied cut across the 12 threads, exactly in the middle of the distance between each tie, leaving little fluffy knots on the thread that tied them together. To mount the fringe on the fichu tie the connecting thread with the same colored wool into the middle of a loop of 7. Miss 8 tufts of fringe, tie again just under the 9th tuft in the 4th loop of 7 from the last. Tie all round in this manner. A second row is put on in exactly the same manner, but must be tied to the 2d of the 3 loops left between the connecting links in the 1st row of fringe. The wool sewn over is cut between each tie.

KNEE CAP.

Materials.—One ounce and a half of fine white knitting wool, four steel knitting needles No. 14, bell gauge.

CAST on 112 stitches on three needles, knit 2 and purl 2 alternately, so as to rib it, for 47 rows. With the 48th row begins middle piece or knee cap, which *throughout* is worked in back and forward going rows of purl 4, knit 4. To form little squares, begin the first of the first four rows with purl 4, knit 4, the first of the second four rows with knit 4, purl 4, and so on, changing the commencement of the first of

stitches is reduced to 12. Then pick up 29 stitches on each side, which completes the original number of 112, and work 47 rows all round, knitting 2 and purling 2 alternately, as before, which, practically, finishes the knee warmer. A pink or blue border in crochet work will add greatly to its appearance.

BLOTTING-BOOK COVER.

THIS blotting-book cover is worked on black cloth, with cloth patterns of different colors sewn on in *appliqué*. The small circle in the centre is of red cloth, with green knotted stitch in the centre, and rays formed of long black stitches. On the oval, pattern of white cloth, edged with blue coral stitch, work four flowers, the two longest of which are of yellow cloth, edged with garnet-colored Mexico stitch; the veining in the centre is worked with chain stitch in black silk, between two other blue veinings; the two smaller flowers are of blue cloth, edged with yellow Mexico stitch, with veinings in chain stitch worked with red and white silk. After the white oval pattern, cut out a large piece of red cloth, embroidered with 4 stars in railway stitch, black silk and yellow knotted

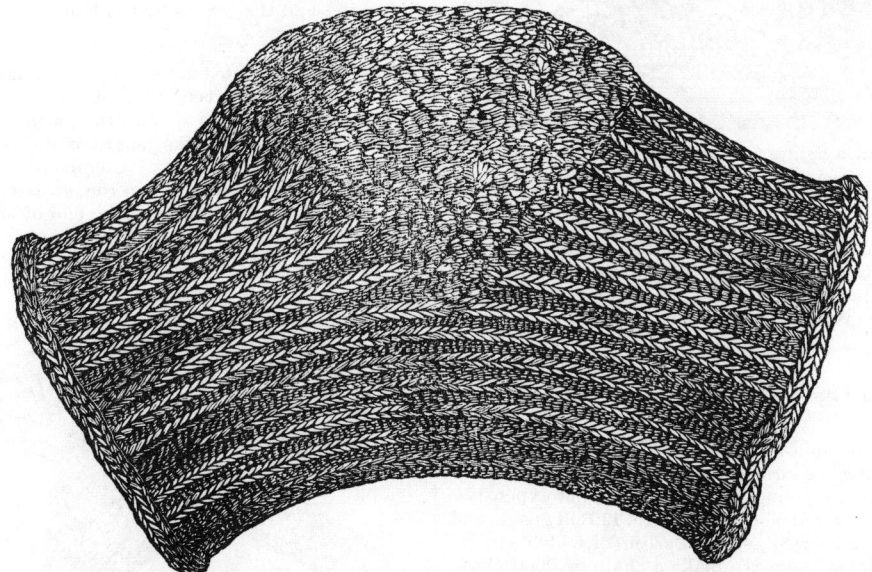

every 4 rows. Now let off 12 stitches of the last knitted row on a needle, knit on them the first row of the middle piece, and at the end of every following row the nearest of the stitches which are remaining on the other needles, so that the number of stitches of the middle piece is augmented by *one* at every needle or row. Do this till only 42 stitches of the ribbed part remain. Now knit the middle piece as before, but take off one stitch at the beginning as well as at the end of every row till the number of

stitch in the centre, and four branches worked in the same manner with green silk. On the edge of the red cloth work yellow herring-bone stitch; close to this, on the black cloth, work a row of herring-bone stitch with lighter yellow silk, and then a third row with white silk. The branches on the black ground are wood-colored between two green shades, and another shade of wood-color between two blue ones. The corner patterns are cut out in red cloth, edged with green Mexico stitch; the veinings in coral stitch are worked with different shades of yellow, the lightest shades in the middle. The branches are blue, in coral stitch, on the black ground. For the border, the lines which form the frame are worked in chain stitch with red silk. Inside these lines work dark green herring-bone stitch,

then a light green row with long white stitch. Between the lines work diamonds in long stitch, blue on one side and yellow on the other, with crosses alternately green and red. The cloth remains without embroidery on the other side of the blotting-book, which must be lined with watered-silk paper; leaves of blotting-paper are fastened in the centre.

MUFF CROCHETED IN IMITATION OF FUR.

THE following articles crocheted in imitation of fur are recommended for the warm winter toilets of young girls, as they are not expensive.

With a fine bone hook, No. 12 Bell guage, and the gray wool, single Berlin (of which you require six ounces), make a chain of 78 stitches.

1st row. Dc (double crochet), at the end 1 ch. *2d.* 1 dc in the first dc, taking up the back of the loop, which is done throughout the work, take up the back of the 2d loop, draw the wool through, pass the wool round the needle, take up the same loop again, making 3 loops on the needle in this one stitch, draw the wool through these 3, then through the 2 on the needle; take up the whole of this row in this manner. *3d.* Plain dc worked from the back of the loop as before. Repeat the 2d and 3d row. Work a piece

wide enough for your muff, then make it up; for this you require blue silk in the piece, two pair of black tassels, some blue ribbon to run in the runner, and a sheet of wadding. Lay your wadding the size of the piece of crochet you have worked, cover it on both sides with

Fig. 1.

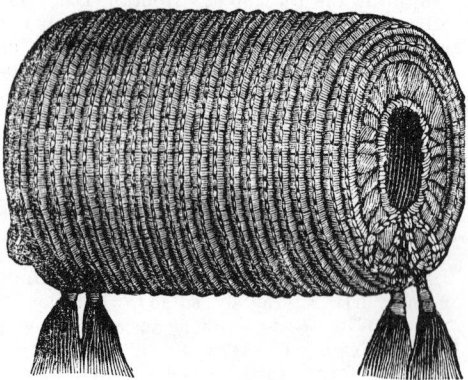

silk, then sew together; make a slot at each outer edge, sew up the piece of crochet, place it over the silk, run the edges of the crochet to the extreme edge of the slot, then pass your ribbon in; add the tassels by the join.

THE BOA.

This is also crocheted in the same stitch as the muff. You require five steel knitting needles, No. 12, for the head as it is knitted, 2 jet buttons for the eyes. For the length of the body make a chain of 117 stitches. Commence with a row of double crochet, then a row of pattern, always working a ch stitch at the end of each row. Work about 8 inches of this crochet for the width of the body. Sew it together, and

Fig. 2.

stuff it with wadding covered with silk. The tail is worked separately, and is crocheted in looped crochet. Make a ch of 20. *1st row.* Dc. *2d.* Take up the back of the loop, pass the wool three times round a mesh one and a quarter inch wide, or your 2 fingers of the left hand, put the needle under these loops, loop the wool over, then take up the st again, draw through, then draw through the 2 on the needle ; work the row in this manner. Work these 2 rows until you have ten rows of loops ; then work 2 more rows, decreasing one stitch on each side now, cut the loops in the middle and comb them with a fine comb. Sew the tail together, then to the body.

The Head is Knitted.—Cast on 10 stitches on each of the 4 needles ; knit a round. Then 3 rounds knit plain. 4*th.* Knit 17. You now commence the increase for the forehead. In the 18th st work 2 st thus : knit 1, then purl 1 ; work the 19th st in the same manner ; 20th st, knit plain ; the 21st and 22d st like the 18th and 19th ; the rest knit plain. 5*th.* Knit plain. 6*th.* Increase like the 4th round in the 2 st on both sides the 22d st. 7*th.* Plain. 8th. Increase like the 4th round on both sides the 24th st ; rest plain. 6 plain rounds. 14*th.* K 7, k 2 together ; k 1, knit 2 together ; knit plain until the last 12 ; then k 2 together, k 1, k 2 together. 15*th.* Plain. 16*th.* K 5, knit 2 together 3 times ; knit plain until the last 11, when knit 2 together 3 times ; knit 5. 17*th.* Plain. 18*th* and 3 next rounds plain. 21*st.* K 5, knit 2 together twice, knit plain until the last 9, then knit 2 together twice, knit 5. 22*d.* Plain. 23*d.* K 7, join the black, knit 2 together in black until the last 7, which knit plain in gray. Knit 8 rounds plain, knitting the black stitches with black, and the gray with gray : cast off. Wad the head to the shape, stitch on the buttons for the eyes, add some shreds of black wool for whiskers, then stitch on the ears, the directions for knitting which follow.

The Ears.—Cast 12 st on 1 needle with gray wool. Knit back. 2*d row.* Purl. 3*d.* Knit 2 together, knit 8, knit 2 together. 4*th.* Purl 2 together, purl all but the last 2, which purl together. Repeat the 3d and 4th rows until you have only one stitch left, then cast off, and sew to the head.

THE CUFFS.

You work the cuffs in the same manner as the body of the animal and the muff. Make a chain of 30 st. This is for the height of the

Fig. 3.

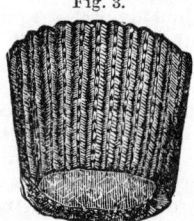

cuff. Work as the muff, until you have enough to pass over the hand. Make a lining of white quilted silk over wadding ; sew neatly to the edges of the crochet, make a runner at the top of the cuff, in which you draw through a ribbon to tie it to the shape of the hand.

JEWEL-STAND OF CRYSTAL BEADS.

Materials.—Large crystal beads, large cut crystal beads, round beads, and eight round crystal buttons, some fine and coarse silver wire, white knitting cotton.

THIS pretty stand is made of crystal beads and wire. First make the frame in the following manner : Take two circles of silver wire, one of which must be eight inches and three-quarters round, and the other eight inches ; the ends must overlap each other about two-fifths of an inch, and be fastened tightly. Wind some knitting cotton closely round these circles. Then cut four pieces of wire, each two inches and three-quarters long, cover them also with cotton, and fasten one large crystal button at the end of each piece of wire ; bend them as seen on illustration, and fasten them on to both wire circles. This frame is then covered with crystal beads threaded on fine silk. For the cup take one large cut crystal bead, draw two ends of fine wire, taken double, two inches and two-fifths long, through this bead, which

must be in the middle of the wire ; fasten a row of larger crystal beads, strung on wire, by drawing the end of the wire through the middle bead, and turning it back underneath it ; then wind this row of beads in coils round the middle bead ; fasten each coil by drawing the beads at regular intervals through the double ends of wire, and crossing two ends of wire close above the row of beads. After the 3d coil fasten another piece of wire between two ends of wire, so that there are now eight double ends of wire all round. On our pattern the cup consists of thirteen coils. Lastly, fasten some large cut crystal beads round the upper edge of the cup, and secure the latter to the frame with silver wire.

GENTLEMAN'S KNITTED SHIRT.

THIS shirt is knitted with white wool. The back and front are worked separately, and sewed together on the sides and on the shoulders. For the front make a foundation of 140 stitches, and knit backward and forward 240 rounds. Then, in order to form the slit, divide the stitches, taking the first 70 on another needle, and knit further 120 rounds. In order to form the contour of the neck, cast off in the 121st round 20 stitches on the widest side next the slit, then in the second following round six stitches, and after this to the 148th round only two stitches in every second following round. On the left side of the front, which counts only

70 stitches, cast off in the 121st round only six stitches, and in the following alternate rounds only two stitches. Besides this it will be necessary to narrow for the shoulder 27 stitches in the following 40 rounds. The narrowing must be as regular as possible. Lastly, knit 12 rounds more without widening or narrowing, after which cast off the front. For the back cast on 130 stitches, beginning on the under edge. Knit first 360 rounds without widening or narrowing, and then 40 rounds, in which narrow as regularly as possible 27 stitches at the beginning and end of the rounds, after which cast off. Join the back and front on the shoulders and on the sides, with the exception of the upper part for the arm-holes. For the sleeve cast on 100 stitches, beginning on the upper edge. Knit 248 rounds, after which work in the round with finer needles for the wrist 58 rounds, alternately one stitch purled and one knitted. Sew the sleeve up, and sew into the arm-hole. Bind the neck and slit, and face the slit, after

which arrange buttons and button-hole fastening.

NEEDLE-CASE IN THE SHAPE OF A FAN.
(*See Engraving, Page* 255.)

THIS case is made of white card-board and purple glacé silk. It consists of twelve parts of exactly the shape seen in illustration, placed so as to form a fan. Six of the silk parts are embroidered in point russe with black silk; in the middle of each part sew on the number of the needles. Then cover the card-board with the silk, always placing an embroidered piece on one side, and a plain one on the other, and piping each division of the fan all round. Each division remains open at the top to push in the papers of needles. At the bottom a bronze screw is fastened in the six parts together; this screw is fastened by means of a bronze button. Instead of a screw two small buttons or beads can be taken, which must be joined together with thick silk or wire, inserting the needle through the six parts at a time.

CROCHET MAT.
(*See Engraving, Page* 255.)

Materials.—Middle-sized gray crochet cotton, red wool.

THIS mat, which can be used for candlesticks, decanters, vases, etc., consists of ten lappets; they are worked alternately with gray cotton and red wool in ribbed crochet stitch, and are sewn together in the manner seen on illustration. Begin each lappet on a foundation chain of 4 stitches, miss the last of these stitches, work 1 double in the 3d and 1st foundation chain, and 3 double in the 2d. Then work 1 chain, turn the work, and work again 1 double in every stitch, and 3 in the middle stitch. Continue to work on in this manner, leaving, however, the last stitch of every row untouched. Work 30 rows in all. In the 31st row work after every 3 double stitches 1 purl as follows: 5 chain, draw the cotton again through the last stitch, keep the loop on the needle, take up a similar loop in the next stitch of the preceding row, cast off the 3 loops on the needle together. The lappets, when finished, are sewn together on the wrong side; the last seam is made only after having worked the centre of the mat in the following manner: Insert the needle into the lower chain of the foundation, and work in each lappet 3 long treble; these stitches are not cast off separately, but together, when all the stitches have been worked, so that the middle opening is completely closed. Then only join the last two lappets together.

NEEDLECASE IN THE SHAPE OF A FAN.
(See Instructions, Page 254.)

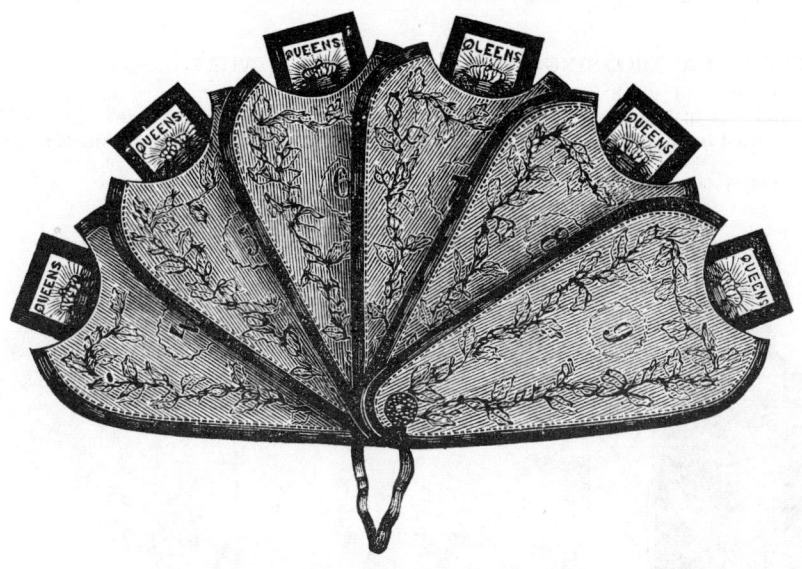

CROCHET MAT.
(See Instructions, Page 254.)

TRAVELLING DRESSING-CASE.

THE outside is of cloth. It is lined with holland, and has inside a narrow embroidered pattern, worked in chain-stitch. The shape of

Fig. 1.

WORK-BASKET.

WORK-BASKET of fancy straw and black split-cane, standing six inches in height, and measuring eight inches in diameter. The lid

Fig. 2.

the fittings may be copied from the design shown open. The outside is bound with sarcenet ribbon, and has strings to fasten together with a hair-roller to draw through after they are tied.

is lined with blue taffetas, and ornamented with embroidered leaves of white cloth (see Fig. 2). The embroidery is worked with dif-

Fig. 1.

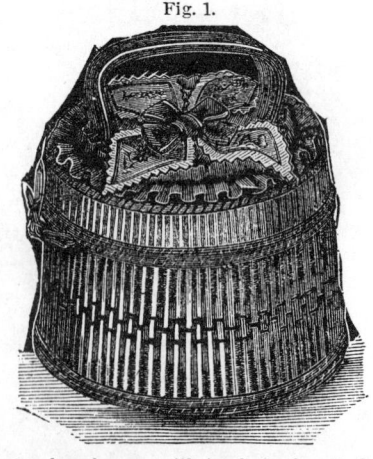

SMOKING-CAP.

IT is simply braided, according to our illustration, with gold soutache on a ground of

brown cloth ; or, if preferred, the pattern may be worked in chain stitch with purse-silk of a different shade from the ground.

ferent colored purse-silk in chain, knotted, and feather stitch, and is edged with gold soutache. The leaf is then vandyked. Outside the lid

Fig. 2.

are similar leaves, and a box plaited ruching and a bow of *gros grain* ribbon.

CROCHET OVER-PETTICOAT AND BODICE, IN ONE PIECE,

FOR CHILD OF TWO YEARS OF AGE.

THIS little dress is worked in white and pink Berlin wool. You work it in one piece. For the length of the back part, make a chain of 92

with the white wool, on this work 9 plain rows of crochet tricotee, this forms half of the back breadth. In the 10th row take up 65 stitches and work back. In the 11th row take up 63

stitches, work back, continue for 18 more rows to take up two stitches less each row. Then in the next 5 rows take up three less each time. Now you work 4 rows, taking up the whole number of stitches, 92, which were left in the 10th row; take these up row by row until all are raised. You then work 7 rows of 81 stitches, leaving the 11 last, which are on the left-hand side of the work, unraised. These 7 rows form the under part of the armhole, In the next row, which is the 46th, at the end of the 81st stitch make a chain of 11, working very loosely, take up these 11 stitches on the needle as loops and work them all back. *47th row.* Work the whole of the last row, then make a chain of 22 stitches, take these stitches up in the same manner as in the last row, and work all off.

Work-Table.—(See Page 259)

Now work 4 more plain whole rows, of·the whole length of 114 stitches; you then leave the twenty-two stitches unworked, and. work 4 plain rows of 92 stitches. You then commence the front gore. Take up 10 stitches only in the row and work off. In the next row take up the last 10 stitches and 3 more, work back; repeat this last little row 4 more times, then work 20 rows, raising 2 more stitches in each row instead of 3. At the end of the 20th of these short rows you should have 65 stitches on the needle; this forms the height of the skirt. Now work 11 rows of 92 stitches, working upon the

55th row; at the end of this row you finish half the little dress. In the next row work 60 stitches, then, instead of taking up the next stitch on the last row make a chain of 32 and work them on the needle, forming another row. You thus form the opening for the front. Work 10 rows plain on the last row, then in the next raise 65 stitches, only work back; in the next 19 rows raise 2 stitches less each row, then 5 rows, raising 3 stitches less each row, and then a row of 10 stitches only. Now work 4 plain rows of the whole length of 92 stitches, then in the next row make a chain of 33, take up these stitches on the needle, and work back. You next work 4 rows the whole length of 114 stitches, now work a row leaving 22 stitches at the end unworked. In the next row, leave the last 11 of the preceding row unworked. Now work 7 rows of 81 stitches only. In the following row make a chain of 11 at the end of the row, take up all the stitches, and on it work 4 plain rows. Then take up 12 stitches, work back. In the next 4 rows take up 3 more stitches each time: In the next 2 rows, 2 more stitches each row, then 9 plain rows of 92 stitches, which finishes the skirt; join up neatly now to the first row, and sew the end of the four rows of 114 stitches to the top of the first and last of the back rows, so forming the shoulder straps. You now work around the little dress with blue wool. The illustration gives the border in an enlarged size. For the border work as follows: 1 dc on the first stitch of the bottom of the petticoat, 5 ch, 1 long on the first of the 5 ch, miss 2 loops on the petticoat, 1 dc on the next, repeat from * all around. In the 2d row work in single crochet to the top of the

top, the fronts, and the armholes, and on it work 2 rows of this border. You add bows, shoulder-knots of blue ribbon, also a sash, which completes the dress.

CASE FOR VISITING CARDS, LETTERS, ETC.

THE material used is Russia leather, the dark gray shades being the most effective. Inside are partitions to receive the cards or letters,

Fig. 1.

and outside is an embroidered medallion worked with chenille and purse-silk, on a ground of gray taffetas. The design for this is given in

Fig. 2.

3d of the 5 ch, and *, then work 5 ch, 1 long on the first of the 5 ch, 1 dc on the 3d of the next 5 ch, repeat from *. Work 6 rows of this border around the bottom of the petticoat, then work a row of plain double crochet all around the

Fig. 2. The violets are formed of violet, and the leaves of green chenille; the veining of the leaves is worked partly in feather stitch, and partly in *point russe*; and the sewing-on is hidden by a fine gold cord.

TRIMMING FOR PETTICOATS.

Figs. 1 and 2.—These trimmings for skirts

Fig. 1.

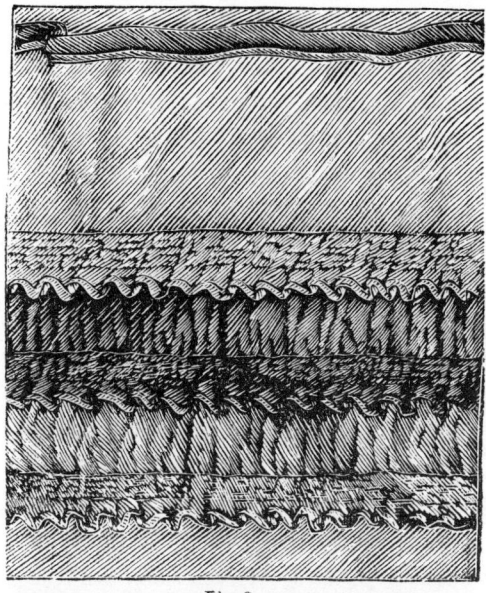

Fig. 2.

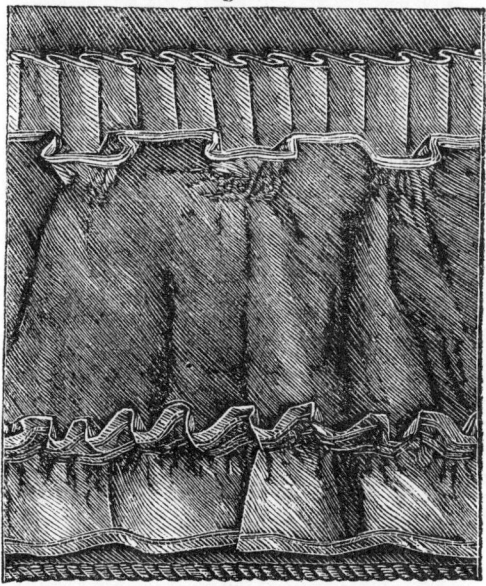

are in reduced size. They **are** different width ruffles bound and gathered.

WORK-TABLE.
(See Engraving, Page 257.)

THE frame is of cane-work, black and yellow. The basket put into it is covered with silk, and trimmed with ribbon, ruching, and

bows. Pockets are put on the outside. These are ornamented with a design in braid-work. The inside is trimmed with quilted sarcenet, and fitted with pockets and straps for scissor.

Fig. 1.—Embroidered Strap.

Fig. 2.—Detail of Strap.

EMBROIDERED STRAPS FOR PLAIDS, CLOAKS, ETC.

THE design given in our illustration is worked on a ground of brown cloth, in satin and overcast stitch, with purse silk of a lighter shade. The cloth is then bound with brown worsted braid.

TOILET CUSHION.

THE toilet cushion foundation is circular, and a good deal raised in the middle. The embroidery may be worked upon Nainsook or book-muslin. The centre pattern is given in the full size in Fig. 2.

The centre is a star shape, cut with the points all round beyond the size of the embroidery,

The row of scallops next the star are quarters of a circle, with the middle point outwards. They are gathered at the top. The size must, of course, depend on the size of the cushion. The edge row consists of half circles, gathered on the straight, and trimmed on the semi-circular side. If the cushion-cover is of book-muslin, a pretty, bright-colored silk lin-

Fig. 1.

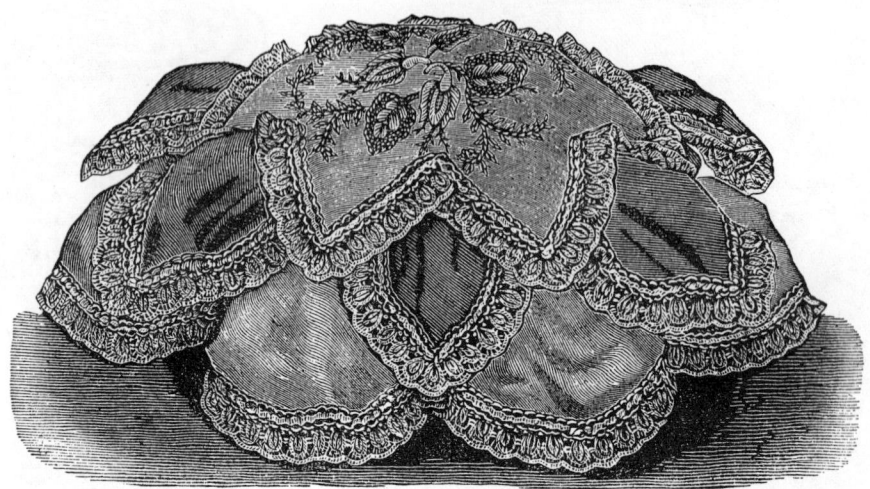

Fig. 2.

and finished with edging. Lace will serve as well as the pattern shown. A narrow gimp is put over the stitches, sewing on the edge.

ing is put beneath. The upper row of points may be of silk or satin, trimmed with lace, if preferred.

TOILET COVER.

THIS cover is made of *piqué;* the border is crochet and fine bobbin cord, worked after the design Fig. 2, which is given on an enlarged scale. Two rows of fine white braid are put round the oval on the *piqué*, and a design is braided in the centre of the *piqué*. For the border use cotton No. 24 and a fine crochet hook. For each leaf work as follows: *The*

3d ch, 2 ch, 1 double long on the first double long in the last vein, 1 double long on the first double long in the first vein, then 13 ch, 1 treble on the 9th ch, 2 ch, 1 long on the 6th ch, 2 ch, 1 double long on the 3d ch, 2 ch, 1 double long on the first double long in the last vein, 1 single on the 1st of the first 16 ch in the first vein. Now work all around the leaves in dc, 2 dc, 4 ch, 2 dc over every 2 ch, and work 4 ch also

Fig. 1.

Fig. 2.

Leaf: For the first vein in the leaf make 16 ch, 1 treble on the 12th, 2 ch, 1 long on the 9th, 2 ch, 1 double long on the 6th, 2 ch, 1 double long on the 3d, then 13 ch, 1 treble on the 9th, 2 ch, 1 long on the 6th, 2 ch, 1 double long on the 3d, 2 ch, 1 double long on the last long in the last vein, 16 ch for the middle vein, 1 treble on the 12th, 2 ch, 1 long on the 9th, 2 ch, 1 double long on the 6th, 2 ch, 1 double long on the 3d ch, 2 ch, 1 double long on the 1st double long in the last vein, then 13 ch; for the 4th vein, 1 treble on the 9th of the 13 ch, 2 ch, 1 long on the 6th ch, 2 ch, 1 double long on the

between the sets of dc, at the top of each vein work 4 loops of ch, and 2 dc between each. Work as many of these leaves as you will require. Then take the bobbin cord and form it in the manner illustrated in the engraving, lay it on a piece of *piqué*, and sew in its proper form, joining the leaves at the same time. Then work a round of chain, and work in single crochet on the picots in the leaves, and the cord where necessary. On this row work a row of 1 treble, * 1 ch, miss a stitch, 1 treble on the next, repeat from *, and sew the last row firmly to the *piqué*.

CHILD'S CROCHET JACKET WITH HOOD.

THIS pretty jacket is worked in crochet à *tricoter* with blue Berlin wool, and trimmed with a crochet border of speckled wool. The hood is partly white, partly blue. The work is done all in one piece, beginning at the bottom on a chain of 177 stitches. Decrease 1 stitch before and after the seam down the middle of the back, and the side seams every 3d row. When you come to the arm-holes crochet the back and fronts separately, still continuing to decrease in the middle of the back, take up the fronts and back together as soon as the

Fig. 1.—Front.

arm-hole is finished, decreasing 2 stitches on either side every alternate row to form the shoulder. For the sleeve cast on 28 stitches, work the 1st row on the 1st 10 stitches, return, then increase 3 stitches at each end of the two next alternate rows and 4 stitches at each end of the 3 following alternate rows. Crochet 22 rows; 1st row, the return as follows : cast off 1, cast off 2 together alternately, 2d rows plain, sew up the sleeve, and crochet 4 rows round the bottom, 1st row blue, 2d row white, 3d row white and gray speckled, 4th row white. Now comes a row of scallops in white and black

Fig. 2.—Back.

wool, as follows : begin with white wool and crochet 1 double stitch over the first stitch of the former row, 5 chain, miss one stitch, 1 double over the following stitch, draw the needle from the loop, and take up the black

wool, 1 double over the stitch that was missed, 5 chain, and 1 double stitch over the following stitch, so that the black scallop lies over the white one ; now leave the black loop, and take up the white loop again, crochet 5 chain and 1 double over the next stitch, and so on to the end of the row, where the ends are fastened off. Next crochet a row of small points in gray and white speckled wool, as follows : 1 double over the 2d stitches of the 4 rows of plain stitches at the bottom of the sleeve, 5 chain, miss the last of these, 2 double, 2 treble stitches into the other 4 chain, miss 2 stitches of the under row, 1 double stitch over the two straight threads of the next stitch, repeat from *. Sew the sleeves into the arm-hole, and trim the jacket all round with a border like that on the sleeves. For the hood, cast on with white wool a chain 1¾ inches longer than the width of the hood from the middle to one of the front corners, and crochet according to the pattern ; make the piece to turn over of blue wool on the cross, beginning with a chain of 2 stitches, sew the hood on to the neck of the jacket, and crochet round the neck—1st row white, 1 double, 1 chain ; 2d row black, like the 1st ; the double stitch over the chain stitch of the preceding row. Run a blue crochet-cord through this edging with small tassels at the end to fasten the jacket in front, and sew on tassels at the bottom of the hood.

KNITTED PETTICOAT.

THE materials required are 2¼ lb. four-thread fleecy, and two wooden pins, No. 8, Bell gauge.

This petticoat is knitted in stripes of seventeen and one-half inches long, and six and one-half inches wide. Ten pieces are required to make one twenty-seven inches long and seventeen inches wide, and twenty-four inches round the waist. If a larger size is needed, eleven pieces will make the waist twenty-seven inches round.

Cast on 16 stitches for the first half of the stripe, and knit 146 rows in plain knitting. Cast off all but last stitch, and pick up the side stitches, taking the front loop of each row. With these stitches, the second half is made by knitting 49 rows plain, and cast off. This forms the first stripe. Knit 9 more the same way, then crochet them together in single crochet on the wrong side, leaving a slit of seven inches long between the two back stripes. The upper edge stitches are then picked up for the top, and in order to make the petticoat set plain in front and at the sides and full behind, the foundation must be decreased in the first row, in the following manner :—Knit 2 plain at the slit, knit 3 together 20 times, knit 2 together 23 times, then knit 1, knit 2 together 10 times, knit the remainder plain to the centre in front, and knit the second half in the reverse way, knit the top backwards and forwards 28 rows.

In the 29th row, through which the string is drawn, knit 2, knit 2 together, thread forward, knit 2 together. In the next row, in the made stitch, knit 1 and purl 1. The next row plain, then cast off; this finishes the top.

For the border, which is knitted separately, cast on 19 stitches, knit 2 rows plain, and purl the 3d. Continue these 3 rows until the stripe is sufficiently long to go round the petticoat rather full. Work on the top of the border 1 row double crochet tightly, and sew it to the bottom of the petticoat on the wrong side. Then with the wool on the wrong side and the crochet-hook on the right side, work a row of loose chain by passing the hook through the join, and drawing the wool through. Repeat this all around, which makes a nice finish, then on the bottom edge of the border work a row of double crochet, with one chain between each double.

For the points: 1 treble in the first loop, 2 chain, 1 treble in the same stitch, 2 chain, miss 2; 1 double in the 3d, 2 chain, and repeat.

STRAP FOR TRAVELLING RUG IN KNITTING AND CROCHET.

THIS strap is of light brown wool, rather loosely knitted crosswise backwards and forwards, and edged with crochet scallops of dark brown wool. The knitting is commenced with a foundation of 14 stitches. *1st row.* Entirely plain. *2d.* Purl. *3d.* Plain. The first stitch of every row is *always* slipped, the last stitch knitted; these two stitches, as they do not belong to the pattern, will not be mentioned again in the following rows. *4th.* Slip 2; these are *always* slipped together as though they were to be purled. Put the thread *behind*

the stitch, 3 plain, slip 2, 3 plain, slip 2. *5th.* Slip 2, bring the wool before, 3 purl, slip 2, 3 purl, slip 2. *6th and 7th.* Like the 4th and 5th. *8th.* Like the 4th. These 8 rows are repeated. Care must be taken that the thread, which in

Fig. 1.

the 4th—8th rows remains behind or before the slipped stitches, is not drawn too tight nor too loose; the length must exactly correspond with the space occupied by the 2 stitches. When the knitting is finished it is edged with a row of purl crochet, with dark brown wool, as follows, alternately: 1 double into the outer edge,

Fig. 2.

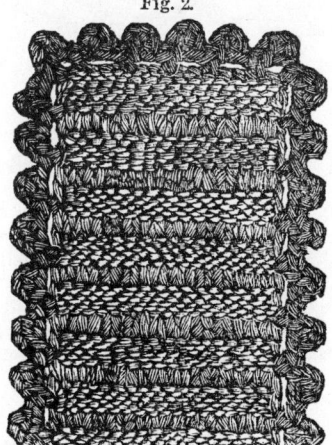

1 purl (5 chain and 1 slip stitch into the 1st), missing a corresponding space of the edge. Then a piece of brown cloth, with a buttonhole, is attached to the ends, and several buttons are sewn on the opposite ones according to Fig. 1, which represents the strap in use. Fig. 2 represents a portion the original size.

COVER FOR KEEPING ROLLS, EGGS, ETC., WARM ON THE TABLE.

THIS simple yet elegant-looking dish is composed of two table napkins, arranged according to Figs. 1 and 2, and placed on a plate or small round dish. Take a square table napkin, fold the four corners to the centre, turn it over and fold the corners again to the centre; turn it again

Fig. 1.

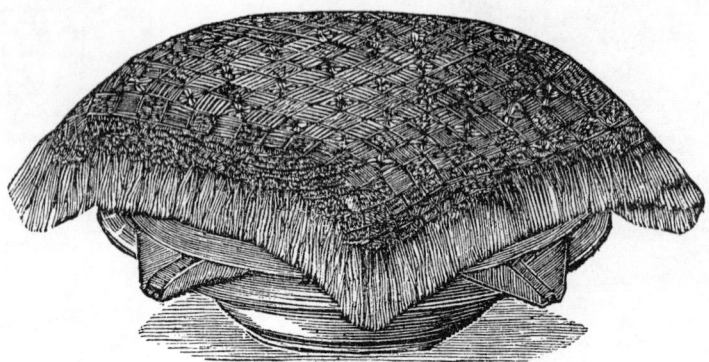

and fold the corners to the centre; turn it once more, lift up the corners meeting in the centre, and bend them back to the edge of the square,

Fig. 2.

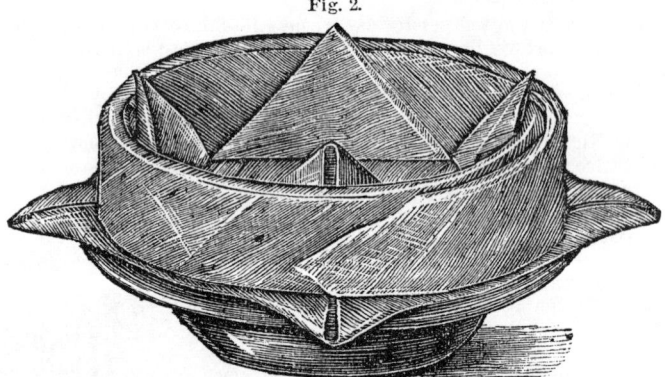

leaving the original corners of the napkin lying at the bottom. Press down all the edges firmly with the hand. Then take another napkin of the same size as the first, fold it to a triangle, and then to a band like a cravat, a little narrower than the depth of the upright corners of the first napkin. Pass this band around the other napkin according to Fig. 2, and fasten the inner and outer ends with a few stitches. The cover is of Java canvas, ornamented with *point russe* embroidery, lined and quilted and edged with wool fringe.

KNITTED RIBBED STOCKING.

CAST on 111 stitches, knit 12 plain rounds, then 140 rounds, knitting 2 and purling 2 alternately (or 70 purls). N.B.—When you commence the 140 rounds, institute a seam stitch thus: There must always be 5 stitches at the end of each round, and the centre of these 5 is the seam stitch, which must be knitted and purled alternately throughout the whole length of leg; the 2 on either side being always plain. After the 140 rounds, you must commence the intakes thus: On each side of the 5 take 2 together, every 3d purl (or 6th round), till you have 79 stitches left on the pins. After these intakes knit 28 purls (or 56 rounds) for the ankle, then divide the stitches for the heel thus: Leave 38 on the 2 pins, and 41 on the other, and this 41 must have the seam stitch in centre. Leave the 38, and with the 41 do 13 purls (or 26 rows), always slipping the 1st stitch, now 6 plain rows without ribbing, then knit plain to within 3 of seam stitch, take 2 together, 3 plain, take 2 together, turn, purl 4, purl 2 together, turn, 5 plain, take 2 together, turn, purl to small hole, purl 2 together, plain to small hole, take 2 together, and so on till all are gone. Off both ends the last row will be a plain one of 22 stitches; the seam stitch is now lost. Pick up 16 and plain, knit them, rib the 38 left on the other needles, then pick up 16 from the other side. Now 10 plain rounds, ribbing the 38 only, and plain knitting the others. Now you must make an intake each side of plain stitches by taking 2 together every 11th row for 8 times (or till you have 38 plain stitches left). Now 12 plain rows all the way around, and no more ribbing. For the toe decrease by taking 2 together every 12th stitch, 8 plain rounds, one round taking 2 together every 10th stitch, 6 plain rounds, a round taking in every 8th stitch, 4 plain rows; then every 6th stitch, 4 plain rows. A round taking in every 4th stitch, 4 plain rows, and take in every 4th. Again 3 plain rows, and take in every 3d stitch, 2 plain, and a round taking in every stitch; then there will be 13 stitches, which must be cast off together. Use Andalusian wool. A pair of stockings will take nearly a quarter of a pound of wool.

WORK-BAG.

THIS bag is made of brown Holland. It is cut into two circles, the outer one measuring fifteen inches, the inner one twelve inches in diameter. They are marked into eight equal divisions. The outer circle is scalloped, and the edges are bound with red braid, and herring-boned with wool. The small circle is

Fig. 2.

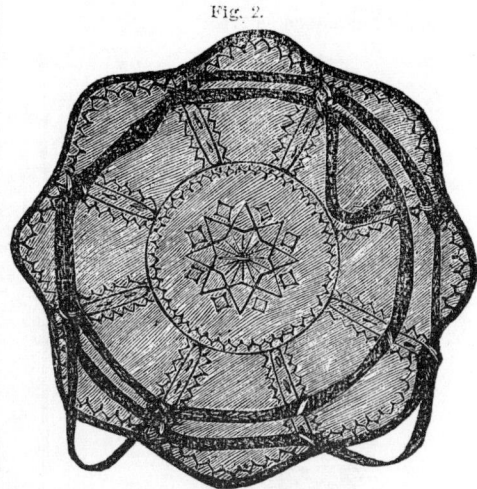

Fig. 1.

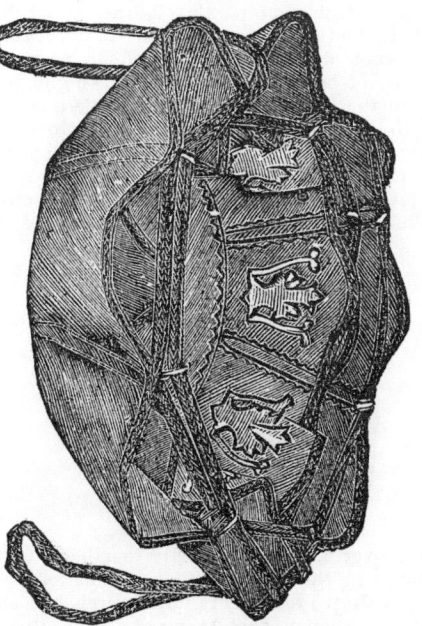

embroidered according to the design shown in the full size in Fig. 3, and herring-boned on the lines marking the divisions, (Fig. 2). A piece of card-board measuring six inches in diameter, is then placed in the centre, between the two pieces of Holland, which must be stitched together around the card-board, and also up the eight stripes separating the divisions forming the pockets for holding the different sewing materials.

Rings are sewn on (as seen in engraving for passing through a double string, by which the bag is drawn up.

BALL OF COLORED WOOL.

TAKE two circles of card-board, 4 inches in diameter; make a hole about the size of a half-penny in the middle. Place a piece of string between the two rings of card-board, and begin winding the wool, as shown in diagram, Fig. 2. Keep winding over and over until the card-board is thickly covered, taking care to keep

Fig. 1.

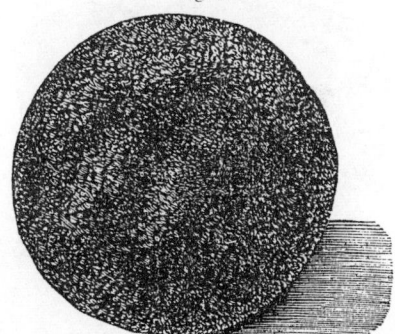

the ends of string outside. When the wool is of sufficient thickness as shown in upper part of diagram, Fig. 3, draw it together in the middle by means of the string, which must be firmly knotted. The wool is then to be cut with a pair of sharp scissors, the pointed blade being inserted between the two rings of card-board. Fig. 3 shows the ball in this stage of progress. When finished, it must be impregnated with steam, and then held before the fire until dry. The ball will then have the appearance shown in Fig. 1. Any odd skeins of wool will be suitable for making this ball; the more varied the colors the better.

Fig. 2.—Ball of Colored Wool.

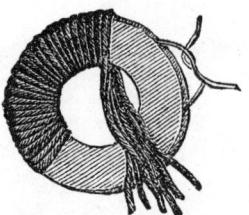

Fig. 3.—Embroidery for Work-Bag.   Page 366.

Fig. 3.—Ball of Colored Wool.

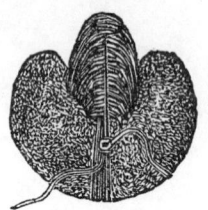

GENTLEMAN'S COLLAR-BOX.

THIS box, with lid, is of stiff card-board, three and a half inches in height, and six inches in diameter.   The inside is lined with glazed paper; the outside is covered with brown cloth —a medium shade—which is ornamented in the manner shown by the illustration, with crochet stripes worked with gray cotton, and with *point*

Fig. 1.

russe embroidery.   The crochet for the edge of the box consists of ten rows, worked lengthwise backwards and forwards as follows: On a foundation the requisite length work the first four rows entirely in double stitches, but in ribbed crochet, namely, always into the front part of each stitch of the last row.   At the end of these rows, before turning, work always 1 chain. *5th row.* 3 chain, which form 1 treble, 1 treble into the next stitch (into *both* top parts) * 2 chain, miss 2 stitches, 2 treble into the 2 next stitches; repeat from * to the end. *6th.* 3 chain, which form 1 treble, then alternately 2 chain,

2 treble into the 2 chain of the last row.   7th to the 10th rows like the 1st to the 4th.   When the requisite number of stripes are worked, they are fastened on to the cloth at regular distances, and connected by means of *point russe* and knotted stitch embroidery of silk in several shades of brown.   This cover is then gummed on to the side of the box, and a piece of the cloth the requisite size on to the bottom outside.   The box is bound around the top and bottom edges with worsted braid the same color, which is first embroidered with cross stitch in paler silk.   The 8 crochet stripes for

Fig. 2.

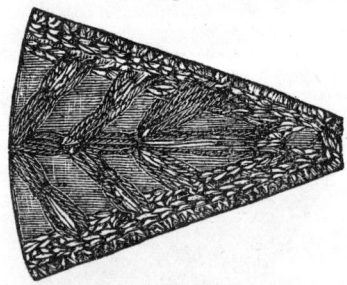

the cover are worked partly together.   Commence in the centre with a foundation of 4 chain, drawn together to form a circle by a slip stitch.   Then crochet 3 rows of double stitches working around, increasing 1 in every stitch in the 1st row; in the 2d and 3d only so many as to make 16 in the last. *4th.* * 30 chain stitches as a foundation for the 1st stripe, miss the last 3, which form 1 treble; work back; 2 treble into the next foundation stitch; 4 times alternately 2 chain, 2 foundation stitches, miss 2 treble into the 2 next foundation stitches, then 3 chain, miss 3 foundation stitches, 7 double into the next 7 foundation, 1 double into the 2d following stitch of the 3d row; repeat from *, working around, and secure the thread. *5th.* This is worked on the *wrong* side, and commenced at the end of a stripe; * 25 double into the foundation stitch of the next stripe of the last row, missing the last 3 and the first 2 stitches; 1 chain, 25 double into the corresponding stitches of the next stripe, 3 slip stitches into the 3 chain, forming 1 treble at the end; repeat from *. In the same way, and in ribbed crochet, work 3 more rows; thus on each side of every stripe towards the centre of the crochet 2 double stitches are decreased, and 1 chain stitch worked between the stripes. The crochet is then, in the manner of Fig. 1, attached to the cloth by means of *point russe* and knotted stitches to the cloth, which is then gummed on to the lid of the box. After this a button, covered with silk and crochet, is put on the centre of the lid, the edge of which is bound with brown braid ornamented with cross stitch.

EMBROIDERED MEMORANDUM BOOK.

THE outside covers of this note-book are of card-board, covered with gray silk rep, em-

tassels according to illustration, a bead hiding the stitches. A strap of double silk, with a layer of stiff paper inside, forms the receptacle for the pencil, and an elastic loop sewn below the upper corner of one of the outer covers serves to keep the leaves together when the book is closed.

CHEST PRESERVER (KNITTING).

Two ounces of scarlet double Berlin wool, and needles No. 7. Cast on 50 stitches, and knit 4 plain rows. Afterwards knit the first 4 and the last 4 stiches plain in every row, and the rest in double knitting, for which 1*st row*, * over, slip 1, put the wool back, 1 plain, passing the wool twice around the needle; repeat from *. 2*d.* * over, take off the double stitch, put the wool back, 1 plain, passing the wool twice around the needle; repeat from *. Continue working this 2d row till the preserver is nearly square, then knit 4 plain rows all across, as at the beginning, and cast off. Fix a piece of ribbon to the two upper corners, sufficiently long to go over the head and keep the preserver at the height desired. If it is thought too thick

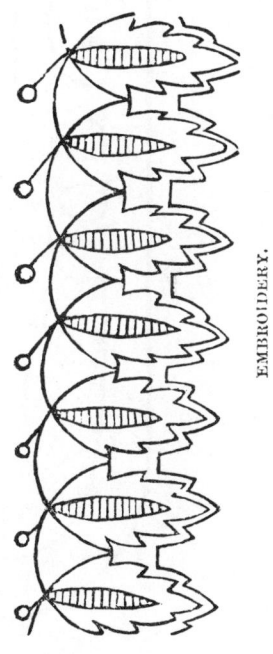

EMBROIDERY.

broidered according to illustration with dark gray silks, and finished at the edge with a fine dark gray silk cord. The six inner leaves are of parchment, and are a trifle smaller than the outside. They are laid between the covers, and fastened to them at one point with a few stitches. At this point is sewn to each of the covers a silk cord, ornamented with beads and

and warm, use single Berlin wool and No. 10 needles, casting on more stitches.

KNITTED SPENCER FOR CHILD.

To be knitted with 3 thread white fleecy wool or Scotch fingering, and needles No. 10. Cast on 140 stitches, knit 2 rows plain, next row 8 plain, * make one by turning wool around needle, knit 2 together, repeat from * till only 8 are left, which knit plain. Next row. All plain ; this makes a row of holes for an elastic or ribbon at waist. Next row. 8 plain, *, wool 10th row, taking care they are the centre 4, and cast on the same number in next row in returning to make the button-hole. After the 48th row, cast off 16th rib from front each side, and then knit fronts and back separately. For

Embroidery for a Cigar Case.　Page 269.

forward, slip one, (taking it off as if about to purl), knit 2 together, repeat from *, knit last 8 plain. Next row. 8 plain, *, wool forward, slip one, knit 2 together (this is brioche stitch), repeat from *, 8 plain for edge. Repeat this row 48 times, that is, till you can count 24 on either side of the work ; but in doing these rows cast off 4 of the 8 stitches in one edge every front, continue button-holes as before, and brioche stitch till you can count 28 rows on each side, then to form shoulder knit all but one rib, return and so on, leaving one more rib each time, till only 3 are knitted, then go all along and return, casting off all but 3 ribs, and edge stitches; knit the other front to correspond. *Back*—Knit straight on with brioche stitch same length as front, and slope for both shoulders in same way, then work all remaining stitches, make a row of holes at the beginning, and cast off. *Sleeve*—Cast on 60 stitches, and work brioche stitch, beginning as before. At 40th row decrease one rib in every three by knitting 5 stitches together, 18 rows plain brioche; 58th row. Decrease one rib by knitting 5 together after 1st rib on one side, decrease again 3 times at intervals of 8 rows; then 30 rows plain brioche, cast off.

BRAIDING PATTERN FOR CHILDREN'S DRESSES.

EMBROIDERY FOR CIGAR-CASE.
(*See Engravings. Page* 268.)

THE foundation is of brown Russia leather, embroidered with purse-silk in two shades of the same color, and curled cord. A few stitches in fine gold cord are occasionally introduced.

CHINESE WORK-BASKET.
(*See Engraving, Page* 270.)

This pretty and useful basket is intended for holding fancy-work and cotton-reels. It is composed of *ecru lawn* or Holland, and bound with red braid or ribbon. It can be made of any size.

GIMP ORNAMENT,
FOR POLONAISES, DRESSES, ETC.

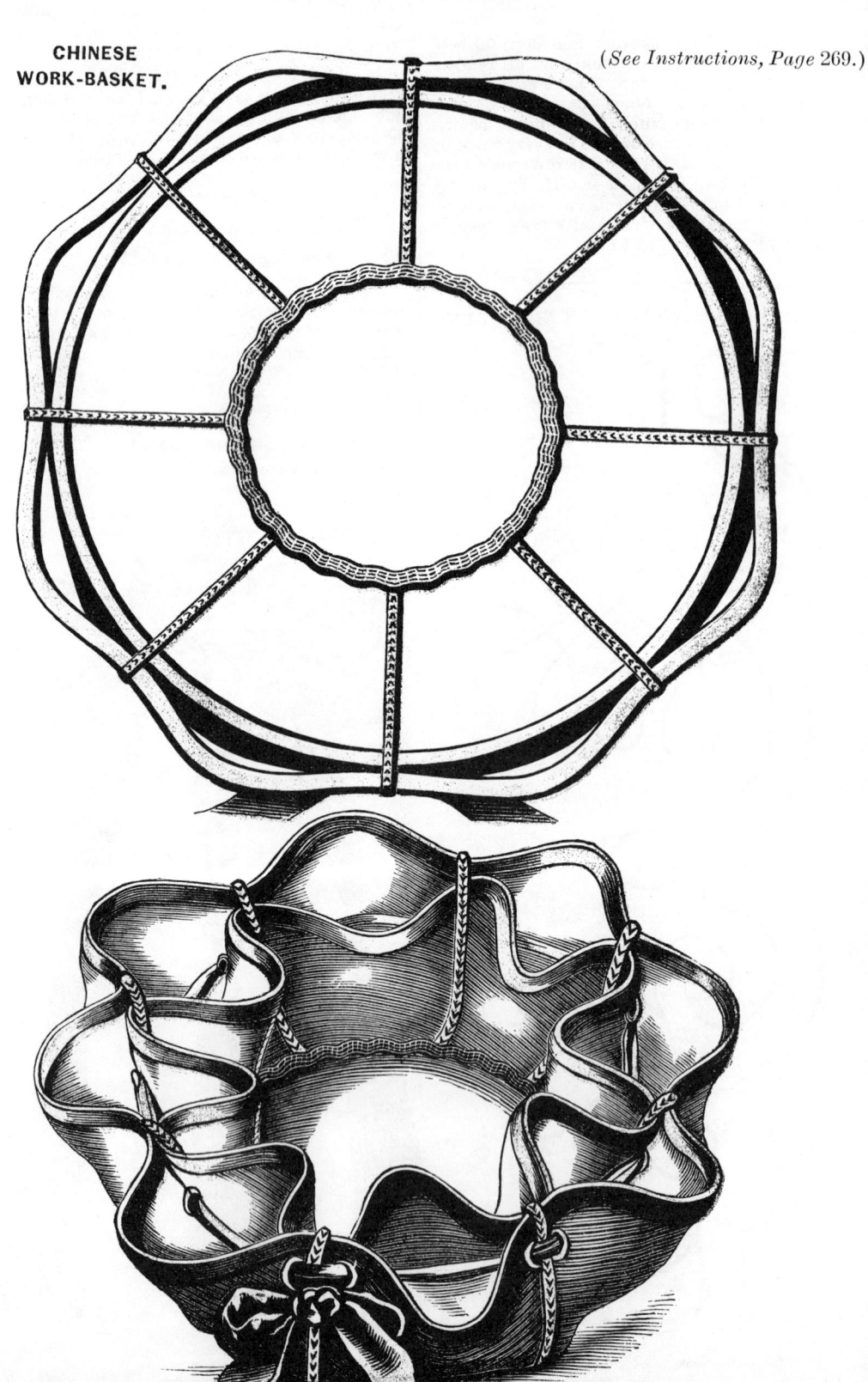

CHINESE WORK-BASKET.

(See Instructions, Page 269.)

BUTTERFLY PEN-WIPER.

THE body of the butterfly is of velvet stuffed with cotton, and entirely covered with gold beads. The eyes are red, and the horns stiff gold cord, with a bead on the ends. The wings can be made of cloth or velvet, the latter, however, is much the richest, and two or more colors should be used; they are to be embroidered with silk, fancy beads, and bugles. Pieces of cloth or flannel are cut the same size of the wings and sewed underneath to wipe the pens on. The size of the engraving is the proper size for the pen-wiper.

BOTTLE-STAND.

Materials.—Colored sarcenet (not too light a shade) —our model is violet; fine straw-colored purse silk; violet silk gimp; four slightly-arched wooden buttons, two of them three-quarters of an inch in diameter and one inch and a quarter in diameter; card-board, etc.

THE tatting of straw-colored silk gives this stand the appearance of a very fine basket frame. The bottom of our model consists of two rounds of card-board, measuring two inches and a quarter, cut together, and separated by a space an eighth of an inch broad and half an inch high. Upon this middle upper surface stands out firmly. This is folded equally on both sides, and firmly sewn on the edges of the cylinder a little below it, and having a puffed-out appearance. The lining, which is placed in with the ruche, is cut out in scallops at the bottom. A silk gimp of the same color covers the place where the under ruche is put on, and a neat paper covers the stitches at the bottom. The tatting, twisted round the bar, and ornamenting the largest button, is worked with one thread, and consists of closed eyes joined at the middle picot, and containing sixteen double knots, with three picots. The eyes of the border contain twenty double knots,

stripe the round middle bar, six inches high and one inch in circumference, is fastened. This is made of card-board, and the edges gummed together in the form of a cylinder, and covered with colored sarcenet; at the top four covered buttons are placed, the arrangement of which is clearly shown in the engraving. The ruche for the whole must correspond, and is of double sarcenet, and a quarter of an inch broad. A strip of card-board, one inch and three-quarters high, corresponding with the round at the bottom, with the narrow edges sewn over each other, and sewn on afterwards, gives the ground for the two glass bottles. The outer covering consists of a strip of sarcenet, two inches broad, arranged in closely-quilted folds a quarter of an inch broad, with a strip of card-board of the same breadth pushed in, by which the with two side picots, a quarter of an inch long, and one short middle picot, which are fastened at the top and bottom with one stitch upon the folds of the glass stand. The double eyes of the third border at the upper edge contain twenty-four double knots, with three picots, and are always joined by one Josephine knot, consisting of five concluding knots; twelve eyes like the latter form the button rosette, which, for the middle, has four eyes of eight double knots, with one picot.

NEEDLE-BOOK, WITH POCKETS FOR SCISSORS, ETC.

THIS needle-book consists of two pieces of card-board five inches long, three inches and one-fifth wide in the middle, pointed off towards the ends ; these are covered on one side with Java canvas, ornamented with embroidery in green purse silk. These parts are bound with green ribbon, two-fifths of an inch wide, fastened with steel beads. A green silk pocket, ornamented with point russe embroidery, is added on each side of the needle-case. A nar-

row green ribbon is drawn through the upper hem of the pockets, and tied in a bow on the top. Inside the leaves of the book fasten some strips of pinked-out flannel for the needles ; stick in pins at regular intervals into the edge, and fasten the book with two green ribbons tied into a bow, as can be seen in illustration.

GENTLEMAN'S COLLAR BOX.

OUR pattern is a round card-board box, measuring five inches and one-fifth across, and being three inches and one-fifth high. The box is covered inside with white calico, the edge of which must be turned down about two-fifths of an inch on the right side, and pasted on ; on the outside the box is covered with a strip of light brown cloth, ornamented from illustration with cross-strips of dark brown cloth, cut out from illustration, and pasted on the lighter strip. The latter is bound at both sides with brown ribbon, two-fifths of an inch wide ; paste it down on the box, and edge the ends of the strip likewise with ribbon imitating binding. The bottom of the box is covered underneath with

cloth. The cover of the box is also made of light brown cloth, on which is pasted a star cut out of dark brown cloth. The cover is bound with brown ribbon like the box ; it is

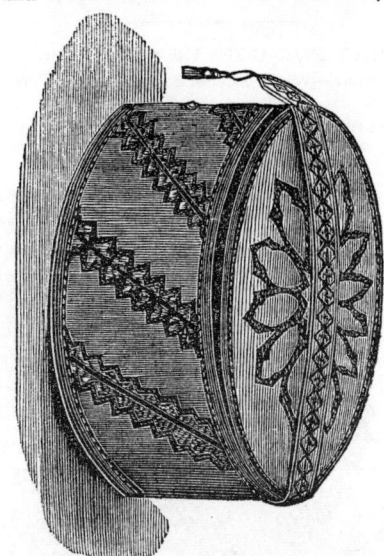

lined inside with card-board and white calico. Lastly, fasten a strip of cloth for the handle by which the box is fastened down ; at the point of the strip sew a loop of elastic, and at the edge of the box a button, as can be seen in illustration

KNITTED SPONGE FOR CHILDREN.

THIS sponge consists of a cushion, measuring four inches across, filled with odd bits and ends of wool, proceeding from knitted woollen

articles which have been unravelled. This cushion is covered with plain knitting in rose-colored wool. Over this cover fasten another one of white wool. Both the covers are fastened together all round with a round of double crochet, in which a row of purl, with red wool, is next worked.

------◆◆------

MAT FOR COFFEE OR TEAPOT.

Materials.—White crochet cotton and steel crochet needle.

THIS mat is very useful to be put under hot coffee or teapots on the table; it may also be

by 1 purl in the following stitch (this purl consists of 5 chain stitches, 1 slip stitch in the first); 3 small purl, missing 2 stitches of the preceding round; 9 double in the following 9 stitches; repeat from * to the end of the round. Observe that at the end of this and of the following rounds, the last double stitch is worked in the last stitch but one, before the first 3 small purl, missing the last double stitch.

41st round. * 3 small purl, 2 treble, divided by 1 purl in each of the next 2 treble of the preced-

used for candlesticks, scent-bottles, etc. The original pattern is worked in rounds with white crochet cotton. Begin in the centre on a foundation chain of 4 stitches, join them into a circle, and work 39 rounds in double stitches, always inserting the needle into the whole stitch, increasing, so that the mat remains quite flat, and that the 39th round has a number of stitches which can be divided by fourteen. In the 40th round begins the open-work border: * 3 small purl (each purl consists of 3 chain stitches, 1 slip stitch in the first), miss 2 stitches of the preceding round under them; 2 treble, divided

ing round; in this, as well as in the following rounds, the 2 treble stitches worked in 1 stitch are only cast off so far as to keep 2 loops on the needle; they are then cast off together with the 1st treble worked in the following stitch (2 stitches cast off together count for 1 stitch in the following round); 3 small purl, missing under them 3 purl of the preceding round and the next double; 7 double in the next 7 stitches. Repeat from *.

42d. * 3 small purl; 3 times 2 treble, divided by 1 purl over the 4 treble of the preceding round; 3 small purl, missing under them the last 3 purl and the next double stitch of the preceding round; 5 double in the 5 middle stitches of the following 7 stitches of the preceding round. Repeat from *.

43d. * 3 small purl; 4 times 2 treble, divided by 1 purl on the 6 treble of the preceding round; 3 small purl, missing under them the next 3 small purl and 1 double of the preceding round; 3 double in the middle 3 of the 5 double stitches of the preceding round. Repeat from *.

44th. * 3 small purl; 9 times 2 treble, divided by 1 purl on the 8 treble of the preceding round; 3 small purl, missing under them the next 3 purl and 1 double of the preceding round; 1 double in the middle one of the 3 double stitches of the preceding round. Repeat from *.

CASE FOR GENTLEMEN'S SHIRTS.

THIS case is made of Java canvas; it is ornamented with point russe embroidery of green filoselle, and lined with Nankeen-colored calico. The flaps on each side of the case must, of course, be folded inside. The upper part of the case is then ornamented with an embroidery pattern; it is worked with green filoselle and black ribbon velvet; the latter is covered with herring-bone stitches of fine gold thread. When the canvas has been thus embroidered, sew in the lining, sewing in a piece of card-board for

elastic, finished off with brass circles or buttons. These are meant for fastening the case, as seen on Fig. 2. Sew on likewise the ribbons from illustration.

TRAVELLING CASE FOR A GLASS OR TUMBLER.

THIS case is made of gray cloth, ornamented

with buttonhole stitch of gray purse silk; it is lined with card-board and black silk, slightly quilted, and stitched through in diamonds with

Fig. 1.—Case Open.

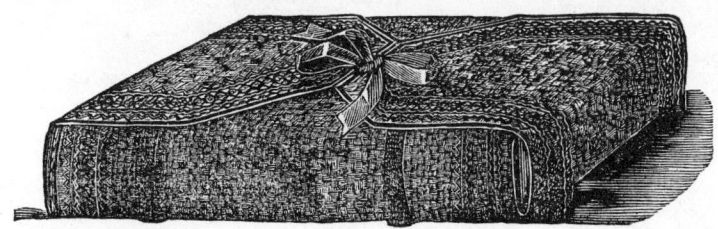

Fig. 2.—Closed.

the bottom of the case, and stitching it all round; it is then bound with green ribbon three-fifths of an inch wide. The flaps are merely hemmed, the ribbon being sewn plain on the lining. Then make a card-board cover corresponding in size to the bottom of the case; cover it on both sides with calico; this cover is not fastened on to the case, but placed loosely on the shirts before shutting it. At the bottom of the case, on the outside, fasten two pieces of

green silk. The cover of the case is kept down by an elastic loop. The cover has an edge which overlaps the case; it is two-fifths of an inch wide. The outer part of the case is then ornamented from illustration with buttonhole stitch of gray silk; then sew in the card-board and the quilted lining. The upper edge of the case is worked round with buttonhole stitch, working over the outside of the lining. The bottom of the case and the lower edge of it are likewise worked round with buttonhole stitch. The inner part of the bottom piece, that is the card-board and the lining, are pasted into the case. When the cover and edge have been joined together with overcast stitch (after having worked both parts round with buttonhole stitch), fasten a strip of cloth on the top of the cover for the handle; then fasten a piece of elastic, about eight inches and four-fifths long, inside the edge of the cover, and sew it fast on to the case underneath the cover with a few stitches (see illustration).

CHINESE PINCUSHION.

Materials.—White velvet or cashmere scarlet velvet, purse sewing silk, and gold cord; cord and tassels.

EMBROIDERY PATTERN IN POINT-RUSSE SATIN-STITCH, AND APPLIQUE.

the rounding parts join the embroidered section. The little cushions may be stuffed with bran or wool; and, when the twelve are made they are joined at the points, and the cushion is finished with the cord and tassels. It will be necessary to allow equal turnings for the scarlet and embroidered sections.

RABBIT PENWIPER (KNITTING).

Materials.—White single Berlin wool, a ball of green moss wool, rather fine knitting cotton, two steel knitting needles No. 12, some scarlet and black cloth, and an ivory mesh, or a strip of firm cardboard three-eighths of an inch wide.

A VERY good imitation of the fur of this little animal is made by knitting in loops with the single Berlin wool wound double, which loops are afterwards cut and carefully combed

THE cushion is formed of twelve little cushions of a triangular shape joined together. These consist of two pieces of plain scarlet velvet and one embroidered part on white cashmere or velvet. The colors may be selected according to taste for embroidering. The little pieces are so arranged that the narrow sides of the scarlet pieces cut to the diagram meet, and

out. Cast on, for the length of the body, 20 stitches, rather loosely, with the cotton, and for the next or loop row use the Berlin wool double, and knit a loop in each of the 20 stitches in the following manner: Insert the right hand needle in the 1st stitch as usual, hold the mesh parallel and close to it with the thumb and first finger of the left hand, take the free end of the double wool, and, holding it between the first and second fingers of the left hand, bring the part of the wool attached to the ball down over the front of the mesh and over the needle, passing it back over the end which is on the first finger; then bring the cotton from the back over the needle only, and knit both cotton and wool together through the stitch. These directions are only for the first stitch of every loop row, the others are more simple. For the next stitch insert the needle as usual, pass the wool down over the front of the mesh and needle to the back, then bring the cotton round the needle only, and knit both through the stitch as before. Continue in this manner, making a loop in each stitch to the end of the row; then cut off the white wool (which is to be done at the end of each loop row), leaving the end rather longer than the width of the mesh, and knit the row back plain with the cotton only (leaving the mesh in), taking great care to take up both the cotton and double wool together in each stitch, as this is what fastens the loops. Now draw out the mesh ready for the next row. A loop row with the wool and cotton, and a plain row with the cotton only, succeed each other alternately

creased at the beginning and end, and after the last plain row cast off all the stitches. This completes one-half of the body of the rabbit; the second half must be knitted to correspond exactly, the two sewn together except on the lower side, and the loops then cut and combed out very carefully and gently. For each ear 8 stitches must be cast on, 2 loop rows knitted, and the stitches cast off after the last plain row. The tail is to be knitted in the same manner, casting on only 5 stitches, and both it and the ears are to be sewn on in their proper position. After the different parts of the little rabbit are put together, a garnet-colored bead must be sewn on with ponceau silk for each eye; the mouth imitated by a few stitches of red silk, and the body thickly stuffed with wool or wadding (the under part being drawn together as best suits the shape), sewn firmly to the stand when this last is ready to receive it. The green part of the ground or stand is knitted with moss wool, a kind of wool in two or three shades of green. Cast on 20 stitches for the

throughout. It is necessary, for the shape of the rabbit, to take in a stitch by knitting 2 together at the beginning of the 2d row of loops, and in the 3d loop row 8 stitches additional at the beginning are required for the head; these are to be cast on with the cotton at the end of the preceding plain row. It will be found rather troublesome to knit the loops into these cast-on stitches, and it is well to use a finer needle than the one you are working with to open each stitch as you come to it, and so render the insertion of the other needle less difficult. In the 4th and 5th rows of loops a stitch is to be diminished at the beginning and end of each row by knitting 2 together as before. In the 6th and 7th loop rows only the first 8 stitches are to be knitted for the head, and after the plain row succeeding the 7th loop row the 8 stitches are to be cast off with the cotton, and also the next 2 stitches (for the neck), and on the remainder knit 2 rows of loops (for the back), in both of which a stitch is to be de-

length, in cotton as before, and knit 15 loop rows for the depth; these loops may be either cut, but not combed out, or left in loops, as may be preferred, to form a contrast with the fur of the animal. By referring to the illustration, it will be easily seen how the rest of the penwiper is intended to be made. The first square projecting beyond the green wool is of scarlet cloth, notched all round the edge. This again rests on a larger piece of card-board, over which some black glazed lining has been strained, and a piece of black cloth projecting slightly beyond the edges, gummed or pasted on the top. Two or three pieces of black cloth, for the practical purpose of wiping the pen, may be placed below this; and the whole firmly sewn through the centre with black thread, the rabbit being first fixed on the green square. The shape of the rabbit may be much improved by the manner in which it is sheared after it has been put together, and the loops cut.

THE WEAVER'S KNOT.

TO FASTEN THREAD OR SILK, IN NETTING OR CROCHET WORK.

FOLLOW with care the figures representing the method of forming this knot. Fig. 1 rep-

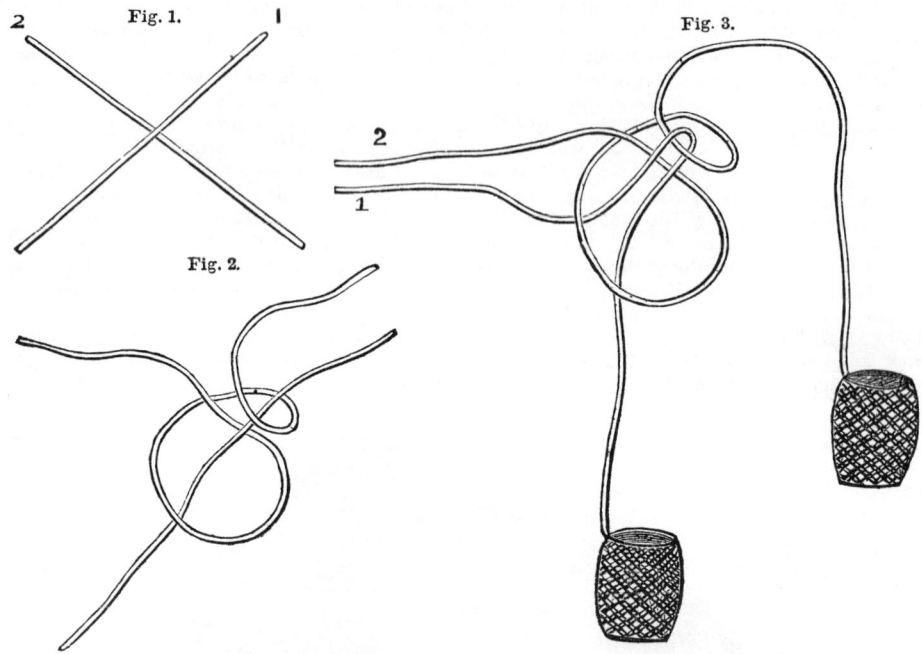

Fig. 1.

Fig. 2.

Fig. 3.

resents the two threads crossed. These threads are held between the thumb and forefinger of the left hand. The thread 2 is placed under thread 1. When the two threads are thus crossed, follow with the right hand the movement of the thread 2 represented in Fig. 2. The thread 1 remains motionless. When you have formed the bow indicated by Fig. 2, lower the thread 1 in the great bow formed by thread 2, as illustrated by Fig. 3. Hold between your thumb and forefinger of left hand the two ends of threads 1 and 2. Then with right hand draw thread 2 to form and tighten the weaver's knot.

EMBROIDERY.

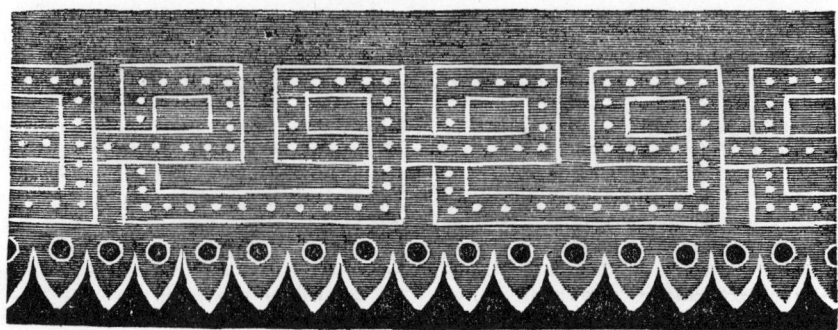

BABY'S SOCK.

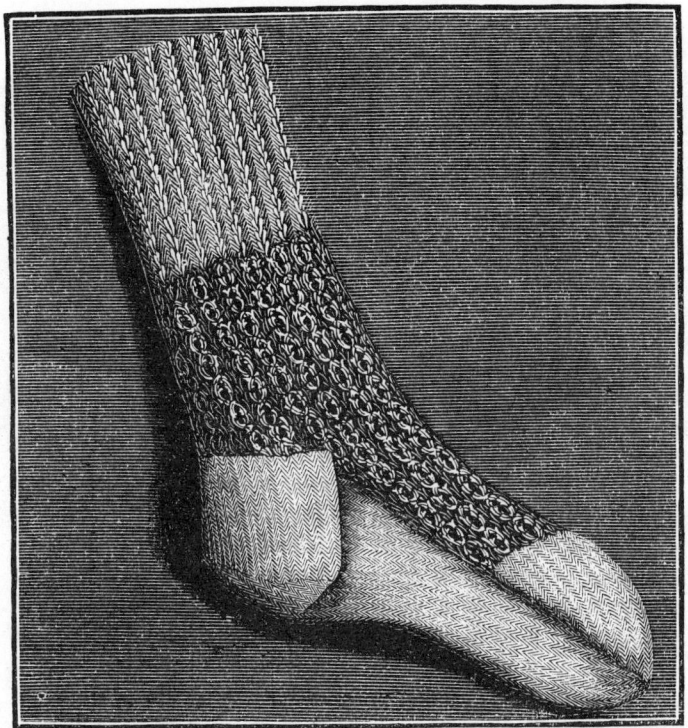

Materials.—Knitting cotton, No. 20.

CAST on 26, 29, 26.

Knit 40 rows; 2 plain and 2 purl—the odd stitch being for the seam, which is made by knitting first round plain, and next purling; so that there will be 20 purled stitches. Then commence the pattern. Purl 2; thread in front; knit 2 together, knit one.

Second row plain, except the 2 purled. Third row: Purl 2; knit one; thread in front; knit 2 together.

This is all the pattern—of which ten patterns go for the leg: the seam stitch for the centre of the heel. The heel is plain knitting, retaining 8 patterns in front; 12 takings-in form the instep, after the heel is closed in the usual way. Ten patterns in front for foot. Six plain, turn beyond, and then close the toe, as is usual, by taking-in on each side the needle, with three rows between, until 12 stitches remain; then close by casting off in the usual way.

EMBROIDERY.

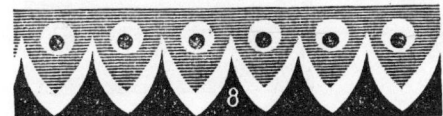

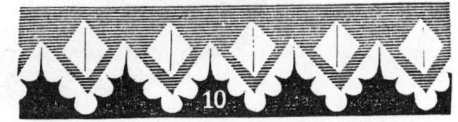

CASE FOR HOLDING EMBROIDERY COTTON.

SUITABLE FOR A CHRISTMAS PRESENT.

Fig. 1.   Fig. 2.

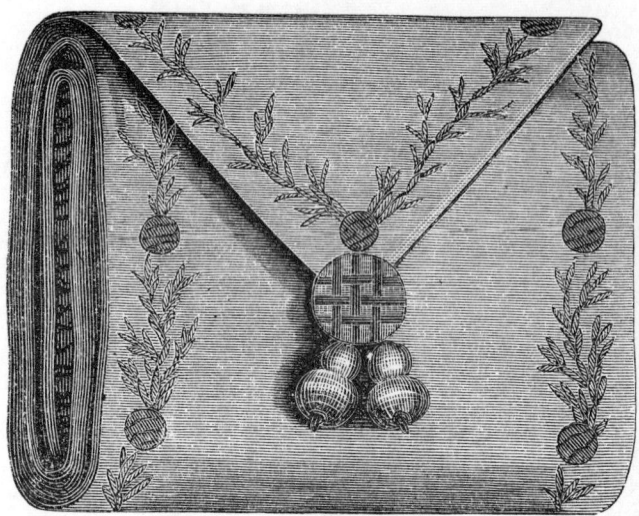

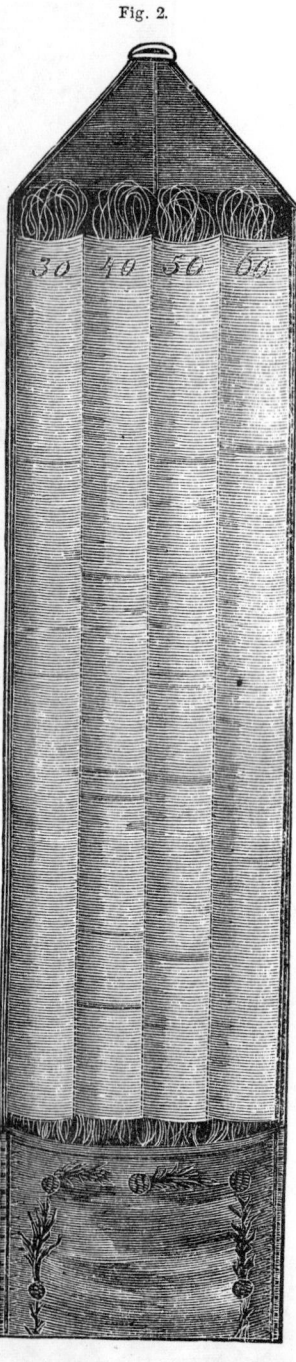

WE give a case intended to contain different sizes of embroidery cotton. Fig. 1 represents the case shut, and of the proper size. Fig. 2 is the case opened. It is made of ribbon, and embroidered on each edge with silk or chenille, as represented in our engraving.

COIFFURE COMPOSED OF PIECES OF BIAS SILK CUT OUT AND BOX-PLAITED.

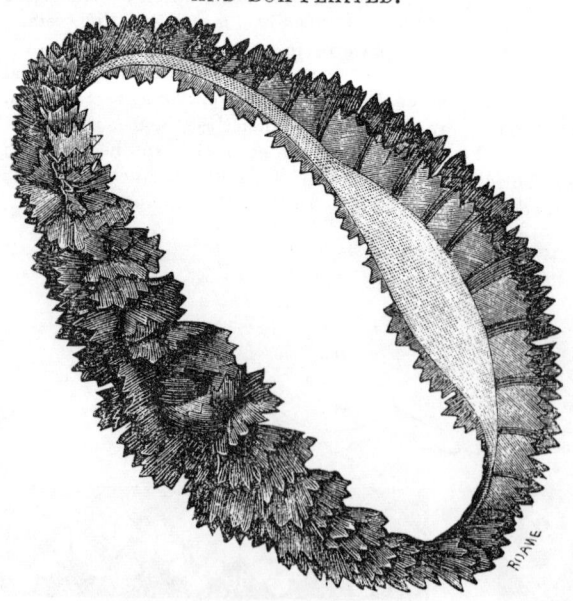

EMBROIDERY.

CHRISTMAS BASKET.
(See Instructions, Page 282.)

CHRISTMAS TABLE BASKET.
(*See Engravings, Page* 281.)

THE pretty, and at the same time inexpensive, little basket which we give in our illustration, is particularly appropriate at this time, when so many friendly entertainments are exchanged, and the young and happy meet together. Where the refreshments consist of cold viands and confectionery, these baskets are exceedingly ornamental. They are very quickly made, only requiring a strip of thin card-board, a little silver paper—pure white is the prettiest—and a few skeins of orange wool. The paper is cut into strips of about three inches wide. It is then cut finely, as if for curling, to the depth of two inches. The method for crimping deserves especial attention for its extreme simplicity and efficiency, and the very pretty effect produced. A great many strips of the cut paper may be all laid together, and folded round and round at the part which is left plain in the cutting. The part which is cut is then crushed and crumpled altogether in the hand into a kind of ball; a little light dexterity alone being required to produce the desired effect. It is then unrolled and the strips separated, when they will be found very prettily crimped. The strip of card-board cut to the size the basket is required to be, is then stitched together at the two ends, and the crimped paper is gummed on it in rows. The card-board must be entirely covered; therefore it requires the rows to be very close to each other. A row of paper roses is then made of the three sizes given in the diagram; six of these, that is, two of each size, form the rose with a little yellow wool for the centre, and are placed close together round the top of the basket and on the handle. We recommend these ornamental little articles, knowing that they are really worthy of being adopted in the numerous and elegant entertainments which will be given during the present season.

NAME FOR MARKING.

BELLOWS PINCUSHION.
A CHRISTMAS ORNAMENT.

THIS little article may be formed of velvet or satin, and ornamented with beads; or it may be made of a small piece of handsome figured ribbon. Two pieces of card-board must be cut out the shape, and covered with either of the above-mentioned materials. The two must be

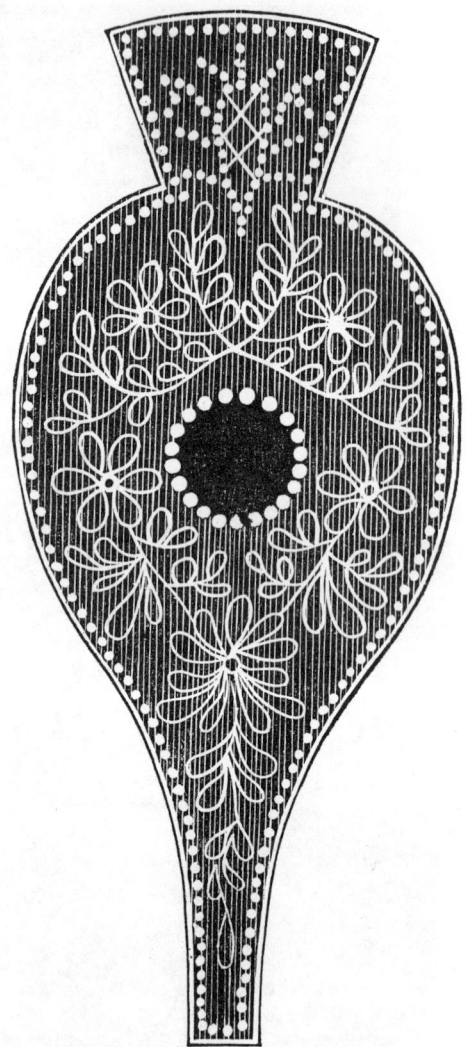

neatly sewn together all round the edges, taking care that they are exactly the same size. The small circle in the centre is in black velvet, fastened down with a row of beads round it. The pins are stuck in all round the edge, and form a little border.

CARRIAGE SLIPPER.

Three oz. of 8-thread drab or stone-colored Berlin wool ; 1 oz. white 4-thread ; 6 skeins of black 4-thread. 1 reel, No. 10 or 12, Boar's Head cotton. Steel crochet hook, No. 16. Pair of steel pins, No. 18.

1st row.—Make a chain of 30 loops, turn back, work a row of long stitches.

2d row.—Turn back, a row of long stitches till within 5 stitches of the end, increase twice by making 2 long into 1 loop, then 1 long into next loop, then 2 long into next, finish with long and turn back.

As all the slipper is worked in long stitches, the repetition of the words "long stitches" will be omitted. After every increased stitch, 1 long to be worked into the next loop.

3d row.—Turn back, take the last 2 loops together in 1.

4th row.—Turn back, till the end of the row, where increase as at 2d row.

5th row.—Turn back, a row without increasing.

6th row.—Turn back, increase as at 2d row.

7th row.—Turn back, increase 1 previous to the last 2 stitches.

8th row.—Turn back, after the 1st stitch increase 1, and when within 7 loops of the end increase 3, working 1 long into the next loop between each increased stitch.

9th row.—Turn back till within 5 loops of the end, increase 2.

10th row.—Turn back, after the 1st long increase twice, and when within 5 loops of the end increase 2.

11th row.—Turn back, increase 3, increase 2 at the end

12th row.—Turn back, increase 1, increase 3 at the end.

13th row.—Turn back, increase 2, not increase at the end.

14th row.—Turn back, 4 dc, the remainder long, till within 7 of the end, where increase 3.

Cut off the wool and draw the end neatly in, now make another piece exactly the same, but before cutting the wool off the last piece, crochet the two corresponding points of the pieces together. After this, the wool must be cut off at every row.

15th row.—2 dc, the 1st on 3d long stitch, then all long till the centre, *which will be where the pieces were joined*, where make 3 long into 1 loop, then all long till the 5th long of last row from the end, then 2 dc.

16th row.—2 dc, the 1st into the 5th loop of last row, then all long, working 3 long into the centre loop of the 3 increased stitches, then all long till the 6th loop of the last row, 2 dc.

17th row.—Same as last row.

18th row.—2 dc, the 1st into the 36th loop from the centre long, *reckoning from left to right,* 34 long, increase 3 as before, 34 long, 2 dc.

19th row.—2 dc, the 1st into the 32d loop from the centre stitch, 30 long, increase 3, 30 long, 2 dc.

20th row.—2 dc, the 1st into the 26th loop from centre stitch in last row, 24 long, increase 3, 24 long, 2 dc.

21st row.—Same as last row.

22d row.—Begin on 1st long stitch, and work the same.

23d row.—2 dc, the 1st into the 22d loop from centre stitch, 20 long, increase 3, 20 long, 2 dc.

24th row.—2 dc, the 1st into the 21st loop from centre loop, 19 long, increase 3, 19 long, 2 dc.

25th row.—2 dc, the 1st in the 17th loop from centre stitch, 15 long, increase 3, 15 long, 2 dc.

26th row.—2 dc, the 1st in the 14th loop from centre stitch, 12 long, increase 3, 12 long, 2 dc.

Work a row of dc along the foot of the slipper, working in the ends and working 3 stitches into the centre loop at the point of the slipper.

Damp well, and press between linen under a heavy weight, then line with Cerise silk, and sew on the inside round a cork sole.

FOR THE TRIMMING ROUND THE LEG AND INSTEP. —On steel pin cast on 15 stitches, knit 2 plain rows, observing always to slip the 1st stitch. Slip 1, knit 1, place the needle through the next stitch, *use the white and black wool double*, place the white wool between the points of the 2 needles, knit off the stitch with cotton; this will bring both cotton and

wool on the right hand needle. For the next stitch, bring the wool tightly round the 2d finger of the left hand, place it between the needles as before, and knit it off with cotton; now knit 1 black stitch, 2 white, 1 black, 2 white, 1 black, 2 white, and 2 plain without wool.

The next row, knit it plain back with cotton, knitting off a cotton and wool stitch together, then cut the loops, comb and lightly shear each row, now knit 2 rows of white, knitting between each row plain, with cotton only, then a row black and white, continue this till there is sufficient to trim the boot, when knit 2 plain rows and cast off, now shear it evenly, and sew round the boot, tie down the front with Cerise ribbon.

With the addition of a gutta percha sole to the cork, this will make an admirable snow boot.

FANCY BASKET.

VERY PRETTY ARTICLES FOR PRESENTS, OR FOR FANCY FAIRS.

Have a frame made of brass wire, and pass fancy ribbons in and out of the wire, as shown in the cut. The handle and sides of the basket can be ornamented by bows or rosettes of ribbon, as taste may dictate.

GLENGARRY CAP IN CROCHET.

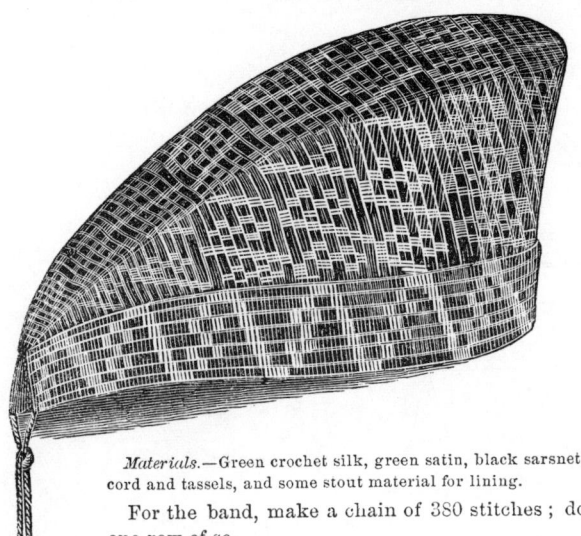

Materials.—Green crochet silk, green satin, black sarsnet, cord and tassels, and some stout material for lining.

For the band, make a chain of 380 stitches; do one row of sc.

1st row.—* 6 dc, 13ch, miss 13 *; repeat to the end.

2d.—* 2 dc, 4 ch, miss 4, 3 dc, 9 ch, miss 9, 1 dc *; repeat to the end.

3d.—* 1 dc, 2 ch, miss 2, 3 dc, 3 ch, miss 3, 3 dc, 6 ch, miss 6, 2 dc *; repeat to the end.

4th.—1 dc, 5 ch, miss 5, * 3 dc over 3 ch of the previous round, 7 ch, miss 7, 3 dc, 6 ch, miss 6 *; repeat to the end.

5th.—1 dc, 2 ch, miss 2, * 3 dc, 3 ch, miss 3 dc of last row, 3 dc, 3 ch, miss 3, 3 dc, 4 ch, miss 4 *; repeat to the end.

6th.—1 dc, 5 ch, miss 5, * 3 dc, 5 ch, miss 5, 3 dc, 8 ch, miss 8 *; repeat to the end.

7th.—7 dc coming on the 5 ch and a dc at each side, and 11 ch before the next dc. This is the last row of the band.

For the crown, make a chain of 140 stitches, and repeat the pattern on it as often as it will permit. These stitches form the extreme width of the crown. A piece of fourteen inches long must be made, which should require about seven repetitions of the pattern.

There now remains to be worked the piece between the band and the crown, and this is done by making a chain of 120 stitches, and doing one pattern; and three rows of the next on this, increasing three stitches at each end of every row. Then work each edge separately, doing first three patterns, then two, then one only; not decreasing all at once, but leaving a few stitches at the *inner* edge of every row.

To make up the cap, cut out the shape first in paper; then in fine tick, or any similar material. Cover this with black on one side, and with green satin on the other. The satin should be rather darker in color than the crochet, which is to be tacked over it. The corners of the oblong piece done for the crown must then be cut off, and all sewed firmly and neatly together. A piece of enamelled leather usually lines the band, and a cord and tassels finish the cap at the back of the head.

EMBROIDERY.

PETTICOAT SUSPENDER.

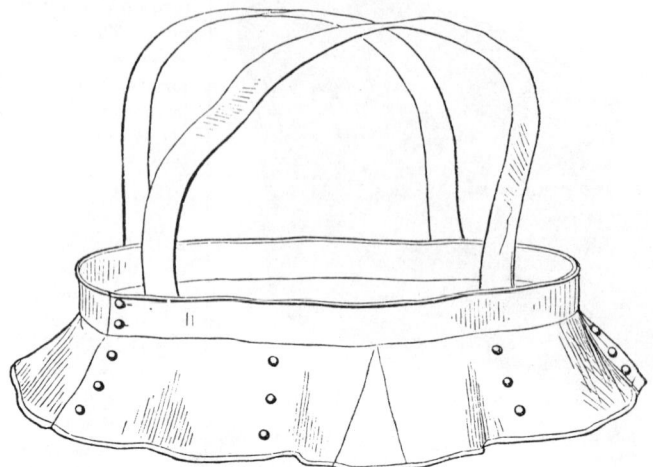

This suspender is attached to a band which is fastened round the waist, and supported by shoulder straps. It is made of some strong material, lined with muslin, and bound with muslin or tape. It can be worn to fasten in front, or on the back. The arrangement of the buttons is marked on the pattern. This suspender has been tried and found to answer very well.

CIGAR-CASE IN APPLICATION.

Materials.—Brown Russia leather, a little green and scarlet ditto; a small quantity of white, black, and scarlet silk braid, and two yards of gold ditto.

The ordinary Russia leather forms the ground of this cigar-case. The black part of the engraving represents the green leather; the inner part, engraved in horizontal lines, is scarlet leather. Both the green and scarlet are very thin, and are cut out in the forms seen in the engraving. The edges of the different leathers are sewed together closely, through a piece of linen which lines the entire case. The engraving is two-thirds the size of the original. The gold braid is marked in the engraving by a narrow *double* line. It will be seen that it covers the joins of the different leathers, and also forms a knot in the centre. The outer line of braiding is scarlet; that on the green is white, and on the scarlet leather is black.

This sort of cigar-case is made up *à ressort*, as the French term it; that is, with a gilt frame, in the same way as the portemonnaies usually are done.

CANADIAN OR TEMPLAR'S CAP, WORN BY GENTLEMEN WHEN DRIVING.

MATERIALS required are four steel needles, No. 12; two bone needles, with knobs, No. 10; three ounces of Berlin fingering wool. The cap is commenced by knitting the head piece. Cast 72 stitches on one of the steel needles; plain knit like a garter until you have done a length of five and a half inches.

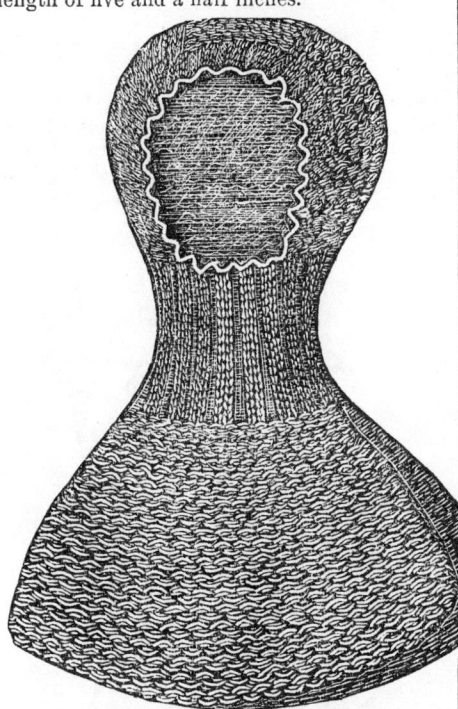

To shape the Head Piece.—Knit plain 47 stitches, knit 2 together, * turn your needle (as you do in forming the heel of a stocking), slip first stitch, knit 22 inches plain, knit 2 together; repeat from * until you have only 24 stitches left on the needle.

You next knit the ribbed bordering which goes around the face. Hold the cap as if on the head, and at the bottom of *right* side, with another needle take up, and as you take up, knit all the stitches there are, then knit on same needle half of the 24 stitches left after shaping the head piece. With a second needle knit the remaining 12 stitches, and take up down the left side the same number of stitches you had on the right. These stitches are to be ribbed backwards and forwards for a depth of two inches. The ribbing is worked thus: Knit 3, purl 3 alternately. If you have not taken up sufficient stitches to bring the ribbing

exact, you must end with knitting or purling as many as there are, but be particular to keep the ribbing right by purling in back row where you knitted before, and *vice versâ.* Cast off. This completes the head piece.

For the Neck.—The four steel needles are now used. Cast 24 stitches on one needle; with a second needle take up, and as you take up, knit (beginning at left side of the head piece) along the neck 45 stitches; with a third needle take up 45 more stitches, which will bring you to the end of the neck. Rib these 114 stitches around and around like a stocking until you have done a length of four inches. The ribbing should be as before. Knit 3, purl 3 alternately.

To arrange the loops for the flaps.—Rib your 24 loops, and on same needle with them rib 16 more stitches. Rib the remaining stitches on next needle on to another. With a third needle rib all the stitches on last needle to within 17 of the end, which 17 you must slip on the needle with the 24 first cast on. You ought to have on it 57 loops.

For the flaps.—Take your bone needles and plain knit the 57 stitches on the one needle backwards and forwards until you have a length of 5 inches. Continue the plain knitting, but to round the corners knit 2 together at the end of *each* row, until you have only 25 stitches left, when cast off.

The flap for the back is worked exactly the same, putting all the stitches on one of the bone needles.

TRIMMING FOR A DRESS.

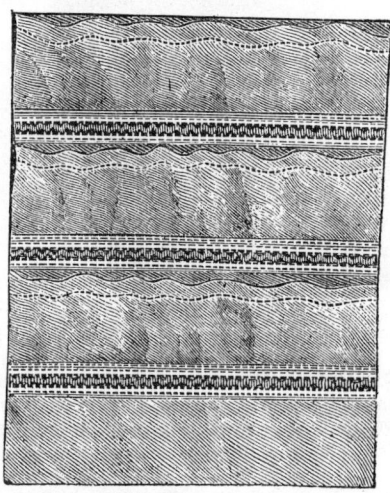

BELL-PULL.

THE foundation is a strip of dark blue cloth the required length, and measuring six inches in width. It is pinked at the edges, and ornamented with braid and medallions. The design for the medallion is shown in the full size in

Fig. 1.

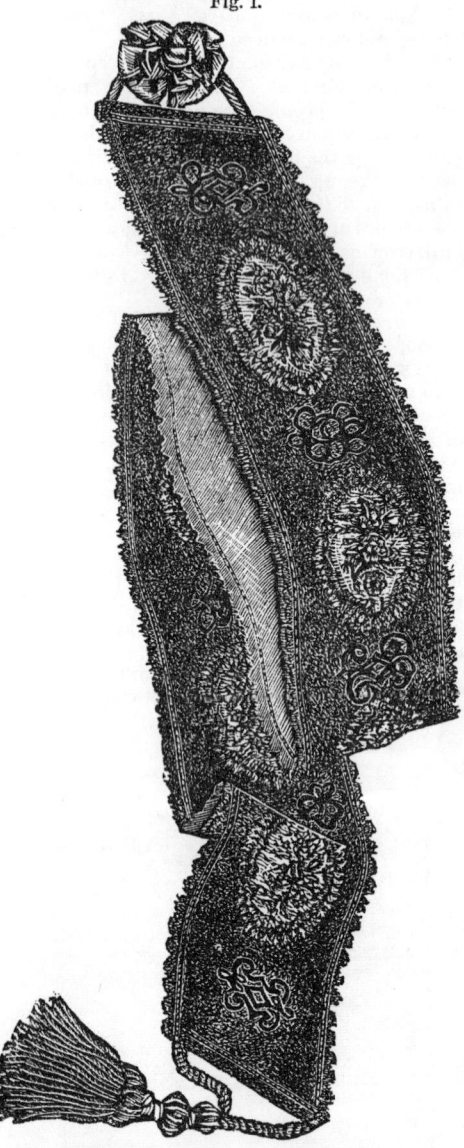

Fig. 2. The foundation is of white cloth. The group of flowers in the centre is composed of woollen braid, of various colors, and green velvet. A moderate amount of ingenuity only is required to arrange this group very effectively. The rose in the centre is yellow; the one at the top, pink; the two smaller ones, scarlet; the bud lying between them, yellow;

and the bud on the opposite side is pink. The leaves are of green velvet, stitched on with lighter green silk. The sprays in coral stitch are brown. This *applique* is button-holed on to the cloth foundation with red purse-silk, and ornamented round with herring-bone stitch in red silk, and a row of long stitch worked with yellow silk (Fig. 2). At the bottom of the bell-pull is placed a cord and tassel the color of the foundation, and at the top a rosette of ribbon of the same color.

TATTED COLLAR.

BEGIN with the three-leaved figure inside the rosettes as follows: Work a circle of 2 double, 9 times alternately 1 purl 2 double; close to this work 2 similar circles, joining them according to illustration; tie the ends of the thread together and cut it off. Around this figure work a row of circles and scallops as

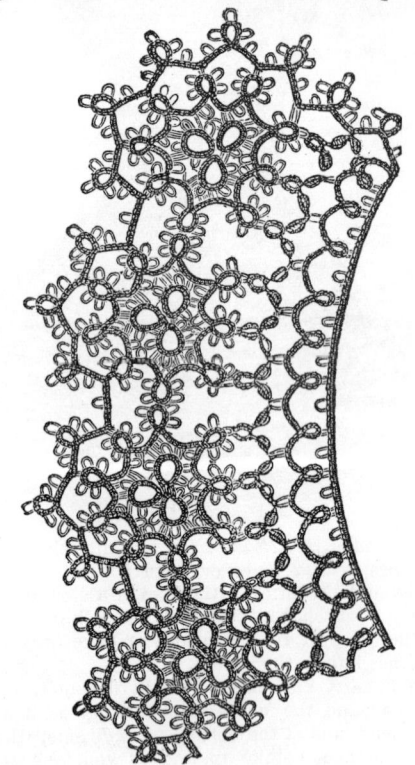

follows: Tie 2 threads together, and * work on 1 thread a circle of 2 double, 5 times alternately 1 purl, 2 double; turn the work, and work on both threads a scallop of 2 double, 1 purl, 2 double, loop into the next purl but one of the nearest circle of the three-leaved figure, 2 double, 1 purl, 2 double; turn the work, work twice alternately a circle and a scallop as above, looping the centre into the 5th and 7th purl of the same circle already connected;

repeat twice from *. At the end of the row tie the ends of the threads together and cut them off. Join the rosettes according to illustration. For the inner edge of the collar work with 2 shuttles as follows: On both threads alternately 4 double, 1 purl, at the end 4 double. In connection with this row work on both threads 1 purl and 4 double; turn the work

follows: Loop the thread into the purl of the first scallop of the last row, work 2 Josephine knots, * turn the work, work a circle of 4 double, loop into the centre purl of the nearest circle of the rosettes, observing to hold the rosettes upwards, 4 double, turn the work, work 1 Josephine knot, loop into the purl of the next scallop, 1 Josephine knot, repeat

Fig. 2.—Medallion Ornament for Bell-pull.   Page 288.

and work on one thread a circle of 3 double, loop into the next purl of the previous row, 3 double; * turn the work and work on two threads a scallop of 4 double, 1 purl, 4 double; turn the work and work on the thread a circle of 4 double, loop into the next purl but one of the 1st row, 4 double, repeat from *; at the end of the row a scallop of 4 double; then tie the ends together and cut them off. The rosettes are connected with the above rows as

from * according to illustration. Around the centre edge of the collar work a row of scallops and circles according to illustration.

BOX FOR HOLDING IRONING APPARATUS.

This convenient receptacle for ironing utensils consists of a cigar-box. It appears open in Fig. 1, which exhibits the various arrangements for receiving the bags of starch and blue, the ironing-cloth, the gauffering-irons, etc. The outside is ornamented with a scalloped border and scalloped beadings of light brown unglazed American cloth, fastened on with small brass nails or upholsterer's pins, and two straps, fastened with buttons according to Fig.

Fig. 1.

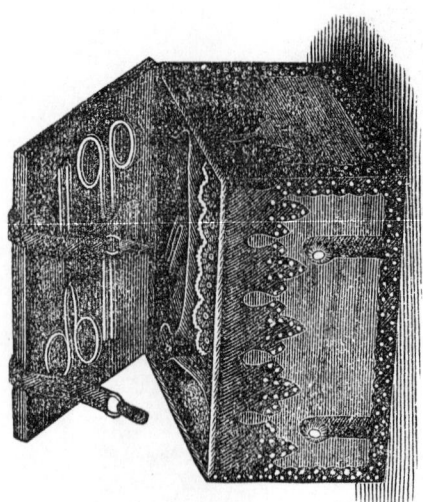

2, in which the box appears closed. Take a cigar-box, about ten inches long, six and a half inches wide, and five inches high, and having carefully removed all traces of paper, and rubbed off the stamp with a piece of glass or

Fig. 2.

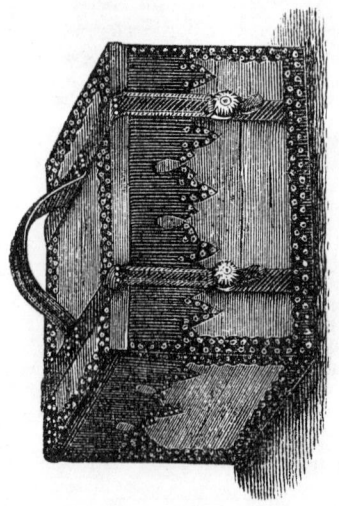

pumice-stone, glue to the box according to illustration two straps of double cloth, three inches long and one inch wide, and fix the upper end with a bronze button by making a hole through the leather and the wood for the shank to pass

through, and passing a wire pin through the eye of the shank inside the box. Then glue over the four side edges of the box strips of cloth, cut into scallops on both sides, fasten them on with brass pins, and put a similar strip, scalloped at the top, round the bottom of the box. Now line it with cloth, making the pieces sufficiently deep to fold over the edge and form the scalloped border, which is fastened down with pins according to illustration. Put in the pockets of double cloth, bound with red worsted braid, and then ornament the lid with a brown leather cloth handle, four inches long and one inch wide, and line it with a piece of brown cloth sufficiently large to fold over the edge and form the scalloped beading, and furnished with a strap according to illustration for holding the irons. Prepare two straps of double cloth fifteen inches long and one inch wide, fasten them to the back of the box and across the lid, thus fixing the lid to the box, and to the other end, which is left loose, attach a brass ring with a leather cloth loop, to be drawn over the bronze button when the box is shut.

WAISTCOAT.—KNITTED OR CROCHET.

THE two stitches that are best adapted for knitting a gentleman's waistcoat, as they will not readily unravel when the pieces are cut into shape, are the "check" and the "moss" stitch. Both will take about the same quantity (12 ounces) of double German wool, and two long needles, No. 11, will be required. For check stitch cast on any even number of stitches, according to the width you require for one front of the waistcoat, remembering that when knitted the stitches measure one-third more than when first cast on. *1st row.* Slip 1, knit 1, * 2 purl, 2 plain; repeat from *. *2d.* Slip 1, purl 1, * 2 plain, 2 purl; repeat from *. *3d.* Slip 1, purl 1, * 2 plain, 2 purl; repeat from *. *4th.* Slip 1, knit 1, * 2 purl, 2 plain; repeat from *. Repeat from 1st row till you have about 27 inches in length; knit a second piece exactly the same, and have them made up at a tailor's. For "moss stitch" cast on any even number of stitches, slip the 1st of each row, and knit 1 plain, 1 purl, alternately throughout, reversing them in the next row, so that a purl stitch may come over a plain, and a plain over a purl stitch, and continue in this manner till you have the required length. The plain tricot stitch is also a good one for gentlemen's waistcoats, as it is not inclined to unravel. Make a chain the width required, raise a loop in every chain, keeping them all on the needle, then work back, drawing the thread through two loops at a time. In the next row raise a stitch in each of the perpendicular loops of the previous row, and work back as before. Repeat 2d row till you have the necessary length.

FLOWER-VASE MAT IN CROCHET.

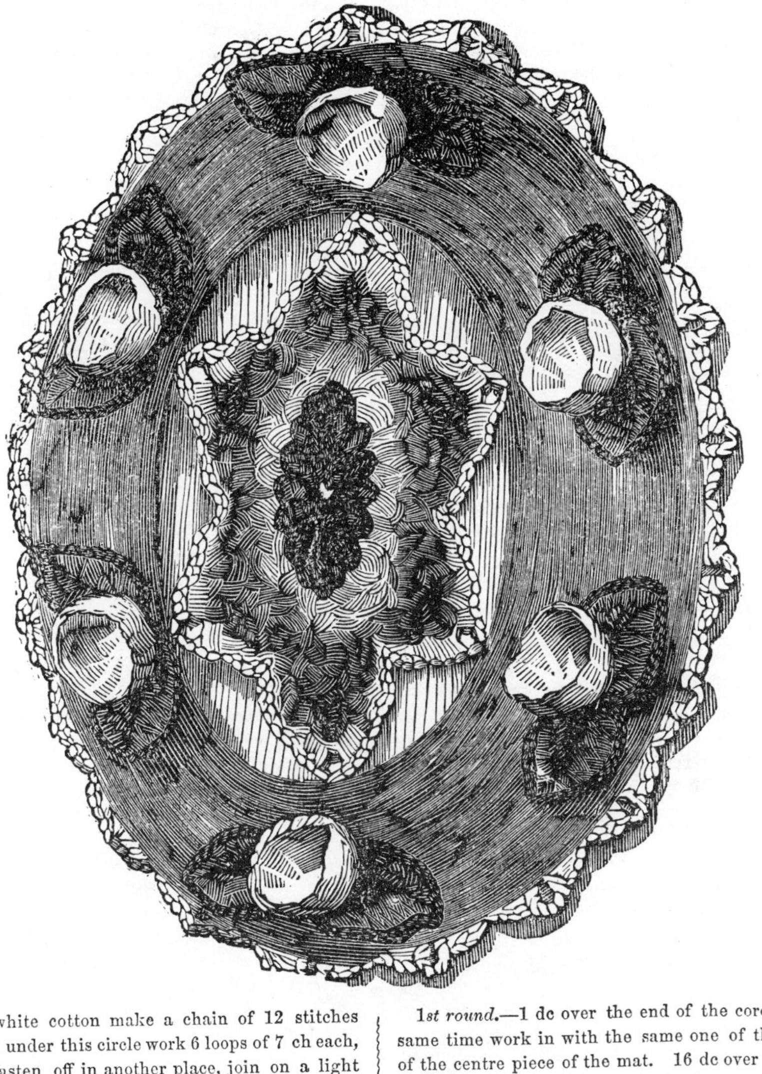

With white cotton make a chain of 12 stitches wide, and under this circle work 6 loops of 7 ch each, dc, and fasten off in another place, join on a light shade of peach, 2 l under the 7th ch, 3 ch, 2 more l under the same loop, 3 ch, repeat under each.

3d round.—A darker shade. 2 loops under the 3d ch between the 4 l, 3 ch, 2 more long under the same, 3d ch dc under next 3 ch, 3 ch, and repeat.

4th.—Next darker shade. 2 l under 3 ch between the 4 l, 4 ch, 2 more long under the same, 4 ch dc over dc, repeat.

5th.—A pale green. 3 l under 4 ch between the 4 l, 5 ch, 3 more l under the same, 3 ch dc under next l, 3 ch dc under next l to this, 3 ch, repeat.

Now with shaded scarlet work six rounds in dc over blind cord.

1st round.—1 dc over the end of the cord; at the same time work in with the same one of the points of the centre piece of the mat. 16 dc over the cord, with the 17th stitch catch up the next point, repeat all around; in each round following this work the stitches close enough to cover the cord. With the pale green used for the centre, work an edge to the mat as follows: 3 l under 1 stitch, taking both meshes of the chain, 5 ch, 3 l, 1 under next stitch, 3 ch, make 3, 1 dc, 3 ch, and repeat. Now make 12 leaves and six white flowers, as follows: For the leaf, with a middle shade of green, make a ch of 7 turn, m 1, 5 l, 1 s c, 1 ch, 1 l in the same loop as the s c, 1 ch, 1 s c in the same loop as the last two, and on the other side of the chain 5 l and 1 s c in the end of the leaf to draw it into shape. Make eleven more like this.

For a flower, with white, make a chain of 5, unite in each stitch, work 2 dc. Next round 1 l in each with a ch between, join the 1st and last stitches together, fasten off and pull it into the shape of a cup, make 5 more and arrange them on the scarlet border, as in the engraving. With the same shade of green as that used for the leaves, make a star for the centre of the mat, to be placed over the cotton work as follows: Make a ch of 5, unite, 7 ch, 1 dc in next stitch, 7 ch, 1 dc the same, repeat all round; you will then have 10 loops of 7 ch each, fasten off. If it is preferred, this mat may be lined with cardboard, covered with white silk, but it is not necessary.

NECKTIE IN TAPISSERIE D'AUXERRE.

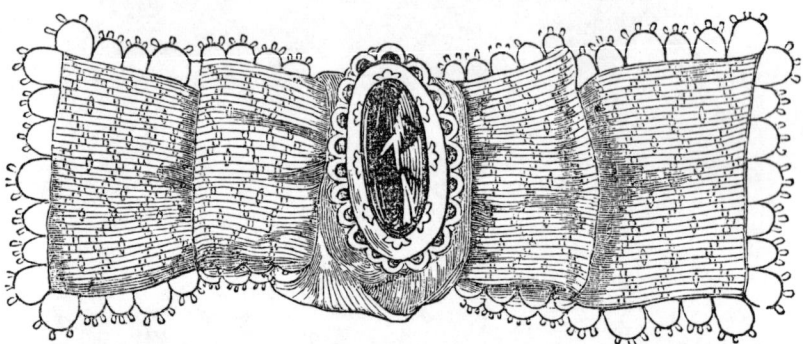

Materials.—Seven skeins of brilliant scarlet chenille; quarter of a yard of black net; one skein of coarse black sewing silk; steel shuttle, and purling pin.

Our readers are aware that the term *tapisserie d'auxerre* is applied to embroidery done by darning on net. The necktie, of which we give an engraving, is not only very comfortable, but also really very *distingué* in appearance, and particularly suitable for wearing in mourning, with a black gilet and jacket.

Cut the net in half, so that each strip is two nails wide; one of these will make the knot and ends, and a sufficient length must be taken from the other to go round the neck. Each end is to be one and a half nails long, and the knot will require two nails. All the pieces are to be darned in the same way, working in the length, the effect being that of parallel zigzag lines.

1st row.—Pass the needle under 2 threads, and over 2 in the entire length. *Begin every row at the same end.*

2d.—* slip the needle under the two threads on a line with the last two raised, *sloping downwards,* over 2, under 1, over 2, under 2, over 3, * repeat.

3d.—Pass the needle under two on the same sloping line, * over 4, under 2, * all the way.

4th.—Again raise the next two threads on the downward line, * over 3, under 2, over 2, under 1, over 2, under 2, * repeat.

5th.—Raise the next two threads on the downward slope, * over 2, under 2, * throughout the line.

6th.—Now raise two threads *sloping downwards,* * over 3, under 2, over 2, under 1, over 2, under 2, * repeat.

7th.—2 *threads upwards,* * over 4, under 2, * repeat.

8th.—2 *threads upwards,* * over 2, under 1, over 2, under 2, over 3, under 2, * repeat.

These eight lines form a pattern, to be repeated until there is as much done as would be wide enough for an ordinary ribbon. Five patterns and a half will do for the ends, and about four for the knot and the piece that goes under the collar.

The ends are edged with tatting, done with the coarse black silk, thus:—

1st loop.—7 double, 1 picot, 4 double, 1 picot, 3 double. (Draw up this, and all the other loops, in the form of a semicircle.)

2d.—3 double, join, * 3 double, 1 picot, * 4 times, 3 double.

3d.—3 double, join; 5 double, 1 picot, * 3 double, 1 picot, * twice, 5 double, 1 picot, 3 double.

4th.—Like 2d.

5th.—3 double, join, * 4 double, 1 picot, * twice, 3 double.

Repeat the last four loops until sufficient is done to trim the ends all round, except at the part which is attached to the knot. The piece for the knot must be twisted into the form of one, and the folds edged also with tatting. The edges of the net are hemmed before the tatting is sewed on; a piece of chenille is sewed at the edge, over the hem, and a loop of chenille is twisted into every loop of tatting.

LOUNGING OR SMOKING-CAP

IN APPLICATION.

Materials.—Very fine cloth, ¾ of a yard by 9 inches; some velvet of the same color; braid, and coarse gold thread of the best quality. Handsome pendent tassel.

THIS cap looks best in coffee brown or rich green. Draw two vine-leaves of different sizes, and cut them out in cardboard. From these cut six velvet ones of each size, or, if preferred, eight, or the number being in inverse ratio to the size. Whatever number is made should be sufficient to go round the cap, without quite touching each other. The leaves are disposed alternately upwards and downwards, and stems and tendrils fill up the spaces between. To draw the pattern, take a piece of stout writing-paper, just long enough to go round the head, and about eight inches wide. Divide the whole length into as many parts as there are to be leaves in outlines (merely creasing the paper), draw the leaf from the cardboard pattern in each of these, add the stems and tendrils, and then, after doing another line of the same with the small leaves, prick all the outlines for a pounced pattern.

Mark the cloth with this; wet the wrong side of the velvet leaves with good thin glue, lay them in their places, and, when dried by slightly pressing them, tack the edges down, and then sew on the braid, with a gold thread on each side of it. The veinings of the leaves are done with gold thread; all the other parts are in braid, with gold thread on each side. The ends must be drawn through the cloth.

The crown is entirely of velvet; it is nearly a round, about five inches in diameter; it is ornamented with a scroll round the edge, in thread and braid, to correspond with the other parts, and there is a scallop round the edge of the cap, done in the same manner.

To make up the cap, line it with sarsenet of the same color, join the sides, gather the top in, and sew it round the crown; add the tassel. The most elegant kind of tassel is made of a large flat plaited button in dead gold, with bullion pendants about nine inches long.

may be filled with point lace stitches. The muslin must be very carefully cut away from the ground.

The edge we have given is suitable in its present dimensions for the frill of the new bishop-sleeve.

Enlarged to twice the size, it would be extremely handsome for the border of a veil. We should advise cambric to be substituted for muslin for the latter purpose.

PATCHWORK.

PATTERNS FOR EMBROIDERY.

BRAID PATTERN.

PAPER FLOWERS.—DOUBLE PINK.

THE materials are cherry-colored (carmine) paper and pale green paper, also blue-green paper, all three without gloss; watered-silk

same way is then slit up one and a quarter inch deep in a fringe-like way, and twisted around a piece of wire, gives the bunch of stamens (shown in Fig. 4); more natural, how-

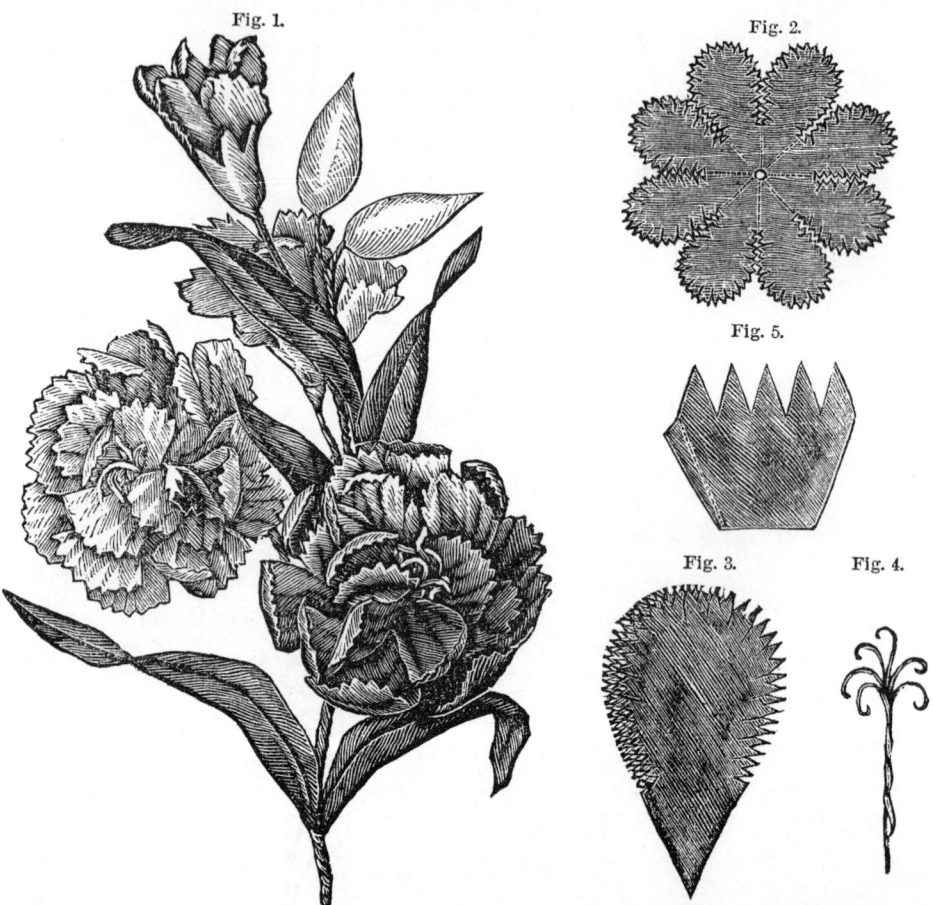

Fig. 1.

Fig. 2.

Fig. 5.

Fig. 3.

Fig. 4.

paper in pink or light lilac, and green; thin flower-wire, etc.

Fig. 1.—Should thin paper be taken for this pink, four petal circles of the same size are required for each; but if the thick so-called carmine paper is used, of which the model flower is made, then three are sufficient. Fig. 2 gives one petal in a small size spread out. Fig. 3 shows the same in the full size folded together eight times. The edges of this folded-together flower part, to be next cut out in points, are to have small slits between every two points; after being opened, the pointed edges are drawn over a knitting-needle or scissors, in order to curve them, and this throughout and only on one side; a narrow stripe of white paper in the

ever, is a small piece from the feather part of a goose-quill. The petal circles are slipped on singly, and tied on the wire stalk, letting the thus-far finished flower slip between the thumb and first finger of the half-closed left hand, so that the petals may come closer together. The calyx of the pink, the edges of which must be pasted over each other, are cut out of the pale green, dull paper, after Fig. 5, filled with a little cotton-wool, and the flower stalk then slipped through. The lower edge of the calyx disappears when caught together by twisting over the flower stalk with green paper. The long, pointed leaves of pale green paper are next broken (folded together, pressed with the finger, and again opened) along the middle, then drawn over the scissors the whole width, and, only at the lower end, finished with a fine wire stalk twisted over with green. Then the green closed pink buds can be formed of cotton-wool, and covered with a mixture of green wax and gum Arabic; but these are so cheap at flower-shops that it is quite unnecessary to make them. Open buds are of one petal circle, and one calyx of only three points.

LEAD CUSHION.

THIS cushion is placed on a case four and a half inches high, which is loaded inside with lead. The cushion itself is of crimson satin, and filled with emery; the case is covered underneath with crimson velvet, edged with Russian leather. Around the cushion is a narrow bronze rim, and in the centre a bronze handle. For the bordering of beads, see Figs. 2 and 3. *1st row.* 3 black beads, 1 bugle, 2 black, 1 bugle, 3 black, 5 gold, turn the work. *2d.* 1 black,

Fig. 1.

the next black bead of the 2d row, 1 gold, thread through the next bugle, 1 black, thread through the next black, 1 bugle, thread through

Fig. 3.

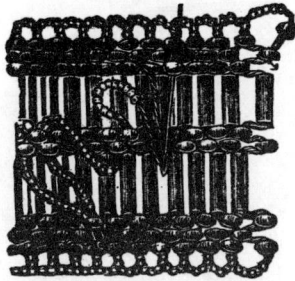

the next bead, 1 black, thread through the next bead and the 2 next gold beads of the 1st row; turn the work and repeat, referring to the illustration. The lighter beads in illustration are gold. The leaf-like figure is then worked in gold beads.

thread through the second black bead of the first row, 1 black, thread through the following bugle, 1 black, thread through the next black

Fig. 2.

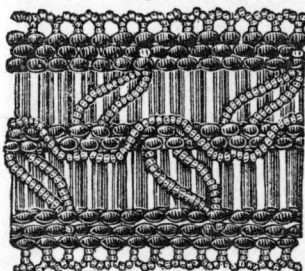

but 1, 1 bugle, thread through the next bead, 1 black, thread through the next bead, 5 gold, turn the work. *3d.* 1 black, thread through

MITTEN.

MITTENS are much worn by ladies in the morning. The pattern shown in the engraving is of fine cloth, embroidered with silk of a contrasting shade.

NETTED NIGHT-CAP.

THIS night-cap is very simple and practical. It consists of two similar three-cornered pieces, sewn together so as to form a double triangle; the point of the triangle is turned back, as seen on illustration, and fastened on the lower half of the same. The cap is edged with a crochet lace; a similar lace covers the seam between both parts of the cap. Our pattern is worked with crochet cotton over a mesh measuring three-quarters of an inch around. Begin each half in the corner; cast on 2 stitches, and work backwards and forwards, increasing 1 stitch at the end of every row, till the number of stitches are 60. Then sew both halves together, and

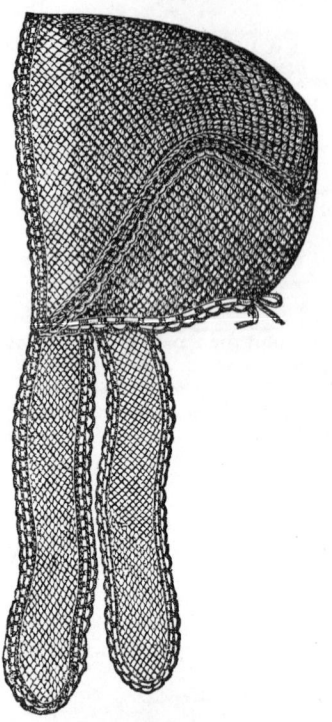

trim the cap and strings with the following lace: work 2 rows of open work treble stitches —the treble stitches are divided by 1 chain— then work 1 row of double, always working 4 double around the chain stitches which divides 2 treble in the preceding row.

KNITTED BORDER FOR COVER-LETS, ETC.

For this border cast on 15 stitches, and work the short way backwards and forwards. *1st row.* Knitted. *2d.* slip 1, knit 11; leave the last 3 on the needle for the next 4 rows. *3d.* Slip 1, purl 11; then crochet from the last stitch a chain of 50 stitches. Take a fresh needle, and take up the crocheted stitches as follows: put the needle in the last crocheted stitch, miss 2, take on 2, and so on, until you have 25 stitches on the needle. *5th.* Slip 1, knit to the end. *6th.* Slip 1, purl 36, cotton forward, knit 3. *7th.* Cast off 3, to do this, slip the first stitch, knit off the next, and pass the slipped stitch over the knitted one; knit the next, and pass the preceding over it; last of all, knit 1 out of the cotton that goes around the needle, and pass the preceding one over it, then cotton forward, purl 1, knit 1, knit 37. *8th.* Cast off 25, knit 11; the last 3 stitches remain untouched for 4 rows. *9th.* Purl. *10th and 11th.* Knitted. *12th.* Slip 1, purl 11, cotton forward, knit 3. *13th.* Cast off 3, cotton forward, purl 1, knit 1, knit 12. *14th.* Slip 1, knit 11; the last 3 stitches are left untouched for 4 rows. *15th to 26th.* Same as 3d to 14th rows. *27th.* Slip 1, purl 11. *28th.* Slip 1, knit 11. *29th.* Slip 1, knit 10. The last stitch of the preceding row is knitted together with the 2 nearest selvedge stitches on the inner crossway edge of the first scallop which is not yet joined to the close part of the work. *30th.* Slip 1, purl 11, cotton forward, knit 3. *31st.* Cast off 3, cotton forward, purl 1, knit 1, knit 11; the last stitch of the preceding row is knitted together with the 2 next stitches of the cross-way edge of the same scallop which was joined to the work in the 29th row. *32d.* Slip 1, knit 11; the last 3 stitches remain untouched during the next 4 rows. Repeat from the 15th to the

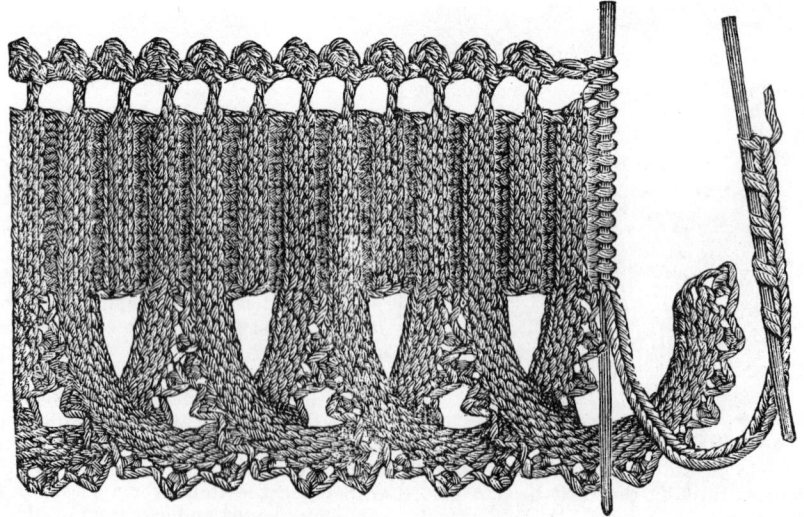

32d row, till the requisite length is completed; twisting the scallops together as shown in illustration.

cotton forward and knit 1. *4th.* 8 times alternately cotton forward and knit 1. *6th.* * cotton forward, knit 2, repeat from *. This

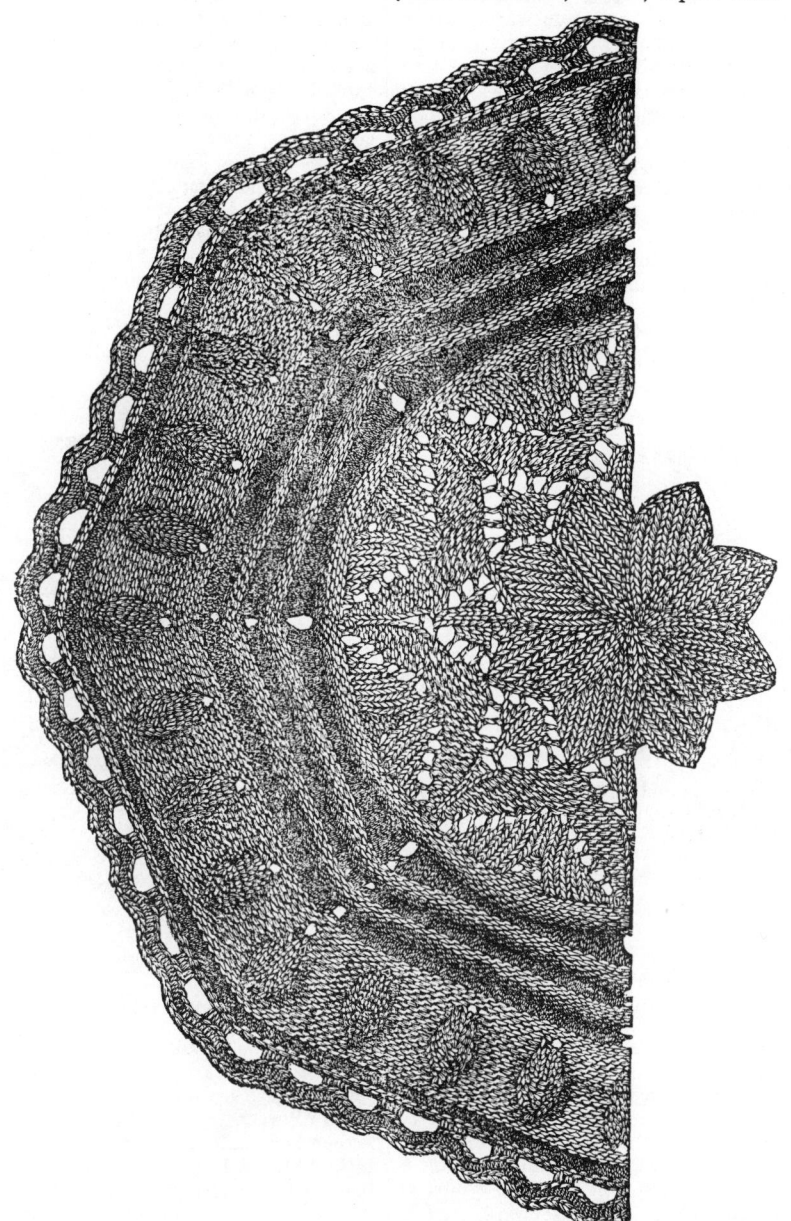

KNITTED OCTAGON FOR COUNTER-PANES, ETC.

THIS octagon looks well in either coarse or fine cotton. It is worked from the centre by casting on 4 stitches, joining them in a circle, and knitting 1 round plain. All the rounds with odd numbers, from 1 to 25 inclusive, are knitted plain. *2d round.* 4 times alternately

repetition will not be mentioned again in the following rows. *8th.* * cotton forward, knit 3. *10th.* * cotton forward, knit 4. *12th.* * cotton forward, knit 5. *14th.* * cotton forward, knit 6. *16th.* * cotton forward, knit 7. *18th.* * cotton forward, knit 2 together, knit 4, knit 2 together. *20th.* * knit 1, cotton forward, knit 2 together, knit 2, knit 2 together. *22d.* * knit

2, cotton forward, knit 2 together, knit 2 together, cotton forward, knit 1. 24*th*. * knit 3, cotton forward, knit 2 together, cotton forward, knit 2. 26*th*. * knit 3, cotton forward, purl 3, cotton forward, knit 2. 27*th*. * knit 1, knit 2 together, purl 5, knit 2 together. 28*th*. * knit 2, cotton forward, purl 5, cotton forward, knit 1. 29*th*. knit 2 together, * purl 7, slip 2; to do this, slip the 1st, knit the 2 next together, and pass the slipped stitch over. The last stitch of this round is passed over the first stitch of the same round, to form the last decrease and to finish the round. 30*th*. * cotton forward, purl 7, cotton forward, knit 1. 31*st*. * purl 9, knit 1. 32*d*. purl 5, * cotton forward, knit 1, cotton forward, purl 4, cotton forward, purl 2 together, purl 4, repeat from * 6 times, cotton forward, knit 1, cotton forward, purl 4, cotton forward,

1. 44*th*. * purl 2 together, cotton forward, knit 6, cotton forward, purl 3, cotton forward, knit 6, cotton forward, purl 2, together, knit 1. 45*th*. Slip 1, * knit 7, purl 5, knit 7, purl 3 together at the end of the row; the 1st and last 2 stitches are purled together. 46*th to* 49*th*. Purled. 50*th*. 8 times alternately knit 20, cotton forward. 51*st*. Knitted, only out of the cotton that is brought forward, knit 1 and purl 1. 52*d and* 53*d*. Same as 50th and 51st, but with a proportionately increased number of stitches, and the cotton brought forward in round 52 must meet with the 2 stitches knitted out of the cotton brought forward in the 50th round. Repeat twice from the 46th to the 53d round. 70*th and* 71*st*. Purl. 73*d*. * knit 1, purl 8. 74*th*. * cotton forward, knit 1, cotton forward, purl 8. 75*th*. * knit 3, purl 8. 76*th*.

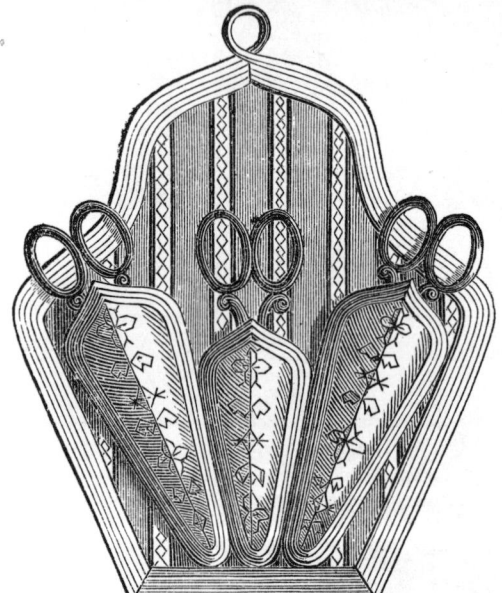

Scissors Case.

Case for Pocket Hankerchiefs.

knit together the first and last stitches of the round. 33*d*. * purl 4, knit 3, purl 4, knit 1. 34*th*. * purl 4, cotton forward, knit 3, cotton forward, purl 4, knit 1. 35*th*. * purl 4, knit 5, purl 4, knit 1. 36*th*. * purl 4, cotton forward, knit 5, cotton forward, purl 4, knit 1. 37*th*. * purl 4, knit 7, purl 4, knit 1. 38*th*. * purl 4, cotton forward, knit 7, cotton forward, purl 4, knit 1. 39*th*. * purl 4, knit 4, purl 1, knit 4, purl 4, knit 1. 40*th*. * purl 4, cotton forward, knit 4, purl 1, knit 4, cotton forward, purl 4, knit 1. 41*st*. * purl 2, knit 2 together, knit 5, purl 1, knit 5, purl 2 together, purl 2, knit 1. 42*d*. * purl 3, cotton forward, knit 5, cotton forward, knit 1, cotton forward, knit 5, cotton forward, purl 3, knit 1. 43*d*. * purl 1, knit 2 together, knit 15, purl 2 together, purl 1, knit

* cotton forward, knit 3, cotton forward, purl 8. 77*th*. * knit 5, purl 8. 78*th*. * cotton forward, knit 5, cotton forward, purl 8, then 3 times alternately, cotton forward, knit 1, knit 3 together, knit 1, cotton forward, purl 8. 79*th*. * knit 2, knit 2 together, knit 3, purl 8 then 3 times alternately, knit 5, purl 8. 80*th*. * knit 3, purl 1, knit 3, purl 8, then 3 times alternately knit 1, knit 3 together, knit 1, purl 8. 81*st*. * knit 3, cotton forward, purl 1, cotton forward, knit 3, purl 8, then 3 times alternately knit 3, purl 8. 82*d*. Knit 3 together, purl 3, knit 3 together, purl 8, then 3 times alternately knit 3 together, purl 8. 83*d and* 84*th*. Purled. 85*th to* 89*th*. Knitted. 90*th*. Purled, cast off. For the border, crochet around the octagon as follows: 3 double in the 1st 3 stitches, 5 chain,

miss 3. *2d round.* 1 double in every stitch. This octagon may be joined to other octagons of the same pattern, or to squares, so as to form large coverlets. In this case the crocheted edging is, of course, omitted.

ORNAMENTAL KNIFE TRAY.

THIS tray is made of either common white wood oiled, or of walnut; the sides are ornamented on one side with embroidery done on leather in colored silks, Fig. 2; the other side,

Fig. 2.

Fig. 3.

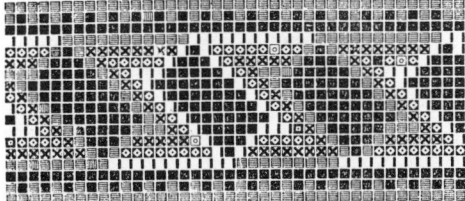

Fig. 3, in beads, of different colors; the ends can be ornamented or not, according to the taste of the worker. The patterns for the sides are given in full size.

CASE FOR POCKET HANDKERCHIEFS.
(*See Engraving, Page* 300.)

THIS case consists of a square card-board box nine and three-fifths inches large, three and one-fifth inches high, with a cover coming far beyond the case. The latter is covered on the outside with blue satin, inside with white silk, having been quilted and stitched in a diamond pattern; the outer covering on the top of the cover is likewise quilted. The edge of the

cover is ornamented with a fluting of blue satin ribbon two and two-fifths inches wide; on the cover fasten a square in guipure d'Art. The cover is moreover ornamented from illustration, with bows of blue satin ribbon; the handle consists of two plaits of narrow cross strips of blue satin, fastened in the middle of the top.

CHILD'S BIB IN KNITTING AND CROCHET.

THIS bib is knitted with soft cotton. Begin at the bottom with a chain of 101 stitches, and work backwards and forwards, * 2 rows to appear purled on the right side, 3 rows to appear plain, 2 rows to appear purled, knitting the 3 middle stitches together in the 3d, 6th, and 7th row. *8th.* Alternately knit 2 together, thread

forward. These 8 rows form 1 pattern; repeat from * 11 times, observing to knit off the threads brought forward like other stitches. In the 1st row of the 9th pattern, increase 1 stitch at the beginning and end of the row, and repeat this increase every 3d row. When 12 patterns are completed, repeat the first 7 rows, knitting off in the last of the 7 the 17 middle stitches for the slope of the neck; continue the rows on each side for 19 rows more, decrease in every other row on the inside, first 5, then 4, then 3 times 2, and at last only 1 stitch; then knit 7 rows like these at the beginning of the work, bringing the shoulder to a point. Make a chain of 20 stitches for the shoulder strap, and knit 95 rows alternately, 3 to appear plain, 2 to appear purled, taking off 1 stitch at the beginning and the end of every 6th row, up to the 36th row. When the strap is finished, cast off, sew a button on at the bottom, and join the strap to the bib on the shoulder. Work a border in crochet to go all around the bib, except at the neck, as follows: Make a chain the required length, and work 1st row. Alternately 3 chain, missing 3 underneath, 1 double long treble, observing to form the corners by working 2 double long treble with 7 chain between them, missing 1 underneath. *2d row.* Work with fine cotton * 1 double on the 1st treble, 6 treble in the centre stitch of the following 3 chain; repeat from *. Repeat this row of scallops on the other side of the foundation chain, making the scallops exactly opposite to each other. 3*d*. 1 treble, 3 chain, working the treble on the back thread of the foundation stitch, into which the double long treble has been worked. 4*th*. Like the 2d. All these rows worked with cotton must be worked very loosely. Around the slope of the neck work 2 rows of scallops opposite each other on the 2 sides of a chain. Sew the border around the bib, putting a colored ribbon underneath the open row, and tie ends of cotton, five inches in length, into the foundation chain at the bottom of the bib, to form a fringe. Make a loop at each side of the bib to draw over the button of the shoulder-strap.

PAINTING ON WHITE WOOD.

To those who employ water-color painting as a pastime and study, painting on unpolished white wood is well worthy their attention. The work is not difficult, and the result is generally so satisfactory that the student is amply repaid. The wood used is the chestnut. In its natural state it is very white in appearance, and the only drawback to it is that in substance it is rather soft, so that in sketching or tracing a design care must be taken not to lean too heavily on the pencil. Besides the agreeable nature of painting on wood, from its smooth surface and the readiness with which it takes the color, articles of use in the drawing-room, boudoir, and for the toilet table, together with those of daily use, can be supplied. Blotting pads in various sizes are most useful and very appropriate on the writing table. Stationery cases and paper knives are made to complete the set. When choosing the wood, try and procure it as white as possible, and that the grain of it should run lengthwise and straight. Blotting pads can be made up in either morocco or leather, and can be mounted singly, with backs of morocco or leather as may be desired.

Floral designs, with an illuminated border, which should correspond throughout the set, look very pretty. Butterflies and birds, from their gay colors, are also appropriate, and small landscapes or a sea piece look excessively well on a blotting pad. For the drawing-room or boudoir such articles can be chosen as book slides, card cases, Swiss card baskets, and stereoscopic slide boxes. The Swiss card baskets, from their shape, may be rendered instructive as well as decorative and useful; they are fitted with a number of panels, on which can be painted views of the principal places in Switzerland. For the toilet table there are glove boxes, handkerchief boxes, jewel boxes and work boxes suitably lined with velvet and silk; fans, made entirely of the white wood; and watch cases. An ornamental or fancy glove painted on the glove box is an appropriate and pretty design. For handkerchief boxes, baskets of flowers or fruit look very well. Wide borders of one color, such as dark or light blue, crimson, scarlet, black, and brown, set off the painting in the centre. The tea caddies in white wood look exceedingly handsome when covered with Chinese figures, which ought to be painted in the brightest colors.

When the design is drawn, before commencing the painting, clean the wood thoroughly with crum of bread; and while coloring, place a piece of paper beneath the hand, so that it should not rest on the wood and soil it in any way. Do not put off the cleansing operation until the design is painted, as in rubbing the color is apt to come off, and thereby necessitates a renewal of the work. Be quite sure that the wood when ready for polishing is perfectly clean, otherwise when polished the marks will show clearly, and cannot be erased. The method of painting in water colors on white wood is the same as that used in painting a fan. The colors should be mixed with Chinese white, which renders them opaque, and also acts as a preventive against their sinking into the wood. Body color imparts brilliancy to the coloring on wood, which, if transparencies were used, would not be so great. In painting reverse the order which is set down for transparent colors, and begin with the dark shades. Work up the different lights, and finally put in the high lights. Do not be afraid to apply dark colors and shades; they become very bright when the painting is varnished, and colors such as Vandyke brown and crimson lake warm up and heighten the brilliancy of the picture. The colors can be obtained in either small tubes or cakes. The ordinary brushes used in water-color painting are the best to employ, although some artists prefer to paint in body color with brushes used in oil-color painting.

When painted, the wood should be polished in the following manner: First pass over the entire wood a coating of patent white size, then wait until it has become thoroughly dry, and repeat the operation. Then, again, be sure it is dry before applying the varnish, which can be done with a large soft brush, working it regularly lengthwise, or from top to bottom; and when this has become dry, another coating can be applied, working the brush from side to side. This process may be continued alternately, until the wood is as polished as may be desired.

The white spirit varnish is the best varnish to use.

SCISSORS CASE.
(*See Engraving, Page 300.*)

MADE of leather, embroidered with silk, and arranged so it can be hung up if desired.

SQUARE FOR QUILTS OR OTHER COVERS—CROCHET.

THIS square is well adapted for quilts, if worked with coarse crochet cotton, or for sofa and carriage blankets worked in single Berlin wool. You commence with a chain of 24, fasten off, and commence again on the next 2 bars of 23 dc; fill in all the four right angles in this manner. You then commence the bor-

joining the squares, the picots are drawn through the corresponding ones on the opposite square.

OPEN KNITTING PATTERNS.

THE following are two easy and open patterns for 4 needles; 13 stitches required for each repetition of the pattern: 1st row. * Knit

der. Work a dc on the first stitch in the corner, then * 5 ch in the corner, and a dc on the first stitch on the next side; now work a row of dc to the next corner, and repeat from *. 2d round. * 1 dc on each of the first 2 ch and dc, 3 dc in the 3d of the 5 ch, 1 dc on each of the two following, and on each stitch of the last row, until you come to the next corner, then repeat from *. 3d. 1 dc on the next dc., * a picot of 6 ch, 1 single on the last dc, 1 dc on the next dc., repeat from *, and fasten off at the end of the round. The star in the centre is now worked with a needle, and the same cotton; it is made in long embroidery stitches; the long leaves of the star have 12 threads in them, and the short cross ones 4 in each. In

2 together twice, over, 1 plain, over, 1 plain, over, 1 plain, over, 1 plain, knit 2 together twice, 1 purl, repeat from *. 2d, 3d, and 4th. Plain; repeat these 4 rows. Another pattern requiring 7 stitches for each repetition. 1st row. * Knit 2 together, 1 plain, over, 1 plain, over, knit 2 together, repeat from *. 2d and every alternate. Plain. 3d. * Knit 2 together, over, 3 plain, over, knit 2 together; repeat from *. 5th. * 1 plain, over, 1 plain, slip 1, knit 2 together, pass slipped stitch over, 1 plain, over, 1 plain; repeat from *. 7th. * 2 plain, over, slip 1, knit 2 together, pass slipped stitch over, over, 2 plain; repeat from *. 8th. Plain.

KNITTING BAG.

Materials.—8 yards of cotton cord; 3 straw-colored silk tassels, and 2 yards of cord to correspond; 1 skein of filoselle to match; 1 skein of light green filoselle; 4 skeins of black Berlin wool; 7 shades of green Berlin wool, and 7 of lilac ditto (2 skeins of each); No. 13 Boulton's crochet-hook, and a mesh one-third of an inch wide.

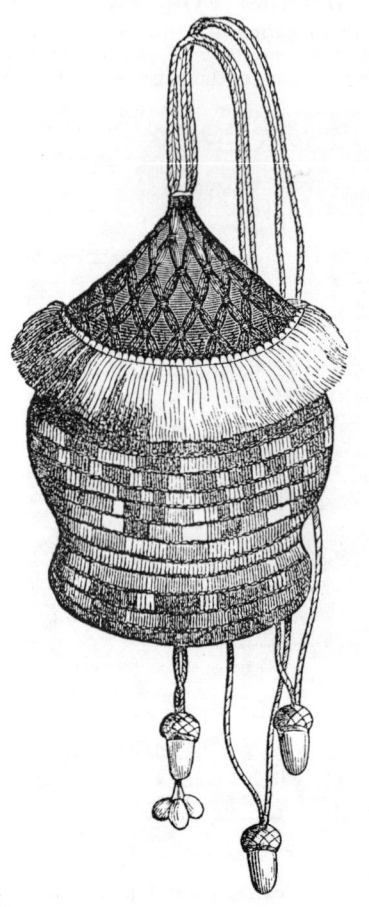

WORK on the end of the cord, with black wool, 10 stitches, which form into a round, on which work 20 stitches.

2d round.—Darkest green wool. Crochet all round, increasing sufficiently to make the work perfectly flat.

3d.—With the next shade of wool, do the same.

4th.—Next shade of wool. Do the same having 60 stitches in the round.

5th.—Next shade of green, and darkest lilac, * 1 lilac, 6 green, on 5 * 10 times.

6th.—Next shade of both colors * 1 lilac, 7 green, on 6 * 10 times.

7th.—Next shades, * 2 lilac, over 1, 1 lilac over green, 5 green, 1 lilac, * 10 times. This is not quite flat.

8th.—Next shades. This round begins the side, and the cord is held in the proper position for that purpose. There is no increase in the *number* of stitches; but they are not quite so close together as in the former round, * 4 lilac, 3 green (coming over the centre of 5 green), 2 lilac, * 10 times.

9th.—Next shade of lilac, green filoselle, * 1 green over the centre of 3 green, and all the rest lilac, working 9 stitches over 8, * 10 times.

10th.—With the lightest lilac work a round, having the same number of stitches; but holding in the cord as tightly as possible to contract the bag.

11th.—Same lilac; darkest green. Contract the round still more, * 4 green, 8 lilac, 2 green, * 7 times.

12th.—Change to the lightest lilac but one, and the next darkest green, altering the lilac to one darker, and the green to one lighter in every future round. Join on the straw silk, * 4 straw, 2 green, 4 lilac, 4 green, * 7 times. Hold the cord looser.

13th.—(Holding the cord still looser), * 2 green, 2 straw, 2 green, 2 lilac, 2 green, 2 lilac, 2 green, * 7 times.

14th.—* 4 green, 4 lilac, 2 green, 2 lilac, 2 green, * 7 times.

15th.—(Lightest green), * 1 green, 5 lilac, 2 green, 5 lilac, 2 green, * 7 times. There is an increase of seven stitches in this round; the cord is also held sufficiently slack to increase the bag a little. The remaining rounds are not increased.

16th.—(Green filoselle, and darkest lilac but one), * 6 silk, 9 lilac, * 7 times.

17th.—Darkest lilac only, without increase. Then do four rounds with the black wool. At the end, cut the cord in a slanting way, so that the top may terminate gradually.

Thread a needle with the darkest green wool, and net all round the top of the bag a single round of common netting: do another round with each shade of green wool, to the lightest: about 24 stitches should be sufficient for the top of the bag. In the last round of netting, the cords are run to draw it up; and the part where the crochet and netting join is trimmed with fringe. A tassel is added at the bottom.

EMBROIDERY.

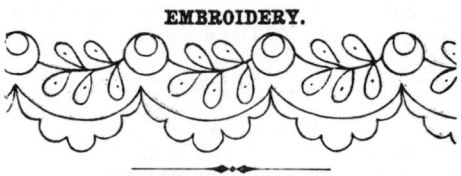

DOG'S COLLAR.

THIS collar consists of a number of brass rings, covered with scarlet wool in crochet. These rings are placed over each other, and held together by three rows of scarlet worsted

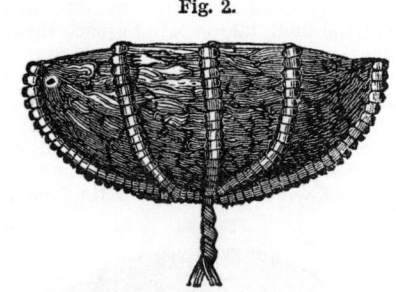

Fig. 2.

braid, placed through them. The ends are finished with scarlet woollen balls.

EMERY CUSHION IN A WALNUT-SHELL.

Fig. 1.

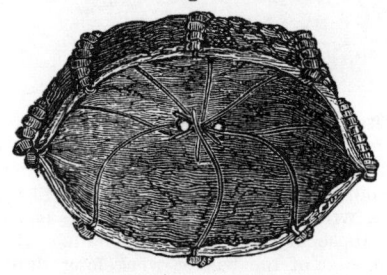

THIS is a very pretty emery cushion, and may be made with half a walnut-shell scraped out carefully with a knife, and varnished out-side to give it a polish. Begin by making two holes at the bottom of the shell, then take four pieces of wire nine inches long, and bend these double; string on to each wire five large round steel beads, and twenty smaller ones at each

Fig. 3.

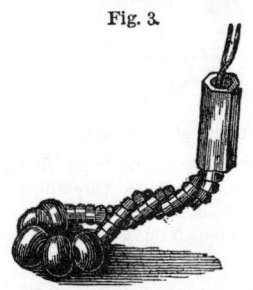

side of the same. Twist the wire together, as shown in Fig. 3, and pass the two ends of each doubled wire through a long steel bead. Now thread on to each of the eight wires a number of small steel beads, and draw them up to the edge of the shell, taking care to place them at regular intervals; bend the wires over the edge, and press them firmly down on the inside of the shell. For the second row of beads belonging to the stand, take four wires five inches long; on to each of these thread six small steel beads, and, having pushed them to the middle of the wire, wind it once round the foot wire

Fig. 4.

between the first and second, and between the fourth and fifth large beads, then thread seven more small beads on each end of the wire, and draw it through two large beads, into which string also the wire of the adjacent foot. Pass all the eight ends through the long bead, and four of them into each of the two holes of the

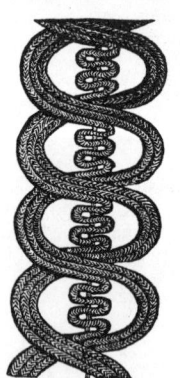

Trimming of braid or cord.

shell, where they should be firmly pressed down. Now glue into the shell an emery cushion, made to fit, and covered with purple velvet and a bead fringe.

TRIMMING OF BRAID OR CORD.

THIS little trimming, which is suitable for heading flounces or trimming children's dresses, may be made at small cost and with very little trouble. Stout silk or thread, the color of the braid, is required. The design is very easy to copy.

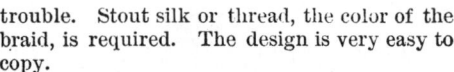

SPOOL BASKET.

THIS basket, for spools of cotton, is covered with a crochet covering of green purse silk and steel beads; at the upper edge sew on a net of green silk; two green ribbon strings are drawn crosswise through the top of the net, so as to fasten the same. The basket is ornamented with a ruche of green satin ribbon. Cut first a round piece of card-board, measuring seven and one-fifth inches across; all round the edge make openings two inches long, at intervals of one and one-fifth of an inch. Turn the thus-formed lappets upwards, and sew them on to one another along the edges, which must overlap each other three-tenths of an inch. The bottom of the thus-formed basket is covered on the outside with green cashmere; fasten three large black buttons for the feet. The inside of the basket is covered with green silk. The covering of the border of the basket on the outside is worked in ribbed crochet stitch with green purse silk and steel beads, in the following manner: Thread several skeins of steel beads on the silk, make with the latter a foundation chain of thirty stitches, and work in rows backwards and forwards till the strip is long enough to go round the upper part of the basket. In every other row of the strip push

up alternately one steel bead in the next three stitches, and then leave three stitches without beads; the bead stitches must be alternated in the course of the work. Lastly, work together on the wrong side the stitches of the last row with those of the foundation chain. At the lower edge of the basket work long slanting bead stitches, imitating a cord. At the upper edge ornament the basket with a ruche of green satin ribbon, one inch wide, the sewing-on of which is covered by a row of beads, imitating a cord. Then sew on the green silk net, five inches deep, worked in slanting netting, as can be seen on illustration.

KNIFE AND FORK CASE.

THIS is a very useful case for keeping knives and forks that are not in use, and when there

Fig. 1.

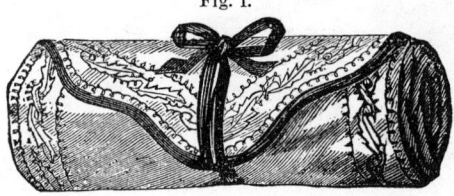

is no box for the purpose, It is made of brown holland, lined with green baize. The bands

WATCH-HOLDER WITH ORIENTAL EMBROIDERY.

Materials.—Red Cashmere; sarcenet to match; wadding; blue, green, brown, yellow, black, and white purse silk; fine gold cord; a red silk cord, fourteen inches long, with tassels at the ends.

THE frame consists of three bronze bars, five inches long and half an inch in circumference, joined together at the top, wound round with a red cord and tassels. The middle bar is fastened with a watch-hook. If, instead of bronze, a wood or cane bar should be used in preserving the weight, a smooth leaden ball may be fastened at the under end for a foot. Inside of the bars, an inch distant from the foot end, the cup is fastened with a bronze edge for the trinkets and the watch-chain, embroidered inside on Cashmere, as shown in full-size illustration, covered outside with red sarcenet, and lined with wadding. According to our model of the embroidery (Fig. 2), the middle star is

Fig. 2.

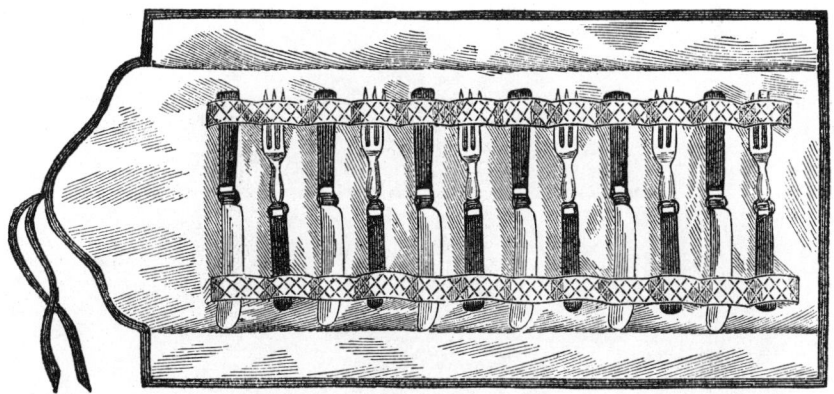

Fig. 3.

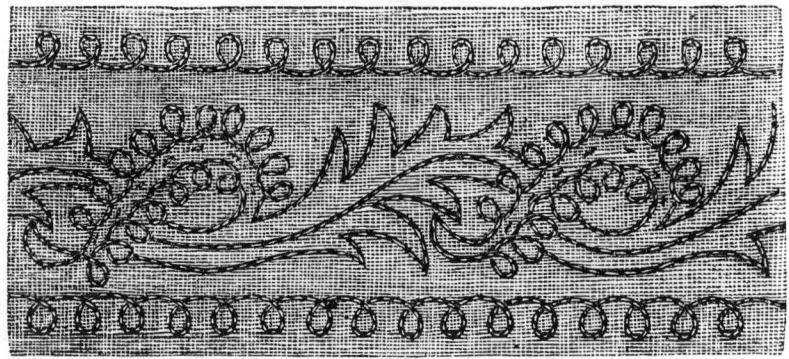

that support them are of holland, decorated with a row of herring-bone stitches in green wool. The border on the outside (given full working size in Fig. 3) is worked in chain stitch with green wool.

ornamented with a gold cross and separate gold stars, each star itself being worked in black and gold embroidery. The adjoining leaves and narrow square patterns are blue, enlivened with red. The separate stars be-

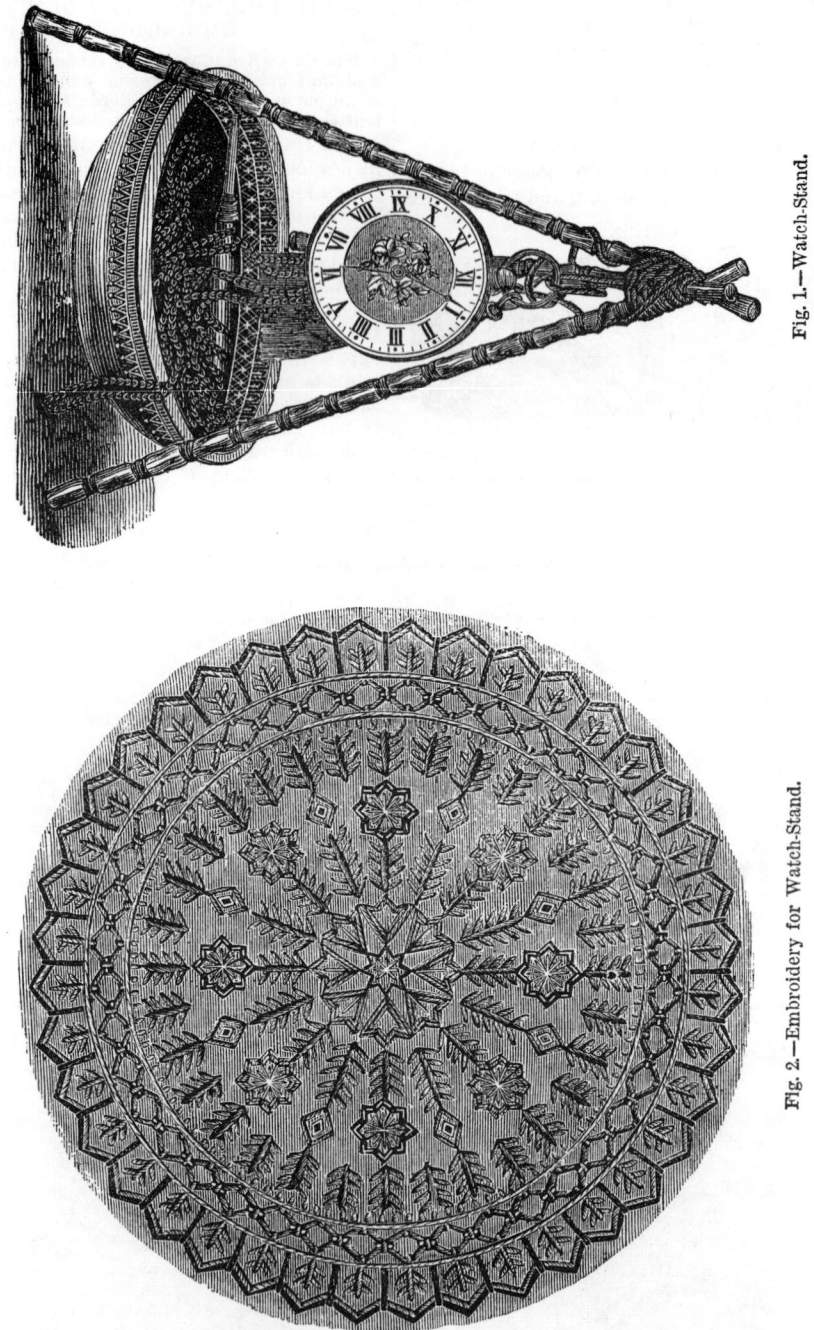

Fig. 1.—Watch-Stand.

Fig. 2.—Embroidery for Watch-Stand.

tween the squares are alternately white and black, enlivened with gold inside. The leaves of the several kinds, which have all brown veins, are worked in yellow and green, whereas those of the outer scallops are entirely white.

The outer scallops are worked with black and yellow silk. The blue square-like pattern of the border is stitched over with yellow stitches, and has an edge of gold cord along the sides, fastened with black cross stitches. Blue loose stitches complete the border.

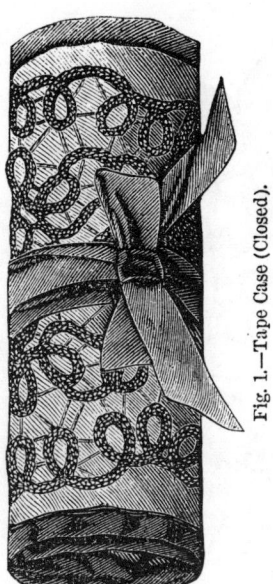

Fig. 1.—Tape Case (Closed).

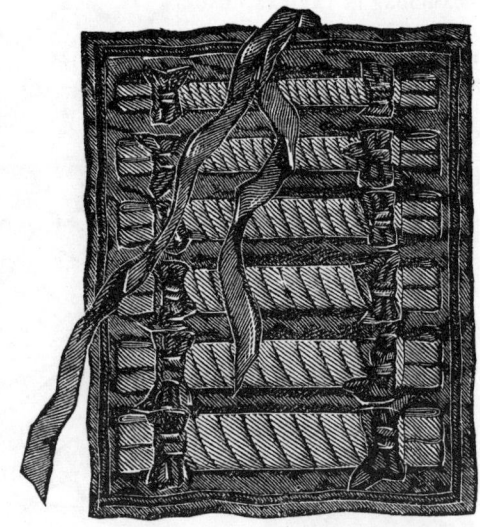

Fig. 2.—Tape Case (Open).

TAPE-CASE (OPEN AND CLOSED).

THE foundation may be of silk, velvet, or Cashmere, neatly lined with a contrasting color, and bound with ribbon. The size of the piece required is eleven and a half by nine and a half inches. Ribbons are sewn on at regular distances, to keep in their proper places six pieces of tape of varied widths. It is almost unnecessary to remark that the outside must be embroidered previous to the lining and binding of the case.

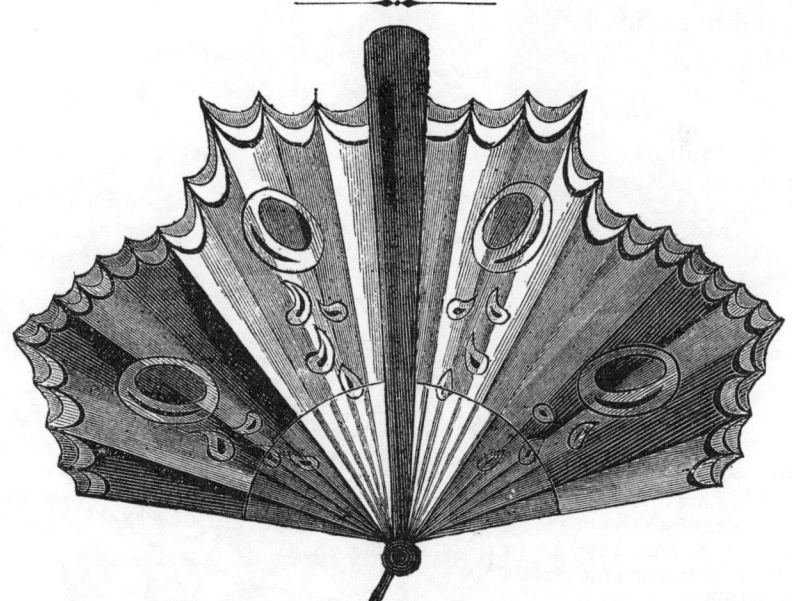

FAN.

THIS fan has an ivory framework. When completed and open it assumes the form of a butterfly. Five equal pieces of violet and of white silk are employed; colored and gold paper are used for the designs, according to the illustration.

WORK-BAG,

WITH MEDALLIONS IN TAPE AND LACE STITCH.

THE upper sections have a foundation of card-board; so have the lower, as far as the straight part of the sides. The lower portion is soft. The outer covering may be of velvet, satin, silk, or Cashmere, and the lining may be of

Fig. 1.

Fig. 2.

Fig. 3.

any pretty colored materials. The sides of the bag are ornamented with medallions, parts of which are shown in the full size in Figs. 2 and 3. In the first place, a tracing of a perfect medallion should be made; next, the tape should be folded according to design, and tacked upon the tracing; then the twisted bars and spun stitches should be worked with thread, No. 1, or coarse Mecklenburgh thread. Tassels of cotton are tied up and fastened to the medallions (see design), and a large one is placed at the bottom of the bag. The lid is fastened by a sliding cord to the bow, by which the bag is fastened up. Pockets for holding cotton, etc., may be placed in the sections inside.

PINCUSHION.

THIS pincushion is made of four triangular pieces the size of Fig. 2. It may, of course, be made any size. The shape should be cut in

Fig. 1.

card-board. Two sides are embroidered on white, two on red; the white sides are worked in red, gold, and blue, as in Fig. 3; the edges, after being sewn together, are herring-boned

over with gold silk; the red sides of the cushion are worked after the illustration Fig. 2 in green and white, with a gold star in the centre.

Fig. 3.

The feather-stitch all around the pattern is worked in gold. The inside of the cushion should be well stuffed, the bottom covered with red velvet or cloth.

Fig. 2.

MAT FOR VASES, ETC.

THE materials required for this mat are stiff muslin, gray lining, and white bobbin-net, besides Berlin wool of different shades of brown and gray. Having tacked the muslin, lining,

Fig. 3.

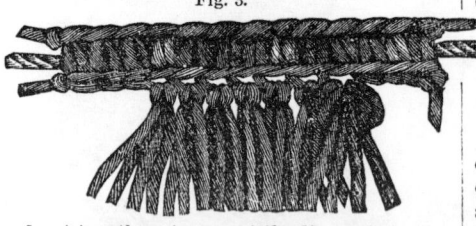

and net together, trace out the lines of the design, as seen in Fig. 2, on the net, observing that each line must run along a line of the holes in the net. Then work with two shades of brown wool the centre star and the diamonds between the points. Then follow two rows of slanting stitches in light and dark gray. Then make the border of the gray by crocheting it as seen in Fig. 3. The fringe is put in the loops by a needle. Fig. 2 shows the star for mat in full size. Any color desired can be substituted for those mentioned.

MAT.

THE foundation may be of any bright-colored cloth. The embroidery is worked in purse-silk of a contrasting color, or in a variety of colors, as fancy may suggest. The mat may be finished with a fringe, a ruche, or an edge of pinked cloth.

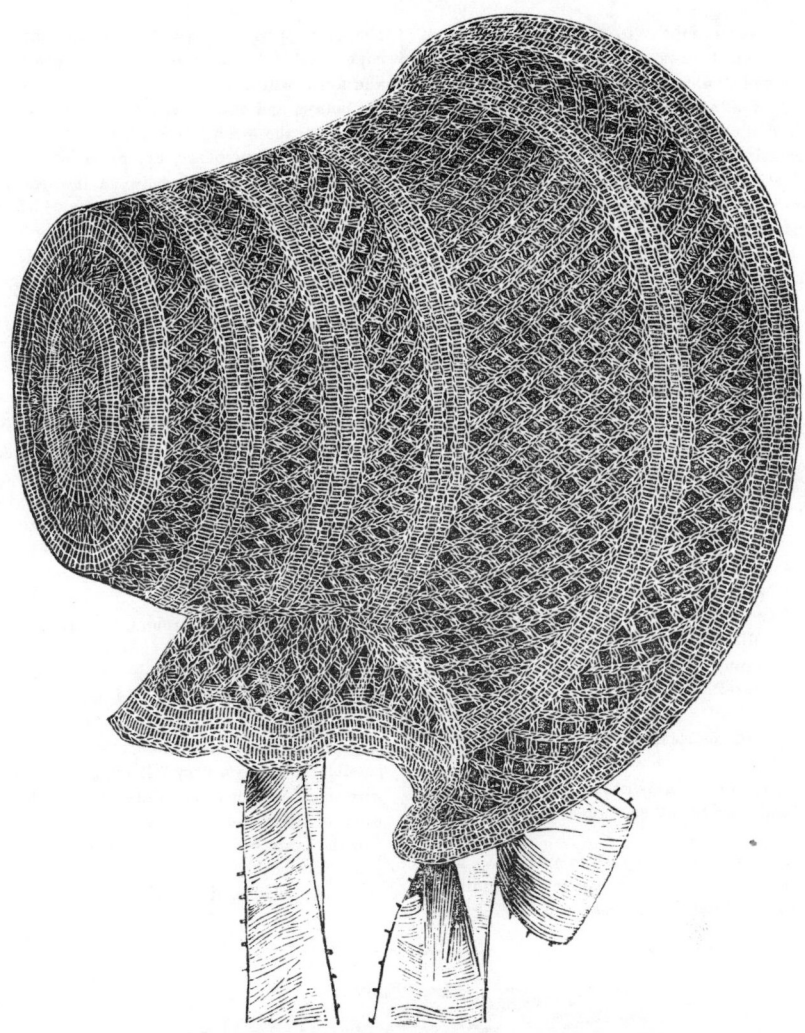

CROCHET.—LADY'S BONNET, SUITABLE FOR THE SEASIDE OR COUNTRY.

Materials.—Dark drape crochet cord; Penelope crochet, No. 3.

MAKE a round foundation of 9 stitches, work 5 rounds in double crochet, increasing in every stitch, in the first, and the same stitch in the succeeding rounds. 6th round, chains of five united to every alternate stitch. 7th, chains of 7, united to the centre stitch of chains; work 3 more rounds, like 7th round, then 6 rounds in double crochet, increasing as it is found requisite. Work 4 more open stitch rounds, in chains of 7 in the first round, missing 2 stitches: between the chains work 6 more rounds in double crochet, without increasing, but decreasing in the second round, by omitting every 8th stitch; work 4 rounds of chains of 7, omitting 3 between each section of chains in the first round. 5th round,

1 double crochet in centre of chain, 3 chain repeat; work 6 rounds of double crochet, 4 rounds of chains as before, then finish with 6 rounds of double crochet, which completes the crown. Make a chain measuring 31 inches for the front; work 2 rows in double crochet, then 4 rows in chains of 7, decreasing at the beginning and end of each row, and working only on the right side; in the first chain row leave 3 stitches between each, and in the last 2 chains work 6 rows in double crochet, continuing to leave a stitch at the beginning and end of row, and decreasing 4 times at regular intervals in each row; this is to form the round shape of the front; work 1 double crochet, 7 chain, miss 4; repeat to end, commencing in centre stitch of chain; work 10 rows of chains of 7, then 1 double crochet in centre stitch

of chain, 3 chain repeat to end; work 5 rows of double crochet, 4 rows of chains of 7, and finish with 3 rows of double crochet, continuing as before to leave the first and last stitches unworked; work 4 rows in double crochet, along the front and each side, increasing at the corners: this completes the front. Make a chain measuring 26 inches for the cape: work 2 rows in double crochet, then 12 rows in chains of 7; it is not requisite to detach the thread, but work 3 single stitches in the first 3 chains at beginning of row, then commence the 7 chains of open, which will form the shape for the cape; work 1 double crochet in centre chain, 3 chain, and finish with 4 rows of double crochet, worked at the bottom and each side, increasing at the corners. Damp on the wrong side with a solution of gum Arabic, and when nearly dry press with a hot iron, placing a piece of cloth between the iron and the crochet; line with blue, or any color which may be preferred, which will harmonize with the bonnet.

We give the above thus early to enable our fair readers to prepare it in time for the coming season.

FLOWER MAT.

Materials.—Two skeins of green crystal wool, one dark and one light; one skein of white ditto; one of lilac ditto. A piece of white satin. Three yards of stout wire. A bone mesh $\frac{1}{2}$ an inch wide, and one $1\frac{1}{4}$ inch wide; also six silvered beads.

THE centre of this mat is of white satin, covered with netting. The latter is done thus: On a foundation make, with the lilac wool, 14 stitches, using the narrowest mesh. Do two plain rows

3d row.—Miss the first stitch, net the second, then the first; continuing this for all the fourteen stitches.

4th and 5th.—Plain netting.

6th.—Like third.

Do altogether fourteen rows, which will make a square piece.

Cover a round of card-board with satin on one side, and calico on the other. Tack this square over the satin.

The flowers are alternately white and lilac. Each one has six petals, which are made by bending a piece of wire in the form of a leaf, and darning them closely (from edge to edge), beginning at the base of each petal, darning to the point, then taking an overcast stitch at the end, and slipping the needle down the centre. Six petals must be tied together, in the form of a flower, and the points bent. A silvered bead is sewed in the centre of each.

FOR THE MOSS.

Bend the wire into a round, exactly the size of the rim of the mat. Bind the ends with wool for greater security. Take a coarse rug needle, and thread it with a very long thread of each of the green wools. Work on the wire in button-hole stitch, over the large mesh, taking the stitches as close together as possible, to make a very full fringe. Work all the wire round in this way. Make another circle, somewhat smaller, and cover it with moss fringe also. Sew the large round at the edge of the mat, and the other just within it, and set the flowers, at equal distances, between the two borders.

FLOWER MAT.—ANOTHER PATTERN

GENTLEMAN'S KNITTED BRACES.

THESE braces are very easy to make. They are knitted plain with gray cotton, and joined together at the back with a piece of gray calico, stitched on double. For each brace, cast on 58 stitches on middle-sized steel knitting-needles,

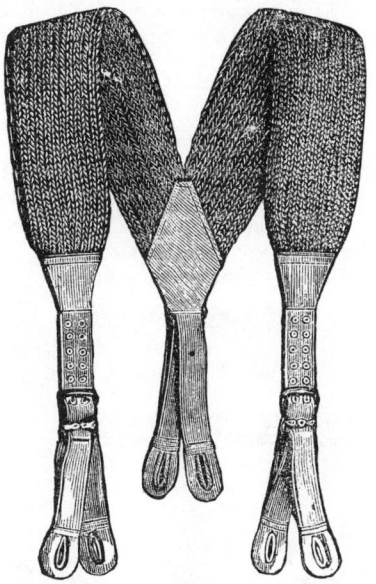

knit the cross way in rows till the brace is long enough. Our pattern is eighteen inches long. The braces are then completed with straps of gray calico, neatly stitched, and fitted up with eyelet-holes and buckles, as seen in illustration. The ends of the straps are finished off with leather; a large buttonhole is worked in the middle of the leather part.

CHILD'S SOCK
KNITTED IN THE SHELL PATTERN.

Materials.—Four needles No. 15, a size smaller for a loose knitter, one ounce of Andalusian wool.

CAST 72 stitches on one needle; knit them off on three needles—26 on two, 20 on the third. Knit 2, seam 2 alternately for 32 rounds. Next round—Knit 2, seam 2 alternately until you reach the 9th stitch of the needle, which has only 20 stitches on it; knit this 9th and the 10th stitch together. The next stitch is called the centre stitch of the back needle. Each round down the leg commences on it, and it must always be seamed.

* Knit 3 rounds plain (remember to seam the 1st or centre stitch). *4th round.* Back needle, seam centre stitch, knit 3, knit 2 together twice, make 1 (by throwing the wool over the needle), and knit 1 twice. You are now at the

end of back needle. Next needle—Make 1 and knit 1 twice, knit 2 together twice, seam 1, knit 2 together twice, make 1 and knit 1 four times, knit 2 together twice, seam 1, knit 2 together twice, make 1 and knit 1 twice. This completes the needle. Knit the next needle exactly the same. You must have 26 stitches always on each of these needles, and, until you begin to reduce, 19 on the back needle. Work the back needle up to centre stitch as follows: make 1 and knit 1 twice, knit 2 together twice, knit 3. Repeat from * 5 times more.

25th. Seam centre stitch, knit 1, knit 2 together, knit plain rest of round to within 3 of the end, when knit 2 together, knit 1. This is for the reducing. *26th and 27th.* Knit plain. *28th.* Knitted like the 4th, only after and before the centre stitch you will have only 2 plain stitches to knit instead of three. *29th, 30th, and 31st.* Knit plain. *32d.* Same as 28th.

Repeat from 25th round twice more, until you have only 13 stitches left on your back needle. Observe after each reducing there will be one less to knit before and after the centre stitch in the pattern rounds. The last time you must knit 2 together immediately after and before the centre stitch. * *49th, 50th, and 51st.* Knit plain. *52d.* Same as the 4th, only omitting to knit 3 after and before the centre stitch. Repeat from * twice more. If you count the patterns, you will find you ought to have worked 15. *61st.* Knit plain. This finishes your sock to the heel. You will have 13 stitches on back needle, 26 on each of the others.

Prepare for heel by knitting to the end of your back needle, and from 1st side (or next needle) knit off on back needle 10 stitches. Knit the other 16 stitches from 1st side needle on another needle. With a third needle knit 2d side needle to within 10 stitches of the end. These 10 you must pass to the heel or back needle without knitting. You will have 33 stitches on heel, 16 on each side needle. The two front needles are not used again until the heel is completed.

HEEL.—The heel is made by working the back needle backwards and forwards, knitting and seaming alternate rows until it is long enough, which it will be after working 26 rows. Slip the 1st stitch in each row, excepting the first time you knit the first row. Seam or knit the centre stitch as required. *27th row.* Slip 1, knit 20, knit 2 together, * turn your needle, slip 1, seam 10, seam 2 together. Again turn your needle, slip 1, knit 10, knit 2 together; repeat from * until you have only 12 stitches left on needle.

With the needle that has the 12 stitches on take up, and, as you take up, knit 15 stitches from side of heel, knit 3 stitches off front needle on the same. Knit plain all the stitches from the 2 front needles, excepting the last 3 on another needle. These 3 must be knitted on a third needle with which take up, and, as you take up, knit 15 stitches from other side of heel ; knit also 6 stitches from next needle on this. You will have 24 stitches on each side needle, 26 on front needle. The next needle is your 1st side needle ; * 1st side needle. Knit plain all till within 5 of the end, when knit 2 together, knit 3. Front needle.—Make 1 and knit 1 twice, knit 2 together twice, seam 1, knit 2 together twice, make 1 and knit 1 four times, knit 2 together twice, seam 1, knit 2 together twice, make 1 and knit 1 twice. *2d side needle.* Knit 3, slip 1, knit 1, pull the slipped stitch over the knitted one ; knit plain to end of needle. Knit plain 3 rounds ; repeat from * until you have only 18 stitches on each side needle. This finishes the reducing for the foot.

The 4 rounds between the last asterisks are now to be repeated, only in the pattern rounds do not reduce on the side needles ; knit all the stitches plain. These rounds must be repeated until, counting the patterns from the top of socks, you have worked 28, and have the three plain rounds beyond.

THE TOE.—This is all done in plain knitting. Put as many stitches on your front needle as you have on the other two together, taking them as fairly as you can off each side needle, two off one end, three off the other. You will have 31 on front needle, 15 on one side needle, 16 on the other. Knit 3 rounds plain and up to the front needle.

TO REDUCE THE TOE.—Front needle. Knit

1, slip 1, knit 1, pull the slipped stitch over the knitted one ; knit plain to within 3 of end, when knit 2 together, knit 1. *1st back needle.* Knit 1, slip 1, knit 1, pull the slipped stitch over the knitted one, knit plain to end of needle. *2d.* Knit plain to within 3 of end, when knit 2 together, knit 1. Knit 2 rounds plain ; repeat from * twice more. Repeat from * again, knitting only one round plain between the reducing rounds, until you have 15 stitches on your front needle, 7 on one back needle, 8 on the other. Knit one round plain, knitting on one needle the stitches off the two back needles. Cast off, knitting the stitches on front and back needles together.

WATCH-POCKET OF WHITE PIQUE.

THIS pretty little watch-pocket is made of white *piqué*, and ornamented with white embroidery and *soutache.* After having traced the pattern on the pocket, work the embroi-

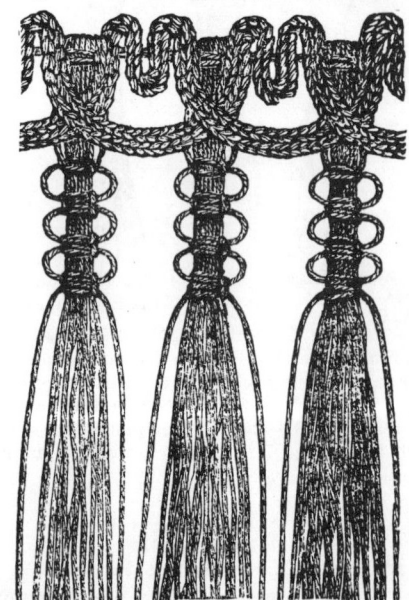

FRINGES KNOTTED OR SEWN.

dery with the knitting cotton, and sew on the *soutache.* Line it with calico, and join the different parts together with buttonhole stitch. Fasten some cotton balls at the bottom, and a circle of buttonhole stitches at the top, by means of which the pocket is hung on the wall.

INDEX